Development Narratives

Development Narratives

The Political Economy of Tamil Nadu

Editors

V.K. Natraj

A. Vaidyanathan

ACADEMIC FOUNDATION

NEW DELHI

www.academicfoundation.com

First published in 2014
by

ACADEMIC FOUNDATION
4772-73 / 23 Bharat Ram Road, (23 Ansari Road),
Darya Ganj, New Delhi - 110 002 (India).
Phones : 23245001 / 02 / 03 / 04.
Fax : +91-11-23245005.
E-mail : books@academicfoundation.com
www.academicfoundation.com

Disclaimer:
The findings/views/opinions expressed in this book are solely those of the authors and do not necessarily reflect the views of the publisher.

Cataloging in Publication Data--DK
Courtesy: D.K. Agencies (P) Ltd. <docinfo@dkagencies.com>

Development narratives : the political economy of Tamil Nadu / editors, V.K. Natraj, A. Vaidyanathan.
p. cm.
Contributed articles.
ISBN 9789332701229

1. Tamil Nadu (India)--Economic conditions. 2. Economic development--India--Tamil Nadu. I. Natraj, V. K. II. Vaidyanathan, A.

DDC 330.95482 23

Typeset by Italics India, New Delhi.

Printed and bound by The Book Mint, New Delhi.
www.thebookmint.in

CONTENTS

Industry

Social Sectors

Environment

List of Tables and Figures

Tables

Figures

About the Editors/ Contributors

Editors:

V.K. Natraj, educated in economics at the University of Mysore and Pembroke College Oxford, has concentrated on interdisciplinary studies relating to decentralisation and panchayat raj institutions (PRIs) and positive discrimination. He worked in the University of York, UK, and the Institute of Development Studies (IDS), University of Mysore, of which he was the Director for a term. He was the Registrar of the University of Mysore. After retirement from Mysore University, he became Director, Madras Institute of Development Studies (MIDS), Chennai (2000 to 2005). He directed a major research study titled: "Delegation to Devolution: A Comparative Study of Tamil Nadu, Karnataka and West Bengal", sponsored by the Development Research Centre for the Future State in the IDS at the University of Sussex, UK. Prof Natraj was a member of the Expert Committee on PR legislation constituted by the Government of Karnataka and was also Co-Chair of the Working Group on Decentralisation of the Tamil Nadu Planning Commission. He was a member of the Advisory Committee of the Shastri Indo-Canadian Institute (1995 to 2005). He was also a member of the Management Committee of the Centre for the Future State at IDS, University of Sussex till 2005. He has to his credit publications in the field of decentralisation as well as positive discrimination and has delivered several major lectures. He was invited to be Visiting Professor at the Centre for Political Studies, JNU in 2008 as also the Devaraj Urs Visiting Professor at IDS, University of Mysore. From 2005 up to 2013, he was the Chair of the Centre for the Study of Culture and Society, Bangalore. He was a trustee and subsequently Chairman of the Malcolm and Elizabeth Adiseshiah Trust Chennai.

A. Vaidyanathan's professional career spans academic and policy-centric research on diverse aspects of development. He worked in the National Council of Applied Economic Research (1956-1962); Planning Commission (1962-1972); as professor in Centre for Development Studies (1976-1984) and Madras Institute of Development Studies (1984-2004); as senior economist in FAO and the World Bank. During this long career, he has combined sustained empirical-analytical research on varied aspects of the country's socioeconomic development with active involvement in planning and policy formulation. Besides numerous articles in professional journals, he has written more than a dozen books some dealing with broader aspects of strategy and policy and others exploring issues relating to specific sectors notably agriculture, water and education. As member of the PM's Economic Advisory Council and the Planning Commission at the Centre and Tamil Nadu, he has first-hand knowledge of the processes of policy-making. He has served or chaired several official committees to review policies in specific areas (such as pricing of irrigation, revitalisation of rural cooperative credit structure and improvement of the current system of agricultural statistics). His areas of interest ranges from critical assessment of recent growth experience and strategies for poverty alleviation, the role of politics and institutions, importance of reliable data for informed policy making, the current state of available data and its utilisation for research. Currently he is honorary fellow, Centre for Development Studies, Thiruvananthapuram,

Contributors:

P. Anbazhagan, Researcher, Madras Institute of Development Studies, Chennai.

P. Balasubramanian, Executive Director, Rural Women's Social Education Centre (RUWSEC), Tamil Nadu.

J. Jeyaranjan, Director, Institute of Development Alternatives, Chennai.

Vinish Kathuria, Associate Professor, SJM School of Management, IIT, Mumbai.

K.S. Kavi Kumar, Professor, Madras School of Economics, Chennai.

G.K. Mini, Research Fellow, Achuta Menon Centre for Health Science Studies, Sree Chitra Tirunal Institute of Medical Sciences.

K. Nagaraj, Professor (Rtd), Madras Institute of Development Studies; currently with the Asian College of Journalism, Chennai.

S. Neelakantan, Former Director, Madras Institute of Development Studies, Chennai.

Meenakshi Rajeev, Professor, Centre for Economic Studies and Policy, Institute of Social and Economic Change, Bangalore.

P. Geetha Rani, Associate Professor, National University of Educational Planning and Administration (NUEPA), New Delhi.

T.K. Sundari Ravindran, Professor, Sree Chitra Tirunal Institute for Medical Sciences and Technology, Thiruvananthapuram.

R. Srinivasan, Associate Professor, Department of Econometrics, Madras University, Chennai

Brinda Viswanathan, Associate Professor, Madras School of Economics, Chennai.

Acknowledgements

We take pleasure in acknowledging our gratitude to: The Malcolm and Elizabeth Adiseshiah Trust for sponsoring this study; Prof C.T. Kurien, Founder-Chairman of the Trust for his constant support; Dr H.B.N. Shetty, Executive Trustee, for his involvement with the work at all stages and gracious help; all our authors for making this volume possible and their patience; Dr G.S. Ganesh Prasad, Member of the Faculty, Madras Institute of Development Studies, for invaluable help in preparing the volume for publication and Ms H.L. Sheela, Mysore, for making available her expertise in word processing and formatting.

Introduction

Tamil Nadu's development experience is worthy of academic inquiry for a variety of reasons. Widely regarded as a very well-administered state, it ranks high in the country in terms of social and economic infrastructure, literacy and health, irrigation facilities, as well as the scale and diversity of its industrial development. Its diversified and modern industrial base has been built by a strong indigenous industrial and commercial entrepreneurial class, more recently supplemented by foreign direct investment for which it has become a favoured destination. It is also highly urbanised, and thanks to the spatial diffusion of urban centres, industrial activity is more widely distributed than in many other states.

Backdrop

In order to appreciate fully the constellation that has brought about this development profile, we would require an analysis couched in a broad historical sweep. And this should encompass the following ingredients: the development policies at the national and state levels, how far the state has utilised the opportunities offered by these policies as also the extent to which it has overcome the constraints imposed on its autonomy by the policies of the centre. And this is by no means an exhaustive list. The role of these and other related features in shaping the course of development in the state, regrettably, could not be addressed fully in this collection. It is nevertheless important to take note of some special features of the state in these respects.

In pre-independent India, Tamil Nadu (Madras Presidency as it then was) gave birth to the Justice Party which started a movement directed at breaking the hegemonic position occupied by the Brahmins in education and service under the state. Initially it was focused on securing reservations for the non-Brahmin castes in education and employment—which is now called positive/protective discrimination. But, largely under the influence of Periyar E.V. Ramawamy the celebrated leader and theoretician of the party, it got transformed over time into a more wide ranging social reform movement that advocated the inculcation of modernity, scientific temper, rational attitudes and equality even as it contained a quite explicit anti-Aryan, anti-Brahmin sentiment.

Other regions of southern India were influenced by the Madras presidency's non-Brahmin movement but they did not emulate its broader dimensions. For example, in princely Mysore, the accent was essentially on securing the benefits of reservation in education and employment. This certainly helped lower castes to secure more access to opportunities in these spheres, but it did not have the same pervasive effects that the movement had in Madras. However, the idea of promoting equity through positive discrimination gained ground and slowly became part of the socio-political dialogue in the south of India. The Constitution incorporated some features of positive discrimination albeit in a limited way to begin with (and this process has continued over time to increase the depth and coverage of policies and constitutional provisions oriented to this end). Tamil Nadu should, however, be recognised as a pioneer in this field. All in all, the southern states were more forward looking in this respect than their counterparts in the north. This should explain to a significant degree the quite different responses of the south and several north Indian states to the recommendations of the Mandal Commission in the 1980s. Acceptance of its recommendations at the national level led to violent reactions in the north, while the south largely remained peaceful. This is to be attributed to the fact that states like Tamil Nadu and Karnataka were not new to measures designed to promote equity through positive discrimination. This makes us recall a witty observation of Devaraj Urs, a long serving chief minister of Karnataka (and one committed to positive discrimination) about the Bihar chief minister Karpoori Thakur who in the late 1970s attempted to introduce progressive policies of reservation but met with fierce resistance. Urs said: "Thakur got into the ring before learning how to box!" The same differentiation was evident subsequently in the early years of this century when necessary legislation for the extension of reservations to the backward classes in educational institutions was proposed. The south more or less accepted it with little protest, while in the north, there was violent opposition spilling out to the streets. It may be noted that even at this point in time, Tamil Nadu has provision for reservation exceeding what is commonly (and by implication judicially) accepted as the limit for reservation, namely 50 per cent. Constraints of space prevent a fuller description of this issue. In this context, it is necessary to draw attention to a feature which is somewhat special to Tamil Nadu as distinct from Karnataka and Andhra Pradesh. The state does not have one or two dominant 'intermediate castes' such as the Reddys and Kammas in Andhra Pradesh and the Lingayats and Vokkaligas in Karnataka who initially posed the challenge to Brahmin supremacy. Tamil Nadu has a fair number of castes that effectively countered the hegemony of Brahmins, and even at present, the state does not witness the 'dominant caste' syndrome as, say, Karnataka.

A second area in which Tamil Nadu stands out is its strong advocacy of adherence to the federal principle. The attempt to make Hindi the national language evoked strong opposition in the state as a manifestation of Aryan domination and hegemony in the 1960s. This apprehension was reinforced by concerns about the asymmetry in powers for resource mobilisation, doubts about the mechanisms for determining the basis of revenue sharing between the centre and the states, central resource transfers and the increasing role of the Planning Commission in determining strategy and priorities of development. While these were widely shared by many states, the government and political parties in Tamil Nadu were vocal advocates of more autonomy for the states, greater share of national financial resources and more respect for their rights. It is no accident that the state was the first to constitute a committee to examine the entire question of centre-state relations (Rajamannar Committee in the early 1970s). It should surprise no one that both the Dravidian political parties, Dravida Munnetra Kazhagam (DMK) and Anna Dravida Munnetra Kazhagam (ADMK), abstained from voting on the 73rd amendment to the Constitution which conferred upon *panchayats* constitutional status as a third tier of governance. This was probably the only issue on which these bitter political rivals ever saw eye to eye. The parties as also several other leaders in the state urge that in the guise of decentralising through the Constitutional Amendment, the union government was actually attempting subtly to strengthen its position in the centre-state power nexus. Critics point out that many of the powers devolved on local government institutions are at the cost of those which belong to the states. The kind of autonomy in local level development for elected *panchayats* that was envisaged by the Constitutional Amendments has not come about in Tamil Nadu but that is a complex question and cannot be analysed here. This patchy performance is indeed the case in most other states but there are distinctive features in relation to Tamil Nadu which are not pursued further.

In 1967, the Congress suffered a crushing electoral defeat in the state, thereafter it was reduced to a marginalised role. Since then, except for brief spells of President's Rule, the two Dravidian parties have shared power. The fact that the Congress needed the support of one of these two parties in national elections made it possible for them to exert influence at the centre as well (and this continues to be the state of the political game presently). This has been strengthened with their direct participation in the central government with both the Congress and Bharatiya Janata Party (BJP)-led coalitions. The state government has used this leverage in its negotiations with the Planning Commission for plan assistance, asserting its priorities under the state plan, lobbying for central projects, etc. An added advantage is the demonstrated and widely recognised capacity of the state administration to implement development programmes. This combination of circumstances has enabled the state to make effective use of resources available by way of central assistance under the plans, and exploit opportunities for growth opened up by liberalisation to reach its present high rank in terms of both social and economic development. It is noteworthy that all governments of the state in the post-independence period have shown a firm commitment to the social sector and the provision of social safety nets. As Natraj and Jeyaranjan's essay in this collection points out, the state has consistently devoted a fairly high proportion of its development expenditure to these programmes. Besides expanding and improving public health care, educational facilities and basic social amenities, other programmes of direct relevance to the poor figure prominently in the state. The principal ones are family planning and welfare, maternal and child health programmes and the public distribution system to provide subsidised supply of food and other essentials to the relatively poorer segments. It has pioneered innovations in all these programmes and also launched on its own initiative several new, state-wide, social protection programmes—including midday meals for school children, child nutrition, pensions for the aged, disabled, and more recently social insurance—which have now become accepted parts of national policy. These schemes are criticised on the ground that they divert scarce public resources from growth-promoting investments, that there are inefficiencies and leakages in their implementation and that the benefits do not reach the targeted segments. While these criticisms are valid to an extent, given their popularity among the people and the fact that a large and wide section of the disadvantaged benefits from them, these social protection programmes cannot all be dismissed as populist. In addition, these criticisms are made across the board about government-sponsored programmes especially in the realm of the social sector in most states. Indeed, a significant contention of the Natraj-Jeyaranjan paper is that the word 'populist' with its negative connotations is not applicable to the Tamil Nadu case.

The papers in this volume highlight significant trends and developments in the following areas: population, labour force and employment, agriculture and irrigation, industrial development, social sectors and environment. The papers are a mix of the descriptive and analytical; some deal with the macro trends in particular sectors or sub-sectors at the state level; some bring out regional variations based on detailed and critical use of available data; a few are based on findings of micro level and other research studies.

Population, Labour Force and Employment

Tamil Nadu has the distinction of reducing both birth and death rates much earlier and faster than most other states, except Kerala. K. Nagaraj's paper describes this process and discusses the role of social factors which influence peoples' attitudes to marriage and desired family size. He also discusses programmes for reducing birth rates, public health services and improvement of maternal and child health in explaining observed trends. The adverse consequences of the reliance on female sterilisations and the inadequacy of public services for maternal and child care are highlighted; Nagaraj's paper probes why and how Tamil Nadu achieved this during a time when its female literacy and social sector development were much less than in Kerala. He examines the knotty issue whether the decline seen in Tamil Nadu as also in Andhra Pradesh is cooperative or coercive. While recognising that there is no overt coercion in either state, he argues that coercion can take place "under a veil of rather impersonal benevolent development processes." He stresses in particular the manner in which patriarchal values coupled with a 'target-driven bureaucracy' leave women with only one form of contraception, sterilisation. He anticipates one possible objection to his conclusion, namely, that women must be better off now because they are spared the suffering resulting from the battering of frequent child births. As he succinctly puts it, "this 'misses the obvious point' that there are alternative routes to fertility decline outside of sterilisation. These routes would ensure women's health while promoting decline in fertility but these would require advances in regard to the social sector and at a more fundamental level a quite different perception of the population problem." This perception, while being more sensitive to gender and health perspectives, is time consuming to implement and is a far cry from the military style campaigns that underlie target-oriented family planning programmes. An equally interesting conclusion of his is that increasing levels of aspirations are not matched by resources with the result that the socioeconomic basis for the fertility transition is weak. Clearly this work can profitably be pursued in the light of the 2011 Census.

Brinda Viswanathan's paper describes in considerable detail the characteristics of labour force, employment and wages and the changes that have occurred between 1987 and 2004. The importance of changing age structure and education in determining the size and composition of labour force, the progressive, though uneven, diversification of employment into non-agricultural activities as a result of urbanisation and industrialisation and increasing importance of employment for rural population outside their villages are highlighted. Of special interest is the in-depth review of variations in the extent and nature of employment of youth, females and socially disadvantaged segments. Labour force participation rates have come down in all age groups, more so for women than men and in urban than rural areas. The status of Muslims appears to be relatively better than in many states and one of the contributory factors may be that Muslims are largely urban in Tamil Nadu. This is, by and large, true of the Scheduled Castes and Scheduled Tribes (SC/ST) population also, although they account for a large proportion of casual labour both in agriculture and in urban areas.

The author also brings to light the fact that work force participation rates vary depending on how seriously education is taken. And this is as true of Tamil Nadu as it is of the country as a whole. She points out that in the 15-19 age group, school attendance is an important determinant of labour force participation. And it should come as no surprise that this is stronger in the case of males than females. Also the female work force participation rate is more volatile in Tamil Nadu than in many other states. Citing a fairly recent study (Ghosh, 2006), she invites attention to the fact that across states, Tamil Nadu has a better nexus between economic growth and human development than many others. A limitation she draws attention to is in regard to the samples in the National Sample Survey Organisation (NSSO) studies and as she suggests, this is an issue that demands more inquiry. Besides highlighting some patterns in these variations, the paper also explores—albeit in a tentative way—the factors underlying them.

In every decennial census, data on key demographic, socioeconomic characteristics of the population as well as access to various amenities for all villages and towns are compiled and published in the Village and Town Directories. Utilising the data from the directories for 1971 and 2001, Vaidyanathan explores patterns of variation in selected socioeconomic characteristics (sex ratios, share in the population of SCs and STs, literacy, work participation rates and extent of diversification in employment) among village groups ranked according to the observed level for each of them. Particularly interesting is the comparison of characteristics and their locations between groups with the lowest and the highest values for each characteristic. Among the several interesting inferences that the paper leads to, we may mention the following. It is seen that the sex ratio in villages has a statistically significant positive correlation with literacy and proportion of agricultural labourers in the work force. It is negatively correlated with the work participation rate, village and household size and proportion of SCs and STs in the population. The paper also examines the relationship of the child sex ratio with these factors. The discussion illustrates the potential of this rich and much neglected source of data for research to track differences in levels of some key aspects of social and economic 'development' and their trends at a disaggregated level.

Agriculture and Irrigation

Neelakantan's papers titled "Declining Significance of Agriculture in Tamil Nadu" and "Changes in the Amaravati Basin" are a qualitative description of the wide ranging and major changes taking place in the state's agriculture and rural society based partly on findings of a recent resurvey of about a dozen villages spread across the state, and on first-hand knowledge and experience of these changes in his native village. Even as the relative importance of agriculture as a source of output and employment in the state has been declining, the rural areas have experienced major changes: population growth has led to proliferation of small holdings but there are also significant changes in the social composition of land ownership; technological change (particularly the use of energised pumps to extract groundwater, mechanisation of farm operations and the advent of new varieties and fertilisers) has reduced the demand for hired labour; modes as well as the terms of their employment in agriculture have changed; importance of the non-agricultural sectors has increased; and more and more people are availing themselves of employment outside the village.

The net impact of these and other internal and external factors has been significant. A village once prosperous which grew two and at times three crops began to experience decline in productivity caused by soil degradation coupled with water scarcity (for irrigation as well as drinking) and this was aggravated by pollution. Neelakantan describes how these trends unravelled themselves and the manner in which two other features emerged. One is the extensive mining of sand from the river with highly deleterious all-round consequences and the growth and later the travails of the dyeing industry. There is a detailed account of how the villages attempted to cope with these changes, as it turned out, unsuccessfully. The principal reason for all this is the progressive decline in the availability of water from the traditional, centuries old, irrigation system in the Amaravati Basin which was the basis of the region's earlier prosperity. This trend followed the construction of an upstream reservoir and subsequently by anarchic expansion of water extraction from the river which increased the irrigated area to nearly three times more than what was intended, by intensive mining of sand from the river bed and spread of pollution caused by the dyeing industry in and around the village. All of these were illegal but the government did little, despite protests from the areas served by the traditional system, to check the trend. Though there were adequate powers to regulate these processes and ensure equitable and sustainable use of the river's water, governments consistently proved unable and unwilling to enforce them because of the political clout of the upper riparians, the sand mining business and the dyeing industry. Although based on the experience of the worst affected region, its findings are of wider relevance. For gross laxity of governance in formulating and enforcing appropriate regulations to ensure efficient, sustainable and equitable use of a strictly finite and environmentally critical common pool resource like water is a regrettably pervasive phenomenon in the state and in the country.

The main features of groundwater irrigation and its growth (between 1979 and 1990) are explored in considerable detail by Anbazhagan. His paper provides a vivid picture of the vast regional differences in the extent of groundwater irrigation overall, as the sole source of irrigation and in combination with water from canals and tanks, and of their impact on land use and cropping pattern compared to other sources of irrigation. What is of special interest is the attempt to explore these aspects across districts and across *talukas* grouped by agro-climatic conditions. An attempt is also made to assess whether and to what degree differences in groundwater irrigation, taken along with surface irrigation and rainfall, impact on overall crop yields. This is another example of the research potential of existing sources of data for exploring important aspects of the development processes at a disaggregated level.

Industry

Kathuria describes the main features of Tamil Nadu's industrial growth and its contribution to the overall economy over the period 1980-2004 and the initiatives and policies of the state government in facilitating the process. This is followed by a discussion of major changes in the overall pattern of industrial growth and of the performance of selected key industries over the period as a whole and during the post-reform period in particular.

Tamil Nadu benefits from the presence of an active entrepreneurial class and good infrastructure. It is a front-ranking state in industry in the country but there are problems as well. One feature of the state's industrial profile is that, unlike in other states, it is more widely distributed across medium and large towns spread across the state. This has had the effect of working as a safety net for the rural poor in times of distress by making possible migration to towns for work.

Although the state has a good record in industrial development (and Kathuria furnishes a wealth of data to illustrate the impressive status of Tamil Nadu in this respect), there are certain trends that need to be taken note of. Despite impressive growth, Tamil Nadu has a high unemployment rate. With falling employment, would it be justifiable to claim that the state is industrialised? Further, since 1996-97, there are noticeable structural shifts. The correlation between state domestic product (SDP) and the value of manufacturing output which was 0.96 in the decade 1981-1991 went down to 0.85 in the next decade. In the post-reform period, we notice that Tamil Nadu's traditionally strong industries such as cotton textiles, food products, leather, etc., have confronted problems. In the textiles segment, the problem is the slow pace of modernisation such as in moving from shuttle to shuttleless looms. Tanneries and the dyeing units have faced problems due to more public awareness about environmental degradation and pollution. Incidentally, this part of Kathuria's analysis should be seen in juxtaposition with the picture presented by Neelakantan in his paper on the Amaravathi Basin. For some industries, the reforms themselves, especially relating to import liberalisation, have resulted in loss of their competitive edge. On the positive side, the state has benefited from a strong engineering base and as mentioned in the beginning of this introduction the presence of a dynamic entrepreneurial class. Again parts of Kathuria's paper should be read in conjunction with Meenakshi Rajiv's study of the information technology (IT) sector. In part, the two complement each other.

Meenkashi Rajiv traces the development of the IT sector in the state, its main characteristics and future prospects and its emergence as an increasingly important source of income and employment. She notes that the government's strategy for promoting IT was not as aggressive as that pursued by Andhra Pradesh and Karnataka and suggests that this was perhaps because the state already possessed a stronger and more diversified industrial base. Though a late starter, the state has intensified its efforts to encourage the industry's expansion through investments in infrastructure and various incentives to increase its share in a growing market and exploit the potential from having a large pool of trained engineers. While this has resulted in quickening the pace of growth in recent years, efforts to diffuse the industry to newer locations, which are desirable, are yet to attract investors in the required degree. She goes on to offer suggestions for remedying this lacuna. The paper draws specific attention to the problems confronted by smaller firms in the IT sector such as inadequate state support. The aggressive push of the government has resulted in significant growth of not only IT and information technology enabled services (ITES) firms but also export revenue. While software industry is the major export earner, ITES segment is also fast catching up. We observe that to begin with software export growth was a mere ₹ 57 crores in 1995-96 which increased to ₹ 10703 crores in the next nine years (in 2004-05) showing an annual average increment of 20 per cent. The major export destination for Tamil Nadu (as for the rest of the country) is the US. Exports to the US have 72 per cent share followed by the UK with 15 per cent share. However, the state has been exporting to other European countries as well. Diversification of export destinations is good for several reasons. The state also earns substantial revenues from data processing. Tamil Nadu is fast catching up with Karnataka in software exports in spite of the latter having a head start. In terms of the share of IT professionals, the southern states appear to have lost ground to Maharashtra and their shares *vis-à-vis* one another are shifting in recent years. An interesting point is that despite all its advantages, Tamil Nadu is not perceived as an ideal IT location. It is not a brand that is promoted. The state is taking steps to promote e-governance and IT training especially in rural areas.

Srinivasan makes extensive and imaginative use of a source that does not figure prominently in most analyses, namely data based on complete enumeration of all establishments engaged in economic activity from the economic censuses of 1990, 1998 and 2005. The paper attempts to assess the contribution of the unorganised sector to the state's economy. Interesting conclusions emerge from this paper including evidence pointing to the social broadening of ownership by caste/class.

An important limitation of the census relates to the absence of an explicit definition of employment. This casts some doubt on the reliability of the data source. And it is possible that total employment is underestimated. In a similar fashion, it classifies ownership of establishments by gender and social classes, which are meaningful only for sole-proprietorship establishments. Classification of establishments by location, use of different sources of power, sources of finance and registration under different acts are interesting facts to highlight the changes in the pattern of establishments in terms of these characteristics. The total number of establishments has more than doubled, whereas employment has increased only by 61 per cent between 1990 and 2005; much of this increase has been between 1998 and 2005.

There are also noticeable differences across regions in the state. Among other findings, we may remark on the following:

- In terms of agricultural and non-agricultural activities, both in absolute numbers and growth rates, the rural areas have larger numbers of both agricultural and non-agricultural establishments. However, in terms of employment, the urban non-agricultural offer more employment.
- Of the 10 major categories in the non-agricultural activities, nearly 90 per cent of the establishments and employment are concentrated in five categories, namely, manufacturing and repair, wholesale and retail trade, hotels and restaurants, financial services and community and personal services. Of the 21 districts in the state, nearly 75 per cent of the establishments and employment are concentrated in 10 districts.

Social Sectors

The theme of the paper by Sundari, Balasubramanian and Mini on inequities in health is obviously important. It is of special interest because unlike most other surveys on health and health-seeking behaviour, it is based on data from a survey of some 2500 households in Dharmapuri—among the least developed districts in the state and one with an unenviable reputation for supposedly high rates of female infanticide. The households are chosen through statistical sampling to capture different socioeconomic groups and health statuses. Also the nature of morbidity is determined on the basis of intensive and closely supervised interviews with respect to symptoms experienced by members of the sample households and the medium and mode in which they are treated. Therefore, it gives a more reliable and comprehensive picture than most other surveys of these aspects and especially about how the more disadvantaged areas and groups cope with health problems. It shows the magnitude of inequalities in the incidence of acute, chronic and reproductive morbidity and its treatment across caste, class, gender, age and education, socioeconomic status and income. The authors use econometric analysis to assess the relative importance of these factors in accounting for variations across the sample units. They find caste, class and gender to be significantly associated with both acute and chronic morbidity. And further that given the well-developed health care system in the state, caste and gender do not make an appreciable difference to seeking treatment as such but they do influence where treatment is sought. This again is a paper which is rooted in a particular location but the methodology as well as the resultant conclusions are of wider relevance.

Geetha Rani concentrates on higher education and its morphology with particular reference to the burgeoning part played by the private sector. In this, we perceive clearly the impact of the overall development policy of the country on an important sub-set such as higher education. In particular, we see the repercussions of the withdrawal of the state from this sphere. She points to the urgent need to address the issue of quality of the human resources in this sector. There is also the problem that information on the quality of education may not be available to those seeking to utilize the sector's facilities. Her plea is for correcting the 'imperfection of information' and for some form of self-regulation in higher education. Given the new policy paradigms in the offing the problems raised by Geetha Rani are relevant to the ongoing national debate on these issues. Her paper also clarifies the position on the role of the private sector in different branches of collegiate education. For instance, she shows that, contrary to common perception, the role of the private sector is not limited to professional/technical education but is important in relation to general arts and science colleges too. Another interesting trend is that while the share of government and aided colleges is declining, they still account for the bulk of student enrolment.

Geetha Rani sees a nexus between the restraint imposed on the state by the Fiscal Responsibility and Budget Management Act (FRBM Act) and the withdrawal of the state from certain spheres of the education sector.

The increasing demand for and the willingness of parents to pay for the education of children in schools, especially private ones offering instruction in English (often of poor quality), are interpreted to mean 'willingness to pay', while in actual fact, it is more likely the result of non-availability of good schools in the state sector. This point is forcefully brought out by Jandhyala Tilak in his Adiseshiah Memorial Lecture in MIDS (2003). To return to the FRBM Act, this has predictably opened up more space for the entry of the private sector which in any case was already an established player. Her analysis illustrates how the education sector as a whole, in particular the professional/technical segment, shows evidence of under-regulation. The other major difficulty for technical education is that places in colleges are beginning to remain unfilled. And the problem of lack of attention towards the quality in recruiting staff is too common. One would expect the majority of technical, especially engineering, colleges to be concentrated in prosperous regions as is indeed the case. She approvingly quotes a well-known statement: "There is a place for the market but the market must be kept in its place." It is clear that the market is beginning to enjoy a free run.

The paper on the social sector by Natraj and Jeyaranjan has already been discussed. It needs to be emphasised that a major conclusion it presents is that what is called, often dismissively 'populism', in fact occupies a central place in the policy frame of Tamil Nadu. It is seen that both the major political parties have, by and large, implemented their electoral promises. The paper also makes an incursion into the impact of the financial crisis that the state experienced in the early years of this century on social sector expenditure. That on the whole social sector survived this crisis, admittedly with some hiccups, has a few lessons for policy makers and researchers alike. Also worth noting is that the trend towards offering benefits, in popular parlance 'freebies', continues into the present.

Environment

In recent times, the environment has come to occupy, and rightly so, a critical position in the development discourse. Kavi Kumar looks at the environment picture in Tamil Nadu and notes that the major forces exercising an impact on the environment are the density of population, especially in the coastal districts, the high degree of urbanisation, and industrial growth in the state. By way of adducing examples of environmental degradation, he cites the rank of Ranipet as one of the 10 most polluted places in the world (Blacksmith Institute) and the severe contamination of groundwater in Dindigul district. Arguing that the state is now at the crossroads in relation to the environment, he reviews the policies of the government to address environmental concerns. He points to the limited successes achieved and locates the reason for the most part in the absence of an integrated policy framework. One result is, as he describes it, emphasis on 'environmental hot spots' to the relative neglect of others. This too indicates the absence of a well-thought-out policy with long-term implications and smacks more of a fire-fighting exercise. Kavi Kumar points out that Tamil Nadu has, like many other states, made use of pressure state impact response (PSIR) to assess the state of the environment of a region. And since Tamil Nadu is relatively more vulnerable to drought and cyclone, a few recent studies in this context are reviewed and the transition of the state in the last decade in its vulnerability to these hazards is analysed. Kavi Kumar makes use of the framework suggested by the Intergovernmental Panel on Climate Change for assessing vulnerability. This framework employs three key components and indicators, namely exposure, sensitivity and adaptive capacity. This paper too discusses the adverse impact of indiscriminate sand mining on the environment. And there is a discussion of the harmful impact of the tanning and dyeing industries on water quality. In this respect, Kavi Kumar's contribution has a common focus in parts with Neelakantan's papers. The response strategies of the state can be seen through three broad categories: (a) strategies towards reducing the pressure; (b) strategies aimed at restoring the state of the environment; and (c) strategies targeted towards the amelioration of impacts caused by the environmental degradation.

Finally, the threats and opportunities for the state in the context of global climate change are discussed. While the potential changes in the rainfall, temperature and sea level could cause significant impacts in the climate sensitive sectors such as agriculture, health and coastal resources, the emerging carbon market through a clean development mechanism also offers opportunities for the state to embark on a sustainable development path.

Summing up

All in all what does one make of the present status of Tamil Nadu in economic, social and political terms? While it has registered impressive progress on many fronts and is well on the way to achieving several of the Millennium Development Goals (MDGs), there are spheres of concern. On the positive side regardless of which method of estimation is used, the state has witnessed decrease in the incidence of poverty but it still remains to be a poor-income state. It has regional imbalances and inequalities related to caste and gender. An area of particular concern is agriculture. In the 1980s and 1990s, Tamil Nadu was a front ranking state in agriculture. Thereafter, agricultural growth has experienced deceleration. Though the proportion of irrigated area is relatively high, there has been little expansion in recent years. Rainfed areas have had to confront several droughts. Agriculture and water conservation, more importantly optimising water utilisation, are areas requiring top priority. On the financial front, there is the problem of a rising debt-GSDP ratio, attributable in part to the weight of subsidies and rising burden of higher salaries and pension liability. Tamil Nadu has a high human development (HD) rank and is regarded highly for performance in sectors such as school education, public distribution, supply of drinking water and public transport. There are the usual and endemic problems in education relating to high dropout rates and the quality of teaching, but there are signs that there are improvements in the state school sector.

A few innovative practices have highlighted the state's development policy. One relates to the social sector, using the term in its broad sense, wherein the flagship programme is the midday meal scheme. Despite criticisms about its implementation, especially regarding the quality of food, it has made a difference to school attendance. The other is the untargeted universal public distribution system (PDS) which has lessons for other parts of India. Another important facet of policy is with respect to the availability of extension services at the grass root level offered by several line departments. Good examples are services rendered by agricultural extension staff and the adequate personnel in the primary health and education departments. We may also note the presence of farmers' markets.

All these are in the nature of social safety nets and explain to a significant extent the relatively lower incidence of farmers' suicides in the state. Although the situation is far from healthy, at least Tamil Nadu has avoided entering the 'black zone' in suicides.

Politically Tamil Nadu is stable with power alternating between the two Dravidian parties with almost pre-determined regularity. As remarked earlier, it is a state where the Congress has little choice except to get a ride as an accompaniment to one of the other two parties. The DMK does not resemble the party and the force it represented in its early days with much of its strident atheist, anti-Brahmanical tone quite diluted. Tamil Nadu is also noticeable for the somewhat underdeveloped Dalit movement. And it is worth exploring whether this is because for long, the Dalit cause was subsumed under the larger and wider canvas of the Dravidian movement. Here too there are some signs of changes in the offing.

It is obvious that the state faces challenges but in the past, it has demonstrated a capacity to meet them and therefore it is likely that the leadership will show the same resilience in the future.

This collection, like most research, raises more questions than it offers solutions for. If it provokes further thought and hopefully results in some pointers for future policy, the effort to put it together would not be unrequited.

We are conscious that in many of the papers, the data are not the latest available. It is our duty to make clear that the authors bear no responsibility for this. Mostly this is the result of delays in the editing of the volume but dare we hope that this limitation does not dilute the validity of the analysis and the diagnoses and the perspectives offered.

References

Ghosh, Madhusudan (2006). "Economic Growth and Human Development in Indian States", *Economic and Political Weekly* XLI(30), July 29.

Tilak, Jandhyala B.G. (2003). *State, Households and Markets in Education*. MIDS.

Population, Labour Force and Employment

1 Fertility Decline in the Southern States

K. Nagaraj

While every region in India has witnessed a significant decline in fertility rates in the recent past, the phenomenon is particularly striking in South India. Of the four southern states, Kerala, as is well known, has a long record in this. Fertility decline in the state set in as early as in the 1960s and today it has the lowest fertility level among all the major states in the country. The rate and nature of fertility decline in the state and the factors underlying it have been studied in detail: The 'Kerala Model' with its high levels of social sector development, and the consequent low fertility levels, is a well-known story by now (see Krishnan, 1967).

The state to follow Kerala was its neighbour, Tamil Nadu. The rapid decline in fertility in Tamil Nadu from around the early 1980s was rather unexpected. Tamil Nadu cannot boast of a very high level of female literacy and a very low level of infant mortality as Kerala can, and as pointed out above, the very high levels of social sector development is seen as the basic factor underlying the low fertility level in Kerala. The fact that Tamil Nadu also has a low fertility level today perhaps points to the fact that the story of fertility decline in this state has to be different from Kerala's.

This particular view—that the story of fertility decline would be different for different socioeconomic regions and states—was reinforced by the example of Andhra Pradesh where fertility decline set in around the middle of 1980s. The level of social sector development in Andhra Pradesh is significantly lower than even in Tamil Nadu. In fact, Andhra Pradesh has just about the same level of social sector development as the country as a whole; the female literacy rate in the state is even lower than the all-India average (see Table 1.2). The fourth state to follow suit, *viz.*, Karnataka, once again has only a moderate level of social sector development: it fares only slightly better than Andhra Pradesh—and all-India average—in this matter.

Today the four southern states have fertility rates which are significantly lower than the all-India average (see Table 1.1). The total fertility rates (TFR) in Kerala and Tamil Nadu are already below the replacement level (of 2.1)—significantly so in Kerala where the TFR is 1.8 and just so in Tamil Nadu with the TFR of 2.0. In Andhra Pradesh and Karnataka, the TFRs (in 2002) are above the replacement level, but given that the rate of decline in the TFR in both these states appears to be quite high, it is likely that both of them will reach the replacement level in the next few years.

However, we would like to reiterate that low and declining fertility rates are perhaps the only common feature in the demographic regimes of these four southern states. They would differ in the manner in which fertility declined in each state and factors underlying the decline. Of the four states, Kerala, of course, would be in a league of its own with high social sector achievements underpinning a rapid decline to a below replacement fertility rate.

Andhra Pradesh—and possibly Karnataka—provides a sharp contrast to Kerala in that conditions in the social sector perhaps provide only a secondary and minor support to fertility decline here. Tamil Nadu, which occupies the middle ground as it was, is also the most complex with a relatively high level of social sector development. On most of the indices relating to social sector, Tamil Nadu ranks quite high, second or third, among the major states in the country—the role played by this sector in the fertility transition in the state cannot be discounted. But social sector developments cannot provide the basis—as the most important determinant—of fertility transition in the state. The rate of decline and the present level of fertility are not what one would expect given the level and improvements in the social sector in the state. One has to bring on board additional socioeconomic factors as explanatory variables for the phenomenon.

This paper attempts to provide a broad, general picture of fertility transition in two of the southern status, *viz.*, Tamil Nadu and Andhra Pradesh. The major issues that it will deal with are the following:

Table 1.1

Birth Rate and Total Fertility Rate in the Southern States

State	Crude Birth Rate (CBR)					Total Fertility Rate (TFR)				
	Average Value of CBR for the 3-Year Period		Rank (in ascending order) among 16 Bigger States		Percentage Change between 1990-1992 and 2000-2002	Average Value for the 3-Year Period		Rank (ing ascendin order) among 16 Bigger States		Percentage Change between 1990-1992 and 2000-2002
	1990-1992	2000-2002	1990-1992	2000-2002		1990-1992	2000-2002	1990-1992	2000-2002	
Kerala	18.5	17.3	1	1	-6.4	1.8	1.8	1	1	Nil
Tamil Nadu	21.0	19.0	2	2	-9.8	2.2	2.0	2	2	-9.3
Andhra Pradesh	25.6	21.0	3	6	-18.0	3.0	2.3	3	4	-22.8
Karnataka	27.1	22.1	6	8	-18.4	3.1	2.4	5	5	-22.2
India	29.6	25.4	-	-	-14.2	3.7	3.1	-	-	-15.5

Sources: 1. Registrar General, India (2004): Sample Registration System (SRS) Statistical Report 2002.

2. Report No. 3 of 2004.

Table 1.2

Literacy Rate and Infant Mortality Rate in the Southern States

State	Literacy Rate				Infant Mortality Rate (IMR)		
	Female Literacy Rate		Total Literacy Rate		Average Value of IMR for the 3-Year Period		Percentage Change between 1990-1992 and 2000-2002
	1991	2001	1991	2001	1990-1992	2000-2002	
Kerala	86.2	87.7	89.8	90.9	16.7	11.7	-29.9
Tamil Nadu	51.3	64.4	62.7	73.5	58.0	48.0	-17.2
Andhra Pradesh	32.7	50.4	44.1	60.5	71.3	64.3	-9.8
Karnataka	44.3	56.9	56.0	66.6	73.3	56.7	-22.6
India	39.3	53.7	52.2	64.8	79.7	65.7	-17.6

Sources: 1. Census of India, 2001.

2. SRS, 2002.

- The extent and nature of fertility decline in Tamil Nadu and Andhra Pradesh.
- The manner in which fertility decline has taken place in the two states: the proximate components which have contributed to the decline.
- The socioeconomic factors that are likely to have provided the basis for fertility decline.
- The consequences of decline—particularly of the manner in which the decline has occurred, specially in relation to maternal and child health issues.

Before we turn to these issues, a word of two about the coverage and scope of the paper, the issues noted above will be dealt with in some detail only in the case of Tamil Nadu. This is for the simple reason that this is the only state whose socioeconomic situation we are familiar with. As for Andhra Pradesh, we should rely largely on a detailed study on fertility decline in that state carried out by James (1999). We shall make some references to Kerala, basically to point out the sharp contrasts that its experience in fertility transition provides in relation to Tamil Nadu and Andhra Pradesh. As for Karnataka, while we do provide some data on it, we have next to nothing to say on it in our discussions.

Extent and Nature of Fertility Decline in Tamil Nadu and Andhra Pradesh

The broad general trends in fertility decline over the last three decades or so—from around the early 1970s—in Tamil Nadu and Andhra Pradesh exhibit some similarities and contrasts. This is clear from the data on birth rates—which can be taken as a reasonable proxy for fertility rates—for the two states given in Tables 1.3 and 1.4.

From around the early 1970s, most of the years witnessed a decline in the birth rate in both Tamil Nadu and Andhra Pradesh, but the rate of decline varied considerably across the years. It appears that there were distinct periods of moderate and rapid decline, and even of stagnation, in the two states. In the case of Tamil Nadu, one can identify three such distinct periods. All through the decade of the 1970s and up to the early

Table 1.3

Birth Rate and Infant Mortality Rate in Tamil Nadu, 1971-1973 to 2000-2002

(3-year moving average)

Year	*Birth Rate*			*Infant Mortality Rate (Total)*
	Total	*Rural*	*Urban*	
1971-1973	31.3	33.4	26.2	114
1972-1974	30.6	32.9	25.0	112
1973-1975	30.0	32.1	25.1	109
1974-1976	30.2	32.1	25.8	109
1975-1977	30.4	31.9	26.9	108
1976-1978	29.8	30.9	27.0	106
1977-1979	28.9	29.8	26.7	103
1978-1980	28.5	29.6	26.0	99
1979-1981	28.3	29.6	25.2	94
1980-1982	27.8	29.4	24.4	89
1981-1983	27.9	29.3	24.9	87
1982-1984	27.9	28.9	26.0	83
1983-1985	26.9	27.5	25.6	82
1984-1986	25.5	25.9	24.7	80
1985-1987	24.1	24.5	23.5	79
1986-1988	23.5	23.9	22.8	76
1987-1989	23.3	23.6	22.5	72
1988-1990	22.5	22.9	21.7	67
1989-1991	21.8	22.0	21.4	62
1990-1992	21.0	21.3	20.6	58
1991-1993	20.3	20.5	20.0	57
1992-1994	19.8	20.2	19.1	58
1993-1995	19.7	20.1	18.7	56
1994-1996	19.7	20.2	18.6	55
1995-1997	19.6	20.1	18.6	53
1996-1998	19.2	19.7	18.3	53
1997-1999	19.2	19.6	18.2	53
1998-2000	19.3	19.8	18.1	52
1999-2001	19.2	19.8	18.0	51
2000-2002	19.0	19.6	17.8	48

Source: SRS.

Table 1.4

Birth Rate and Infant Mortality Rate in Andhra Pradesh, 1971-1973 to 2000-2002

(3-year moving average)

Year	*Birth Rate*			*Infant Mortality Rate (Total)*
	Total	*Rural*	*Urban*	
1971-1973	34.1	34.3	33.1	109
1972-1974	33.9	34.0	33.3	111
1973-1975	33.6	34.1	31.2	113
1974-1976	34.2	35.0	30.7	119
1975-1977	33.6	34.6	29.2	123
1976-1978	33.2	34.2	28.7	121
1977-1979	32.6	33.5	28.5	116
1978-1980	32.2	33.1	28.3	105
1979-1981	31.6	32.5	27.9	95
1980-1982	31.3	32.2	27.5	86
1981-1983	31.2	32.1	28.0	81
1982-1984	31.1	31.6	29.0	78
1983-1985	30.6	30.9	29.7	79
1984-1986	30.9	31.2	29.8	81
1985-1987	30.6	31.0	29.0	81
1986-1988	29.7	30.3	27.7	81
1987-1989	27.8	28.3	26.3	81
1988-1990	26.5	26.9	25.3	78
1989-1991	26.1	26.5	24.6	74
1990-1992	25.6	26.1	24.0	71
1991-1993	24.9	25.4	23.4	69
1992-1994	24.2	24.6	22.9	66
1993-1995	24.1	24.5	22.9	65
1994-1996	23.6	24.1	21.8	66
1995-1997	23.2	23.8	21.2	65
1996-1998	22.6	23.1	20.7	65
1997-1999	22.2	22.6	20.7	65
1998-2000	21.8	22.2	20.6	66
1999-2001	21.3	21.7	20.1	66
2000-2002	21.0	21.4	19.7	64

Source: SRS.

1980s, the birth rate here registered a modest decline. If we consider the 3-year averages for 1971-1973 and 1982-1984, the decline in birth rate was from 31.3 to 27.9, a modest drop of 3.4 points over an 11 year span (corresponding to an annual rate of decline of just 1.1%). The decline in birth rate in the next decade—from the early 1980s to early 1990s—was, in sharp contrast, very rapid: between 1982-1984 and 1992-1994, the decline was of the order of 8.1 points (corresponding to an annual rate of decline of 3.5%). A period of stagnation in birth rates followed thereafter, from the early 1990s onwards: between 1992-1994 and 2000-2002, the birth rate dropped by less than a point (with an annual rate of decline of just 0.5%).

The pattern in Andhra Pradesh is somewhat different: right up to the mid-1980s, the decline in birth rate here was sluggish. Between 1971-1973 and 1985-1987—over a period of nearly a decade and a half—the decline in birth rate was from 34.1 to 30.6, a modest drop of 3.5 points (corresponding to an annual rate of decline of just 0.8%). A rapid burst of decline set in after that, from around the mid-1980s to early 1990s: between 1985-1987 and 1992-1994, the birth rate declined by 6.4 points (annual rate of decline of 3.4 per unit). This short burst of rapid decline was followed, from around the early 1990s, by a period when there was a distinct deceleration in the rate of decline in the birth rate in the state. Between 1992-1994 and 2000-2002, this rate was 1.8 per unit per annum.

Two important points emerge from this discussion: first, it is the decade of 1980s when rapid decline in birth rates occurred in both Tamil Nadu and Andhra Pradesh. This span of rapid decline stretched for about a decade, from the early 1980s to early 1990s in Tamil Nadu, and accounted for nearly two-thirds of the decline in birth rate over the entire three-decade long span from 1971 to 2002. This burst of rapid decline occurred over a short span in Andhra Pradesh, from around the mid-1980s to early 1990s, and accounted for nearly half of the total decline in birth rate from 1971 to 2002. Certain socioeconomic factors—state policies in particular—underlie this phenomenon in the 1980s; we shall return to this issue later in the paper.

The second important point to note is that this rapid burst of fertility decline in the 1980s could not be sustained during the 1990 either in Tamil Nadu or in Andhra Pradesh: while in Andhra Pradesh, the rate of decline in birth rate decelerated considerably during the 1990s, Tamil Nadu witnessed a virtual stagnation in the birth rate during this decade. Part of the reason for the phenomenon could be the fact that at lower levels of birth rate, further reduction in it becomes increasingly difficult. But this could only be a partial explanation for the simple reason that neither of the two states has reached the 'lower limits'—if there be such limits—of birth rates. The fact that birth rate in Kerala today (at 19 in 2002) is lower than in Andhra Pradesh (20.7) or slightly higher than in Tamil Nadu (18.5) would testify to this. Given this, the phenomenon of decelerating decline or stagnation of birth rates in the two states may be because of broader socioeconomic factors or state policies. It may even be that the very manner in which fertility decline occurred in the two states might have created conditions or counter-currents, as it were which may render the process of fertility decline unsustainable. We will discuss this later.

There is another important issue to be noted from Tables 1.3 and 1.4. In Tamil Nadu as well as in Andhra Pradesh, the trajectory of decline in the rural birth rate seems to differ from the urban trajectory. This is particularly true during periods in which the overall birth rate (rural and urban combined) declined at a sluggish rate. Thus in Tamil Nadu, the rural birth rate declined at a significant, but moderate, rate (1.3%) during the first phase up to the early 1980s, while the urban birth rate hardly registered any overall decline but fluctuated considerably. Thereafter, there was considerable convergence in the two trajectories. The period of 1980s witnessed a rapid decline in both the rates, even though the decline appears to be faster in rural areas. The stagnation in the 1990s was witnessed in both the rural and urban birth rates, although the phenomenon was particularly striking in rural areas.

In Andhra Pradesh in the first phase up to the mid-1980s, the rural birth rate declined steadily, but at a low, sluggish rate, while the urban birth rate witnessed a roller coaster ride as it were: it declined sharply up to the early 1980s and thereafter in fact started increasing up to the mid-1980s. The second phase from the mid-1980s to early 1990s—the phase of rapid decline in overall birth rate—was one where both rural and urban rates declined sharply. And during the third phase of 1990s, the rate of decline decelerated in both rural and urban areas.

Thus, both in Tamil Nadu and Andhra Pradesh, while there was a considerable degree of divergence between the rural and urban birth rate trajectories until the phase of rapid fertility decline set in in the 1980s, there was a convergence, as it were, of the trajectories after that: the phase of rapid decline in birth rates was one when both rural and urban rates declined rapidly; the phase of deceleration or stagnation during the 1990s was one when both rural and urban rates either declined at low rates (as in Andhra Pradesh) or remained stagnant (as in Tamil Nadu).

There is another important dimension to this phenomenon of convergence which needs to be noted. The patterns of decline in birth rates in rural and urban areas from around the early 1970s in the two states have resulted in a situation where the differentials between the rural and the urban rates have declined considerably. And this is particularly true in Tamil Nadu. The rural-urban differential which was 7.2 points in 1971-1973 practically disappeared, to 0.5 point, by the early 1990s; during the phase of stagnation in birth rates in the 1990s, this differential widened a bit, but even by 2000-2002, it stood at a low 1.8 points. Even in Andhra Pradesh, there was a large and widening rural-urban differential in birth rates in the 1980s and remained low thereafter. In 2000-2002, this differential in Andhra Pradesh was just 1.7 points. We may note here that the corresponding figure for the country as a whole (in 2000-2002) was 7.2 points.

This phenomenon of convergence is observed not just across the rural and urban sectors in the two states, but across various socioeconomic groups also (see Table 1.5). The National Family Health Survey-2 (NFHS-2) data for the year 1998-99 clearly reveal that the differentials in TFR across various socioeconomic groups—defined by residence, mother's educational level, religion, caste and standard of living—are of a much lower order in the four southern states compared to the country as a whole. It is interesting to note that these differentials are particularly low if we consider a volitional variable like the (mean) 'ideal number of children' as reported by the women respondents in the NFHS. And this is particularly true for Tamil Nadu: except for the STs, whose numerical presence in the state is very low, no social group in the state today considers a family size of more than 2.1 children as being ideal.

Table 1.5

Variations in Actual and Wanted Fertility by Background Characteristics of Women in the Southern States, 1998-99

Background Characteristics		*Kerala*		*Tamil Nadu*		*Andhra Pradesh*		*Karnataka*		*India*	
		Mean Ideal Numbers of Children	*TFR*	*Mean Ideal Numbers of Children*	*TFR*	*Mean Ideal Numbers of Children*	*TFR*	*Mean Ideal Numbers of Children*	*TFR*	*Mean Ideal Numbers of Children*	*TFR*
Residence	Urban	2.3	1.51	2.0	2.11	2.3	2.07	2.0	1.89	2.3	2.27
	Rural	2.6	2.07	2.1	2.23	2.4	2.32	2.3	2.25	2.8	3.07
Mother's education	Illiterate	2.9	2.22	2.1	2.49	2.6	2.35	2.3	2.57	2.9	3.47
	Literate, below mid-school	2.8	2.02	2.0	2.37	2.2	2.22	2.1	2.09	2.5	2.64
	Middle school	2.5	2.14	2.0	2.21	2.1	1.94	2.0	2.06	2.2	2.26
	High school and above	2.2	2.02	1.9	1.85	2.1	2.20	1.9	1.89	2.1	1.99
Religion	Hindu	2.2	1.64	2.0	2.16	2.4	2.20	2.1	2.04	2.6	2.78
	Muslim	3.3	2.46	2.1	2.57	2.8	2.53	2.5	2.84	3.1	3.59
	Christian	2.3	1.88	2.1	2.14	2.4	2.53	2.0	1.57	2.7	2.44
Caste	SC	2.3	1.52	2.1	2.25	2.5	2.51	2.2	2.49	2.7	3.15
	ST	2.4	-	(2.2)	(2.39)	2.6	2.75	2.4	2.38	3.0	3.06
	OBC	2.6	1.90	2.0	2.18	2.4	2.26	2.1	1.85	2.6	2.83
	Other	2.5	1.85	1.8	1.69	2.3	2.00	2.2	2.24	2.5	2.66
Standard of living	Low	2.5	1.78	2.1	2.39	2.5	2.29	2.4	2.53	2.9	2.37
	Medium	2.6	1.98	2.1	2.10	2.4	2.32	2.2	2.03	2.7	2.85
	High	2.5	1.98	1.9	1.93	2.3	1.99	2.0	1.81	2.3	2.10
All		2.5	1.96	2.0	2.19	2.4	2.25	2.2	2.13	2.7	2.85

Note: OBC, other backward classes.

Source: NFHS-2.

Two important implications follow from our discussions on the phenomenon of convergence in birth rates across socioeconomic groups. Firstly, it is clear that the process of fertility decline in both Tamil Nadu and Andhra Pradesh has a wide social base and is not confined to any specific social group. It is a phenomenon that is observed in rural as well as urban areas, among the illiterate as well as literate, among Hindus as well as Muslims, among the rich and the poor and among the Dalits as well as the non-Dalits. Secondly, while the process of fertility transition has not bypassed any social group, the trajectory each of these groups has adopted in this transition is likely to be distinct. This is because of the simple reason that the 'initial conditions' from which each of these groups started would be different: given that the rural birth rate in Tamil Nadu at the beginning of 1970s was considerably higher than the urban rate, convergence in these rates by the early 1990s was possible because the pattern and rate of transition for the rural birth rate was different from the urban birth rate.

Two corollaries follow from the point made above. Firstly, if the socially deprived sections had a higher fertility rate at the beginning of this process of fertility transition, the 'burden' of this transition has fallen largely on them: it has fallen more on the rural than the urban, more on the illiterate compared to the literate and possibly more on the poor compared to the better off sections. The second corollary is methodological. The overall process of fertility transition, either in Tamil Nadu or in Andhra Pradesh, subsumes within it many strands, each corresponding to a different socioeconomic section of the population. Each of these strands has its own pattern and rate of transition and hence possibly a different set of factors underlying this transition. Fertility transition even within a state is a very complex phenomenon and monocasual explanations would hardly do justice to this complexity.

Coming back to the issue of convergence discussed above, we have so far dealt with it only in terms of birth rates. But this process of convergence, we believe, has a wider ambience. It is more in the nature of homogenisation of the fertility regime involving dimensions like the components of fertility decline and the manner in which the decline has come about, the methods adopted in this transition, etc. Let us turn to a brief discussion of these issues.

Proximate Components of Fertility Decline in Tamil Nadu and Andhra Pradesh

There are three distinct ways in which fertility rate of a population can decline: 1) an increase in age at marriage, of females in particular, 2) an increase in spacing between births and 3) a decline in the average number of children born during the reproductive span of women.

The relative contribution of these three proximate components—aptly termed as 'later', 'longer' and 'fewer' by the Chinese—provides important clues as to the manner in which fertility decline takes place and the larger socioeconomic factors underlying the decline. In Kerala, for example, the initial thrust to fertility decline was provided by an increase in female age at marriage which in turn was related to high and increasing female literacy levels. Family limitation followed thereafter and there is some evidence that birth intervals are increasing in the state in the recent past. So, the low fertility level in Kerala today is a consequence of high female age at marriage, family limitation and a high and increasing birth interval: all the three proximate factors seem to contribute to it.

The picture in Andhra Pradesh seems to provide a sharp contrast to Kerala. In terms of later marriage for females, the record of Andhra Pradesh appears to be poor. The age at marriage of females did increase, from a very low 16.3 years in 1971 to 18.3 years in 1991. This increase perhaps was one of the factors underlying rapid fertility decline during the 1980s. But the increase during 1990s—the phase of sluggish decline in birth rates—was very modest and Andhra Pradesh even today has an effective age at marriage of females which is 18.9 years—lower than the all India average (20.0 years). Slightly more than 80 per cent of the marriages in Andhra Pradesh take place with the age of the female 20 years or less; the corresponding all-India figure is much lower at around 63 per cent (see Table 1.6). The corresponding percentage, for Kerala, it may be noted, is much lower, at around 30 per cent. Thus one can safely argue that age at marriage does not seem to be a major factor underlying the low fertility level in Andhra Pradesh today.

The picture with respect to birth intervals is only marginally better: the median birth interval in Andhra Pradesh according to NFHS-2 was 31.1 months, which is only marginally better than the corresponding all-India

Table 1.6

Mean Age at Marriage in the Southern States

State	*Singulate Mean Age at Marriage of Females*					*Data for 2002*				
	1971	*1981*	*1991*	*NFHS-1 (1992-93)*	*NFHS-2 (1998-99)*	*Mean Age at Effective Marriage of Females*	*Percentage Distribution of Female by Age at Effective Marriage*			
							< 18 Years	*18-20 Years*	*21+ Years*	*Total*
Kerala	21.3	22.1	22.2	22.1	21.5	22.3	3.3	27.3	69.3	100.0
Tamil Nadu	19.6	20.3	20.9	20.5	20.9	21.3	2.2	41.5	56.2	100.0
Andhra Pradesh	16.3	17.3	18.3	18.1	18.3	18.9	19.9	61.2	18.9	100.0
Karnataka	17.9	19.3	20.1	19.6	20.1	19.5	14.6	56.6	28.8	100.0
India	17.2	18.4	19.3	20.0	19.7	20.0	11.6	52.2	36.2	100.0

Sources: 1. NFHS–1 and NFHS–2; 2. SRS, 2002; 3. Census of India.

average of 30.8 months (see Table 1.7). But what is worrisome is that the birth interval in fact registered a decline in the 1990s—from 33.4 months in 1992-93 to 31.1 months in 1998-99. Nearly 27 per cent of births in Andhra Pradesh took place with a birth interval of less than 24 months in 1998-99; the corresponding percentage in 1992-93 was around 23 per cent. While this phenomenon of declining birth intervals is observed in Tamil Nadu and Karnataka as well as the country as a whole, the striking contrast which Kerala provides is noteworthy: the median birth interval in 1992-93 in Kerala at 34.9 years was highest among the southern states, and it increased to 38.1 years by 1998-99.

Table 1.7

Birth Interval in the Southern States

State	*Year*	*Percentage Distribution of Births During the Five Years Proceeding the Survey by Interval in Months Since Previous Birth*						*Median (closed) Birth Interval (in months)*
		<12 Months	*12-17 Months*	*18-23 Months*	*24-35 Months*	*36-47 Months*	*48+ Months*	
Kerala	1992-93 (NFHS-1)	1.4	8.3	13.5	28.5	19.7	28.6	34.9
	1998-99 (NFHS-2)	1.2	8.4	11.7	24.4	18.1	36.2	38.1
Tamil Nadu	1992-93 (NFHS-1)	0.9	9.7	16.5	33.1	18.5	21.3	31.6
	1998-99 (NFHS-2)	1.7	11.3	17.3	33.0	16.5	20.3	30.5
Andhra Pradesh	1992-93 (NFHS-1)	1.8	8.0	12.9	33.7	21.2	22.5	33.4
	1998-99 (NFHS-2)	2.4	10.1	14.8	35.0	19.1	18.5	31.1
Karnataka	1992-93 (NFHS-1)	2.0	9.7	16.9	36.9	18.4	16.2	29.9
	1998-99 (NFHS-2)	1.1	9.9	19.3	35.5	18.4	15.8	29.7
India	1992-93 (NFHS-1)	2.0	9.8	15.1	33.8	20.8	18.6	31.6
	1998-99 (NFHS-2)	2.5	10.1	15.7	34.2	19.6	17.9	30.8

Sources: NFHS-1 and NFHS-2.

While the contribution of later marriages and longer birth intervals to the low fertility levels in Andhra Pradesh seem marginal or modest, it is the third component of family limitation of fewer children which has a major, overwhelming role in this. This is clear from Table 1.8 which gives the percentage distribution of live births by birth order for the southern states. The lower-order births, i.e., births of first and second order, account for an overwhelming proportion, more than 85 per cent of the total births in Andhra Pradesh today. The obverse of this is that the higher order births—births of the third order and above—account for a small proportion, just around one in seven, of the total births today. The contrast with the all-India picture is quite striking. The lower order births i.e., births of the first and second order, account for about 62 per cent of total births in the country as a whole in 2002, and obversely the higher order births account for around 38 per cent of total births. It is worth nothing that the proportion of higher order births in Andhra Pradesh in 2002 was even lower compared to Tamil Nadu, where about a fifth of the births were of the third order and above.

Table 1.8

Distribution of Live Births by Birth Order in the Southern States

State	*Year*	*Distribution of Live Births by Birth Order*			
		1st	*2nd*	*3rd*	*4th and Above*
Kerala	1984	35.9	27.4	18.0	18.7
	1992	44.6	34.8	13.7	6.9
	2002	47.2	37.7	10.8	4.2
Tamil Nadu	1984	32.9	26.1	18.7	22.3
	1992	47.6	30.5	14.4	7.4
	2002	42.5	37.7	14.1	5.7
Andhra Pradesh	1984	30.8	25.4	19.5	24.3
	1992	36.8	30.9	16.4	16.0
	2002	47.0	39.5	10.1	3.4
Karnataka	1984	28.3	23.0	17.6	31.1
	1992	37.2	29.4	16.5	16.9
	2002	41.2	34.0	14.5	10.4
India	1984	26.9	22.1	17.7	33.3
	1992	34.6	28.1	16.7	19.6
	2002	33.7	27.9	16.9	21.5

Source: NFHS-2.

What is also striking is the rapid decline in the importance of higher-order births over time in Andhra Pradesh. Births of the third order and above accounted for nearly half, around 44 per cent, of total births in the state in 1984; over the phase of rapid fertility decline, between 1984 and 1992, this proportion declined to around 32 per cent; and the sharp decline in this proportion continued even during the third phase when the rate of fertility decline in the state had decelerated. The decline in this proportion over this entire period, from 1984 to 2002, is of a much lower order, from around 51 per cent to 38 per cent, in the country as a whole.

Thus the rapid fertility decline in Andhra Pradesh, as well as its low fertility today, is based almost solely on family limitation where a large, and increasing, proportion of couples limit the number of children to just two. Later marriages or longer birth intervals appear to play only a modest role, if any, in this process.

The picture in Tamil Nadu has some similarities as well as differences with the picture in Andhra Pradesh. Late marriages do seem to have a role here unlike in Andhra Pradesh. The age at marriage of females, at 21.3 years in 2002, is higher than the all India average (of 20.0 years); it also appears that there has been a modest increase in the age at marriage, from 19.6 years in 1971 to 21.3 in 2002. But it is also worth noting that even today close to half, nearly 44 per cent, of the marriages in Tamil Nadu occur when the bride's age is 20 years or less. Early marriages are not rare in Tamil Nadu; they are still an important phenomenon.

It is in terms of birth intervals that Tamil Nadu's record appears to be particularly poor. The median birth interval in the state in 2002 is 30.5 months which in fact is slightly lower than the all India average (of 30.8 months). Bunching of births around low birth intervals is quite high: close to 30 per cent of the births in the state occur with a birth interval of less than 24 months. What is more as in Andhra Pradesh and in sharp contrast to Kerala, the birth interval in Tamil Nadu has declined over the 1990s, and the phenomenon of bunching of births around low birth intervals has got strengthened.

The third proximate factor, *viz.*, family limitation, has played a very dominant role in fertility reduction in Tamil Nadu, as in Andhra Pradesh. The higher order (3+) births account for just about a fifth of the total births in the state in 2002, and there has been a sharp decline in this proportion over the years. It declined very sharply, from 41 per cent to just around 22 per cent during the 1980s, the period when fertility declined very sharply in the state. The decline in higher order births as a proportion of total births was very modest in the next decade when birth rates in the state were stagnant: from around 22 per cent in 1992, it declined to around 20 per cent in 2002. The close links that the phenomenon of family limitation has with fertility decline in Tamil Nadu are indeed striking.

Let us summarise: family limitation appears to be the dominant factor underlying the transition to a low fertility regime in both Tamil Nadu and Andhra Pradesh. Of the other two proximate components later marriages and longer birth intervals—the former seems to have played some role in Tamil Nadu, although the state's record in terms of the latter, *viz.*, longer birth intervals, is quite poor. In Andhra Pradesh, on the other hand neither of the two factors later marriages and longer birth intervals seems to have played any significant role in its transition to a low fertility regime.

It is clear from the foregoing that the dominant fertility behaviour in Andhra Pradesh is the one where an early marriage is followed by the birth of two children in quick succession and the family size is limited to that. The picture in Tamil Nadu is substantially the same except that marriages generally take place at a later age here. And this dominant fertility behaviour has its reflection, as it were, in the pattern of contraceptive use in the two states. This comes out clearly from Table 1.9.

The temporary methods of contraception which would aid spacing have no role to play in fertility control in the two states, and the reliance in both the states has overwhelmingly been on a permanent method, *viz.*, female sterilisation. This phenomenon is particularly striking in Andhra Pradesh: in 1992-93, only around 4 per cent of the women who used any contraceptive method went in for a temporary method, almost all of the remaining 95 per cent opting for a permanent method. And within the permanent methods, only a handful, 14 per cent of the total, went in for male sterilisation, the rest opting for female sterilisation. In 1998-99, the overwhelming reliance on permanent methods, had continued with 96 per cent opting for them, but within these methods, the role of female sterilisation had increased, while that of male sterilisation has declined. In Tamil Nadu, the role of permanent methods increased between 1992-93 and 1998-99 and this increase could be attributed solely to an increasing

Table 1.9

Percentage Distribution of Currently Married Women using Contraceptives by Contraceptive Method Used in the Southern States

State	Year	Modern Methods							Any Modern Method	Any Traditional Method
		Permanent Methods			Temporary Methods					
		Female Sterilisation	Male Sterilisation	Total	Pill	IUD	Condom	Total		
Kerala	1992-93	66.0	103	76.3	0.8	4.3	4.6	9.6	85.9	14.1
	1998-99	76.1	3.9	80.0	0.6	2.5	4.9	8.0	88.1	11.9
Tamil Nadu	1992-93	75.3	4.0	79.3	1.2	7.0	3.2	11.4	90.8	9.2
	1998-99	86.8	1.5	88.3	0.6	4.8	2.9	8.3	96.5	3.5
Andhra Pradesh	1992-93	81.1	14.0	95.1	1.1	1.3	1.5	3.8	98.9	1.1
	1998-99	88.4	7.2	95.6	0.8	1.0	1.2	3.0	98.8	0.8
Karnataka	1992-93	83.5	3.1	86.6	0.8	6.5	2.4	9.8	96.3	3.7
	1998-99	88.3	1.2	89.5	1.0	4.8	1.7	7.5	96.9	2.9
India	1992-93	67.2	8.4	75.6	3.0	4.7	5.9	16.5	89.4	10.6
	1998-99	71.0	3.9	74.9	4.4	3.3	6.4	14.4	88.8	10.4

Note: Date refer to contraceptive method currently used. (IUD: intrauterine device)

Source: NFHS-1 and NFHS-2.

role of female sterilisation; the role of male sterilisation which was already of a marginal significance in 1992-93 went down even further by 1998-99 to a mere 1.5 per cent of the total. We may note here that the dominant role of female sterilisation in fertility decline, as well as an increase in this dominance over time, is a phenomenon observed all over the country, including Kerala. It is just that the extent of this dominance in quantitative terms appears to be higher in Andhra Pradesh and Tamil Nadu compared to most other states (including Kerala).

In sum, the homogenisation of the fertility regime in Andhra Pradesh and Tamil Nadu has occurred not just in terms of bridging the fertility gaps across social groups but also in terms of the dominance of certain pathways and methods adopted in the process of fertility transition. Fertility transition in the two states seems to have encompassed almost all the social groups most of whom seem to have adopted some standard pathways and methods. All the same, one should not lose sight of the fact that homogenisation is an outcome of many strands of transition each with its 'initial conditions', trajectories and rate, and different sets of factors underlying each of them. Let us now turn to a brief discussion of these likely factors.

Factors Underlying Fertility Decline

As pointed out earlier, overall fertility transition in Andhra Pradesh or Tamil Nadu is likely to subsume within it a number of different strands each with specific factors underlying it. And hence any mono-causal explanation for fertility decline in either of the states would be totally inadequate. But we shall not attempt to provide a comprehensive explanatory scheme for fertility decline in either of the states here. And hence the discussions in this section will be somewhat sketchy and will concentrate only on two broad issues:

- The role of state policies in fertility decline: here we shall deal with two sets of state policies: a) policies with respect to social sector development and poverty alleviation and b) the family planning programmes implemented by the state.
- The broader socioeconomic, cultural and political dimensions which may have a bearing on fertility levels.

We would also like to reiterate that discussions in this section will be largely confined to Tamil Nadu given our relatively better familiarity with the socioeconomic situation in this state.

Role of State Policies in Fertility Decline

State Policies with Respect to Social Sector Development and Poverty Alleviation

We had noted earlier that the level of social sector development in Andhra Pradesh can hardly provide the basis for the low level of fertility prevailing there: female literacy and infant mortality rate—two indices usually taken as barometers of social sector development—are around the same as the all-India average, while the fertility rate in the state is significantly lower than the all-India average.

Social sector development in Tamil Nadu on the other hand would have played a more important role as a basis for its low level of fertility. In terms of both female literacy and infant mortality, Tamil Nadu is one of the better performing states. All the same, a comparison with Kerala would point out that while social sector development may be a significant factor behind its low fertility, it cannot be as in Kerala the dominant explanatory factor: while the fertility rate in Tamil Nadu is close to that of Kerala, it falls much behind Kerala in terms of social sector development. Female literacy rate in Tamil Nadu in 2001 is 64 per cent which is considerably lower than what Kerala had achieved even a decade earlier, by 1991 (86%); infant mortality rate (IMR) in Tamil Nadu today is around 4 times as high (at 48) compared to Kerala (12).

However, improvements in social sector conditions certainly seem to have provided the basis for a decline in fertility levels in Tamil Nadu, particularly in the 1980s when fertility declined rather sharply here. This is clear if we look at the trend in infant mortality in the state (see Table 1.3). A declining trend in infant mortality as a basis for a decline in fertility is perhaps one of the most consistently observed relationships in demography. And Tamil Nadu seems to be no exception to this: the infant mortality rate has steadily declined, albeit from a high level, from around the middle of 1970s up to the early 1990s in the state: over a span of around 14 years from 1976-1978 to 1990-1992, IMR declined by as much as 48 points (corresponding to annual rate of decline of 4.4%). Thus decline in IMR seems to precede, as it were, the decline in fertility in Tamil Nadu. But what is noteworthy is that the period of 1980s, when fertility declined sharply, was also the period of rapid decline in IMR in the state, and this is particularly true of the latter half of 1980s: between 1985-1987 and 1990-1992, IMR declined at an annual rate of 6.4 per cent. The remarkable fit between decline in IMR and decline in fertility in the state is visible even in the 1990s: during this decade, birth rate remains stagnant, so does IMR.

A complex set of socioeconomic factors underline this decline in IMR. We do not propose to get into these issues in any detail except to point out the role played in this decline particularly in the 1980s by important state interventions, particularly in relation to maternal and child health: the most important of these interventions is the by now the well-known Noon Meal Scheme, covering all children in the age group of 3-15 years, which was introduced in 1982. In spite of the many problems that this scheme faces, its impact in terms of improving the general nutrition and health status of children perhaps is undeniable. But equally important is the fact that this major intervention programme provided the focus, or nucleus, as it were, for a number of other interventions with respect to ante-natal care and child care provisions. State intervention to control tetanus deaths is a case in point: in the late 1970s, a major cause of infant death in Tamil Nadu was tetanus, and this was particularly so in the rural areas. A sharp increase in the coverage of pregnant women by anti-tetanus injections in the 1980s was a major factor behind the sharp decline in infant deaths in this decade.

The link between decline in IMR and fertility decline appears to be rather weak in the case of Andhra Pradesh: while the phase of rapid decline in fertility from around the mid 1980s was preceded by a sharp decline in IMR from around the mid 1970s to early 1980s, there was a virtual stagnation in IMR for a few years around the middle of 1980s when fertility was declining quite rapidly. A short period from around the late 1980s to early 1990s is the only one when IMR and fertility rates seem to decline in unison. It is also noteworthy that from around the early 1990s, IMR has remained virtually stagnant in Andhra Pradesh. We may recall that this is the period when a significant deceleration in fertility decline sets in in the state (Table 1.4).

A detailed district level study on fertility decline in Andhra Pradesh by K.S. James also comes to similar conclusions: female literacy or infant mortality across the districts in the state correlated poorly with fertility rates. But James does point to a number of important state interventions in the 1980s which might have been responsible for rapid decline in fertility in Andhra Pradesh in that decade. The chief among them are 1) significant progress made during the decade in ante-natal care of pregnant women; 2) improvements in child health programmes, particularly in immunisation; 3) a vigorous public distribution systems (PDS): the subsidised rice scheme at ₹ 2 per kilo which was implemented in 1983 was a major nutritional intervention programme; and 4) vigorous implementation of various poverty alleviation programmes.

In sum, the foregoing discussion points to the complexity of the relationship between social sector development and fertility decline; a cross-sectional comparison between Andhra Pradesh and Tamil Nadu on the one hand and Kerala on the other would point out that unlike in the latter, social sector development was not a dominant factor in the two former states in terms of their low fertility level today. All the same, it appears that decline in IMR even from a high initial level does have a significant effect on fertility. As James points out, there seems to be no threshold level for IMR or female literacy at which fertility starts declining. Given this, state interventions in social sector development and poverty alleviation do have a significant bearing on fertility decline, as the examples of Tamil Nadu and Andhra Pradesh in the 1980 clearly demonstrate. Stagnation of IMR in both states from the early 1990s onwards and the concurrent stagnation or deceleration in fertility in the two states lend support to the above contention. Neo-liberal policies pursued in this decade which led to a dilution or withdrawal of state commitment to social sector and poverty alleviation were obviously responsible for this phenomenon observed in the 1990s. But, as we shall point out later, that is only a part of the story, albeit perhaps the major part.

Role of Family Planning Programme in Fertility Decline

It is often claimed that state policies with respect to family planning as such are central to fertility decline in Tamil Nadu. The main points made by the proponents of this view, consisting mostly of serving and retired bureaucrats in the state, regarding the elements crucial to this decline are: 1) strong political will to implement the family planning programme which is related to the fact that Dravidian parties, which have had an almost uninterrupted rule in the state since the mid 1960s, have a strong ideological commitment to the small family norm; 2) bureaucratic efficiency, which is partly due to the fact that resources of many government departments and not just of the Department of Health and Family Welfare as in other states were utilised for motivating and organizing family planning services; and 3) effective communication strategies.

The family planning programme in Tamil Nadu does appear to be relatively more 'efficient' compared to most of the states in the country, perhaps even in comparison with Kerala in that while it has had a better spread and reach across space as well as social groups, it is also better targeted towards more fertile couples. But this 'efficiency' of the programme hides certain imbalances: there is total lack of emphasis in the programme on the female age at marriage or on the delivery of temporary methods of contraception; it relies excessively on female sterilisation, and this is not accidental. The family planning programme in Tamil Nadu was essentially target driven, as it was all over the country. Driven by a desire to obtain quick results in terms of a rapid decline in the birth rate, the state, it appears, had devoted its energies to a single, 'effective' technique, *viz.*, female sterilisation. This technique, along with the birth-based approach adopted in its family planning drive would yield quick and reliable results. In contrast, the spacing methods would be less reliable and the logistical problems involved in their delivery are also perhaps more intractable, and hence these methods are given a go by in the official family planning programmes. Thus the 'efficiency' of the family planning programme in Tamil Nadu and the imbalances in the programme seem to be two sides of the same coin.

The discussions above would also point to a number of congruences between characteristics of fertility transition on the one hand and aspects of the family planning programme on the other, in Tamil Nadu. Thus, the fact that fertility transition in Tamil Nadu took place very largely through family limitation, with later marriages and longer birth intervals not having an important role in it, has its congruence or reflection in the imbalances in the family planning programme where the reliance has been overwhelmingly on female sterilisation with spacing methods and age at marriage given a go by. Similarly the increasing homogenisation of fertility also finds its expression in the relatively better spread and reach across space and social groups of the family planning programme in the state.

Now, to claim on the basis of such congruencies that the family planning programme in the state is the factor responsible for the fertility transition, a leap from correlations to causation would, in our view, be untenable. Such an assertion would have to rely on either of the two underlying assumptions, each of which we believe would be unsustainable. The first such assumption would be that the demand for family planning services has been quite high for sometime in Tamil Nadu, but a large part of it was unmet earlier, and the recent fertility transition is an outcome of an increasingly efficient family planning programme which has met a larger and larger proportion of this overall demand. Such an assumption of a more or less static overall demand for family planning services is hardly tenable.

The available data clearly indicate a decline in the 'desired family size' and consequently an increase for family planning services in Tamil Nadu over the last three to four decades.

If the demand for family planning services has increased over time, the claim that the family planning programme in the state is the major factor underlying fertility transition in Tamil Nadu would have to assume that the very increase in the demand for the family planning services is to be ascribed to the programme. Arguments which emphasise that a major factor behind fertility decline was the effective communication strategies and programmes which spread the message of the small family norm seem to rely on such an assumption.

Such a view, we believe, is simplistic. The demographic regime is moulded by basic socioeconomic factors, and one has to look into these factors to understand why the desired family size would decline and the demand for family planning services would increase in a region. Once these basic socioeconomic factors are at work, the communication strategies adopted in the family planning programme may play a supportive role in creating the demand for various types of services. And once this demand has been generated, an 'efficient' family planning programme may be necessary to fulfil the demand, and hence it can play a supportive role in fertility decline. But to understand the phenomenon of fertility decline, one has to look deeper into the basic socioeconomic structure and the transformations in it.

The Role of Socioeconomic Factors in Fertility Decline

A promising line of enquiry regarding socioeconomic factors underlying fertility decline in Tamil Nadu would be to view it as a consequence of increasing aspirations of the population, the poor included, on the one hand, and the continuation of absolute deprivation, on the other. This would lead to unfulfilled aspirations and in an effort to bridge these aspiration gaps, limitation of family size would be taken recource to. A number of surveys based on Focus Groups Discussions in different parts of Tamil Nadu by Sundari Ravindran and P.M. Kulkarni support this contention.

The perspective outlined above is very much within the tradition of social mobility approaches to fertility which has a long history in population studies, dating back perhaps to Arsene Dumont's theory of 'social capillarity', put forward in 1890 to explain the French experience of rapid fertility decline in the 18th and the early 19th centuries. According to this theory, in a hierarchical society which is also witnessing considerable social mobility or circulation, the drive towards social recognition by the individual or the household would result in low fertility since a large family size is an encumbrance to upward social mobility. Just as a liquid has to be thin to facilitate its movement upwards in a capillary, a family needs to be small to facilitate its upward social mobility. Such pressures towards family limitation to facilitate an upward social mobility would be particularly strong if the family also happens to be a deprived one.

If social capillarity is to be seen as a factor that underlies rapid fertility decline in Tamil Nadu in the 1980s, one has to look for the socioeconomic factors that would provide the basis for such a phenomenon in and around the 1980s. Apart from the reasonably high literacy rates, there are a number of other socioeconomic factors responsible for this phenomenon, some of which are noted below in brief.

Role of Strong Rural-Urban Linkages

The rural-urban linkages in Tamil Nadu are quite strong compared to other states in the country (with the possible exception of Kerala). Apart from the fact that it has the highest degree of urbanisation among all the states in the country, the urban population in the state is distributed over a large number of towns and these towns are also fairly evenly spread out over space within the state. These strong rural-urban linkages in Tamil Nadu can act as an effective mechanism for the transmission of urban values to rural areas in terms of the small family norm, but perhaps more importantly in terms of norms and aspirations regarding lifestyles. This spread of urbanism got strengthened particularly during the 1970s and 1980s in the state for a number of reasons. 1) The period 1960s-1980s witnessed a very significant increase in the spread and development of the road network of 'minor' roads, *viz.*, roads other than highways and major district roads in particular and of transportation facilities, of public transportation in particular. 2) There appear to be significant changes in the migratory patterns in the state during the 1970s and 1980s, when circulatory movements between rural and urban areas increased as also urban to rural migration: both of these would have helped in the spread of urbanism in rural areas. 3) High and increasing levels of exposure to mass media.

Nature of Agrarian Transformation and Fertility Decline

The Green Revolution in the late 1960s and the 1970s in Tamil Nadu had a higher intensity and depth, as also a wider reach and spread in spatial as well as social terms compared to most other states in the country. The wider spatial and social reach of this transformation is due to the fact that it is largely based on what is termed as the 'pump set revolution'. The gainers from the Green Revolution were drawn from a large number of castes and communities, even though within each of these castes and communities only a few gained and the gainers also had a larger spatial spread. And it is these small number of gainers in different communities and localities who would have set the trend in terms of elite-emulation, and over the years, their lifestyles and norms provided the desideratum to which others in the community and locality aspired to, without, it may be noted, the means to live such lifestyles and norms.

Changes in Marriage System and Fertility Decline

One of the striking characteristics of the marriage system in Tamil Nadu is the high incidence of consanguinity in the state, but there is considerable evidence to the effect that the importance of consanguinity in the state was declining over the 1970s and the 1980s. While urbanisation and increase in educational levels may be partly responsible for this decline in consanguinity, the major factor underlying it in rural Tamil Nadu perhaps is the nature of agrarian transformation that was outlined above: there is some evidence to the effect the gainers from the Green Revolution in different communities and localities, who often set the lifestyle norms for the others to aspire to, often utilised marriage as a means to social mobility, often bypassing the traditional rules of consanguinity. And dowry was frequently used as a means to do so.

Now the age at marriage within the consanguineous system generally is quite low and hence the decline in this system would have provided an upward thrust to age at marriage. And this could be one of the factors underlying fertility decline in the state.

We may also point out that the emergence of dowry, a concomitant of the decline in consanguinity, is often seen as the basis of the pernicious practice of female infanticide and foeticide, a practice which appears to be quite common among certain communities and localities in Tamil Nadu today. It is far from our contention that there is any direct link between fertility decline on the one hand and the practices of female infanticide or foeticide on the other. But it is also worth noting that some of the socioeconomic factors which provide the basis for fertility decline are also the ones which result in a devaluation of female life.

The Dravadian Movement and Fertility Decline

As pointed out earlier, it is often claimed that one of the factors responsible for rapid fertility decline is the strong ideological commitment to the small family norm of the Dravidian parties which have ruled the state since the mid 1960s. This is debatable because for the Dravidian Movement, as at least for its founder leader E.V. Ramaswamy, family planning did not just stop at family limitation; it encompassed late marriage (for women) and female education, issues to which the family planning programme under the dispensation of Dravidian parties has hardly paid any attention. But it is undeniable that the Dravidian Movement in the state, at least in its initial phases, did create space for the middle and the lower castes to assert their rights and identities and hence created the space for social mobility and circulation, a space which was essential for the phenomenon of social capillarity to operate.

Our discussions so far have identified some of the factors that underlie rapid fertility decline in Tamil Nadu. We had also noted, in passing, that the dilution of state commitment to the social sector and to poverty alleviation programmes in the 1990s as part of its neo-liberal policies may be a factor responsible for the stagnation of IMR as well as of fertility in this decade. We had also hinted there that it could only be a partial explanation. Our contention in fact is that the very manner in which fertility transition has taken place in Tamil Nadu as well as in Andhra Pradesh can have consequences for maternal and child health which in turn can effect IMR and birth rates. Let us turn to a brief discussion of these issues now.

Consequences of the Manner in which Fertility Transition Has Taken Place in Tamil Nadu and Andhra Pradesh

We had noted earlier that the dominant fertility behaviour in Andhra Pradesh today is the one where an early marriage is followed by the birth of two children in quick succession after which the mother resorts to female sterilisation. The picture in Tamil Nadu is substantially the same except that the percentage of early marriages here is not high as in Andhra Pradesh.

Such fertility behaviour can lead to a high incidence of high-risk pregnancies. The data on high-risk pregnancies from the NFHS-1 for the year 1992-93 are given in Table 1.10. Nearly half the births in Andhra Pradesh in 1992-93 were in the high-risk category, a proportion which was only marginally lower than the all-India average. The proportion is lower in Tamil Nadu at around 38 per cent, which, it is to be noted, is significantly higher than the proportion of high-risk pregnancies in Kerala. What is also worth noting is that both in Andhra Pradesh and Tamil Nadu, while the proportion of pregnancies with 'traditional' forms of risk (as with birth order >3 and mother age >34 years) is low, risks accompanying emerging fertility behaviour associated with early marriages and short birth intervals are indeed quite high: traditional forms of risky pregnancies are being replaced not so much with risk-free pregnancies but with new forms of risky pregnancies. It is worth noting that while in Andhra Pradesh, early marriages are the most important factor behind high-risk pregnancies, in Tamil Nadu, it is the short birth intervals. Unfortunately, the NFHS-2 has not provided similar data for the year 1998-99. But given the fact that the dominant fertility behaviour in Andhra Pradesh and Tamil Nadu has not changed significantly and the incidence of births with low birth intervals has increased between 1992-93 and 1998-99, it would be a safe surmise that the incidence of pregnancies at risk would not have declined during this period in either state.

It is perhaps to state the obvious that high-risk pregnancies can have serious consequences for maternal and child health. They can lead to a high incidence of spontaneous abortions as in Tamil Nadu, with important consequences for maternal health. The strong relationship between high-

Table 1.10

High-Risk Fertility Behaviour in the Southern States, 1992-93

State	Percentage of Children Born in the Last Five Years at Elevated Risk of Mortality, According to Category of Increased Risk												
	Single High-Risk Category					Multiple High-Risk Category							
	Mother's Age <18 yrs	Mother's Age >34 yrs	Birth Interval (BI) <24 Months	Birth Order (BO) >3	Sub Total	Age <18 and BI <24	Age >34 and BI <24	Age >34 and BO <3	Age 34 and BI<24 and BO >3	BI <24 and BO >3	Sub Total	In Any High-Risk Category	In Risk Categorical with Age <18 and /or BI <24
Kerala	3.0	1.2	11.2	7.3	22.8	0.3	0.1	2.0	0.1	2.1	4.6	27.3	14.5
Tamil Nadu	7.6	0.6	12.9	10.3	31.4	0.9	0.2	2.1	0.2	2.9	6.3	37.7	21.4
Andhra Pradesh	17.0	0.3	8.5	15.9	41.7	2.5	-	1.9	0.1	4.7	9.2	50.9	28.0
Karnataka	13.1	0.6	10.3	17.2	41.1	2.1	0.1	1.9	0.4	7.2	11.7	52.9	25.5
India	9.0	0.4	10.2	19.2	38.9	1.3	-	4.1	0.6	7.4	13.5	52.3	20.5

Source: NFHS-2.

Table 1.11

Mother's Age, Birth Interval and Infant Mortality: 1988-1999

Variable	Value	Kerala			Tamil Nadu			Andhra Pradesh			Karnataka			India		
		Neonatal Mortality	Post-neonatal Mortality	Infant Mortality	Neonatal Mortality	Post-neonatal Mortality	Infant Mortality	Neonatal Mortality	Post-neonatal Mortality	Infant Mortality	Neonatal Mortality	Post-neonatal Mortality	Infant Mortality	Neonatal Mortality	Post-neonatal Mortality	Infant Mortality
Mother' age at birth (years)	<20	16.0	2.9	18.9	43.2	16.3	59.5	52.1	31.8	84.0	55.2	19.3	74.4	63.1	29.7	92.7
	20-29	12.5	5.4	18.0	33.8	13.6	47.4	42.9	17.2	60.1	36.6	16.7	53.3	40.7	22.6	63.3
	30-39	30.7	9.7	40.4	35.5	19.8	55.2	52.3	22.8	75.1	52.8	20.4	73.2	48.7	27.9	76.7
	40-49	NA	NA	NA	NA	NA	NA	NA	NA	NA	NA	NA	NA	61.9	44.3	106.2
Previous birth interval (months)	<24 months	22.1	9.5	31.6	53.8	31.8	85.6	77.6	27.9	105.5	68.3	30.5	98.8	71.7	37.8	109.5
	24-47 months	10.0	4.7	14.6	35.4	12.5	47.9	35.0	22.6	57.6	29.0	16.1	45.1	35.5	22.6	58.1
	48+ months	11.5	4.1	15.6	18.8	9.5	28.4	20.3	13.0	33.3	25.2	7.1	32.3	24.1	14.4	38.5

Source: NFHS-2.

Table 1.12

Infant Mortality Rate and its Components in the Southern States

Year	Kerala			Tamil Nadu			Andhra Pradesh			Karnataka			India		
	Neonatal Mortality	Post-neonatal Mortality	Infant Mortality	Neonatal Mortality	Post-neonatal Mortality	Infant Mortality	Neonatal Mortality	Post-neonatal Mortality	Infant Mortality	Neonatal Mortality	Post-neonatal Mortality	Infant Mortality	Neonatal Mortality	Post-neonatal Mortality	Infant Mortality
1981	37	26	11	91	63	28	86	60	26	69	49	29	10	70	40
1986	27	19	8	80	57	23	82	57	25	73	54	19	96	60	36
1992	17	11	6	58	43	15	71	52	18	73	54	19	79	50	29
2001	11	9	2	49	32	17	66	40	26	58	40	18	66	40	26
2002	10	7	3	44	30	14	62	41	21	55	38	17	63	40	23

Source: SRS.

risk pregnancies and child health is brought out sharply in Table 1.11 which relates different high-risk variables to components of infant mortality: high-risk variables like low birth intervals and pregnancies at early ages are very strongly related to both neonatal as well as post-neonatal infant mortalities and hence to exceedingly high levels of IMR in Andhra Pradesh as well as Tamil Nadu.

Given this, it should not come as a surprise that the infant mortality rates have remained stagnant at high levels both in Andhra Pradesh and Tamil Nadu during the 1990s: the stagnation in IMR in the 1990s, it appears, is largely due to stagnation (as in Tamil Nadu) or even an increase (as in Andhra Pradesh) in the post-neonatal rate (Table 1.12). A look at Table 1.11 should clarify the reason for this. In Tamil Nadu where the incidence of short birth intervals is high and increasing, the post-neonatal rate is very sensitive to this variable: post-neonatal mortality rate (PNMR) for births with short birth intervals is at least 2½ times as high as for births with higher intervals. In Andhra Pradesh, a similar role is played by early child birth and we may recall that the proportion of early marriages is very high in the state.

In sum, one can identify two sets of factors which in combination have resulted in a situation in the 1990s when the infant mortality rate and consequently the birth rate have remained stagnant in Andhra Pradesh and Tamil Nadu: the first set of factors seems internal to the demographic regime. The manner in which fertility transition has taken place in the two states has generated tendencies with serious consequences for maternal and child health. The second set of policies relates to the withdrawal of the state from the social sector and poverty alleviation programmes.

Concluding Observations

After exploring in some detail the extent, nature and the manner in which fertility decline took place in the two southern states, this paper has attempted to delineate the larger socioeconomic factors including aspects of state policies which underlie this decline. Given our emphasis on studying the broader socioeconomic issues, a crucial question regarding the nature of this transition is not explicitly taken up for consideration so far, and the question is: is this transition, either in Andhra Pradesh or in Tamil Nadu, cooperative or coercive?

If one were to equate a coercive transition essentially with overt forms of coercion stipulated and enforced by the state as in the imposition of a two-child norm or of disqualification of those with more than two children from contesting *panchayat* elections, etc., the transition either in Andhra Pradesh or Tamil Nadu cannot be characterised as being coercive. But coercion takes many forms: it may be direct or indirect, over or covert. And just as exploitation can take place under a veil of market relations, coercion can take place under a veil of rather impersonal, "benevolent" development processes. Viewed from this broader perspective, there are, we believe, strong elements of coercion in the manner in which fertility transition took place in Andhra Pradesh and Tamil Nadu, and the following reasons are offered as explanations:

- The fertility transition takes place in a context where women seem to have next to no choice in terms of the method of contraception: patriarchal values that govern the society on the one hand and concerns of a target-driven bureaucracy on the other provide women here with only one choice: female sterilisation.
- The transition has imposed costs in terms of health status on both women and children.
- The socioeconomic basis for this transition is one where increasing levels of aspirations have not been matched by the 'resources' to meet them: persistence of absolute deprivation appears to be a factor necessary for this transition to occur. This is so at least in the case of Tamil Nadu. We may also note here that some of the socioeconomic factors underlying fertility transition have also led concurrently to the emergence of dowry and hence to a devaluation of status of women.

To anticipate an objection to the above line of reasoning, it may be argued that even a fertility transition of the nature witnessed in Andhra Pradesh and Tamil Nadu would result in enormous benefits to women 'battered by over frequent child births' and on the whole, the 'benefits' would outweigh the 'costs' to the women. Such an argument, we believe, misses the obvious point that there are alternative routes to fertility transition through social sector advances and empowerment of women which would avoid these costs but confer the same benefits. That this alternative route would require an entirely different perspective on the so-called 'population problem' and a different set of state policies to buttress it is another matter.

References

James, K.S. (1999). "Fertility Decline in Andhra Pradesh: A Search for Alternative Hypotheses", *Economic and Political Weekly*, February 20-26.

Krishnan, T.N. (1967). "Demographic Transition in Kerala: Facts and Factors", *Economic and Political Weekly*: 1203-24 (Special No; 1976).

2 Trend and Pattern of Employment in Tamil Nadu

Some Recent Trends, 1980s versus 1990s

Brinda Viswanathan

Introduction

Tamil Nadu is among the more developed and faster developing states of the country in most conventional socioeconomic indicators. According to the 2011 census provisional results, Tamil Nadu accounts for 5.96 per cent of India's population at 72.1 million. Decadal growth rate of population has been higher at about 15.6 per cent (17.64% for all India and 4.86 per cent for Kerala) in the recent inter-census period of 2001 and 2011 as against 11.7 per cent between 1991 and 2001, and the higher rate is being attributed to increase in in-migration to the state.[1] The literacy rate of the population (aged 7 years and above) increased from about 50 per cent in 1981 to 80 per cent in 2011 with the male literacy rates going up from 68 per cent to 87 per cent and female literacy rates from 40 per cent to 74 per cent during the same period. There has been a decline in total fertility rate (TFR) from 3.4 per cent in the early 1980s to 2.1 per cent in the early 21st century.

The state is more urbanised than most other states. The pace of urbanisation continues with the proportion of population residing in cities and towns increasing from 33 per cent in 1981 to 44 per cent in 2001 with the rate for 2011 still awaited. It has a well-developed infrastructure and a diversified economy. A large proportion of its farm land is irrigated and productivity of land is also relatively high. Manufacturing is developed and

1. The census related information is from the recent census report provided at *http://censusindia.gov.in/2011-prov-results/data_files/Tamil Nadu/1.PPT%201%20TN%20-%20Intro.pdf* and accessed on 30th May 2011.

accounts for a larger proportion of income and employment compared to other parts of the country.

According to Rao and Singh (2005), Tamil Nadu accounted for 8 per cent of the total net state domestic product (NSDP) of the country in 2001 while its population share was about 6 per cent. Tamil Nadu's annual growth rate in NSDP has been on the upswing since the 1980s. Panagariya (2010) observes that annual growth rate increased from 4.8 per cent in 1981-1988 to 5.5 per cent in 1988-2003 and 8.6 per cent for the period 2003-2009. As per the economic appraisal done in 2008-09, the gross state domestic product (GSDP) (at constant 1999-2000 prices) of the state grew at 4.6 per cent (Government of Tamil Nadu, 2009).

Considering the per capita GSDP, Tamil Nadu grew at a rate (compound growth rate) of 3.88 per cent per annum compared to an average of 3.02 per cent per annum for all states put together in the 1980s. In the following decade, the per capita GSDP growth for all states increased to 3.8 per cent per annum, while for Tamil Nadu, it surged up to 5.52 per cent, the highest after Karnataka and Gujarat. In terms of the sectoral composition of the domestic product, the share of primary sector for the state has been among the lower end values compared to most other states even three decades back. In the early 1980s, share of agriculture in Tamil Nadu's NSDP was about 25 per cent which declined further to about 17 per cent by 2000 and the share of service sector by this time was close to 50 per cent (EPWRF, 2001). In 2008-09, the primary sector recorded a negative growth of 1.92 per cent, while the secondary sector declined to 1.0 per cent from 2.25 per cent and the services sector also showed a decline to 7.62 per cent from 8.17 per cent compared to the previous year (Government of Tamil Nadu, 2009). Though the current trend in the state's income including sectoral growth has been very encouraging, the state has been shown to have done well in reducing intra-state regional disparity. Kurian (2000) identifies Tamil Nadu as one of those states successful in reducing intra-state disparities, even though the natural endowments of the regions vary substantially.

This paper documents the main features of changes in overall structure and characteristics of employment during this period of significant demographic changes and rapid improvements in the indicators of socioeconomic development. The focus is not only on the overall picture but also on rural-urban and gender differences and to a limited extent on changes in select, relatively disadvantaged religious and social groups. In most sections, comparison is drawn between Tamil Nadu and the all-India picture in these respects. The study is based on data from quinquennial employment and unemployment surveys conducted by the National Sample Survey Organisation (NSSO) for the years 1987-88, 1999-2000 and 2004-05. The analysis is largely based on unit record data of these employment rounds and supplemented with information provided in the detailed tables in published reports of NSSO.

Section 1 analyses the changes in age-specific labour force participation rates (LFPR) and section 2 discusses the employment and under-employment patterns among rural men, urban men, rural women and urban women separately. This section in particular focuses on the trends in unemployment among youth and the educated for the four segments mentioned above. Section 3 focuses on the trends and patterns in the employment states—self-employed, regular salaried and casual labour, while section 4 deals with the changes in sectoral shares of employment looking at nine major segments including agriculture, manufacturing, construction and services. This section also looks at the changes in real daily wage rates in the state and across some regions of the state. Section 5 analyses the labour market features across social and religious groups, while section 6 concludes the study.

Changes in Age-Specific Participation Rates: 1987-88 to 2004-05

Demographic Structure

As per the NSSO estimates, the population of Tamil Nadu increased from 50 million in 1987-88 to 52.6 million in 1999-2000 to 55.7 million in 2004-05. About 33 per cent of the population was below the age of 15 years in 1987-88, declining to 27 per cent in 1999-2000 while maintaining the same rate in 2004-05 as well with the rural sector contributing to most of this change. Evidently, this resulted in an increase in the prime working age population (25-54 years) going up from 18.5 million in 1987-88 to 24 million in 2004-05. However, the share of Tamil Nadu in this age group in India declined from about 7.7 per cent in 1987-88 to 6.6 per cent by 2004-05. How do these demographic changes affect the change in LFPR and more so is the pattern of change similar in rural and urban areas, and, between men and women?

The overall LFPR has been consistently higher than the national average, in rural and urban areas and among males as well as females as shown in Table 2.1. Given the rise in the share of working age population, one would have expected LFPR to have risen during the period from 1987-88 to 2004-05. However, this has not happened and it will be useful to analyse further the age-specific participation rates and changes over time.

Table 2.1

Trends in Labour Force Participation Rates (Principal and Subsidiary Status) Tamil Nadu and All India: 1987-88, 1999-2000 and 2004-05

	Tamil Nadu			*All India*		
	1987-88	*1999-00*	*2004-05*	*1987-88*	*1999-00*	*2004-05*
Overall	56.0	52.6	49.5	48.6	45.8	43.0
Rural	61.0	56.9	52.2	51.0	48.1	44.6
Urban	47.0	44.7	43.1	40.3	39.1	38.2
Male	67.8	66.2	60.4	62.2	60.9	55.5
Female	44.3	38.8	37.7	34.1	29.9	33.3

As shown in Table 2.2, in Tamil Nadu as well as all India, rural areas have a larger proportion of population in the young age groups with lower participation rates compared to the main 15+ working age group. Participation rate of females in all age groups is lower than that of males; differences in these respects are more marked in urban areas resulting in lower participation rates overall in urban areas. Given that the decline in LFPR is more marked in Tamil Nadu than at the national level, this trend could perhaps be explained by a combination of several factors: a progressive fall in the proportion of the 5-19 age group in the population reflects progressive reduction in birth rates and equally importantly a remarkable decline in child labour, that is, a decline in the LFPRs among this age group reflects progressive increase in the proportion attending school.

Changes in Age-Specific Participation Rates: Younger Cohorts

Sundaram (2001) observed that a major reason for the decline in overall labour force participation in India in the 1990s was the increase in

Table 2.2

Trends in Age-Specific Labour Force Participation Rate (PS+SS), Tamil Nadu and All India: 1987-88, 1999-2000 and 2004-05

	TN	*5-14*	*15-19*	*20-24*	*25-29*	*30-54*	*55-59*	*Above 59*	*All*
				Tamil Nadu					
ALL	1987-88	10.7	55.4	70.4	77.2	81.2	69.4	44.9	56.0
	1999-2000	3.8	42.3	63.5	72.1	77.7	67.7	38.1	52.6
	2004-05	1.6	40.1	65.1	72.0	80.2	68.9	38.3	49.5
Males	1987-88	10.0	63.3	91.8	97.3	97.6	89.4	61.9	67.8
	1999-2000	4.0	49.2	87.0	96.7	97.6	86.5	52.6	66.2
	2004-05	1.3	44.0	83.9	98.5	97.7	89.6	51.3	60.7
Females	1987-88	11.4	48.0	51.0	57.7	64.9	49.8	27.3	44.3
	1999-2000	3.5	35.0	42.3	49.8	57.8	50.6	23.1	38.8
	2004-05	1.9	35.8	47.8	49.1	63.1	49.8	26.5	38.5
Rural	1987-88	12.5	63.9	76.4	83.1	86.9	75.8	52.1	61.0
	1999-2000	4.3	46.6	69.3	77.3	83.3	74.7	45.1	56.9
	2004-05	1.5	45.5	71.3	78.4	87.4	78.7	46.3	53.4
Urban	1987-88	7.3	42.0	61.7	67.5	70.2	55.6	31.1	47.0
	1999-2000	2.8	33.9	53.8	63.3	67.7	53.7	25.8	44.7
	2004-05	1.7	31.8	56.7	63.3	69.6	52.7	23.7	43.4
				All India					
ALL	1987-88	8.66	46.89	64.29	71.95	75.50	66.60	42.22	48.57
	1999-2000	4.20	38.01	60.22	69.19	73.88	64.54	38.04	45.78
	2004-05	3.44	39.28	61.87	71.48	75.75	67.23	39.39	43.00
Males	1987-88	9.06	56.49	86.43	96.17	97.16	90.24	62.47	62.19
	1999-2000	4.27	48.43	84.62	97.00	97.97	89.52	57.76	60.85
	2004-05	3.50	48.82	85.35	97.44	98.19	90.54	57.77	55.90
Females	1987-88	8.22	35.91	43.49	48.05	52.73	41.59	20.68	34.08
	1999-2000	4.11	25.76	36.38	42.66	49.07	39.67	18.51	29.93
	2004-05	3.36	28.12	38.48	45.79	52.91	43.49	21.54	29.43
Rural	1987-88	9.89	52.12	68.50	75.31	78.35	69.87	45.51	51.02
	1999-2000	4.73	42.85	64.72	72.95	77.55	68.59	42.48	48.13
	2004-05	3.71	43.71	65.64	75.00	79.74	72.10	44.82	44.62
Urban	1987-88	4.12	30.87	51.80	61.66	66.15	54.32	29.18	40.29
	1999-2000	2.39	25.34	48.77	59.14	64.16	51.81	23.55	39.05
	2004-05	2.47	27.32	52.64	62.60	65.26	53.31	22.79	38.25

attendance in educational institutions in younger age groups. This is also the case in Tamil Nadu. Table 2.3 gives the overall workforce (principal and subsidiary) participation rates and attendance in educational institutions for three young subgroups—5-14 years, 15-19 years and 20-24 years for four different segments: rural males, rural females, urban males and urban females.

Table 2.3

Workforce Participation and Attendance in Educational Institutions (Principal Status), 1987-88, 1999-2000 and 2004-05: Tamil Nadu

	In Workforce			In School			Others		
	1987-88	1999-2000	2004-05	1987-88	1999-2000	2004-05	1987-88	1999-2000	2004-05
				Rural					
Males									
5-14	9.6	2.8	1.2	54.2	86.2	97.7	36.2	11.0	1.1
15-19	62.6	43.2	41.4	28.3	46.9	51.6	9.1	9.9	7.0
20-24	87.7	85.0	84.0	2.5	7.3	8.2	9.8	7.7	7.8
Females									
5-14	13.6	1.8	1.8	42.9	82.7	94.1	43.4	15.6	4.1
15-19	59.0	23.4	39.9	12.6	38.0	32.0	28.4	38.6	28.1
20-24	57.3	39.2	50.0	1.3	6.0	4.7	41.4	54.8	45.3
				Urban					
Males									
5-14	6.5	2.1	1.2	84.5	90.1	97.7	9.0	7.8	1.1
15-19	47.0	34.6	35.7	37.9	57.5	58.2	15.1	7.9	6.1
20-24	73.3	73.0	67.5	8.5	17.2	22.8	18.2	9.9	9.8
Females									
5-14	6.1	0.2	1.5	77.5	85.5	95.7	16.4	14.3	2.8
15-19	23.6	9.2	16.4	27.0	61.9	63.4	49.4	29.0	20.3
20-24	29.9	10.2	29.1	4.1	17.2	14.1	66.0	72.6	56.8

Close to half in rural areas and over 80 per cent in urban areas were in school in 1987. Gender disparity in this respect was very marked but only in rural areas. The proportion of children out of school was relatively high among rural children and much more so among females. The situation changed: by 1999, more than 80 per cent of both male and female children were in school in rural as well as urban areas which increased to about 95 per cent in 2004-05. Gender and rural-urban disparity in this respect has been more or less eliminated and increase in enrolment rates corresponds to a decline in participation rates for all the segments. Reported work participation rates in 1987 were quite low for children in the 5-14 year age group (less than 15% among rural females and less than 10% among males) and negligible in urban areas; even if one included 'others' or 'nowhere children' as they are referred to, still the numbers seem to be small. These rates have fallen to less than 2 per cent in all categories by 2004. The veracity of these figures of working children is under question, and there are reasons to believe that they understate the incidence of child labour. This could be because this table is based on principal status alone and the children could still be working after or between school hours, and further home-based unpaid work could still be largely unreported or under-reported. The increase in school attendance from the 1980s to the mid 2000s could be divided into two parts: the 1990s saw a movement out of the labour force, while the 2000s saw a larger share of 'nowhere' children also drawn into the schools with boys having an edge over girls.

In the 15-19 age group, there is a clear indication that school attendance is an important determinant of LFPR but this change is more apparent among males than females and more so between the 1980s and the 1990s than between the next five years. Higher school participation goes with lower LFPR in all groups and over time, but this impact is much stronger among males than among females. In 1987, in urban areas, a larger proportion of males in this age group was in school and their LFPR was also higher compared to rural areas. In both segments, there has been a sharp rise in these indicators. The proportion of those who are neither in school nor in the labour force is relatively small.

The picture is quite different in the case of females—in both rural and urban areas, LFPR declined substantially between 1980s and 1990s but then increased by 2004, though not to the same extent as the late 1980s. In 2004, though there is an increase in LFPR among females in both rural and urban areas, this seems to have decreased 'in school' share as well as the 'others' in rural areas, while in urban areas the share of 'in school' also increased marginally and 'others' share declined substantially since 1987 from 49 per cent to 20.3 per cent. Of course, this decline was sharper from 1980s to 1990s than from 1990s to 2000s. This pattern of decline in share of 'others' is similar to men in both rural and urban areas but not so for rural females which showed a 10 percentage point increase to 38 per cent in 1999 from 1987 and a decline back to 28 per cent in 2004.

In the 20-24 age groups participation rates are higher, and enrolment rates are lower, than in the 15-19 age bracket in all the years but there are rural-urban and male-female differences in the pattern which change over time. The proportion in 'others' category is very small among males which probably reflects the fact that the proportion of population in this group continuing education is quite small and that a large majority of them have entered the labour force. Compared to males, the proportion of females in workforce is much smaller, a large majority being out of labour force at least in principal status. It is quite likely that this age group would be engaged in child care and household chores and hence shows lower participation rates when compared to men, but the differences in temporal changes between men and women are important to take note of.

The school attendance which improved substantially between 1987 and 1999 declined in rural areas between 1999 and 2004, while it increased only marginally in urban areas similar to males. However, in rural areas, the withdrawal from the workforce which got translated into increase in school attendance was lower than for other segments while the share of 'others' increased more. More importantly, the workforce participation rate (WFPR) in 2004-05 got restored to rates similar to 1987-88 with a small decline in the share of school attendance rates and more substantially a decline in the share of 'others'. Thus, it appears that this cohort may be behaving like surplus labour but the increased participation could be due to two reasons. One is that it may be due to higher human capital for this age group which is expected given that many of the women in this cohort may have attended school as compared with the previous NSS round. Alternately, second is that participation rates for women could increase when the wages are depressed in the labour market leading to lower incomes for the households thereby drawing more women into the labour force to supplement household income. Since the changes are noticed in both rural and urban areas and given the liberalisation and demand for female labour in urban areas and poorly performing agriculture in most states, both these conditions may be prevailing in Tamil Nadu. A more detailed analysis of the wages and participation rates for more recent years may be helpful in getting at the root of this pattern of change over time.

Changes in Age-Specific Participation Rates: Middle-aged and Older Cohorts

Referring back to Table 2.2, one notices that for the age group 30-54, the overall participation rate's decline between 1987 and 1999 and increase again by 2004 were similar for Tamil Nadu and at the national level. This change is similar in both rural and urban areas but not so for men and women: men have almost similar participation rates across all the three rounds in the 30-54 age group but it is the women who seem to be contributing to this change. For the 55-59 age group also, there is a marginal decline in 1999 from 1987 but then increases back by 2004 in overall rates. Here the changes are similar for men and women. The above 59 age group shows an overall decline from 1987 to 1999 and settles down at the same level in 2004 and is similar for Tamil Nadu and all India. The pattern for males is very similar to the overall pattern, while for women after the decline in 1999, the rates pick up by 2004. However, there has been a secular decline in urban areas while rural follows the overall pattern.

Female LFPRs among adults are lower than those of males in all age groups. They show an across the board decline between 1987 and 1999. But the age group variations follow a different pattern compared to that observed among males. Participation rates of adult women are low partly because responsibilities of child bearing, child care and household work severely limit their availability for outside work. The other reason is that time spent on collection of fuel, tending cattle and other similar unpaid activities are excluded in the concept of labour force used by the Census and the NSSO.[2] Women's occasional and part-time involvement in economic activity is treated as subsidiary work and accounts for a significant portion of their LFPRs. Their magnitude does not show a clear pattern over time.[3]

In sum, focusing on the 20-60 age group, the overall participation rates have declined since 1987-88. This is contributed mainly by women, as for men, this decline is either very small in some age groups or remains

2. The proportion of women who spent time collecting domestic goods along with household chores remained the same at about 9 per cent for Tamil Nadu during this period, while at the all India level where about 15 per cent women spent their time in this activity in 1987-88, it increased further to 17 per cent by 1999-2000. Recent surveys by NSS provide a more comprehensive picture of the time spent by women on different activities and their relative importance.

3. In Tamil Nadu, the incidence of subsidiary employment in the labour force (6.1% in 1987-88) is lower than the national average (7.4%). It had nearly halved to 3.2 per cent in Tamil Nadu by 1999-2000 which is much steeper than the decline in the national average which was around 6 per cent in the same year. It is to be noted that in 2004-05, subsidiary employment remained at similar levels as the previous NSS round for 1999-2000 and that the increase seemed to come from an increase in principal status employment.

stable, while for women the decline is more prominent. This has impacted on both the rural and urban labour markets. In Tamil Nadu, the female participation rates have all along been higher than all India in each of the age segments within 20-59 years, but the rates have fallen further at the national level. Further analysis of this phenomenon is essential to understand the regional changes and the factors causing these changes

Unemployment and Underemployment

Not all those in the labour force (i.e. available and seeking employment) find jobs all the time. Those who do not have any work during the previous 365 days are categorised as 'usually unemployed'. The proportion of the labour force reporting this status to the total labour force is a measure of the unemployment rate. A sizeable proportion of labour force does not have employment throughout the year, these constitute the 'underemployed'. The rate of underemployment is measured as the ratio of the number of days on which the labour force reports lack of work to the total number of days for which they are available for work. These estimates for Tamil Nadu and all India are presented in Table 2.4.

Table 2.4

Unemployment Rates (Percentage) according to Usual and Daily Status: Tamil Nadu and All-India (in brackets)

	Rural				*Urban*			
	Males		*Females*		*Males*		*Females*	
	Usual Status	*Daily Status*	*Usual Status*	*Daily Status*	*Usual Status*	*Daily Status*	*Usual Status*	*Daily Status*
1987-88	2.6 (1.8)	8.4 (4.6)	3.1 (2.4)	10.7 (6.7)	6.2 (5.2)	12.3 (8.8)	6.6 (6.2)	13.2 (12.0)
1993-94	1.8 (1.4)	12.8 (5.6)	0.6 (0.8)	11.3 (5.6)	4.3 (4.0)	8.6 (6.7)	6.8 (6.2)	12.7 (10.5)
1999-2000	2.7 (1.7)	14.3 (7.2)	1.0 (1.0)	12.3 (7.0)	3.6 (4.5)	9.0 (7.3)	5.1 (5.7)	8.6 (9.4)
2004-05	1.2 (1.6)	15.3 (8.0)	1.1 (1.8)	14.9 (8.7)	2.9 (3.8)	8.1 (7.5)	4.8 (6.9)	9.8 (11.6)

Source: Various Reports of NSSO.

Trends in Unemployment and Underemployment Rates: Tamil Nadu and All India

The rate of usual status unemployment in rural areas of both Tamil Nadu and all India is relatively low—these rates are generally higher among females than among males. Reported unemployment rates in urban areas are much higher ranging from 3 to 6.8 per cent in Tamil Nadu which is sometimes higher and sometimes lower than the all-India rates. These rates do not show a clear trend in rural areas over time. But they show a larger and more sustained decline among both males and females in urban Tamil Nadu compared to the national picture.

Underemployment rates are much higher than unemployment rates in Tamil Nadu. The difference between the two is also far more pronounced in rural than in urban areas. Underemployment rate in the state is generally higher (nearly double in several cases) than the corresponding national averages. Over time, rural underemployment rates in Tamil Nadu show a progressive and steeper rise than in the country as a whole. By contrast, urban underemployment rates in the state show a decline between 1987-88 and 2004-05 which is more sustained but somewhat less pronounced among males than among females and also compared to the national pattern. Increasing underemployment rates seem to go with increasing proportions of casual wage labour in the labour force. NSSO also collects information on the reason for being unemployed or underemployed. An analysis of this data could help us better understand the factors underlying these trends.

Unemployment Rates among Youth and the Educated in Tamil Nadu

Focusing on Tamil Nadu, one observes that unemployment is largely concentrated among youth, in the age group 15-24 (Table 2.5). For each of the NSS rounds, the unemployment rate (4-8 per cent in rural and in urban areas) in the 15-19 age group was two to three times the overall rate for males as well as females with a decline in the reported rate in the 19-24 and 24-29 age groups and yet this is above the overall rate. The urban rates are higher than rural rates and the better-educated report far higher rates than the others.

High rates of youth unemployment are associated with high rates of unemployment among the educated: unemployment rates in the population with middle level education are about twice that for the below primary group; the rate for those with more than secondary-level education is five times that of the below primary group for males and higher by many more times among females. This pattern holds both in rural and urban areas.

Table 2.5

Unemployment Rates (Principal Status) Among Youth and Among Educated for Age Groups 15 Years and Above, Tamil Nadu 1987-88, 1999-2000 and 2004-05

(Percentage)

		Age Specific				Education Specific		
		15-19	*20-24*	*25-29*	*All age>=15*	*Below Primary*	*Primary and Middle*	*Secondary and Above*
All	1987-88	10.2	12.0	6.3	5.0	2.7	5.3	13.7
	1999-2000	13.4	13.6	7.2	4.5	0.3	2.2	8.5
	2004-05	8.4	9.0	3.4	2.7	0.7	1.7	7.7
Males	1987-88	12.1	13.6	6.3	5.0	2.0	5.8	10.8
	1999-2000	14.7	13.1	7.2	4.5	0.6	2.6	7.2
	2004-05	8.6	8.2	2.4	2.3	0.4	1.6	5.4
Females	1987-88	7.8	9.3	6.3	5.0	3.3	3.6	24.3
	1999-2000	9.9	15.1	7.2	4.4	0.1	1.0	14.0
	2004-05	8.1	10.3	5.1	3.2	0.9	2.0	15.1
Rural	1987-88	6.7	8.5	5.0	4.0	2.6	3.8	15.5
	1999-2000	8.2	6.4	3.0	2.1	0.2	1.7	10.8
	2004-05	6.6	6.7	2.7	2.1	0.8	1.4	8.5
Urban	1987-88	18.5	18.2	9.0	7.3	3.0	7.7	12.5
	1999-2000	14.9	15.0	8.1	5.1	1.1	3.3	6.7
	2004-05	12.3	12.8	4.4	3.8	0.3	2.3	7.1

The overall unemployment rate above the age 15 has declined over these NSS rounds but the rate of decline is faster between 1999 and 2004 than between 1987 and 1999. However, across age groups, there was an increase between 1987 and 1999 in the 15-19 and 20-24 year age groups in Tamil Nadu mainly due to higher rates among females than males. Also while urban rates showed a decline all along rural rates increased and then decreased. The education-specific rates have also declined and more substantially for women from 24.3 per cent in 1987-88 to about 14 per cent in 2004-05 in the upper end of the education segment but the rates for women are still the highest. All over the world, this is a known phenomenon that unemployment rates are higher for women than for men.

A further classification of the person-days employed shows that except for rural men the person-days of employment increased in 2004 after a decline in 1999 since 1987 and that it increased secularly to about 10 percentage points in urban areas for women (Table 2.6). Alongside this change, there has also been an increase in the unemployed in rural areas alone; this has more than doubled since 1987.

Table 2.6

Distribution of Person-days of Usually Employed (Principal and Subsidiary Status) by their Broad Current Daily Status (Percentage)

	Rural			*Urban*		
	Employed	*Unemployed*	*Not in Labour Force*	*Employed*	*Unemployed*	*Not in Labour Force*
			Males			
1987-88	90.6	5.6	3.8	91.2	6.5	2.3
1999-2000	82.7	11.2	6.2	91.4	5.2	3.4
2004-05	83.9	13.8	2.3	93.3	5.0	1.7
			Females			
1987-88	72.1	5.4	22.5	77.7	5.1	17.2
1999-2000	70.2	8.9	20.9	82.1	3.0	14.9
2004-05	76.4	12.1	11.5	88.2	4.5	7.3

Thus, once again the female unemployment rates seem to be different when compared to males and that it is a far more serious problem in urban areas and among youth with secondary- and higher-level education. But there are welcome signs as there has been a decline across all the segments. Reported unemployment rate in rural areas is quite small but here underemployment is a more serious problem both in terms of level and the fact that it seems to be increasing.

These changes in LFPR need to be assessed in terms of the type of employment, that is self-employed, casual labour and regular employment and more so for women as is done in the following section.

Employment Status and Some Related Features

Employment status as reported by NSSO is categorised into self-employment and wage employment which can be further classified as regular-salaried and casual labour. There are significant gender and rural-urban differences in these respects which are shown in Tables 2.7 and 2.8.

Table 2.7

Distribution Across Employment Status of Workers as a Proportion of Total Workers in Tamil Nadu from 1987-88 to 2004-05

	Rural				*Urban*			
	SE/TW	*RE/TW*	*CL/TW*	*WL/TW*	*SE/TW*	*RE/TW*	*CL/TW*	*WL/TW*
				Males				
1987-88	44.6	13.7	41.7	55.4	33.7	47.4	18.9	66.3
1993-94	41.4	12.5	46.1	58.6	34.5	40.3	25.2	65.5
1999-2000	35.8	15.3	48.9	64.2	34.5	40.3	25.2	65.5
2004-05	39.9	13.4	46.7	60.1	38.0	45.2	16.7	62.0
				Females				
1987-88	46.0	6.9	47.1	54.0	45.4	30.0	24.6	54.6
1993-94	41.9	5.2	52.9	58.1	39.4	30.1	30.2	60.3
1999-2000	38.0	6.9	55.1	62.0	39.4	30.1	30.2	60.3
2004-05	46.1	6.6	47.3	53.9	44.3	41.2	14.5	55.7

Notes: TW: Total Workers (= RE+CL+SE); SE: Self-employed, RE: Regular Employed, CL: Casual and Other Labour.

The following features are noteworthy:

- Shares of self-employment and wage labour are in the ratio of 45:55 for women, while they are about 40:60 for men in both rural and urban areas.
- Among men, the share of wage labour has been on the decline in urban areas while it has been on the rise in rural areas.
- For women, there was a dip in the 1990s in the share of self-employment resulting in an increase in the share of casual labourers but this returned to initial values similar to 1987 by 2004 in both rural and urban areas.
- Among wage labour, the share of regular employed is far lower in rural than urban areas but once again, there are distinct patterns for men and women. For rural women, regular employment is just about 7 per cent while it is about 13 per cent for men; in urban areas, the share of regular wage has been increasing reaching comparable proportions by 2004.

Table 2.8

Employment Status and Education Level in the Workforce Aged 15 Years and Above, 1987-88 and 1999-2000, Tamil Nadu

SE/TW	*Year*	*Not literate*	*Lit+bel prim*	*Prim+ Mid*	*Sec+ hisec*	*Post-hisec*	*All*
All	1987-88	39.0	45.6	48.9	34.4	26.2	42.0
	1999-2000	32.3	39.7	40.7	34.2	28.4	35.9
	2004-05	40.7	39.0	44.2	43.1	30.5	41.1
Males	1987-88	34.2	42.1	44.9	33.1	26.3	39.0
	1999-2000	30.3	36.7	37.2	33.7	32.8	34.5
	2004-05	38.6	35.7	41.0	41.6	34.0	39.2
Females	1987-88	42.3	54.4	61.9	39.9	25.6	46.7
	1999-2000	33.7	46.2	51.2	36.6	13.1	38.3
	2004-05	42.1	44.2	52.1	48.6	16.3	44.3
Rural	1987-88	38.7	47.4	55.0	43.5	35.8	44.4
	1999-2000	31.3	39.2	42.5	38.3	37.6	36.5
	2004-05	40.3	38.3	44.7	47.6	37.1	42.1
Urban	1987-88	40.2	40.9	38.9	27.2	22.4	36.2
	1999-2000	38.5	41.3	37.1	30.2	25.7	34.5
	2004-05	42.8	40.9	43.2	39.0	28.0	39.2

RE/WL	*Year*	*Not literate*	*Lit+bel prim*	*Prim+ Mid*	*Sec+ hisec*	*Post-hisec*	*All*
All	1987-88	12.1	28.8	48.4	89.3	99.0	35.2
	1999-2000	10.0	22.1	35.9	73.1	97.9	33.7
	2004-05	10.9	19.9	36.6	73.7	96.1	37.3
Males	1987-88	13.2	30.4	50.2	88.4	98.8	42.7
	1999-2000	10.2	23.6	37.2	72.1	97.3	39.5
	2004-05	11.0	19.3	37.5	72.9	95.0	42.4
Females	1987-88	11.1	23.5	40.1	93.2	100.0	21.8
	1999-2000	9.8	18.3	30.9	77.7	99.7	23.2
	2004-05	10.8	20.9	33.8	77.2	99.5	28.1
Rural	1987-88	7.8	20.6	30.4	80.3	96.8	19.9
	1999-2000	6.0	12.2	24.2	58.8	93.2	18.7
	2004-05	4.9	11.1	19.7	53.9	88.7	18.1
Urban	1987-88	34.8	46.9	70.3	94.8	99.7	66.9
	1999-2000	36.6	52.5	58.2	85.7	99.1	67.8
	2004-05	44.3	46.9	66.6	89.3	98.5	73.5

Notes: SE: Self employed; TW: total workers; RE: Regular employed; WL: wage labour; Not literate: not literates; literate: includes literates and below primary; prim+mid: completed primary or middle school; Sec+hisec: completed secondary or higher secondary school; Others: diploma holders, graduates and above.

Source: Own calculations from unit record data.

- The share of self-employed declines with improvement in education levels and more secularly in urban areas but over time the share of self-employed has increased more prominently in the upper education levels. Though similar changes are noticed for men, there is a reverse trend for women.
- The share of regular employment shows a very sharp increase across education levels constituting about 90 per cent at the higher education levels and is similar among men and women in both rural and urban areas.

Based on the unit record data, further analysis for the period 1987-88, 1999-2000 and 2004-05 shows that the decline in self-employment for men in rural areas increased the share of casual labourers substantially with a very small increase in the unemployment rate. Since the decline in self-employment came from agriculture and the labour-land ratio in Tamil Nadu has gone up substantially with an increase in landless households from 57 per cent to 67 per cent in 1999-2000, most of them were employed as casual labourers. Interestingly this argument cannot be extended further to 2004-05. The share of landless households increased to nearly 72 per cent but still the share of casual labourers came down (Eswaran *et al.*, 2007). This essentially suggests that the change in the last quinquennium perhaps came from an increase in the share of self-employment in non-agriculture. In this context, it must be noted that 1993-94 had not been a good year when both regular and self-employment decreased compared to 1987-88, while regular employment picked up marginally and self-employment declined further in 1999-2000 picking up substantially in 2004-05.

Sectoral Distribution of Employment

The share of non-agricultural employment in rural areas was higher in Tamil Nadu than the all-India average since the late 1970s. Though the share of agricultural employment had marginally declined between 1987 and 1999, it increased substantially in 2004 mainly due to an 8-9 per cent increase in female employment since 1987 (Table 2.9). There has been a decline in manufacturing employment as per the recent NSS round and more substantially in rural areas from about 13-14 per cent to about 8 per cent. This decline is from food-, textile- and leather-based manufacturing

Table 2.9

Trends in Sectoral Distribution of Employment in Tamil Nadu

Sectors	*All*	*Rural*	*Urban*	*Males*	*Females*
			1987-88		
Agriculture	51.0	69.1	9.2	43.9	63.5
Mining	0.5	0.6	0.3	0.5	0.3
Manuf-1	13.3	10.1	20.7	12.7	14.4
Manuf-2	5.9	3.1	12.5	7.1	3.8
Manufac-T	19.2	13.2	33.1	19.8	18.2
Utilities	0.4	0.3	0.7	0.6	0.0
Construction	3.8	2.6	6.8	4.8	2.2
Trade etc.	9.9	6.0	19.0	12.0	6.2
Transport	3.3	1.8	6.7	5.0	0.3
Services-1	1.5	0.5	3.6	2.2	0.2
Services-2	10.4	6.0	20.6	11.1	9.1
			1999-2000		
Agriculture	49.6	67.6	7.9	42.7	62.4
Mining	0.5	0.5	0.3	0.5	0.4
Manuf-1	10.3	8.2	15.4	9.5	12.0
Manuf-2	7.9	5.8	12.9	8.9	6.3
Manufac-T	18.3	14.0	28.3	18.3	18.2
Utilities	0.3	0.2	0.7	0.5	0.1
Construction	5.2	4.1	7.8	6.8	2.3
Trade etc.	11.5	5.7	24.9	14.4	6.2
Transport	4.6	2.7	9.2	6.6	1.0
Services-1	1.7	0.6	4.1	2.3	0.5
Services-2	8.2	4.6	16.7	7.9	8.9
			2004-05		
Agriculture	56.1	70.8	7.6	50.5	71.0
Mining	0.6	0.6	0.8	0.7	0.4
Manuf-1	5.9	4.2	11.6	5.3	7.6
Manuf-2	5.8	3.9	12.2	6.7	3.5
Manufac-T	11.8	8.1	23.8	12.0	11.1
Utilities	0.3	0.2	0.7	0.4	0.0
Construction	6.1	5.4	8.4	7.6	2.2
Trade etc.	11.0	6.7	25.3	13.4	4.5
Transport	4.2	2.8	9.1	5.7	0.4
Services-1	1.7	0.5	5.5	2.1	0.7
Services-2	8.2	5.0	18.9	7.7	9.7

Notes: Manufac-T: all manufacturing; Manuf-1: food-, tobacco-, textiles- and leather-based manufacturing; Trade: wholesale and retail trade and hotel and restaurant business; Transport: Transport and communication; Services-1: Banking and business etc.; Services-2: Public administration, education, etc.

Source: Author's own calculations using unit record data.

which had started to show a decline since 1987. Employment in the construction sector picked up in all segments except for women from 1999 to 2004, while the share of trade, transport and services sector remained nearly the same in 2004 and has been so since 1999. Though overall share of services related to public administration declined from 1987, the urban share went up in 2004 compared to 1999 and this contribution seems to be coming from the increase in female employment.

Changes in Real Daily Wage Rates for Agricultural Wages

At the all-India level, the 1990s showed a slower growth rate in wages along with a low growth in employment and a decline in the number of days of wage employment, compared to the earlier decades (Himanshu, 2006). Table 2.10 presents regional analysis of wage rates for the state which shows that the northern coastal region always had the lowest wage rate for both men and women. More importantly, the growth rate in the late 1990s for this region was far higher for male wages. The female wage rates grew more slowly in the second half as compared to the first. The gap between female-male wages was the highest in the inland districts and lowest in the southern districts and has been growing over the decades.

Table 2.10

Average Daily Wage Rates in Agriculture

	Males			*Females*		
	1983	*1993-1994*	*1999-2000*	*1983*	*1993-1994*	*1999-2000*
Coastal North	21.3	35.9	48.2	10.9	20.7	26.0
		(5.1)	(5.0)		(6.3)	(3.9)
Coastal	22.9	42.5	52.7	13.7	24.5	30.5
		(6.1)	(3.7)		(5.7)	(3.7)
Inland	26.8	40.9	57.0	12.5	23.8	31.1
		(4.1)	(5.7)		(6.3)	(4.6)
Southern	23.6	43.6	52.3	14.8	26.7	33.4
		(6.0)	(3.1)		(5.8)	(3.8)

Note: Values in brackets are annual growth rates.

Source: Himanshu (2006).

Based on this same study, one can also make some inter-state comparisons. Tamil Nadu was among the high-growth states in real wages but as mentioned earlier, within the region growth rates varied. Real wages in Tamil Nadu when compared to most other regions were in the middle range for men whereas states like Kerala, some regions of Punjab and Haryana had much higher rates. Wages for women across regions were near the average and improved far more slowly in Tamil Nadu compared to other states.

Several other studies have also worked out regional trends in agricultural wages based on data collected by the Directorate of Statistics as well as by the Rural Labour Enquiries (RLE) which form a part of the NSSO. One such study by Chavan and Bedmatta (2006) showed that Tamil Nadu was among the lower end states in the 1960s and 1970s for both male and female wages. The wages in 1990s showed a significant improvement growing at more than 1.5 per cent for males in some of the districts and a lower growth rate for female wages around 0.7 per cent. During this decade, several states showed negative growth rates and Tamil Nadu had a significant improvement and was among the top end values leaving behind the earlier front runner states in wage rate growth. The RLE on the other hand showed a larger variation in growth rates for these two decades. The period between 1983 and 1987-88 showed a growth rate of 22 per cent for males (high value compared to most other states) and 9 per cent for females (middle level value compared to other states). The subsequent period of 1987-88 to 1993-94 and 1993-94 to 1999-2000 had values of 6 per cent and 3.6 per cent for males and 5.6 per cent and 3.2 per cent for females, respectively. One finds that not only were the growth rates for female wages much lower than for males, but also the male to female earnings ratio was increasing from about 0.9 in 1983 to 1.7 in 1999-2000. Further, the study also highlighted that male wages in 2004 were far above the minimum wage (for ploughing and weeding), while it was lower by about ₹ 15 for females. Most states in India showed this differential between male and female wages.

In a comparison of labour productivity and land productivity, Jha (2007) finds that though both have increased over the years, the growth rates in these declined in the recent past and more so for land than for labour. Compared to all India, the distribution of land was more skewed in Tamil Nadu and more than 70 per cent of the households in rural areas did not have land in 2004-05 compared to the all-India value of about 43 per cent. Eswaran *et al.* (2007) show that the labour to land ratio in Tamil Nadu was as high as 350 in 1999-2000, while in Kerala, Haryana and Punjab, it was about 100. Apart from Tamil Nadu, Andhra Pradesh had about 400 and Bihar 550. The important distinction between Bihar and Tamil Nadu according to the results of this study was that they were nearly in the same coordinates in terms of land-labour ratio and real daily wages in 1983. While Tamil Nadu's position improved substantially with respect to the latter, Bihar showed a large increase with regard to the labour-land relationship and much less with respect to real wages. Perhaps one could infer that there was a productivity increase among those who were employed in agriculture despite the increase in labour-land ratio. Interestingly, Jha (2007) finds that not all of the growth in real wages in agriculture can be explained through improvements in productivity but statutory minimum wages (SMW) also played a significant role. Tamil Nadu and Kerala were the two states where the SMW increased nearly fourfold in the decade of 1990s and hence were among those few states where this also impacted the increases in real wages.

Labour Market Characteristics of Social and Religious Groups

Apart from the sectoral and gendered analysis, a study of the labour market for the socially disadvantaged sections of the population forms an important part of the analysis. This section reviews characteristics of employment and trends therein for the more vulnerable disadvantaged religious and caste groups relative to others. Table 2.11 shows that as for the other castes the participation rates of the Scheduled Castes and Scheduled Tribes (SC/ST) has also been higher in Tamil Nadu compared to all India. However, the gap in female participation rates between SC/ST and 'Others'—higher for the former—is similar for Tamil Nadu and all India. A more important and noteworthy change that has occurred is the decline in participation rates of SC/ST women between 1987 and 2004, while it has remained the same or increased among 'Others' and this has been the case at the national level as well.

Among the religious groups, Muslims have lower participation rates in Tamil Nadu and all India but for Christians, the rates are lower in Tamil Nadu but not so at the national level (Table 2.11). For most years and most sub-groups of population, the minority religions have lower participation rates for Tamil Nadu when compared to all India but that for Hindus is far higher than the all-India rate. The LFPR for Muslims in urban areas for both men and women and rural women was higher in Tamil Nadu in comparison to all India in 1987-88 but this also changed by 2004-05. Though the participation rates have declined in all segments of the population for Tamil Nadu and all-India, the rate of decline appears highest for Muslims. Clearly these changes need further exploration.

Table 2.11

Trends in LFPR of Social and Religious Groups in Tamil Nadu and All India

		1987-88		*1999-2000*		*2004-05*	
		Tamil Nadu	*All India*	*Tamil Nadu*	*All India*	*Tamil Nadu*	*All India*
				Social Groups			
Rural Males	SC/ST	59.0	55.7	58.9	54.9	58.1	55.9
	Others	61.0	54.2	61.9	53.7	61.3	55.3
Rural Females	SC/ST	52.6	40.1	46.8	37.0	48.3	37.9
	Others	46.4	30.0	40.7	27.5	46.0	31.2
Urban Males	SC/ST	66.5	52.3	55.3	52.4	58.7	56.3
	Others	66.6	53.6	58.9	54.7	61.5	57.2
Urban Females	SC/ST	36.3	22.3	28.4	19.7	33.7	21.8
	Others	23.2	15.1	21.8	13.7	24.0	17.0
				Religious Groups			
Rural Males	Hindus	69.5	63.0	67.8	61.6	61.1	56.1
	Muslims	53.5	60.0	57.3	56.8	48.6	50.5
	Christians	62.0	64.3	65.0	64.6	53.6	57.7
Rural Females	Hindus	55.5	40.1	48.6	36.4	47.9	35.0
	Muslims	31.0	24.7	14.4	19.6	14.8	18.5
	Christians	41.6	46.3	31.9	38.0	39.2	38.5
Urban Males	Hindus	67.1	60.4	65.0	60.5	62.2	57.6
	Muslims	63.2	60.1	64.3	58.4	53.0	54.6
	Christians	63.7	59.5	54.7	56.6	55.7	53.5
Urban Females	Hindus	55.5	40.1	48.6	36.4	47.9	35.0
	Muslims	31.0	24.7	14.4	19.6	14.8	18.5
	Christians	41.6	46.3	31.9	38.0	39.2	38.5

Focussing only on 2004-05, Table 2.12 shows the distribution of each social and religious group across the employment status of self-employed, regular employed, casual labour and unemployed. The share of regular

Table 2.12

Employment Status across Social and Religious Groups in Tamil Nadu, 2004-05

		Tamil Nadu				*All India*			
		SE	*RE*	*CL*	*UE*	*SE*	*RE*	*CL*	*UE*
					Social Groups				
Rural Males	SCST	20.3	12.7	64.6	2.4	42.2	7.5	48.3	2.0
	Others	45.6	13.2	39.7	1.5	63.1	9.6	25.1	2.2
Rural Females	SCST	22.2	6.6	68.1	3.1	43.7	3.8	50.5	1.9
	Others	52.7	6.7	38.4	2.2	61.1	5.1	29.9	3.9
Urban Males	SCST	22.0	45.3	28.7	3.9	30.6	39.5	24.1	5.8
	Others	39.3	43.4	14.2	3.1	45.3	39.0	11.6	4.1
Urban Females	SCST	24.9	44.9	25.0	5.3	27.2	39.0	28.0	5.8
	Others	43.3	40.0	11.3	5.4	39.5	38.2	12.2	10.1
					Religious Groups				
Rural Males	Hindus	39.1	12.4	47.0	1.6	56.5	8.9	32.6	2.0
	Muslims	42.2	31.7	18.2	8.0	58.0	7.1	32.4	2.5
	Christians	37.9	18.9	41.3	2.0	54.4	13.8	28.2	3.6
Rural Females	Hindus	43.2	6.4	48.1	2.3	54.5	4.4	38.6	2.6
	Muslims	88.0	5.9	0.4	5.7	61.0	3.9	28.3	6.8
	Christians	52.2	14.2	27.6	6.0	54.5	13.6	20.7	11.2
Urban Males	Hindus	35.3	44.5	17.3	2.9	40.7	41.5	13.5	4.3
	Muslims	50.1	35.3	8.7	5.9	52.8	27.1	15.8	4.3
	Christians	36.3	46.0	11.1	6.7	32.1	45.1	16.3	6.5
Urban Females	Hindus	39.8	40.4	14.9	4.9	35.2	39.3	16.7	8.8
	Muslims	65.8	21.1	7.6	5.4	58.8	21.8	11.3	8.1
	Christians	21.5	60.9	5.2	12.4	22.4	54.1	6.8	16.7

Note: SE: Self-employed, RE: Regular Employed, CL: Casual Labour, UE: Unemployed.

employed among SC/ST in urban areas is higher than the 'Others' in Tamil Nadu when compared to all India. The share of casual labourers is far higher among the rural SC/ST when compared to 'Others' and this is reversed in the case of self-employed. When compared to all India, the share of casual labourers in rural Tamil Nadu is far higher than rural all India but this does not hold for urban areas. Similarly, the gap in the share of self-employment between Tamil Nadu and the national picture is more apparent in rural than in urban areas.

The share of self-employed among Muslims is higher than among Hindus and Christians, and for women particularly in rural areas of Tamil Nadu it is as high as 88 per cent (Table 2.12).The share of casual labourers among rural Christian men is higher than for Hindus while the share of regular employed among urban women is much above the average rates. The unemployment rates are also far higher among the Christians.

In sum, the social and religious groups do not seem to follow a pattern.

Conclusion

The trend and pattern of employment is influenced by the changes in demographic structure that reflect the changes in working age population, the skill level of the population broadly assessed by improvements in literacy rates and educational attainment and the structural change in the domestic product shifting away from agriculture towards industry and the service sector. These factors not only influence the numbers in the labour force but also the remuneration received affecting the well-being of the population. This study highlights these changes for Tamil Nadu and also across socially deprived population groups whose economic and social status improvement is essential for overall improvement in well-being.

The analysis carried out in this study on the labour market shows that the choice of the time points could make for changes in the overall picture. Two dots are sufficient for drawing a line but if several dots are scattered all over, then the line will mostly likely not pass through all of them. In a similar way, the trends in the labour market are different when the comparison is between 1987-88 and 1993-94, between 1987-88 and 1999-2000 and now 2004-05. These changes are also different for rural and urban and differ between men and women and expectedly state-level changes are different from all-India changes. What has come to stay is that the population is getting more educated with the share of agriculture declining and the share of public administration declining, but this also seems to be showing a different pattern in 2004-05 compared to the previous NSS rounds.

Beginning from 1987-88, there was a decline in the working population in Tamil Nadu and this has not added to the unemployment rates as noted by Sundaram (2001) for all India. Similar inferences can also be drawn for Tamil Nadu that the participation rates have come down across all age groups and more for rural than urban, and more for women than for men and hence cannot be attributed solely to the shift in the population's age structure. The share of child labour has come down significantly while there has been a withdrawal of women in higher age groups. The 2004-05 data set shows that the participation rates had actually fallen overall despite the increase in working age population but female participation rates increased. The turnaround in the share of agricultural employment in 2004-05 is another issue to be explored and so is the turnaround in the share of self-employed among women in rural areas and regular employed in urban areas. Whether this will stay on or change once again with the new NSS round expected soon is to be seen. This analysis has only been able to document the trends and patterns but the onerous and important task of what is bringing about the changes is left for future studies. The nature of data collection including sampling and non-sampling biases should also form an important aspect of further analysis.

The Sachar Committee report brought to focus the lower social and economic status of the Muslim community in India. In Tamil Nadu by virtue of the fact that most Muslims are in urban areas and have a very small share in agriculture in rural areas, they seem to be better off than elsewhere in India. Their share among the less educated has been coming down. The SC/ST in Tamil Nadu though better off in terms of their education status compared to all India still form a substantial proportion of casual labourers in agriculture as well as in urban areas. Alongside this, SC/ST also constitute a higher share of the regular salaried, though the proportion of above secondary education among the regular salaried is about 20 per cent with a small increase in the last decade.

Female labour market participation rates are more volatile for Tamil Nadu than all India and changes are also extreme as shown by increased share of casual labourers and self-employed workers in the late 1990s in rural areas while the share of regular employed is going up along with a withdrawal from the labour market. Several of these changes do not carry through to the recent round of NSS data in 2004-05.

Male and female labour markets may appear segregated in terms of the work and skill profiles, but when there is a reduction in the demand for labour, women may be laid off from paid work and in that sense form the 'surplus' labour. However, increase in the share of unpaid self-employment for women showed that there was a labour requirement elsewhere but perhaps it was seen as a cost cutting measure so that those who need not be paid can be employed. In this sense, a small proportion of women who moved out of self-employment into casual labour in agriculture and self-employment in unpaid family work could be in a worse-off situation. On the other hand, a higher LFPR of women among the poorer sections is seen as an economic necessity and their withdrawal from the labour force could be seen as betterment in the economic status of their households. A more detailed and careful analyses of the data may take us close to the assessment of the groups which could have become worse off or better off. However, data sets across time points are necessary to answer such questions effectively, particularly while making inter-temporal comparisons.

References

Chavan, P. and R. Bedmatta (2006). "Trends in Agricultural Wages in India", *Economic and Political Weekly* 41(38), September 23-September 29.

EPW Research Foundation Database (2001).

Eswaran, M., A. Kotwal, B. Ramaswami and W. Wadhwa (2007). "How Does Poverty Decline? Evidence from India, 1983-1999", *Mimeograph*. Delhi: Indian Statistical Institute.

Government of Tamil Nadu (2009). *Economic Appraisal*.

Himanshu (2006). "Agrarian Crisis and Wage Labour: A Regional Perspective", *Indian Journal of Labour Economics* 49(4): 827-46.

Jha, B. (2007). "Agricultural Wages in India: A State Level Analysis", *Indian Journal of Labour Economics* 50(2): 293-302.

Kurian, N.J. (2000). "Widening Regional Disparities in India: Some Indicators", *Economic and Political Weekly*, February 7.

NSSO (1996a). *Employment and Unemployment Situation in India: Fifth Quinquennial Survey NSS fiftieth round (July 1993-June 1994)*, Report No. 409, Department of Statistics, Government of India, New Delhi.

———. (1996b). *Sarvekshana* XX(68): 137-38, July-September. Department of Statistics, Government of India.

———. (2001). *Employment and Unemployment Situation in India: 1999-2000 (Part I)*. Report No. 458, Department of Statistics, Government of India, New Delhi.

———. (2006). *Employment and Unemployment Situation in India: 2004-05*, NSS 61st Round (July 2004–June 2005). Report No. 515(61/10/1). New Delhi: Ministry of Statistics & Programme Implementation, Government of India.

Panagariya, A. (2010). "India on the Growth Turnpike: No State Left Behind". *http://www.columbia.edu/~ap2231/Policy%20Papers/Kelkar%20Vijay%20Festschrift%20Panagariya.pdf*

Rao, M. Govinda and Nirvikar Singh (2005). *Political Economy of Federalism in India*. New Delhi: Oxford University Press.

Sundaram, K. (2001). "Employment-Unemployment Situation in 1990s: Some Results from NSS 55th Round", *Economics and Political Weekly* 36(11): 931-40, March 17-23.

Vaidyanathan, A. (2001). "Employment in India: 1977-78 to 1999-00: Characteristics and Trends", *Journal of Indian School of Political Economy* 13(2): 217-54.

———. (2007). "Private Sector in Education: Trends, Causes and Consequences", *C.D. Deshmukh Memorial Lecture. Hyderabad:* Council for Social Development.

3 Socioeconomic Characteristics of Tamil Nadu Villages 2001

A. Vaidyanathan

Background

Rural India is undergoing significant changes since Independence in practically every aspect of economic, social and political life. The nature and extent of these changes, the forces driving them and their significance have been widely discussed by social scientists, political and social activists and in the media. For the most part, these discussions deal with particular aspects of rural economy and society at the national, state and sometimes regional levels. Comprehensive assessment and interpretation of regional variations and temporal changes even at the macro level are rather rare. In any case, given the country's vastness and diversity, national and state level studies need to be complemented by in-depth studies of structure and change at the sub-regional and village levels. Such analyses are obviously relevant for local level planning for improving socioeconomic welfare keeping in view differences in current conditions and potentials for improvement. They have become the more important as the resources, responsibility and authority for local development are vested, as envisaged by the 73rd amendment to the Constitution, with elected panchayat raj institutions (PRIs) from the district down to the village level.

This calls for a great deal of information. It so happens that India has a great wealth of it thanks to a long and continuing tradition of public agencies collecting socioeconomic data through censuses of various kinds and sample surveys capable of providing considerably more details at the sub-regional levels. The decennial population censuses—conducted regularly for over 100 years—collect information on basic demographic and economic characteristics of the entire population through a complete enumeration of all settlements and households in the country. The census reports provide tabulated information on these characteristics, by district, for the population as a whole and for rural and urban areas separately, by religion and for Scheduled Castes (SCs) and Scheduled Tribes (STs). Beginning 1961, the Registrar-General (RG) has been publishing Village and Town Directories as part of District Census Handbooks giving basic demographic and economic characteristics individually for all villages (and ward-wise information for towns) as well as data on cultivated and irrigated areas, availability of various amenities (including schools, hospitals, bus services, post offices, telephones and other amenities) within the village and their connectivity to the outside world.

In addition, village-wise data are available on several other aspects from quinquennial agricultural censuses (which compile data on land use, irrigation and cultivation by size class of holdings from village records) and economic censuses (which collect through complete enumeration, the number of commercial, industrial and service establishments and their characteristics down to the village level). Livestock censuses, minor irrigation censuses and national education surveys are other sources that, though not as frequent and regular as the above-mentioned sources, provide data on important socioeconomic features of all villages on a comparable basis for several points of time.

The potential value of these data for local and regional development planning has remained largely unexploited. Planners and policymakers in government, political parties and academics are generally unaware of the existence of so much information relevant to track changes in socioeconomic indicators at the grass root level. However, those who are aware have made little effort to collate, assay and organise the information. Published data provide selective tabulations of particular characteristics mostly at the state and district levels. Even these are not readily accessible. Primary data are not properly preserved in most cases but some (notably the census and economic census) are being digitised. Access to primary data, even when digitised, is severely restricted. There has been hardly any effort at using them for assessing spatial patterns of socioeconomic change or for analytical research to explore factors underlying these patterns and their implications for policy. An essential condition for this is to ensure digitisation of all the data and make them freely and widely available in the public domain. Since all these data are collected at public expense ostensibly for public policy purposes, they must be considered public goods.

Scope of This Paper

This paper is a modest attempt to use the data available in Village Directories published by the RG to explore some selected socioeconomic characteristics of Tamil Nadu villages. Data for 1991 and 2001 are available in digitised form and were obtained from the RG's office at a nominal fee. Village level data for the earlier censuses (1971 and 1981) are available only in hard copy. These have also been digitised as part of a project undertaken and funded by the Centre for Development Studies, Thiruvananthapuram.[1]

The idea was to map the selected characteristics at the level of districts and individual villages and their changes over these three decades and to examine whether they show any distinct patterns and the factors that may account for such patterns. It was hoped that this would help assess the extent to which villages individually or grouped by district and fractiles have improved their absolute and relative position in respect of various characteristics. But given changes in district boundaries, difficulties of matching village names across censuses and getting information on infrastructure and amenities, this exercise has to be deferred hoping that other researchers will take up the challenge. This paper is therefore limited to describing the situation in 2001 and exploring the spatial patterns of variation in each characteristic and its association with other characteristics.

We focus on six characteristics: sex ratio, literacy and proportion of SCs and STs (as indicators of social condition), work participation rate, proportion of workers in agriculture and ratio of agricultural labour to total agricultural workers (which relate to economic structure). The extent and pattern of variations in each of these characteristics, and their association with other characteristics across all villages ranked according to its level and grouped into deciles, are reviewed in the next section. This is followed

1. Digitisation of Kerala data was done mainly by Ajit Menon at Kerala Research Programme on Local Level Development (KRPLLD) while that of Tamil Nadu was done in Chennai by Hemalatha under the supervision of A. Vaidyanathan and N. Krishnaji. Ajit Menon, J. Saravanan and R. Sugumari (the latter two are from the Dhan foundation) did much of the tabulation.

by a comparison of the characteristics of 500 villages which are most disadvantaged and an equal number of those which are best placed in terms of each of the social and economic indicators. For this purpose, villages in the lowest (highest) decile of literacy and sex ratio and highest (lowest) incidence of SC/ST are considered to be in most (least) disadvantaged social situation. On the economic front, those in the lowest (top) decile in terms of work participation rates and topmost (lowest) decile in terms of proportion of agricultural workers and incidence of wage labour in agriculture are taken to be the least (most) economically advantaged groups.

Social Indicators

Size of Villages

In 2001, the state had 15,400 inhabited villages. The average population per village is around 2500. The size of villages varies from less than 50 to 34,000. About 4 per cent of villages have less than 500 inhabitants; and 31 per cent have less than 1000 inhabitants. The large majority (60%) have populations ranging between 1000 and 5000. Villages with more than 5000 population comprise a tenth of the total. Close to 300 villages (1.9% of the total number) have more than 10,000 inhabitants.

The average population per village ranges from 2224 in Dharmapuri to nearly 3700 in Kanniyakumari. These variations reflect differences in the size distribution of villages. Broadly speaking, districts at the lower end of the size scale tend to have a larger proportion of small villages (<1000 people) and a relatively small proportion of large-sized (>5000 persons) villages. Among districts which rank high in terms of population size, the proportion of relatively small villages is much lower and that of large villages considerably higher, compared to the state averages.

Sex Ratio

Sex ratio (SR) is widely used as an indicator of gender disparity in a population. In a closed population (i.e., in the absence of in and out migration), a rough parity between the number of females and males is considered to be normal and desirable. In India, the number of females is fewer than males: the ratio in 2001 was 933. The ratio in Tamil Nadu is considerably higher at 986 overall and 989 in rural areas but still below parity.

Table 3.1 presents the mean value of SRs and of selected socio-economic characteristics across districts ranked in ascending order of SRs and grouped into 10 equal segments (called deciles): the average ratio ranges from less than 650 females per thousand males in some 250 villages (0.18% of all villages) to over 1200 in some 3000 villages (2.2% of the total). It ranges between 950 and 1050 in close to 60 per cent of villages; and in the range of 850-1100 in nearly 90 per cent of villages.

Variations in characteristics across villages grouped by their overall SR show diverse patterns. Broadly speaking, there is clear tendency for higher SRs to be associated with higher dependence on agriculture and agricultural labour, and higher proportion of women reporting to be at work. With the exception of the groups with lowest SRs, higher SRs go with higher overall literacy rates. Villages with very low and very high SRs tend to be, on the average, smaller than those in groups with SR ranging between 850-1050, and also to have a lower incidence of SC/ST in their populations.

Table 3.1

Distribution of Villages according to Overall Sex Ratios and their Socioeconomic Characteristics

Sex Ratio Range	*Mean*	*% of Villages*	*Average Village Size*	*0-6%*	*% SC/ ST*	*Literacy Rate*	*WPRF*	*%ag/tw*	*%al/tw*
<650	574	0.18	1407	8.5	12.7	75.9	22.2	14.1	4.0
650-750	713	0.31	2313	10.2	25.0	68.3	27.6	20.0	5.5
750-850	821	1.86	2195	11.7	15.6	55.6	37.3	33.7	8.3
850-950	920	18.46	2372	12.0	22.1	58.5	38.6	39.3	11.4
950-1050	993	59.51	2750	11.8	24.5	61.3	36.9	35.6	12.2
1050-1100	1070	11.35	2055	12.1	24.4	61.4	40.3	38.3	13.0
1100-1150	1120	4.41	1482	12.2	22.2	62.1	38.0	41.0	13.5
1150-1200	1173	1.71	1447	11.9	18.5	64.3	38.9	42.1	12.4
1200+	1292	2.21	1219	11.7	14.9	70.1	31.0	31.6	9.5

Note: WPRF: Work participation rate for females; Ag/tw: Agricultural workers/total workers; Al/tw: Agricultural labour/total workers

Variations in overall SRs are in part due to variations in child SRs. Adjusting for this, adult SRs show a stronger rising trend across groups. This could reflect gender differentials in mortality and migration. The latter is generally considered to be more important. Low overall SRs are largely a reflection of differences in the extent of male migration into and out of the village in search of employment (female migration is mostly due to shift of residence after marriage and very little in search of employment). Low SR villages have far more males relative to females both in their populations and their workforce. The fact that they are predominantly non-agricultural suggests that they attract more male migrants and more literate male migrants; villages with SRs exceeding 1100 point to high rates of male emigration which is plausible given that they are much smaller than average in size and more heavily dependent on agriculture. Those with SR greater than 1200 and especially those with ratios of 1500 and more (and some more than 2000) need closer scrutiny.

Child Sex Ratios

Child SRs vary over a much wider range than overall SRs. The range varies from 100 to 150. The ratio is less than 650 in about 4 per cent of villages, and less than 850 in about a fourth of villages. It is more than 1050 in one-fourth of villages and exceeds 1200 in 8 per cent of them. Roughly half the villages are in the modal group with ratios in the range of 850-1050 (Table 3.2).

Table 3.2

Distribution of Villages according to Child Sex Ratios and their Socioeconomic Characteristics

Child Sex Ratio		*% of Villages*	*Average Village Size*	*Sex Ratio All*	*0-6%*	*% SC/ ST*	*F lit*	*WPRF*	*%ag/tw*
Range	*Mean*								
0-450	381	0.78	119	865	10.8	31.2	48.1	53.0	60.6
450-550	510	0.88	483	925	10.7	20.4	50.5	48.0	47.1
550-650	608	2.18	948	906	11.7	18.3	45.0	48.1	47.8
650-750	707	6.39	1668	926	12.0	21.1	44.6	45.4	44.8
750-850	808	15.53	2138	966	12.0	23.9	48.0	44.0	42.1
850-950	905	26.35	2989	985	12.0	24.0	51.6	38.4	36.9
950-1050	991	24.00	3467	996	11.7	22.1	56.1	32.1	30.2
1050-1100	1072	7.30	2267	1020	12.0	26.1	51.2	37.9	38.2
1100-1200	1140	8.28	1619	1028	11.9	27.7	50.6	38.7	35.6
1200 +	1320	8.31	877	1047	11.8	29.8	49.2	40.7	45.5

Note: felit: Female literacy.

Higher child SRs go with higher overall SRs. But the former are lower than the ratio for the total population in most groups. The average CSR is less than half the overall SR and nearly a third of the adult SR among districts where the ratio is less than 450. The differential however narrows progressively as average CSRs increase to reach parity and subsequently rise above the overall SR. Gender discrimination among children is obviously very high in areas with very low overall SRs. It diminishes progressively and sharply as average CSRs increase. This pattern is even more sharply manifested when comparing CSRs with adult SRs.

It is well known that there is a marked preference in India for male children, that selective abortions of female foetuses and female infanticide are quite widely prevalent and that infant and child mortality among females is relatively high compared to males. The incidence of these features however varies depending among other things on the age composition of adult females, the nature and extent of female participation in economic activities, attitudes to bearing and rearing children especially female children, as well as the quality of water supply, sanitation and health care facilities.

Across Tamil Nadu villages, low CSRs are associated with higher degree of dependence on agriculture and higher work participation rates among females. It seems likely that access to health facilities is better in larger villages and higher female literacy goes with lower incidence of discrimination against female children. But these relationships are not seen across all groups. Thus, village size increases progressively with CSR only over the first 7 groups, but thereafter higher CSR goes with smaller village size. Similarly, the positive association between literacy and CSRs is noticeable only across groups where the latter lies between 650 and 1050. Female literacy rates at the lower and upper ends of the spectrum tend to decline with increasing CSRs. Better understanding of the relative roles of different sociodemographic characteristics in determining SRs of different groups would require more refined analysis that recognises and allows for interactions among them.

Scheduled Castes and Scheduled Tribes

Being the most disadvantaged segments of the population socially and economically, the characteristics of this social group need special attention. Table 3.3 gives a picture of the characteristics of villages grouped into deciles on the basis of the proportion of SC and ST in their population. More than 1000 villages in the state do not have any persons belonging to this group. Their numbers are more or less evenly diffused in the middle groups (with proportions ranging between 0% and 60%) and account for the bulk of the population in this category. SC and ST comprise, on the average, 90 per cent or more of the population in over 400 (4%) of villages. Some 93 of them are wholly SC/ST villages.

Table 3.3

Association between Incidence of SC/ST in Population and Select Characteristics of Tamil Nadu Villages

Class Interval Range	*% SC/ST*	*% of Villages*	*Average Village Size*	*S Ratio Overall*	*S Ratio SC/ST*	*Literacy % Overall*	*WPRF*	*%ag/tw*	*al/tw*
0	0.0	6.94	691	999	0	62.0	36.4	44.4	12.0
0-10	10.1	17.50	2572	984	996	65.4	31.3	30.9	8.5
10-20	14.9	19.44	3410	988	997	61.9	36.6	35.7	10.6
20-30	24.7	17.79	2836	991	995	59.2	40.7	38.0	11.8
30-40	34.4	13.18	2445	991	997	59.0	39.9	38.4	14.4
40-60	48.2	14.66	1891	996	997	58.3	39.5	38.9	16.6
60-70	64.7	3.84	1373	997	997	56.9	41.3	40.2	20.2
70-80	74.3	2.51	1079	992	993	55.7	43.8	38.8	20.7
80-90	84.6	1.44	1006	986	987	50.2	47.0	48.9	20.3
90+	97.0	2.69	736	983	984	38.1	53.2	61.2	13.6

Note: Ag/tw: Agricultural workers/total workers; Al/tw: Agricultural labour/total workers.

Villages with no SC and ST are, on the average, much smaller in size, more dependent on agriculture and with higher female work participation rate than those groups with low incidence of this social group. Among the rest, higher incidence of SC/ST is associated with higher female work participation rates, higher dependence on agriculture and agricultural labour for livelihood and lower literacy rates. Except for the groups with the lowest proportion of SC/ST, average village size declines progressively as this proportion increases. Villages with SC/ST comprising more than 90 per cent of population are very small, predominantly agricultural, have low literacy rate and a high rate of women's participation as workers. The other notable feature is that average SC/ST SR is higher by about 12 per cent in villages where this group comprises less than 10 per cent of the population. Thereafter, the differential narrows progressively to reach parity in villages of the 60-70 per cent category and then falls below the overall ratio.

Literacy

Literacy rates (LRs) in rural Tamil Nadu—overall (61%), males (70%) and females (52%)—are well above the national average and among the highest in the country. The large majority (nearly two thirds) of villages report LRs between 60 and 70 per cent. The overall rate is less than 40 per cent in about 5 per cent of villages; it is less than 30 per cent in 250 villages and less than 20 per cent in about 100 villages. The rate exceeds 70 per cent in about a fifth of the villages and is above 80 per cent only in 3 per cent of them.

LRs bear a strong positive correlation with average village size across all groups—those with the lowest literacy are very small villages and those in the highest group have more than 4400 people on the average. A plausible explanation is that smaller villages tend not to have schools within accessible distance and that larger villages are likely to have more schools up to higher levels within the village or at an accessible distance. On the other hand, it is noteworthy that villages at low levels of literacy have relatively high proportion of children in their population, both of which decline progressively at higher rates of literacy. The population of the least literate group of villages consists almost entirely of SC and ST. Their proportion diminishes rapidly in more literate groups to less than 10 per cent in the most literate group. Also noteworthy is the strong negative correlation between LRs and work participation rates (WPRs) and degree of dependence on agriculture and agricultural labour. Low literate villages are predominantly agricultural and the proportion of workers in the population is very high. The most literate group has a WPR which is a little over half the rate in the lowest group, and over 95 per cent of the workers are in non-agricultural activities.

Table 3.4

Frequency Distribution of Villages according to Literacy Rate, 2001

Class Interval	*Literacy % Overall*	*% of Villages*	*Average Village Size*	*0-6%*	*% SC/ ST*	*WPR All*	*% ag/tw*	*% al/tw*	*Mlit*	*Flit*
0-10	6.2	0.23	515	18.4	94.7	61.6	77.5	15.9	8.9	3.5
10-20	15.4	0.46	900	17.0	78.0	57.5	76.2	15.0	20.6	10.0
20-30	26.1	0.90	1137	15.6	45.2	58.6	66.3	13.6	33.4	18.4
30-40	36.2	3.33	1553	14.4	29.5	55.7	56.6	14.8	45.3	26.7
40-50	46.2	14.48	1978	13.1	26.2	55.0	49.9	14.9	56.4	35.7
50-60	55.4	37.90	2279	12.1	26.4	53.0	42.8	13.7	65.8	45.0
60-70	64.4	29.10	2457	11.8	25.4	46.7	33.5	12.4	73.3	55.4
70-80	74.9	10.88	3720	10.9	15.7	37.1	14.1	5.6	80.2	69.6
80+	82.7	2.71	4426	9.1	8.4	34.4	3.5	1.1	85.9	79.4

Note: Mlit: male literacy; Felit: female literacy.

The overall LR is the weighted average of the rates among males and females. While the two are highly correlated, female literacy is consistently lower, but the differential declines progressively as male literacy increases. Thus in the least literate group, LR among females (3.5%) is only two-fifths of the rate among males (8-9%). In the highest literacy group, female LR is close to 70 per cent compared to 80 per cent among males. Variations in overall LRs are thus largely a reflection of variations in female literacy.

WPRs among males remain more or less at different levels of their literacy in a majority of the village groups. It is only in the highest groups that higher literacy goes with lower work participation among males but the decline is moderate. In sharp contrast, female WPR declines progressively from 48.5 per cent in the least literate group to less than 20 per cent in the most literate group. This tendency is rather more marked at the higher levels of literacy.

Economic Characteristics

Work Participation Rates

WPR gives a measure of the proportion of population working in various economic activities and thereby generating the means for meeting their own livelihood needs and of their dependents. A higher ratio implies that those generating the means of livelihood are more numerous relative to their dependents. A low ratio implies that a worker has more dependents to take care of. A higher proportion of working members means more earners relative to population. But this does not necessarily translate into proportionately higher incomes insofar as high participation rates arise from the necessity to ensure means of subsistence—as it often is among poor and socially disadvantaged.

In rural Tamil Nadu, WPR averages around 48 per cent implying that on the average one worker supports one dependent. It ranges between less than 20 per cent to more than 90 per cent. In about a fifth of the villages, less than 40 per cent of the population is reported to be working. The proportion lies between 40 and 60 per cent in a large majority (62%) of villages and exceeds 60 per cent in the remaining fifth of villages. Some 330 villages (2.1% of the total) report rates exceeding 70 per cent.

Table 3.5

Frequency Distribution of Villages according to Overall Work Participation Rate, 2001

Class Interval	*WPR All %*	*% of Villages*	*Average Village Size*	*Hh size*	*S_ Ratio*	*0-6%*	*%SC/ST*	*Lit all*	*% ag/tw*
30-	27.1	3.08	1729	4.74	1031	11.7	19.2	71.4	16.3
30-40	34.9	15.71	4030	4.46	985	11.3	17.5	71.6	14.0
40-50	45.3	26.27	2399	4.31	993	12.4	26.8	60.1	36.4
50-60	54.9	35.50	2281	4.18	988	12.3	25.8	55.5	43.5
60-70	63.4	17.31	1780	3.95	987	11.3	25.0	53.3	47.0
70-80	72.7	1.92	1213	3.68	980	9.4	26.2	53.1	51.5
80+	83.3	0.22	461	3.87	930	9.8	41.0	43.7	61.2

Note: Hh: household.

Numerous factors—age and sex composition of households, socio-cultural factors influencing the nature and extent of participation by gender, religion and caste in economic activity, education—account for these variations. With available data, it is possible to obtain some idea of the association between variations in WPR and some selected village characteristics. Villages with higher LRs and those with larger average household size and larger populations tend to have lower overall WPRs. On the other hand, villages with higher proportion of children in their population and greater dependence on agriculture and higher proportion of SC/ST tend to have higher overall participation rates.

Variation in overall WPR is largely due to difference in WPR of females. Female participation rate is on the average lower in all groups than that of males. While higher female WPR goes with higher male WPR, it shows a much wider range of variation. It is also noteworthy that the differential between them narrows as male WPRs increase. Both male WPR and female WPR are inversely related to their respective literacy rates. The tendency for WPR to decline as levels of literacy increase is much stronger among females.

Table 3.6

Literacy and WPR among Males and Females

Class Interval	*Mlit*	*WPRM*	*Flit*	*WPRF*	*Fli/Mlit*	*WPRF/WPRM*
30	76.8	45.9	66.2	8.9	86.2	0.19
30-40	77.4	53.9	65.7	15.7	85.0	0.29
40-50	69.1	57.1	51.1	33.5	73.9	0.59
50-60	65.5	60.4	45.3	49.4	69.2	0.82
60-70	63.8	65.6	42.6	61.2	66.8	0.93
70-80	64.0	73.7	42.0	71.6	65.6	0.97
80+	52.7	83.6	34.0	83.1	64.6	0.99

Note: WPRM: work participation rate for males; WPRF: work participation rates for females.

These patterns of association are not uniform across districts with different levels of overall WPR. Across villages in the top decile, as with all villages, WPR bears a strong negative correlation with village size, household size and sex ratio but a much weaker negative relation with literacy and incidence of agricultural labour. Correlations between WPR and SC/ST as well as dependence on agriculture are much weaker. In the lowest decile, as across all villages, WPR is negatively correlated with household size, sex ratio, SC/ST, and literacy but the coefficients for all except household size are much weaker. While across all villages WPR is negatively correlated with village size and incidence of agricultural labour, these correlations in the lowest decile are negative. The correlation with dependence on agriculture is negative and much weaker than in the state as a whole.

Employment Diversification

The importance of agriculture as a source of employment in Tamil Nadu (37% of the working population) is conspicuously less than the national average and one of the lowest among major states. Agriculture employs the major proportion of workers in less than two-fifth of the villages. Roughly one-sixth of villages report more than 70 per cent of their workers in agriculture and about 4 per cent are almost exclusively dependent on agriculture. In a majority of villages (62% to be exact), agriculture employs less than half the work force. This proportion is below 30 per cent in more than a third of villages. About one-eighth of villages are predominantly nonagricultural with such activity employing more than 90 per cent of the local working population. Some 130 villages depend entirely on non-agricultural employment.

Greater the dependence on agriculture (and smaller the proportion engaged in non-agricultural activity), smaller is the village size and lower the literacy rate (both among males and females). Villages that are exclusively non-agricultural or predominantly non-agricultural are much smaller in size than average. Among the rest, groups that are more dependent on agriculture also tend to be smaller, have a higher proportion of children and SC/ST in their population and have higher WPRs among both males and females. All these associations are strong. Household size, proportion of children and of SC/ST bear weaker positive correlation with dependence on agriculture.

Table 3.7

Frequency Distribution of Villages according to Percentage of Workers in Agriculture, 2001

Class Interval	*%ag/tw*	*% of Villages*	*Average Village Size*	*Sex Ratio*	*0-6%*	*% SC/ST*	*Lit %*	*WPR t*	*% al/tw*
0	0.0	0.85	978	1038.4	12.2	10.5	74.6	35.6	0.0
0-10	3.4	11.94	4507	980.4	11.0	17.1	72.8	37.4	0.7
10.1-30	20.4	23.76	2661	995.9	12.0	25.5	61.0	47.9	5.8
30-50	39.5	25.26	2411	988.1	11.9	25.6	57.3	51.5	12.4
50-70	59.1	20.70	2102	988.6	12.4	24.2	55.0	52.9	19.6
70-80	74.7	7.39	1612	996.6	12.4	25.3	53.8	53.7	27.2
80-90	84.4	6.24	1348	993.8	12.6	29.6	52.8	54.5	33.1
90+	93.8	3.87	800	993.5	12.9	38.3	48.5	56.7	35.9

The composition of workers varies with the degree of diversification. Villages with higher dependence on agriculture tend to have: 1) a smaller proportion of males among agricultural workers and among cultivators; 2) a higher proportion of agricultural labourers relative to cultivators; and 3) the proportion of males among agricultural labourers is generally lower than among cultivators in all groups. It is nearly half in districts where less than 10 per cent of workers are in agriculture and tends to decrease as dependence on agriculture increases up to a point and then increases progressively to more than two-fifths in predominantly agricultural districts.

The importance of females in agricultural workforce, overall and among cultivators, thus increases as the degree of dependence on agriculture varies from 30-35 per cent in predominantly non-agricultural districts to 10-48 per cent in the predominantly agricultural group. Females comprise a larger proportion of labourers than among cultivators, accounting for the majority in the lowest group and increase progressively to nearly two-third up to the middle groups and then rises to about 58 per cent in the predominantly agricultural groups. The share of females among non-agricultural workers is much smaller compared to agriculture ranging from less than a fourth to a maximum of 40 per cent.

Table 3.8

Composition of Workers at Different Levels of Employment Diversification

% ag/tw	*m/t age workers*	*clm/clt*	*alm/alt*	*% non-agr workers*	*% m/non-agr workers*
0.0	0	0.0	0.0	100.0	76.7
3.4	64.4	68.7	47.6	96.6	74.5
20.4	59.8	68.6	37.7	79.6	61.9
39.5	55.3	63.9	36.6	60.5	60.3
59.1	53.7	62.2	36.4	40.9	60.7
74.7	52.6	61.2	37.6	25.3	62.6
84.4	52.9	61.1	40.3	15.6	65.3
93.8	52.4	58.9	42.0	6.2	64.3

Note: m/t: Male workers/total workers; clm/clt: Male cultivators/total cultivators; alm/alt: Agricultural labour(male)/total agricultural labour.

Incidence of Agricultural Labour

Workers in agriculture consist of cultivators and labourers. The latter largely belong to SC/ST and other socially disadvantaged groups who have little or no productive assets, depend mostly on wage employment for their livelihood and comprise the lowest income groups. The proportion of agricultural labourers among agricultural workers is therefore indicative of the incidence of economically weak groups in the population.

Over a tenth of the villages have no agricultural labourers; they comprise less than 10 per cent of the workforce in the next lowest group covering 45 per cent of the villages. In three-fourths of the villages, the share of labourers to all workers lies in the range of 0-30 per cent. Barely 2 per cent report this share to be more than 70 per cent.

Higher share of agricultural labourers goes with higher share of agriculture in the total workforce. Their share in the total agricultural workforce is about 11 per cent in the lowest group and thereafter increases progressively to a maximum of more than 90 per cent. In predominantly agricultural districts (with agriculture employing more than 90 per cent of the workforce), labourers comprise practically the entire agricultural work force. Villages that have higher percentage of agricultural labour in the workforce tend to be smaller in size, less literate but go with higher proportion of SC/ST and of children in the population, lower literacy and higher proportion of females in the population and the workforce.

Table 3.9

Frequency Distribution of Villages according to Per cent of Workers who are Agricultural Labourers, 2001

Class Interval	*% al/tw*	*% of Villages*	*Average Village Size*	*0-6%*	*S_ Ratio 06*	*% SC/ ST*	*Lit t*	*WPRF*	*WPRF/ WPRM*	*% ag/tw*	*al/ag Workers*
0	0.0	11.18	1181	11.3	953.3	19.2	68.3	26.5	0.47	20.3	0.0
0-10	3.1	45.89	2988	11.6	937.4	21.8	62.6	35.8	0.61	26.4	11.8
10+-20	14.4	16.20	2700	12.2	926.8	24.2	57.9	40.9	0.70	43.3	33.4
20-30	24.4	10.02	2461	12.4	935.0	26.5	57.0	41.5	0.71	52.1	46.7
30-40	34.4	6.25	2051	12.4	942.0	29.4	57.1	40.7	0.70	60.2	57.1
40-50	44.5	4.37	1622	12.4	946.2	32.7	56.8	42.3	0.73	67.7	65.7
50-60	54.2	2.57	1315	12.5	958.2	34.7	55.2	43.3	0.75	74.7	72.6
60-70	64.6	1.59	1240	12.5	946.7	36.8	57.5	42.5	0.74	80.0	80.7
70-80	74.0	1.13	1047	12.6	976.0	42.4	56.3	43.0	0.75	86.0	86.0
80-90	84.2	0.48	856	13.1	974.8	48.2	54.1	46.6	0.79	90.7	92.9
90+	93.3	0.35	480	13.3	1021.5	44.3	50.7	49.3	0.84	95.4	97.9

Variations at the Village Level

The directory data make it possible to explore variations in selected indicators of socioeconomic conditions across villages. This section presents the association between each of the indicators and other characteristics across 15,400 villages in the state and across villages with the lowest and highest deciles in respect of different indicators.

Simple correlations across all villages taken together suggest that across villages SRs bear a statistically significant positive correlation with literacy and with the proportion of agricultural labourers in the workforce. They are negatively correlated with WPRs, village size, household size and the proportion of SCs and STs. Also noteworthy is the fact that higher overall SRs go with higher SRs among children (cc 0.267) and SCs and STs (cc 0.121).

Table 3.10

Simple Correlations between Sex Ratio and Selected Village Characteristics

Pop	*Hh size*	*% 0-6*	*% SC/ST*	*WPR*	*Lit*	*% ag*	*al/agwkr*
-0.068	-0.040	-0.008	-0.028	-0.092	0.125	-0.016	0.025

As with overall SR, higher child SRs are associated with lower work participation rate, smaller village size and greater dependence on agriculture. However, associations with other characteristics are different. Villages with larger average size of households, higher proportion of children, higher literacy and larger proportion of SC/ST in their population tend to have higher child SR. Also noteworthy is the fact that most of the correlations are much weaker compared to those observed in the case of overall SR.

Table 3.11

Simple Correlations between Child Sex Ratio and Selected Village Characteristics

Pop	*Hh size*	*SR*	*% SC/ST*	*WPR*	*Lit*	*% ag*	*al/ag wkr*
-0.038	0.028	0.267	0.047	-0.049	0.035	-0.011	0.032

Variations in the proportion of SC/ST across all villages and their association with different sociodemographic characteristics suggest that higher proportion of SC/ST goes with higher incidence of wage labour in agriculture and less strongly with dependence on agriculture and overall work participation rate. Villages with higher proportion of SC/ST tend to have higher proportion of children in their population. Villages with higher proportion of SC/ST tend to be less literate, are smaller in size and also have smaller households on the average.

Table 3.12

Simple Correlations between % SC/ST and Selected Village Characteristics

Pop	*Hh size*	*% 0-6*	*SR*	*Lit*	*WPR*	*% ag wkrs*	*al/ag wkr*
-0.130	-0.008	0.219	-0.028	-0.278	0.080	0.032	0.170

Villages with higher overall literacy rates tend to be larger in size and have larger households. However more literate villages tend to have lower WPRs, greater dependence on agriculture and smaller proportion of SC/ST. The association between the latter characteristics and literacy is much stronger than with population or household size.

Table 3.13

Simple Correlations between Literacy Rate and Selected Village Characteristics

Pop	*Hh size*	*SR*	*% 0-6*	*SC/ST*	*WPR*	*% ag wkr*	*al/ag wkr*
0.165	0.023	0.125	-0.424	-0.278	-0.427	-0.336	0.027

Villages with higher LRs, larger average household size, larger populations, higher proportion of agricultural labourers in the workforce and larger proportion of children in their population tend to have lower overall WPRs. WPRs are negatively correlated to the overall SR. These associations are strongest in the case of literacy and household size. On the other hand, villages with higher dependence on agriculture and higher proportion of SC/ST tend to have higher overall participation rates.

Table 3.14

Simple Correlations between Work Participation Rate and Selected Village Characteristics

Pop	*Hh size*	*0-0.6 %*	*SR*	*SC/ST*	*Lit*	*% agwkr*	*al/ag wkr*
-0.160	-0.253	-0.080	-0.092	0.080	-0.427	0.327	-0.148

Higher the dependence on agriculture for work, the lower tends to be literacy, smaller the village size, and lower the SRs. Conversely, villages with higher proportion of workers in non-agriculture are much more literate and much larger in size. Villages that are more dependent on agriculture also tend to have a higher WPR and a larger proportion of agricultural labourers in the work force. All these associations are strong. Household size, proportion of children and of SC/ST bear a weaker positive correlation with dependence on agriculture.

Table 3.15

Simple Correlations between % of Workers in Agriculture and Selected Village Characteristics

Pop	*Hh size*	*0-0.6 %*	*SR*	*SC/ST*	*Lit*	*WPR*	*al/ag wkr*
-0.221	0.077	0.065	-0.016	0.032	-0.336	0.327	0.213

The share of agricultural labourers in the working population and that of agriculture as a whole are strongly correlated. The characteristics associated with the two are also similar in some respects but differ in strength and also direction in others. Thus, villages with larger proportion of labourers, like those with greater dependence on agriculture, tend to be smaller but have larger households, a higher proportion of SC/ST and more children relative to total population. The correlation with the proportion of children is however much stronger than in the case of overall agricultural dependence. Also unlike with overall agricultural dependence, higher incidence of agricultural labour goes with lower WPRs, higher literacy and higher SRs.

Table 3.16

Simple Correlations between % of Agricultural Labour in Workforce and Selected Village Characteristics

Pop	*Hh size*	*0-0.6 %*	*SR*	*SC/ST*	*Lit*	*WPR*	*% ag wkr*
-0.039	0.047	0.106	0.025	0.170	0.027	-0.148	0.213

Given that the data base relates to averages for households from over 15,000 villages, the values of the coefficients, though apparently small, do indicate a statistically significant relationship between these variables. Their low values are partly due to a high level of 'noise' in data collected through several thousands of interviewers from close to 200 million households. They are also a reflection of the high degree of variability in the strength and direction of these associations across regions and within groups at different levels of attainment.

Intra-decile Variations

This is brought out in the correlations between different socioeconomic indicators and associated characteristics across villages in the bottom and top decile of attainment in each indicator. A comparison with the correlations for all villages and between the two groups of villages shows the wide differences in both the direction and pattern of associations.

Inter-district Variations

District-wise distribution of villages in the lowest and highest deciles in terms of selected socioeconomic indicators and their incidence is given in Tables 3.17 and 3.18, respectively. Districts with a larger number of total villages tend to have larger number of villages in both deciles for all indicators. Of greater interest is the interdistrict variation in the number of villages in each that fall within the two deciles of the selected indicators as a percentage of its total villages. The range of inter- district variations in incidence differs between indicators but is large in both deciles. Incidence of more than 10 per cent (which is decile average in all cases) may be considered as 'high' and those below this figure as 'low incidence'. On this basis, the proportion of high incidence ranges between 25 per cent (SR) and 60 per cent (WPR) in the bottom decile and from 40 per cent (SR) to 60 per cent (SC/ST) in the top decile. The number of districts with high incidence (on the above definition) is larger in the top decile but the range of variation in this index is narrower in all but one indicator compared to the least well-placed districts.

Table 3.17

Association between Indicators and Characteristics across Deciles with the Lowest and the Highest Attainment, 2001

SR	*Pop*	*Hh size*	*SR 0-6*	*% SC/ST*	*Lit*	*WPR*	*% ag wkr*	
Bottom decile	0.007	-0.202	0.179	0.084	-0.091	0.042	0.102	
Top decile	-0.080	0.182	-0.020	-0.082	0.124	-0.109	0.028	
% SC/ST								
	Pop	*Hh size*	*SR*	*Lit*	*WPR*	*% ag wkr*	*al/ag wkr*	
Bottom decile	0.057	-0.028	-0.028	-0.058	0.047	0.012	0.055	
Top decile	-0.237	-0.013	-0.037	-0.465	0.200	0.155	-0.146	
% literacy								
	Pop	*Hh size*	*SR*	*SC/ST*	*Litf/Litm*	*WPR*	*% ag wkr*	
Bottom decile	0.195	-0.009	0.040	-0.368	0.181	-0.141	-0.090	
Top decile	0.043	0.063	0.066	-0.264	0.534	-0.250	-0.252	
WPR								
	Pop	*Hh size*	*SR*	*SC/ST*	*Lit*	*Litf/m*	*% ag wkr*	*al/ag wkr*
Bottom decile	0.166	-0.252	-0.179	-0.004	-0.013	-0.034	-0.113	0.081
Top decile	-0.172	-0.147	-0.138	0.027	-0.040	-0.073	0.049	-0.079
%ag wkr								
	Pop	*Hh size*	*SR*	*SC/ST*	*WPR*	*Lit*	*Litf/m*	*al/ag wkr*
Bottom decile	-0.157	-0.091	0.025	0.143	0.145	-0.172	-0.165	0.157
Top decile	-0.309	0.011	0.075	0.089	0.087	-0.118	-0.047	-0.041
al/ag wkr								
	Pop	*Hh size*	*SR*	*SC/ST*	*WPR*	*Lit*	*Litf/m*	*% ag wkr*
Bottom decile	mostly have little or no agricultural labourers							
Top decile	-0.258	-0.035	0.058	0.078	-0.017	-0.020	0.070	0.017

Tables 3.18

District Level Variations in Incidence of Villages in Bottom and Top Deciles

	Bottom Decile		*Top Decile*	
	Range	*Districts with >10% Incidence*	*Range*	*Districts with >10% Incidence*
Sex ratio	2.4 – 31.4	7	2.1 – 16.2	11
%SC/ST	7.5 – 14	10	7.4 – 14.5	17
% literacy	4.3 – 16	11	5.8 – 14.6	13
WPR	6.9 – 13.1	17	7.3 – 14.9	15
%agr workers	5.9 – 17.1	11	4.8 – 13.6	16
Al/ag workers	0 – 14	14	6.9 – 15.7	15

For the most part, both individually and collectively, indicators with higher than average incidence differ between districts in the two groups. However, there are some instances in which the same indicator figures in both groups. This is noticed in the case of SR (6 districts), % SC/ST (7), literacy (5), WPR (7), % agriculture workers (8), and al/ag (5). A few districts share two or more of the same indicators in both groups: Salem (5), Ramanathapuram (4), Dharmapuri and Sivaganaga (3 each), and Coimbatore, Thanjavur, Nagapattinam, Madurai and Nilgiris (2 each). This could indicate the existence of concentration of villages in these indicators at both ends of the spectrum within villages.

The distribution of districts by the number of indicators with high incidence is highly uneven (see Table 3.18). None of the indicators figure in this category in three districts of the bottom decile and in four of the top decile. The number of indicators with higher than average incidence ranges from 1 to 3 in 18 districts and 4 to 6 in 7 districts of the bottom decile. In the top decile, this distribution is more skewed: 14 districts have high incidence in 1 to 3 indicators, while 14 districts with 4 to 6 indicators have this characteristic.

Table 3.19

Frequency Distribution of Districts according to the Number of Indicators with High Incidence

No. of Indicators	*None*	*1*	*2*	*3*	*4*	*5*	*6*
Bottom decile villages	3	7	7	4	3	3	1
Top decile villages	4	2	5	7	8	1	1

The distribution of districts in the two groups with 3 or fewer indicators of lower than average (denoted as 'low incidence') and those with 4 or more such indicators ('high incidence') shows some interesting patterns of clustering.

HbHt	*HbLt*	*LbHt*	*LbLh*
Salem R'puram	Namakkal Nagapattinam, Nilgiris Dharmapuri Theni	Tiruvallore Kancheepuram Krishnagiri Coimbatore Thanjavur Sivaganga Tiruvannamalai Virudunagar Tirunelveli	Cuddalore, Vellore, Erode Thiruvarur Thiruchi.. Karur, Perambalur Pudukottai, Madurai, Dindigal Tirunelveli Toothukudi

Note: H = high incidence; L = low incidence; b = bottom decile; t = top decile.

Of the 21 districts in the first group with 3 or less higher than average incidence, as many as 13 also figure in the same category in the second. The remaining 8 figure among districts in the second group with 4 or more indicators. Of the 7 districts in the first group that have 4 or more indicators of higher than average incidence, only 2 figure in the same category in the second group. The rest figure among those with 3 or less of such indicators. Ten 'high-incidence' districts in the second group figure among the low-incidence districts of the first group. The significance of this pattern of clustering and the factors underlying it is an area for further research.

Tables 3.20

District-wise Distribution of the Bottom Decile of the State's Villages in Selected Socioeconomic Indicators of Status, 2001

	*High Sex Ratio***		*Low SC/ST**		*High Literacy***		*High WPR***		*Low % ag wkrs**		*Low Al/ag wkrs**	
	Number	*Per cent*	*Number*	*Per cent*	*Number*	*Per cent*	*Number*	*Per cent*	*Number*	*Per cent*	*Number*	*Per cent*
Thiruvallur	90	14.5	63	10.2	67	10.8	65	10.5	51	8.2	60	9.7
Kancheepuram	168	16.2	107	10.3	102	9.9	107	10.3	106	10.2	105	10.1
Cuddalore	61	7.7	71	9.0	75	9.5	67	8.5	66	8.4	87	11.0
Villupuram	66	6.2	92	8.6	99	9.3	118	11.1	104	9.7	126	11.8
Vellore	118	11.3	94	9.0	112	10.7	101	9.7	100	9.6	110	10.5
Tiruvannamalai	160	11.2	142	9.9	123	8.6	157	11.0	146	10.2	145	10.1
Salem	25	4.5	78	14.0	56	10.1	72	12.9	60	10.8	78	14.0
Namakkal	23	6.2	40	10.8	33	8.9	31	8.4	40	10.8	35	9.4
Erode	28	7.3	40	10.4	46	11.9	36	9.4	38	9.9	37	9.6
Dharmapuri	1	2.4	5	12.2	6	14.6	3	7.3	7	17.1	3	7.3
Krishnagiri	27	6.7	44	11.0	41	10.2	34	8.5	45	11.2	41	10.2
Coimbatore	25	7.4	32	9.5	40	11.9	33	9.8	35	10.4	34	10.1
Thanjavur	6	3.4	17	9.7	18	10.3	25	14.3	20	11.4	18	10.3
Thiruvarur	26	5.9	42	9.6	43	9.8	55	12.5	54	12.3	45	10.3
Nagapattinam	4	2.8	11	7.7	9	6.3	15	10.5	13	9.1	18	12.6
Tiruchirappalli	4	2.1	23	12.2	18	9.6	22	11.7	11	5.9	20	10.6
Karur	84	10.4	78	9.7	83	10.3	82	10.2	73	9.0	61	7.6
Perambalur	46	9.4	45	9.2	48	9.9	41	8.4	39	8.0	47	9.7
Pudukkottai	65	12.5	54	10.4	51	9.8	64	12.3	50	9.6	52	10.0
Madurai	75	9.6	84	10.7	84	10.7	69	8.8	90	11.5	82	10.4
Theni	107	14.5	82	11.1	73	9.9	74	10.1	73	9.9	71	9.6
Dindigul	75	14.7	57	11.2	64	12.5	41	8.0	56	11.0	43	8.4
Ramanathapuram	51	9.3	57	10.4	59	10.7	61	11.1	60	10.9	48	8.7
Sivaganga	3	3.7	9	11.1	8	9.9	6	7.4	10	12.3	4	4.9
Virudhunagar	74	14.8	51	10.2	58	11.6	52	10.4	55	11.0	53	10.6
Tirunelveli	43	11.2	43	11.2	37	9.6	36	9.4	35	9.1	29	7.5
Thoothukkudi	50	11.7	32	7.5	37	8.6	38	8.9	44	10.3	45	10.5
The Nilgiris	29	6.5	42	9.4	44	9.8	46	10.3	47	10.5	38	8.5
Kanniyakumari	4	5.8	8	11.6			6	8.8	6	8.7		

Notes: * Relates to the lowest decile of villages ranked according to the level of the specific indicator.

** Relates to the highest decile of villages ranked according to the level of the specific indicator.

Table 3.21

District-wise Distribution of the State's Villages with Highest Levels of Select Socioeconomic Indicators, 2001

	*High Sex Ratio** Low*		*Low SC/ST**		*High Literacy***		*High WPR***		*Low %ag wkrs**		*LowAl/ag wkrs**	
	Number	*Per cent*	*Number*	*Per cent*	*Number*	*Per cent*	*Number*	*Per cent*	*Number*	*Per cent*	*Number*	*Per cent*
Tiruvallur	90	14.5	63	10.2	67	10.8	65	10.5	51	8.2	60	9.7
Kanchipuram	168	16.2	107	10.3	102	9.9	107	10.3	106	10.2	105	10.1
Cuddalore	61	7.7	71	9.0	75	9.5	67	8.5	66	8.4	87	11.0
Villupuram	66	6.2	92	8.6	99	9.3	118	11.1	104	9.7	126	11.8
Vellore	118	11.3	94	9.0	112	10.7	101	9.7	100	9.6	110	10.5
Tiruvannamalai	160	11.2	142	9.9	123	8.6	157	11.0	146	10.2	145	10.1
Salem	25	4.5	78	14.0	56	10.1	72	12.9	60	10.8	78	14.0
Namakkal	23	6.2	40	10.8	33	8.9	31	8.4	40	10.8	35	9.4
Erode	28	7.3	40	10.4	46	11.9	36	9.4	38	9.9	37	9.6
Dharmapuri	1	2.4	5	12.2	6	14.6	3	7.3	7	17.1	3	7.3
Krishnagiri	27	6.7	44	11.0	41	10.2	34	8.5	45	11.2	41	10.2
Coimbatore	25	7.4	32	9.5	40	11.9	33	9.8	35	10.4	34	10.1
Thanjavur	6	3.4	17	9.7	18	10.3	25	14.3	20	11.4	18	10.3
Thiruvarur	26	5.9	42	9.6	43	9.8	55	12.5	54	12.3	45	10.3
Nagapattinam	4	2.8	11	7.7	9	6.3	15	10.5	13	9.1	18	12.6
Tiruchirappalli	4	2.1	23	12.2	18	9.6	22	11.7	11	5.9	20	10.6
Karur	84	10.4	78	9.7	83	10.3	82	10.2	73	9.0	61	7.6
Perambalur	46	9.4	45	9.2	48	9.9	41	8.4	39	8.0	47	9.7
Pudukkottai	65	12.5	54	10.4	51	9.8	64	12.3	50	9.6	52	10.0
Madurai	75	9.6	84	10.7	84	10.7	69	8.8	90	11.5	82	10.4
Theni	107	14.5	82	11.1	73	9.9	74	10.1	73	9.9	71	9.6
Dindigul	75	14.7	57	11.2	64	12.5	41	8.0	56	11.0	43	8.4
Ramanathapuram	51	9.3	57	10.4	59	10.7	61	11.1	60	10.9	48	8.7
Sivaganga	3	3.7	9	11.1	8	9.9	6	7.4	10	12.3	4	4.9
Virudhunagar	74	14.8	51	10.2	58	11.6	52	10.4	55	11.0	53	10.6
Tirunelveli	43	11.2	43	11.2	37	9.6	36	9.4	35	9.1	29	7.5
Thoothukkudi	50	11.7	32	7.5	37	8.6	38	8.9	44	10.3	45	10.5
The Nilgiris	29	6.5	42	9.4	44	9.8	46	10.3	47	10.5	38	8.5
Kanniyakumari	4	5.8	8	11.6			6	8.8	6	8.7		

Notes: * Relates to the lowest decile of villages ranked according to the level of the specific indicator.

** Relates to the highest decile of villages ranked according to the level of the specific indicator.

Conclusion

This paper is largely descriptive of the patterns observed in the distribution of villages according to the level of attainment of a few (obviously far from exhaustive) socioeconomic indicators and their association with different village characteristics. Explaining the factors that account for these patterns calls for formulation and testing of hypotheses regarding the factors that influence different characteristics. A number of such hypotheses are available in the literature. But testing them would require far more data on socioeconomic infrastructure than was available to the author. (For a limited exploratory attempt see Vaidyanathan, 1996). The range and scope of analysis of the dynamics of change at a disaggregated level (down to villages) can be further extended by making use of village level data on infrastructure (available in the village directories).

Reference

Vaidyanathan, A. (1996). *Socioeconomic Characteristics of Villages of North Arcot: Exploratory Study—Review of Development and Change*. MIDS.

Agriculture and Irrigation

4 Declining Significance of Agriculture in Tamil Nadu

An Overview

S. Neelakantan

This paper contains two parts. The first part gives a bird's eye view of the agrarian transformation in Tamil Nadu. The declining importance of agriculture is clearly discernable in it. The second part is a 'leg' eye view of the change. I look at the same transformation more closely at the ground level, sometimes as a participant observer and sometimes as a general observer. Therefore, it contains more micro-details.

PART I

A comparison of the wedding invitations of rural families in the 1950s with the present dramatically publicises the fact that the agricultural sector in Tamil Nadu has lost its pre-eminence in the state's economy. Almost all the invitations of the 1950s would proudly announce that the families of either bride or groom or both were 'Mirasdars' or 'Nilakizhars'—meaning that they were landowners even if the ownership was only a tiny plot!. But no marriage invitation now contains the term, even among large land-holding families. Agricultural activity has no special esteem attached to it at present.

The approach paper to Tamil Nadu's current Five Year Plan states that the contribution of the primary sector to state's gross domestic product (GDP) has fallen to 13.2 per cent this year. This steep fall must be compared to its share at the time of independence, which was around 45 per cent. The secondary sector's share has increased from around 20 per cent to 30 per cent and the share of the tertiary sector has jumped up from 35 per cent to 55 per cent during the same period.

The percentage of population dependent on agriculture and allied activities has also fallen from around 75 per cent at the time of independence to the current 56 per cent. There is an increase in absolute numbers because of population growth, but the relative importance in employment of the agricultural sector has fallen.

Peter Timmer (1988) has theorised that such a decline is inevitable. "The declining importance of agriculture is uniform and pervasive, a tendency obviously driven by powerful forces inherent in the development process, whether in socialist or capitalist countries, Asian, Latin American or African, currently developed or still poor." Timmer recognises that industrial development dictates simultaneous agricultural development as agriculture would have to supply wage goods and also a portion of the raw materials for industrial growth. Yet he asserts that the importance of agriculture would continuously decline. He ascribes this apparent paradox to two mechanisms, Engel's law and rapid rise in agricultural productivity.

General Features of Rural Change in Tamil Nadu

I wish to situate this declining significance of agriculture in the overall setting of the changes taking place in the rural economy of Tamil Nadu.

I had the opportunity to go through a set of village studies of a number of villages in Tamil Nadu commissioned by the Centre for Development Studies under its Kerala Research Programme of Local Level Development in the period 2001-2003. I sum up the overall changes in rural conditions in Tamil Nadu perceived by me from the study of these papers and by observations in my own hamlet.

Population has increased in all the villages. However, the rate of increase has fallen in the last decade in all these villages. A noteworthy feature is that the number of households has increased fast and their rate of increase is greater than the rate of increase of the population. The implication is very clear. Even in the villages, nuclear families have become the norm and extended families are on the wane.

A positive feature is that in all those villages, literacy levels are going up. However, the growth is uneven among sexes as well as castes. Women lag behind men, and Scheduled Castes (SCs) lag behind other castes in most villages.

The landholding pattern continues to remain highly skewed in all the villages. The natural growth of population and the emergence of nuclear families have led to division of large estates among family members. This causes some decline in large-size farms and some enlargement of small-size farms.

Absentee landlordism is everywhere declining. Owners of large farms very often move out of the village to live in nearby towns. There is very little evidence to show that the large farmers are attempting to purchase additional land with the surplus generated from their farms.[1] On the contrary, new purchasers are generally from the towns or from among the persons who have saved money out of wages or salaries or other income generated outside the villages concerned. Many local marginal and small farmers have also acquired land out of their savings.

A positive feature is that the SCs, who practically owned no cultivable land at independence, have started acquiring land now. They also encroach on village poramboke or tank foreshore lands but mainly for construction of houses. They have acquired only small pieces of relatively unfertile lands or lands with least access to water.

Among the SCs, it is mostly persons who generate income by working or earning outside their villages who seem to have acquired land. Many SCs from outside the village have purchased land in other villages. While some of them purchase land, small and marginal farmers in many villages have also started selling land. It may be for raising finance to get employment outside, either in India or abroad, or to educate their children or because urban dwellers offer high prices to start factories or for real estate speculation. It may also be because they have not been able to invest heavily for digging or drilling wells and install pump sets in areas where the water table is falling fast. This has forced some of the erstwhile landowners to join the ranks of landless labourers.

Mechanisation has spread to all the villages surveyed. Resistance to introduction of tractors was found in 1970s in Thanjavur district but soon the labourers themselves acquiesced in the introduction of tractors and other farm machines. Machinery mostly replaced the jobs previously done

1. In the stagnant village, Vengidengal, palatial houses are getting dilapidated because the owners are unable to maintain them.

by male labourers. However, in many places, the conjunctive use of well and river/tank water has increased the cropping intensity, which to a great extent has increased the demand for labour.

The introduction of tractors and threshers has certainly been the cause for the rapid decline of draught animals in all villages.

The pump set revolution received tremendous impetus after 1970s through the state policy of subsidised and later, free electricity to agriculture. The pump set revolution has had several consequences. It extended the irrigated area and made conjunctive use of water possible in many villages. It helped change the crop mix and cropping pattern. It converted mono-crop areas into double-crop areas. It led to competitive digging of wells. It caused the water table to fall rapidly. It has also created a market for irrigation water in some villages. Worst of all, it has altered a substantial portion of agricultural activities from daytime to night.

The impact of this revolution has not been uniform among all villages. It has provided those who possess groundwater with security. By and large, it is the large and medium landowners who have benefited most from well water. In the long run, the change in crop mix, especially the changeover to sugarcane, proved to be unsustainable in many areas. With the fall in groundwater levels, the previously extended area irrigated is no longer getting assured water supply. Digging wells and securing electricity connections are costly operations and drive many farmers into the debt trap. The conjunctive use of well water with river/canal/tank water initially increased the certainty of water availability till the crop cycle was completed. But competitive deepening of wells/bore wells combined with uncertainty in the flows of river/canal/tank water has of late increased the uncertainty again.

After 1970s, in the existing canal and tank irrigated areas of Tamil Nadu, additional lands beyond the originally envisaged *ayacut* were given the right to access water. In the newly constructed dams and tanks also, the anticipated area irrigated was increased by adding new land or by introducing the turn system. These were accomplished either through legal means or those of doubtful validity. The second category predominates. At the same time, the catchments of river valleys and tank foreshores are getting encroached. In the rivers, sand cover is excessively mined. Water bodies are getting polluted by urban and industrial effluents. An unholy alliance between politicians and officials makes such activities possible. They have succeeded in blunting the enforceability of the rights which the original *ayacutdars* were enjoying for long in the past. In the case of inter-state rivers, the upper riparians are asserting their rights to get water at the expense of the lower riparians residing in Tamil Nadu. The macro consequences are a fall in the availability and quality of water for irrigation and considerable increase in the uncertainty of the farmers regarding availability of water till the end of the season when their crop matures. This is one of the important causes for the post-1990 stagnation in the yields of crops.

In all the villages, the status-oriented, traditional labour arrangement, which "ties up" a labourer to his master through an advance payment in kind or cash, called "Pannayal" or "Padiyal", is fast disappearing. Unless there are special local circumstances, permanent "tie-up" arrangements might totally disappear soon.

Another general feature is the replacement of wages in kind by wages in cash. In almost all the villages, this trend is visible. Payment of wages in kind as well as in the form of food is also disappearing, except during sowing, harvesting and threshing of food grains, especially paddy.

Mechanisation, pump set revolution and technological changes have decreased the demand for the services of many local artisans, who were receiving payments in kind according to the local variations of the '*jajmani*' system (called '*mirasu* rights' in Arkavadi). This system is also seen to be disappearing in almost all places.

Along with mechanisation, pump set revolution and green revolution, it is observed that for all the labour-intensive and time critical operations, such as sowing, harvesting and threshing, the 'contract system' of engaging labour has spread widely. In most villages, supply of food to the labourers during these critical operations in paddy cultivation continues. This continuation of wages in kind, while contract wages are in cash, is the accepted practice in other operations such as cutting of sugarcane and indicates that the relative bargaining power of the labourers is greater than that of the landowners during such critical operations. Both sides implicitly acknowledge the relative change in their bargaining positions.

The same reasons impel small and marginal farmers to engage in reciprocal exchange of labour services of family members among themselves for these operations.

In all villages, the tasks performed by men and women labourers are different due to cultural practices. Everywhere women are paid less as wage than men. Even when contracted wages are paid to a 'pair', the share of the woman *vis-à-vis* the man is lower. Even militant trade unionism in East Thanjavur is not able to beak this gender discrimination.

At the time when mechanisation and pump-set revolution were replacing labourers in the 1970s, when *'pannayal'* system, was breaking down and payments in kind were being replaced by cash payments, real wages might have been falling. But in the last decade, real wages are increasing in most villages.

Increase in real wages is surprising because the availability of employment in agriculture is declining in most of the villages in the last decade, mainly because the availability of water for the second crop has become uncertain. The cultivated area is also falling. These should have reduced the demand for labour in the villages.

However, non-farm employment within the villages and farm and non-farm employment outside the villages have increased. Urban demand for labour from far away places draws away a portion of the labour force. Labourers out-migrate to perform agricultural operations such as sugarcane cutting on contract basis or for non-farm operations in places as far away as Chennai, Bangalore or Goa. Some attempt to obtain employment outside the country. Educated persons out-migrate to get salaried employment in government and private sectors. It is this diversion of the rural labour to non-agricultural occupations which is the cause for the increase in real wages.

More and more consumer durables, especially TV, two-wheelers and gas stoves, are entering the villages, though their distribution is highly skewed.

Labourers everywhere have discontinued regular consumption of coarse cereals such as cumbu or ragi. The labouring classes have ceased to consume the more nutritious cereals and have shifted to the less nutritious rice; and the public distribution system (PDS) has played an enabling role for this unfortunate shift, though the shift itself is mainly due to the labouring class imitating the food habits of the superior classes—a Veblenesque behaviour due to 'sanskritisation'.

The common property resources are getting neglected in almost all the villages. Encroachments of *poramboku* lands are reported in many villages. Unlike in the past, the encroachers are not merely the rich. Many poor people have also encroached upon these resources mainly to build houses.

The traditional methods of tank management, especially maintenance and allocation, continue to function with modifications in some places. In other places, they have been replaced. On the whole, the maintenance and allocation do not function as efficiently as they did in the past.[2]

The *panchayat*, where it works harmoniously, is able to deliver many benefits to the villages. But in many, there is increasing caste conflict which hinders progress. The Dalits are seen asserting their right everywhere, and this is resisted by the locally dominant castes. The tide is slowly turning in favour of the Dalits, even though atrocities against them are reported to be continuing. Right from the *panchayat* level, a routine of giving 'cuts' from the funds sanctioned for public programmes to politicians and bureaucrats on a pre-determined pattern has been established and practised.

Almost all the villages are connected by bus or mini-bus thanks to improved roads. There is telephone connection to most villages. Cell phones, television sets and mopeds are common. All the villages have an elementary school. But the preference is for English medium education, and in most villages, school vans from private schools come to pick up fee paying students. Drinking water is now supplied by the *panchayat* in all the villages. However, individual house connection is given only in a few villages and very few Dalits have this privilege. Practically all the villages have street lights.

In the provision of basic needs such as drinking water, street lighting, transport access and primary schooling, the state's role is certainly positive.

2. Rajagopal's contention that the Common Property Resources are relatively better managed where a single dominant caste wields control than in places where that control is divided among castes is supported by the experience in Alappakkam and Enathimelpakkam.

In places where there is harmony among castes, the *panchayat* effectively functions and provides all these amenities. Opinion about the role of PDS is mixed.

In all the villages, a section of the SCs has succeeded in getting concrete houses built for them, while the others are awaiting their turn. State assistance in this direction has proved to be of importance. In most villages, there is improvement in housing.

Land sales and mortgages have now become a common feature. Purchase of land for non-agricultural purposes (for real estate sales in villages around urban centres and for industrial use in other villages) is reported in many studies. Sale of land by small and/or marginal farmers to raise finance for seeking employment opportunities outside the villages is taking place. Similarly, many out-migrants who have earned sufficient money come back to purchase land in their native village. In a few villages, new immigrants belonging to the dominant caste of the locality have purchased land and settled. Living standards for most inhabitants in the villages have improved. The families whose farm income is supplemented by income from non-farm employment are better off than those who depend on farm income alone.

PART II

My Chettipalayam Experience as a Participant Observer

I hail from Chetttipalayam, a hamlet of Appipalayam village in Karur taluka, where I own and operate a farm. So I have a 'leg' eye view of the changes, i.e., a ground level perspective. I have witnessed the alterations in cropping patterns and the labour conditions in my region over the last 50 years.[3] Similar transformation, subject to local variations, has taken place in all parts of Tamil Nadu. I propose to narrate them in some detail, referring to my Chettipalayam experience wherever necessary.

The decline of agriculture in Tamil Nadu has not occurred at a uniform pace. In fact, we can distinguish three phases in which this change has taken place, each phase having some unique characteristics.

3. The details are more completely given in Neelakantan (2002, 2003).

First Phase 1947-1965

In this period, both area cultivated and area irrigated increased. This was a period in which public investment in irrigation and power was initiated and expanded.

In Tamil Nadu, all the rivers are seasonal. It was at this time that the state started constructing reservoirs across most of the rivers to give assured water supply to existing canals and to build new canals. The 'system' tanks which received water from the canals branching from rivers benefited by this activity. New canals were constructed in the Cauvery Delta also.

Simultaneously, fresh land was brought under the plough. The area cultivated increased because of the availability of water through new canals. The intensity of land use increased.

The completion of a dam over the Amaravathi River in 1958 induced the farmers in Chettipalayam area to irrigate their drylands by tapping river water directly without authorisation. The revenue authorities initially levied penal rates on such unauthorised irrigated lands. But after a period of time, the landlords jointly and severally influenced politicians and officials to 'regularise' the unauthorised irrigation. In this way, new lands began to get irrigation which was not originally envisaged in the construction plans of the dam.

In this period, the villages were relatively isolated and, therefore, attempted to be nearly self-reliant at least in respect of their necessities. Then, as now, there were different strata of agriculturists—absentee landlords who cultivated with their own overseers or leased out lands, supervisory landlords who lived in the villages and operated their farms, small and marginal farmers who cultivated their own land or leased in land from others and landless agricultural labourers. Even among the landless, the SCs formed the bottom strata.

Land ownership was highly skewed. It was respected and honoured. Agricultural work was the primary function of the villagers. All other work served a customary and complementary role. The blacksmith fixing wheels of carts and sharpening the ploughshare, the carpenter making the wooden plough or repairing the wheels of carts and the cobbler making and mending the water bucket (*'pari'*) were all rewarded not by a wage, but by a customary payment in kind. The other service castes performed essential functions such as washing (*dhobis*), supplying mud pots (potter), beating of drums (*thottis*), carrying messages on life-cycle ceremonies such as birth, marriage and death by designated persons, performance of regular *poojas* by *pandaram* and the Brahmin and were rewarded with customary payments mostly in kind. A hierarchy of interconnected occupations preserved and maintained an accustomed way of life. Those who performed their functions pre-ordained on them by the caste hierarchy received a customary moiety which enabled them to survive, but did not give them much opportunity to improve their lot in life. Stated differently, wages were mostly paid in kind. The staple food of the land-owning class was rice. The working class depended almost entirely on coarse cereals and a meal of rice was a luxury. Upward mobility was possible mainly through cultivation or trade. Land ownership was negligible among SCs and trade was on an insignificant scale in many hamlets.

The supervisory class engaged a set of permanent farm labourers[4] who themselves worked in the farms and also oversaw the work of daily wage workers. In many places, they were 'bonded' labourers in the sense that they were given advances by the landlords and were working in the farms as a form of interest for the advances. For regular agricultural work, local labourers, both male and female, were available in sufficient numbers. This kept the relative wage level stagnant. However, in regions where new lands were brought under the plough, labour scarcity began to appear, forcing wages upwards.

Most landowners owned draught and milk cattle. Draught animals were the main source for drawing water from wells, the source of power for the plough team and also the chief means of transport of agricultural commodities. Cattle were the most prestigious form of a farmer's wealth. Big landowners were proud of their cattle and sheep pens. The men who specialised in training the draught animals for agricultural work commanded a lot of respect in the villages. The swirls in the body of the cattle were supposed to determine the fortunes of the owners, and there were experts who would predict fortunes on the basis of those swirls. Shepherds were employed to guard the cattle and sheep pens. It was

4. Termed as '*pannayal*' in Thanjavur, and there were many local variations.

common practice in our region in those days for the shepherds to live in the houses of the landlords. This was necessary because feeding and tending to cattle and sheep was a 24-hour task. Most of the shepherds were 'attached' labourers who were supplied food in the houses of the landlords and received an annual payment of two or three bags of coarse cereals in addition to a little cash. Most shepherds knew 'home remedies' for cattle diseases. The cattle and sheep provided manure for the lands of the farmers.

In the drylands, the coarse cereals or pulses such as cumbu, cholam, varagu, horse gram, groundnut, *tur dhaal* and *naripayir* were the main crops. The general practice was to sow—say *cholam* (*jowar*)—mixed with other crops. In the borders of every *paathi* (segment), the pulses were sown and interspersed along with the main crop, long-duration crops such as castor. The main crop would be a mix of short duration (*cholam*), middle duration (pulses) and long-duration crops (castor). This crop mix ensured continuous engagement for family labourers and also some insurance against risk of monsoon failure. In the wetlands, long-duration paddy crop of 140-160 days was the norm. It was common for labourers from dry villages to come to work in wet villages at the time of work-intensive periods such as sowing, harvesting or threshing.

Till the mid-1960s traditional cropping pattern continued in the old *ayacut* areas, including the newly irrigated lands also, with one major exception. Sugarcane became a preferred crop in all places where sugar mills existed or new sugar mills were started. The sugar mills supplied crossbred cane seedlings. Co-operative societies and banks provided credit for raising sugarcane. This annual commercial crop was the most profitable crop for the average farmer in those days. Of course, it needed regular watering throughout the year. Therefore, only those who had lands in the head reaches of channels, or wells as a supplementary source, raised sugarcane.

In this phase, a strong trade union movement backed by the Communist party was emerging in the agricultural belt of Thanjavur District. Partly due to its pressures and partly due to the ideological commitments of the then ruling Congress party, the state went through a phase of rapid passage of land reform legislation. It abolished all intermediary tenures such as *zamindari* by passing the 'Madras State

Estates (Abolition and Conversion into Ryotwari) Act, 1948'. The agitational approach in support of tenants got rewarded in the passage of the 'Madras Estate (Reduction of Rent) Act, 1947'. 'The Tanjore Tenant and Pannayal Protection Act, 1955', as the very name suggests, was passed to protect the rights of the tenants and permanent labourers in Thanjavur District. Tenancy was to be recorded in village records and tenants were given protection from eviction. This formed the basis of the more general 'The Madras Cultivating Tenants Protection Act and Rules, 1955'. Landlords began to evict the tenants before they could get their names recorded in the village records. Therefore, the very next year, its scope was further extended by 'The Madras Cultivating Tenants (Protection from Eviction) Act, 1956'. 'The Madras Cultivating Tenants (Fair Rent) Act, 1956, fixed the fair rent at 40 per cent of the gross produce if canal or tank irrigation was supplemented by lift irrigation and 33.33 per cent in other cases. To prevent eviction of tenants from farm houses, 'The Madras Occupants and Kudiyiruppu (Protection from Eviction) Act' of 1966 was passed, which was later modified in 1971. A 'Minimum Wages Act' was passed in 1954. Bonded labour was abolished. The 'Tamil Nadu Land Reform (Fixation of Ceilings on Land) Act, 1961' fixed a ceiling of 30 'standard' acres per family of five. (In the next phase, in 1970, the ceiling was reduced to 15 'standard' acres.) However, Tamil Nadu did not pass any legislation to consolidate fragmented holdings.

The land reform legislations had many loopholes built into them. Successive state governments were not firm in implementing them. The landlord class exploited the loopholes but had to pay a 'price' to the bureaucracy for allowing them to avoid, evade or escape the clutches of the law. Corrupt politicians and officials did not enforce the provisions of the land reform legislation. This increased the transaction costs for the landlord class of protecting their rights and enforcing their decisions. The strong trade union movement in Thanjavur District was agitating for the vigorous implementation of the ceiling, tenancy and wage legislations and this had its echo in other areas too. In our region, this took the form of an agitation for recognition of rights of 'watering man' as a tenancy right. A brief description follows.

In the lower reaches of the Amaravathi River, the common practice then was to make a customary payment in kind—usually two bags of paddy per *'Kani'*—[about one and one-third acre] to the 'watering man', whose specialised job was to divert canal water from the sluices to the farmer's wet fields. The farmers would perform all the farm operations inclusive of ploughing, preparation of fields, transplantation of paddy seedlings and manuring and fertilising. Then they would 'hand over' the fields to the 'watering men'. These 'watering men' were mainly from the SC communities, though a few higher caste men also performed this task. In the 1950s when tenancy protection legislation was enacted, the 'watering men' claimed that they were tenants and should not be evicted. The Brahmin landlords of the region were the most affected in the beginning. Being a minority, they were unable to organise any resistance to the claims of the 'watering men', which became more and more exorbitant with the passage of years. But the landlords belonging to the dominant backward communities of this region such as Vellala Gounders, Vvettuva Gounders, Mutharaiyars, etc., began to resist their claims. Using the community network, they managed to get the 'watering men' of their communities to switch loyalties to their side. Only the SC 'watering men' were forced to fight the battle against the landlords. What was originally a class conflict became, in effect, a caste conflict. This conflict began gathering momentum in the late 1950s.

The caste network allowed the supervisory landlords living in villages to forge alliances with small and marginal landholders of their own and other backward castes. The SCs formed a sizable proportion of non-landowning agricultural labourers (even though they were not a majority) and their attempts to protect their rights were painted with a caste colour. Thus, in many places in this region, the confrontation between landlords and agricultural workers was perceived as a conflict between 'superior' castes and SCs.

The caste conflict over the issue of the rights of 'watering men' intensified and reached a climax in 1962. A violent struggle took place in Pallapalayam village on the bank of the Amaravathi River opposite Chettipalayam hamlet. Men were injured on both sides, but the SCs suffered more.[5] The upper castes had better leadership, more influence

5. On similar grounds, but over a different issue, the worst atrocity took place in Keelavenmani in Thanjavur District on 25/12/1968 where the hut in which Dalits had assembled in the night was set on fire by upper caste and 44 Dalits were burnt alive.

and more resources. Court battles followed, which ended mainly in favour of the upper castes. One of the immediate results was that the minority landlords of the forward castes, mostly Brahmin landlords in the region, began to sell their lands. They were afraid that they could not continue as absentee landlords or even as supervisory landlords. Many of them had their families in urban centres. Numerous marginal and small landholders from the backward castes purchased their lands. Land transfers in large numbers from Brahmins to others took place in the 1960s and 1970s.

One striking feature in the post-independence period detected in all the villages is that most families, irrespective of the class to which they belonged, sent their children to school and to jobs outside agriculture. Children who studied well were encouraged to migrate to towns, mainly for salaried jobs. This caused and still causes an 'adverse selection' by which the least competent children were left to fend for themselves in the villages in agriculture while the relatively more efficient 'escaped' to other sectors. This tendency commenced from the first phase. This is a contributory cause for the progressive deterioration of the quality of labour and management in agriculture over a period of time.

The Second Phase: 1965-1990

This phase marked the beginning and spread of the green revolution in Tamil Nadu. Use of high-yielding variety (HYV) seeds, chemical fertilisers, pesticides, insecticides, conjunctive use of water, mechanisation, replacement of wages in kind by wages in cash and gang contract spread in this phase.

It was during this phase that the state government aggressively extended electricity connectivity. It helped the villages in many ways, freeing the village folk from the tedium of fetching water from distant places. However, it brought a dramatic change in the pattern of agricultural activities. Till electricity came to the farms, agriculture was mostly a daytime activity. Except for the tending of the cattle in the night, most agricultural operations were done only during the day. However, when electric pumps entered the rural-areas and when electricity was rationed and was made available continuously only at night, many agricultural activities were obliged to be shifted from day to the night with consequential changes which are described later.

The green revolution ushered in HYV paddy. Hybrid crops were introduced during the 'green revolution'. Hybrid *cholam*, *cumbu* and cotton were also introduced in the late 1960s. All of them had certain common features.

The durations of the new hybrid crops were shorter. Conventional paddy such as *'kichidi-samba'* matured in 160 days, whereas the hybrid varieties matured in 130 days. Spread variety of groundnut was a 150 day crop, whereas the bunch variety was a 110 day crop. The yields were higher.

The input requirements were higher; i.e. more fertilisers, more water and more pesticides and insecticides.

The labour intensity for these crops was also high. Within a short time, the agricultural operations had to be completed. The farmers began to raise two crops in succession on their wetlands. Thus, in wetlands of Chettipalayam area, instead of the pre-independence practice of cultivating a long-duration paddy followed by a dry crop such as *cholam*, they began to cultivate two paddy crops in succession.

The hybrid introduced in the 1960s became popular quickly. Agricultural operations such as preparation of land, sowing and harvesting had to be completed within a very short time and the next crop had to follow immediately. Farm mechanisation became inevitable.

To raise the new crops, more labour than was available within the village was required. They came from different dry villages surrounding the hamlets. The types of work and skills demanded from the labourers also changed. Old established skills such as *Kavalai* (water-bucket) lifting, ploughing with draught animals, making ploughs, *pari* (water-bucket), etc., were less in demand. Spraying pesticides, driving and repairing tractors, preparing the land for cultivation and making *'pars'*—that is, rows—or planting sugarcane, etc., were the new skills demanded. Because of the scarcity of labour, agricultural wages both in money terms, and after a while, in real terms began to rise slowly.

The growth of manufacturing and trade in urban centres increased urban demand for labour in this same period. Karur town, which is only 10 km away from Chettipalayam hamlet, became an exporter of textiles. The demand for labour there grew exponentially. Off- and non-farm employment also began to increase. Customary practices gave way to market determined transactions. Payment of wages in kind began to decline, and wages in cash replaced them. Contract labour gangs appeared on the agricultural scene. Old established practices began to give way to new practices. For example, the cobbler's traditional right to a share in the produce began to disappear because water was lifted with pump sets and not by *'pari'*—the leather bucket. Employment opportunities in tea shops, cycle shops, as tractor drivers, cart men to transport sand and sugarcane and for repairs of tractors, agricultural implements, tyre carts, etc., began to increase.

An interesting feature was the decline of a class of shepherds, who lived in the families of big farmers living virtually as members of the family. Sheep farming was always profitable. But with the new irrigation pattern, the drylands which used to produce *cumbu* and *cholam* were irrigated and converted into paddy or sugarcane fields. The wage level began to increase and keeping a shepherd became costly. Cooking for the shepherd in the homes became a burden for the housewife because domestic help (especially girl children) began to dwindle fast after 1970. The net result was that the shepherd class disappeared altogether from many hamlets by 1990s.

The demand for draught animals for ploughing fell as also their demand for *Kavalai*. Individual farmers raised more animals for milk. The crop residue from wetlands, especially paddy straw, sugarcane stalks and groundnut plant after harvest, were brought in bundles by landless labour households who began to raise cattle. Labourers demanded sugarcane stalks after sugarcane harvest as a right, and landowners had to concede this because of labour scarcity. After 1970s, the Integrated Rural Development Programme (IRDP) loans also helped intensify this trend of landless labourers keeping animals for milk.

Fall in the number of sheep and other cattle reduced the amount of farmyard manure available in the hamlet. At the same time, the increase in area irrigated and the introduction of hybrid crops increased the demand for fertilisers. The farmers began to use more and more chemical fertilisers from this period onwards.

As long as human muscle power and animal draught power were the only means to lift water, and earthen bunds the only means to convey water, the irrigated area was confined to the regions where water naturally flowed or was caused to flow by dams, tanks and canals, or where open wells could be dug. But in the post 1965 period, changes in technology radically altered this scenario.

Diesel and electrical pumps could lift water to much greater heights. Water could be conveyed over long distances by pipelines. Technological change enabled irrigated area to be expanded provided there was adequate water. In the past, many regions near the catchment areas of rivers and tanks could not use most of the rainwater because the elevations were steep and human and animal power could not lift it up from the stream flowing down below. With the new technology that could be done. Water, which normally flowed to the lower reaches in rivers, canals or tank systems, was partly diverted along new directions to newer lands through mechanised means. In the older irrigated areas also, for similar reasons, vast stretches of land adjacent to the originally irrigated tracks were supplied with water. As long as there was adequate rainfall to cater to the demands, there was no problem. But when monsoons failed, problems began to appear.

Throughout the 1970s and 1980s, individual farmers both in the head reaches and tail ends of water courses were expanding area cultivated with a more water-intensive crop mix by digging more wells and/or by deepening the existing wells. Conjunctive use of well water with canal or tank water became common. Free or subsidised electricity to agriculture encouraged this. The groundwater levels began to fall, in some places to an alarming extent. Farmers began to switch more and more to cultivation of commercial crops. Sugarcane was the most favoured crop in areas where the right amount of water was available. Many new sugar mills came into existence in this period. The cultivation of coarse cereals began to dwindle. In Chettipalayam region, all these changes were discernable.

Mechanisation was an inevitable by-product of this changing crop mix. Time management became critical with the introduction of second paddy crop and tractors came in in a big way. They replaced draught animals both for ploughing and transporting. There was resistance to the introduction of machines in some parts of Thanjavur District since they reduced the demand for (male) labour. But labour soon realised that a second crop could not be raised unless the critical operations were completed in a very short time. They reconciled themselves to the introduction of tractors since the employment provided by the raising of the second crop was larger than what was replaced by mechanisation. The tractors were used exclusively by big landlords in the beginning. Once the system of 'hiring by the hour' or 'charging per acre' was introduced, it became possible for small and marginal landowners also to use tractors. Motor pumps and submersible pumps or compressor-driven pumps came with deep, open wells and deep bore wells.

Mechanisation spelt the doom for some traditional skills. With this, the traditional Jajmani system of rewards for artisans also began to disappear. The landowners who paid cash for hiring machines attempted also cash payment of wages. Though it was resisted for some time and kind payments continued, ultimately cash wages had become the norm everywhere except for sowing, harvesting and threshing.

Mechanisation also destroyed the rationale behind the permanent attached labour contract such as the *pannayal* system. The new water regime dictated that fields should be irrigated in the nights. Since electricity generation was inadequate especially in summer, electric supply was made available for agricultural operations throughout the night, while daytime electricity supply was getting restricted. This meant that a permanent attached labourer had to work at night. This was not part of their traditional contract. Their supervisory functions over ploughing and baling of water in the traditional system which gave them prestige had also disappeared. Bonded labour was legally prohibited. Slowly the *pannayal* system began to wither away.

This period is marked by the beginnings of labour scarcity in many villages. This gave more bargaining power for the labouring class. Agricultural labourers used their bargaining power to reduce the hours of work and to increase the wage levels. The working day in Chettipalayam region in the late 1960s was from 8 AM to 5.30 PM with a break for lunch. In the late 1980s, the working day was shortened to 8 AM to 3 PM with a lunch break. The position of working women improved. Many of them secured jobs in urban industries just like their male counterparts. They began to commute from villages to towns. The town buses were a boon for them. They gained their 'dignity' and more and more women chose not to accept employment as 'domestic help.' However, gender disparity in the fixation of wages continued.

A new form of labour contract gained popularity in most parts of Tamil Nadu in this phase. That was the gang contract system. A group of labourers would enter into a contract with the landowner to complete a piece of agricultural work in a given period of time for a stipulated amount of cash or grain. A group would agree to harvest an acre of paddy in one day for a payment of 300 kg of paddy. The contracted amounts were generally much higher than the regular wages that would have been paid for the work in an extended period of time. The effort required here was much higher and the time available to complete it extremely limited. These tasks required teamwork and monitoring. Given these circumstances, in the 'contract' system, the benefits seemed to be greater than the disadvantages for both landowners and labourers. The labourers earned more than the regular wages; the landlord could complete the agricultural operation in time without the need for much supervision. 'Gang contracts' became the norm in our region for sowing and harvesting of paddy, sugarcane cutting and for harvesting of turmeric. 'Gang contract' system has spread to all parts of Tamil Nadu now. Even in 'gang contracts', gender disparity of wages continues.

Small and marginal landowners revived the *'Moi'* work (reciprocal work) system in this period. In periods when labour was not easily available, farmer A and his family members would work in farmer B's fields, and farmer B and his family, in turn, would work in farmer A's fields. As the working hours began to shorten, it was not uncommon for marginal farmer households to go to work for a wage and then return to work in their own fields after 3 PM.

The decline of the supervisory class of landowners started in this period. The cost of cultivation began to increase because of the introduction of new crops, new methods of cultivation and extensive application of chemical fertilisers, pesticides and insecticides. Real wages began to rise because urban demand induced the labourers to migrate towards towns. Agency problems in managing agricultural land began to multiply because the traditional pattern of management through *pannayals* started disappearing. But the most important reason was their inability to monitor the labourer's performance in the night. There were frequent failures of electricity. Supervisory landowners in Chettipalayam region were unable to know whether their servants were irrigating their fields in the night or not until the next morning. The wages for night time work were also very high.

The Third and Last Phase: 1990 and 2008

The natural growth of population and the emergence of nuclear families have led to division of large estates among family members. This has caused decline in large-size farms and some enlargement of small-size farms. A feature of this phase is that the yields of HYV crops reached a plateau.

It is in the control and regulation of water that the state has miserably failed. Both with respect to surface and groundwater, demand exceeds supply. But there is no effective rationing, regulation or pricing policy. Individual farmers have been permitted access to both sources of water depending on their ability to influence the revenue and Public Works Department (PWD) authorities. Free supply of electricity has encouraged farmers to maximise their water use unmindful of the consequences on others. And this has led to collective disaster, especially in years when monsoons have failed. This has caused alarming depletion of the groundwater table in several districts.

The immediate response of the farmers to drying up of open wells was to switch to digging deep bore wells. It started in the late 1980s and reached a peak level in the drought years 2002-2004. Competitive digging of bore wells brought collective ruin in that period. In many wells, the yields decreased. New, deeper wells were dug. Many bore wells dug in the 1980s which were giving good yields till then turned dry in this period. Within a 2 km^2 area in Chettipalayam region, more than 100 bore wells were dug. Now more than 70 bore wells are dry or have reduced yields. The water security which the rich farmers enjoyed due to conjunctive use of river and well water began to decline at an alarming rate.

Simultaneously, the state has allowed legal and illegal sand mining on a massive scale in all the river beds of Tamil Nadu taking away a key source of recharge for groundwater. It has also reduced the flow of percolation water in the rivers. Since electric supply for agricultural use is available in the nights, farmers have enlarged the size of the *vayals* or *paathis* (segments) so that they will have to do fewer water diversions from *vayal* to *vayal*. This causes enormous waste of water. In Chettipalayam region, the groundwater level has fallen significantly. The sand cover in the Amaravathi River in this locality has been mined with the help of earth moving machinery. Spring water from the sand cover in the river is not adequate to meet the drinking water needs of the surrounding villages in summer.

The common property resources are getting neglected in almost all the villages. The traditional methods of tank management, especially maintenance and allocation, continue to function with modifications in some places and have been replaced in others. In many places, tank beds are encroached which has caused reduction in the supply of water for crops.

A combination of these, and the increasing diversion of water for non-agricultural uses, has made it impossible to sustain the two crop regime introduced during the 'Green Revolution'. The expansion of textile industry in Karur has resulted in the location of many dyeing units along the two channels of the nearby Amaravathi River. These units extract water from the river and let out the effluents into the channels or the river. The water in the channels and river has been polluted. This affects agricultural yields. There is increasing conflict between the dyeing unit owners and agriculturists for the use of channel and river water. With their money power, the dyeing units are able to influence politicians and bureaucrats to side with them. The agriculturists are generally the losers in these conflicts. With the increasing uncertainty in the availability of water, the farmers in Chettipalayam region have completely given up the cultivation of sugarcane.

More generally, a large number of industries, including dyeing and tanning industries, extract canal water or groundwater claiming that it is for agricultural use and divert it to their industries. This enables them to claim free electricity. In any case, the demand for water for non-agricultural use has increased enormously. The effluents let out by industries and the agricultural chemicals flowing out of the fields in the upper reaches have adversely affected the quality of water reaching the lower riparians. While the total supply of water has remained constant or diminished, the total demand has increased. This has made the cropping pattern of the 1980s unsustainable for the farmers. Even the small and marginal farmers find it difficult to break even in the existing environment, and most supervisory landlords suffer losses.

The younger generation in the villages are going to schools in larger numbers. Parents do not want their children to return to agricultural work after they complete their schooling. Urban industries send their buses and vans to rural areas to pick up workers for service in their companies. Compared with agricultural work which is hard in a harsh natural environment, work in factories and industries is in a relatively more pleasant environment and is comparatively easy. Wages are much higher in factories than in agriculture. Therefore, a large number of rural workers go for non-agricultural work. Non-farm employment in the villages is also increasing. Workers available for agricultural work in rural areas are diminishing every year. The remaining labourers in the villages are old and infirm.

The scarcity of labour has increased the agricultural wages of all categories. In the last decade, the real wages have increased. In the 1950s and 1960s, the trade union movement in Thanjavur was responsible for wresting higher wages from the landlords. But in the last decade, this increase has occurred everywhere in Tamil Nadu simply due to scarcity of supply. Between 1980 and 2008, the money wages of male casual labour have increased from around ₹ 12 to ₹ 100 per day in Chettipalayam region. The wages of female casual labour have increased from ₹ 6 to ₹ 60 per day. At the same time, the length of the working day has fallen from 9 hours/day in 1980 to 6 hours/day. However, agricultural wages are still lower than the wages of industrial or construction workers. This induces labour to move out of agriculture in large numbers. The better connectivity of villages through mini buses encourages this trend. In Chettipalayam, the scarcity of labour for agricultural work increased dramatically after the introduction of mini buses in 1998.

The cultivated area has started shrinking since the 1990s. A land sale which was a rare event in the 1950s has now become an everyday activity. Many supervisory landlords are selling their lands and moving to urban areas. The Kerala Research Programme on Local Level Development (KRPLLD) survey of Venkidengal (which is within 10 km of Keelavenmani—the place where 44 Dalits were burnt alive) discloses that the landlords of the minority community there complain of lack of purchasers—they are willing to sell but there are no takers. Large areas of agricultural land are diverted for urban and non-agricultural uses. The farmers willingly and readily agree to sell land clearly indicating the non-viability of agriculture. In Chettipalayam region, the expectation is that the lands in the hamlet and its surroundings would soon be taken over by the Karur agglomeration. This has caused land prices to rise. But most farmers expect further rise and are waiting for better prospects.

The cost of production has increased all round for the agriculturists, whereas the returns have become more and more uncertain. The costs of inputs and wages have increased. The absentee and supervisory landlords suffer losses. The self-cultivating peasants are able to earn only their opportunity costs. Sometimes, they are unable to earn even this. The state has intervened piecemeal in several directions subsidising agricultural inputs and credit and providing price support for some crops. But 'rent-seeking' activities by politicians and bureaucrats have actually robbed agriculturists of a sizable portion of the benefits which should have accrued to them. The severe drought of 2002-2004 and the unprecedented floods that followed have forced the farmers into the 'debt trap' from which even the writing off of co-operative loans could offer not much real relief.

Living standards for most inhabitants in the villages have improved, but it is not due to agricultural prosperity. It is due to the wages earned by the villagers and their earnings from non-farm activities. There is better access and connectivity to the villages. Drinking water supply has improved. Electricity is available. Housing conditions are better. Literacy levels have increased and more women are getting educated. In the last decade at least, the rate of growth of population is slowing down. All villages have schools at least up to primary level. However, the younger generation complains about their deprivation in comparison to their urban counterparts.

More and more consumer durables, especially TV, two wheelers and gas stoves, are entering the villages, though their distribution is highly skewed. This acts as an additional inducement for the youth to leave the rural areas in search of better opportunities elsewhere.

To sum up, the average size of the farms is becoming smaller. The decline in agriculture has gained momentum in this third phase. Available supply of water is inadequate to meet the existing demand. In most places, there is scarcity of agricultural labour. Employment in agriculture has ceased to be attractive even though real wages are increasing. It is because the real wages in alternative employments are much higher and the working conditions more agreeable. The Green Revolution technology has become a spent force with yields reaching a plateau. Agency problems are multiplying for supervisory landlord class. Even self-cultivators are not getting a guaranteed positive return in agriculture.

In rural Tamil Nadu, there is a sense of defeat and a mood of pessimism. There is restlessness and frustration. People cling to agriculture only because they find no immediate substitute for it.

References

Timmer, Peter (1988). "The Agrarian Transformation", Ch. 8 in H. Chenery and T.N. Srinivasan (ed.), *Handbook of Development Economics* (Vol.1). Amsterdam: North Holland.

Neelakantan (2002). "Change and Continuity: A Contrasting Account of Urban and Rural Transformation", *Journal of Indian School of Political Economy* 14(1), Jan.–Mar.

———. (2003). "A Gossipmonger's Revisit To Chettipalayam", *Working Paper No*. 182. Chennai: MIDS. An expanded and revised Tamil version is "Oru Nagaramum, Oru Gramamum" (2008) MIDS and Kalachuvadu, Nagercoil.

Note: This paper is based on my paper entitled 'Changes in the Amaravati Basin with Special Reference to Karur' which provides a detailed account of the development of water resources in the Amaravati Basin, changing patterns of their use across its different segments, their impact on economy and society in the lower portions of the basin, emerging problems and how they have been managed. Partly due to limitations of length for contributions to this collection, it has been abridged and edited by Prof A.Vaidyanathan with his own additional inputs to highlight the problems of ensuring sustainable, efficient and equitable use of water resources in the light of the Amaravati experience. Thanks are due to him as well as Prof Natraj. This experience is typical of much of water resource planning and management in the country. MIDS Working Paper No.182, "A Gossipmonger's Revisit to Chettipalayam" (2003) by the author provides a more detailed elucidation of the Amaravati experience.

5 Groundwater Irrigation in Tamil Nadu 1970-1990

Characteristics and Impact

P. Anbazhagan

In Tamil Nadu, as in the rest of the country, cultivated area reporting irrigation from groundwater grew rapidly in absolute terms from 0.8 million ha in the early 1970s to 1.1 million ha in the late 1980s. Over the same period, its importance has increased both in terms of the proportion of cultivated area served by this source (from 13% to 20%); and of total irrigated area (from around 31% to 46%) (see Table 5.1). It is noteworthy that increase in total irrigated area in this period came entirely from groundwater sources; area reported to be under surface sources actually declined. This paper describes the main features of groundwater irrigation, its regional distribution and impact on land use, cropping patterns and productivity of land in these two periods.

Table 5.1

Irrigation by Source in Tamil Nadu, Three-Year Moving Averages

(Area in '000 hectares)

Item	*1971-72 to 1973-74*		*1981-82 to 1983-84*		*1988-89 to 1990-91*	
	ha	*%*	*ha*	*%*	*ha*	*%*
Groundwater	831	30.7	1023	40.8	1100	45.5
Canals	918	33.9	849	33.8	790	32.7
Tanks	923	34.1	615	24.5	511	21.2
Other sources	34	1.3	23	0.9	14	0.6
NIA	2706	100	2510	100	2415	100
NSA	6283	43.1*	5453	46.0*	5570	44.0*

Note: *NIA: net irrigated area; NSA: net sown area;* *: % of NSA.

Source: Compiled from *Season and Crop Reports for Tamil Nadu*, various issues.

Wells are of two types: open or dug wells of relatively shallow depth and tubewells that draw water from deeper aquifers. In 1970-71, dug wells accounted for most (close to 99%) of all wells both in terms of numbers and area irrigated. By 1990-91, dug wells continued to be predominant (95%) in numbers but their share in area under groundwater irrigation fell to 85 per cent because of a six-fold increase in the number of tubewells and 14-fold rise in area irrigated by them.

Table 5.2

Growth Profile of Well Irrigation in Tamil Nadu, 1951-1990

(Nos in '000s and Area '000 ha)

Item		*1971-72*	*1981-82*	*1990-91*
No. of Dug Wells	000 nos	1303	1567	1667
No. of Tubewells	000 nos	16	57	98
Total No. of Wells	000 nos	1319	1624	1765
Area Irrigated by Dug Wells	000 ha	947	1011	890
Area Irrigated by Tubewells	000 ha	14	125	169
Total Area Irrigated by All Wells		961	1136	1059
Avg area/ow	ha	1.01	.65	.53
Avg area/tw	ha	.88	2.25	1.72

Note: ow: open well; tw: tubewell.

Source: Govt. of Tamil Nadu, *Season and Crop Reports*, various years.

The spread of groundwater irrigation has come about by an increase in the number of dug wells and in the use of energised pump sets for lifting water whose number has risen from a mere 0.6 million in 1971 to over 1.2 million in 1990-91 (Table 5.3). The expansion in the number of wells and energisation have come about as a result of government policy. Government has for long followed a policy of actively encouraging development of well irrigation. Public institutional finance for minor irrigation (most of which went to support groundwater development) accounted for more than half of the total state plan outlay on irrigation during the past four decades.

In 1971, only 45 per cent of all wells were energised with over 90 per cent of them being run with electricity. By 1990-91 nearly 70 per cent of all wells were energised but the proportion using electrical pumps fell to 77 per cent. There has been a rapid rise in the use of diesel-operated pumps over this period. Another noteworthy feature is that most tubewells use energised pumps, but more than half the dug wells were not energised in 1970 and about 30 per cent were not even by 1990-91.

Table 5.3

Energisation of Groundwater Irrigation, 1971-1992

(Nos in '000)

Item	*1971-72*	*1981-82*	*1991-92*
Electric pumps	530	720	962
Diesel pumps	52	150	285
Elec pumps/diesel pumps	10.0	4.8	3.4
% dug wells energised	44.7	51.7	69.1

Source: *Tamil Nadu: An Economic Appraisal,* various issues.

Groundwater is mostly used as a sole source of irrigation. Practically the entire increase in the number of wells and in net area irrigated by groundwater has been on account of wells and tubewells used as a sole source. But wells are also used to supplement surface water in canal and tank commands. In 1971, supplementary wells comprised more than a third of sole wells in terms of numbers but less than a fifth the area under sole wells. Their reported number is the same in 1991 but the area irrigated by them has halved in absolute terms and decreased to less than 10 per cent of that under sole wells (Table 5.4).

Table 5.4

Growth of Sole and Supplementing Wells and Area Irrigated by them

Item		*1971-72*	*1981-82*	*1990-91*
No. of Sole Wells	000 nos	964	1311	1407
No. of Supplementing wells	000 nos	355	371	358
Area Irrigated by Sole Wells	000 ha	820	1044	1059
Area Irrigated by Supplementing Wells	000 ha	141	92	75
Area/sole wells	ha	.85	.80	.75
Area/supp wells	ha	.40	.25	.21

Source: Same as Table 5.3.

A striking feature is that even as the number of wells and energised pump sets has grown rapidly, area irrigated per well has declined. This points to declining yields per well—a tendency evident both in respect of dug wells and tubewells. This is probably because of progressive deepening of wells which increases the energy required to pump water and may also be indicative of over-exploitation of groundwater.

Several factors have contributed to these trends. The growing importance of groundwater is in part a reflection of the relatively slow growth in surface irrigation. During the first two plan periods, a number of new major and medium projects were constructed adding an estimated 250,000 ha to the potential. Since then, the surface water resource available to the state has been more or less fully harnessed, leaving little scope for further expansion. There has been little addition by major and medium irrigation potential since the mid-1960. However, the subsequent decline —the reported figure for the later 1980s being about 10 per cent below that for 1971-1973—is more difficult to explain.

A similar trend—a rise in irrigated area during the first two decades followed by a decline in the subsequent two decades—is also noticed in the case of tanks and small local storages which have played an important role in Tamil Nadu. They accounted for nearly 35 per cent of all irrigation in the early 1950s. Unlike the major and medium projects for canal irrigation, hardly any new tanks were constructed after the 1950s. Nor was the scale of renovation of old tanks large enough to make a significant difference. Investment in minor surface irrigation has been meagre. Continued neglect of tanks with very poor maintenance, which has been the case for a long time, even before independence, is widely believed to have eroded their capacity to provide irrigation.

It is however difficult to explain the trends revealed by the official data. Area irrigated by tanks is known to be much more volatile than other sources and there is some indication that these fluctuations are due to variations in local rainfall. The sharp rise in tank-irrigated area during the 1950s could be due to the relatively low rainfall in the early 1950 and the better rainfall in the subsequent part of the decade. There is in fact a significant positive correlation between rainfall during the north-east monsoon and the area irrigated by tanks over the four decades ending in 1990. The relatively low level of tank-irrigated area in the early 1950s and the decline in the 1980s seem to be due, in part, to the less than average rainfall in these periods. But the steep and progressive decline in the 1970s and 1980s is puzzling. Most of the area under tank irrigation is accounted for by Public Works Department (PWD) tanks and the available studies—though limited—do not indicate any significant reduction in effective command compared to registered *ayacut* (Vaidyanathan and Janakarajan, 1989; Vaidyanathan, 1996).

Regional Variations in Groundwater Irrigation

The role of groundwater as a sole source of irrigation is far from uniform across different parts of the state. According to official statistics, during the late 1980s the proportion of net sown area using groundwater as the sole source of irrigation (groundwater irrigation rate) ranged from a mere 4.5 per cent in Thanjavur to around 37 per cent in Chengalpattu. This proportion is higher than the state average in Chengalpattu, North Arcot and South Arcot Districts, and well below the state average in the districts of Salem, Ramanathapuram, Tirunelveli and Thanjavur. The proportion of area irrigated by groundwater to net irrigated area by all sources, which measures the importance of groundwater relative to other irrigational sources, also varies from a mere 5 per cent in Thanjavur to 94 per cent in North Arcot (see Tables 5.5 and 5.6). Groundwater is the dominant source of irrigation (accounting for 60% or more of net irrigated area) in South Arcot, North Arcot and Salem. It is the major source in Coimbatore, Chengalpattu and Madurai and considerably less important than surface sources in other districts. Across districts, higher overall irrigation ratio does not go with higher dependence on groundwater as a source of irrigation. But districts where surface sources account for a higher proportion of irrigated land tend to depend less on groundwater as a source of irrigation.

Salem includes Dharmapuri, Coimbatore includes Periyar, Trichy includes Pudukottai, Madurai includes Dindugul, Ramanathapuram includes Kamarajar and Pasum Pon Muthu Ramalingar and Tirunelveli includes V.O. Chidambaranar.

Table 5.5

Groundwater Irrigation as a Sole Source, Relative to NSA and NIA, 1988-1990: District-wise

(Area in '000 ha)

District	*NSA*	*NIA*	*NIAGW*	*NIA/ NSA %*	*NIAGW/ NSA %*	*NIAGW/ NIA %*
1	*2*	*3*	*4*	*5*	*6*	*7*
Chengalpattu	297	209	111	70.3	37.3	53.1
South Arcot	542	274	174	50.5	32.1	63.6
North Arcot	433	162	152	37.4	35.1	93.8
Salem	875	216	172	24.7	19.6	79.6
Coimbatore	635	261	138	41.1	21.7	52.8
Trichy	636	233	90	36.2	14.1	38.6
Thanjavur	528	453	24	85.8	4.5	5.3
Madurai	549	231	128	42.1	23.3	55.4
Ramanathapuram	490	201	54	41.0	11.0	26.9
Tirunelveli	402	144	55	35.8	13.6	38.2
State	5387	2384	1098	44.3	20.4	46.1

Note: NIAGW refers to net irrigated area from groundwater.

Source: GoTN, *Season and Crop Reports*, Various Issues.

Table 5.6

Numbers of Wells per ha. of NSA

District	*NSA ('000 ha)*	*No. of Sole Wells ('000s)*	*No. of Wells/NSA (ha)*	*NIAGW ('000 ha)*
Chengalpattu	297	74	0.249	111
South Arcot	542	161	0.297	174
North Arcot	433	231	0.533	152
Salem	875	329	0.376	172
Coimbatore	635	154	0.242	138
Trichy	636	203	0.319	90
Thanjavur	528	Neg	Ng	24
Madurai	549	131	0.23.	128
Ramanathapuram	490	65	0.133	54
Tirunelveli	402	106	0.263	55
State	5387	1454	0.269	1098

Source: Same as Table 5.5.

The reported extent of supplementary use of groundwater also differs widely: in terms of numbers—wells and tubewells used as a supplementary source comprise about one-fourth of total number of wells and tubewells used as sole source. Thanjavur has no wells in this category; among the rest, the ratio of supplementary to sole wells is least in Coimbatore (about 9%); in a majority of the other districts, this ratio is between 15 and 20 per cent. The incidence of supplementary wells relative to sole wells is highest (over 30%) in Chengalpattu, Ramanathapuram and North Arcot. On the average, the area reported to be irrigated by supplementary wells is only 7 per cent of the area under sole wells. This proportion is lower than the state average in all districts except Chengalpattu, North Arcot and Salem.

However, the recording of supplemental well irrigation is particularly difficult: what does 'area irrigated' mean when the quantum and number of times well water is used can vary greatly? There is also reason to believe that *Karnams* (or village officers) may be somewhat casual about verifying the extent of supplemental irrigation. Even the classification of wells as 'sole' and 'supplementary' is open to some doubt: for instance, in North Arcot, the area under surface irrigation is now reported to be nearly zero, and yet there are a large number of supplementary wells each irrigating a miniscule area. More importantly, recent field studies do not present much evidence of any significant permanent decline in surface irrigation (especially tanks) on the scale suggested by the official data. Micro-level surveys of some 80 tanks in Periyar Vaigai Basin suggest that the number of wells may be properly recorded but the area benefited seems generally underestimated.

Differences between districts in the extent of groundwater development and its use are due to several factors including rainfall and terrain, potential availability of groundwater, the extent of its utilisation and the characteristics of wells (the relative importance of dug wells and tubewells, the density of wells per unit area, aquifer characteristics, depth of water table and nature of lifting devices used).

Table 5.7

Indicators of Utilisation of Groundwater in Tamil Nadu, 1992-93

District	*Utilisable Ground Water Potential (MCM)*	*Per ha NSA '000 cm*	*Utilised Potential (MCM)*	*% of Potential Utilised*	*NIAgw '000 ha*	*No of Wells/ Ha NSA*	*% Energised*	*Utilised Volume/ Ha NIAGW*	*Average NIA/Well ha*	*Utilised Volume per well ('000 cm)*
Chengalpattu	1829	6.2	1117	61.0	111	0.249	52	8.8	1.6	14.0
South Arcot	3585	6.8	2608	72.7	174	0.297	95	14.5	1.3	6.1
North Arcot	2981	6.9	1862	62.5	152	0.533	64	11.6	.8	5.8
Salem	2458	2.8	1884	76.6	172	0.376	58	10.5	.6	8.1
Coimbatore	1848	2.9	1599	86.5	138	0.242	77	11.1	.7	5.7
Trichy	2898	4.6	1220	42.1	90	0.319	57	12.8	.5	7.8
Thanjavur	1315	2.5	532	40.4	24	0.1	27	13.2	.01	7.4
Madurai	1911	3.5	1077	56.3	128	0.230	66	8.1	1.0	5.7
Ramanathapuram	1518	3.3	422	27.8	54	0.133	44	6.7	.9	5.9
Tirunelveli	1247	3.1	669	53.6	55	0.263	44	11.0	.7	7.5
State	20790	–	12990	60.1	1098	–	–	5.6	–	–

Source: GoTN, *Report of the Ground Water Estimation Group, 1997.*

Season and Crop Reports, Various Issues

The State Groundwater Board estimates the annual groundwater recharge in different districts of the state on the basis of recommendations by an Expert Committee of the Central Ground Water Board. The annual volume of recharge (in 1992-93) is placed at 26400 mcm. Deducting the requirement for drinking, domestic and other non-agricultural uses, the quantum potentially available for irrigation is placed at 20790 mcm. Relative to cultivated area, potential is lowest at 2500 cm per ha in Thanjavur and 6900 cm per ha in North Arcot.

Relative to cultivated area, the potential is highest in Chengalpattu, South Arcot and North Arcot, all of which are made up by unconsolidated or semi-consolidated formations and have relatively high rainfall. These formations are also widespread in Ramanathapuram but recharge is limited by low rainfall. In Salem, Coimbatore, Madurai and Tirunelveli—where rainfall is relatively low and consolidated formations are predominant—the potential is low. Overall, utilisable water per hectare of net sown area seems positively related to rainfall and the proportion of area under surface irrigation.

Estimated actual utilisation in 1992-93 is placed at 61 per cent of the potential. It is highest in Coimbatore, followed by Salem and then South Arcot, North Arcot and Chengalpattu. Utilisation is lowest in Ramanathapuram, despite being a relatively dry area and the productivity impact of irrigation being much higher than elsewhere. Low rate of utilisation in Thanjavur may be because of relative abundance of surface water. These data need to be used with caution because the volume of groundwater actually used is an estimate and not based on any measurement of actual extraction.

We need to distinguish between dug wells and tube wells. Tube wells tap deeper aquifers and invariably use electric or diesel pumps, have larger pumping capacity and irrigate larger areas. These are relatively small in number overall but are important in South Arcot and one would therefore expect that the larger the proportion of tube wells to dug wells, the larger will be the area irrigated by a given total number of wells. Dug wells, on the other hand, cover a wide range in terms of water yields and area irrigated depending on the aquifer characteristics, depth and lifting devices used.

A majority of dug wells now use energised pumps. However, a sizeable proportion continues to use traditional, manually operated or animal-driven lifting devices. The proportion of dug wells with energised pumps varies from around 27 per cent in Thanjavur to 95 per cent in South Arcot.

The density of sole wells (including tube wells) in the state averaged around 27 per 100 ha net sown area in the late 1980s. Thanjavur has very few wells. Among others, the density varies from 0.133 wells/ha of NSA (Tirunelveli) to 0.533 per ha (South Arcot). The average area irrigated per well again excluding Thanjavur varies from 0.5 ha (Tiruchy) to 1.6 ha in Chengalpattu. The proportion of energised wells ranges from 44 per cent (Ramanathapuram and Tirunelveli) to 95 per cent in South Arcot.

Broadly speaking, districts with larger groundwater potential relative to cultivated area also tend to have a higher rate of exploitation of potential, greater well density, a higher degree of energisation and larger area irrigated per well. These characteristics do not seem to be a significant factor in explaining variations in the estimated volume of water extracted per well (ranging between 6700 cm and 14500 cm) and volume used per ha of irrigated area (5700 cm to 14000 cm). These variations probably reflect differences in aquifer characteristics, the relative importance of dug wells and deeper bore wells and tube wells and crop patterns, and they need closer study.

The spatial variations are brought out more sharply when we examine these patterns at the *taluka* level. Data relating to land use, irrigated area by source and cropped area compiled from village level records are available from the World Agricultural Census conducted periodically since 1970-71 and from the files of the Directorate of Statistics. The state has been divided into the following seven distinct agro-climatic zones based on rainfall and its distribution, soil characteristics, geological features, irrigation and crop patterns and social characteristics:[1] (1) North Eastern, (2) North Western, (3) Western, (4) Delta, (5) Southern, (6) High Rainfall and (7) Hill. Our subsequent discussion relates to the first five zones. The high rainfall zone and hill zone are not of much interest for the present paper as groundwater irrigation is relatively unimportant in these areas.

1. GoTN, Agricultural University, 1985.

The number of *talukas* in the state has increased over time from 125 in 1970-71 to 169 due to division and sub-division of *talukas*. In order to facilitate comparison over time, the data for 1986-1988 relating to 169 *talukas* has been reworked to get estimates for the original 125 *talukas*. This is possible because the details of the boundary changes of *talukas* are known.

Table 5.8

Distribution of Talukas according to the Agro-Climatic Zone, Tamil Nadu

Sl. No.	*District*	*Zone*	*No. of Talukas from Districts*
1	Chengalpattu	North Eastern	12
2	South Arcot		7
3	North Arcot		13
4	Trichy		3
5	Salem	North Western	7
6	Dharmapuri		8
7	Madurai		2
8	Coimbatore	Western	9
9	Madurai		6
10	Salem		1
11	Trichy		1
12	Thanjavur	Delta	12
13	Trichy		7
14	South Arcot		1
15	Ramanathapuram	Southern	17
16	Tirunelveli		13
17	Madurai		3
18	Trichy		3

Source: GoTN, Tamil Nadu Agricultural University, 1985.

The distribution of districts and *talukas* among the five major zones is indicated in Table 5.8. All or most *talukas* in a majority of districts fall into one of these zones. A few districts fall over more than one zone. The North-Eastern zone comprises all the *talukas* of Chengalpattu and North Arcot Districts, all but 1 of the *talukas* of South Arcot and 3 out of 12 of Tiruchy *talukas*. The North-Western zone comprises all but one of the *talukas* of Salem and Dharmapuri Districts and 2 *talukas* of Madurai District. In the entire Coimbatore District, a majority of the *talukas* in Madurai District together with a *taluka* each from Tiruchy and Salem districts form the Western zone. The Delta zone consists of the entire Thanjavur District, a good part of Tiruchy District and one *taluka* of South Arcot District. The districts of Tirunelveli and Ramanathapuram fall wholly in the Southern zone which includes in addition a few *talukas* of Madurai and Trichy districts.

During 1986-1988, the mean overall irrigation ratio (NIA/NSA) was highest in *talukas* of the delta followed by the North-Eastern zone; the lowest was in the Western zone and the second lowest in the Southern zone. About one-sixth of the *talukas* had an overall irrigation ratio of less than 25 per cent, while nearly half had more than 50 per cent. The proportion of *talukas* with high irrigation ratio (more than 50%) was the highest in the Delta and North Eastern zones and the lowest in the North-Western zone (see Table 5.9).

Table 5.9

Frequency Distribution of Irrigation Ratio by Agro-Climatic Zone, 1986-1988

Sl. No.	*Zone*	*Below 25%*	*25-50%*	*50-75%*	*More than 75%*
1	North Eastern	2	11	13	9
2	North Western	7	7	2	1
3	Western	3	10	4	0
4	Delta	0	5	4	11
5	Southern	8	11	11	6
6	All	20	44	34	27

Source: See Annexure 3, GoTN, Tamil Nadu Agricultural University, 1985.

Twenty-three *talukas* have a relatively high percentage of their cultivated lands irrigated by groundwater. Another 26 *talukas* have between 25 and 30 per cent of their lands under groundwater irrigation. These *talukas* are concentrated in the (1) North-East zone whose rainfall, geology, and topography are highly favourable for groundwater extraction; (2) *talukas* along the foot of the Western Ghats and the Palni Hills where underground seepage in the upper reaches drains into aquifers and provides copious groundwater supplies; (3) *talukas* along the Cauvery between

Mettur and Grand Anicut and where there is very little canal irrigation; and (4) the upper reaches of the Vaigai and Tamraparani basins, some of which benefit from their location at the foot of the hills and where the terrain is not suitable for large-scale surface irrigation.

At the other extreme, 32 *talukas* have little or no groundwater irrigation, the proportion of NSA irrigated by this source being less than 5 per cent. A few of them (like Kodaikanal and Yercaud) are hilly regions; several are in the dry upland areas of Madurai and Ramanathapuram. A strikingly large concentration is to be found in the Cauvery Delta. Though groundwater supply is abundant, practically the entire area is irrigated by canals and the supply has been relatively assured (till recently). It is likely that under these conditions, the returns to supplemental well irrigation relative to the costs are not high enough to induce farmers to invest in conjunctive use. The quality of groundwater in the lower reach of the Delta may also be a problem. A similar situation seems to exist in the Tamraparani basin, where geology may be an additional constraint.

Table 5.10

Distribution of Talukas across Agro-Climatic Zone by the Level of Importance of Groundwater to NSA, 1986-1988

Sl. No.	*Zone*	*Less than 5%*	*5-25%*	*25-50%*	*50-75%*	*More than 75%*	*All*
1	North Eastern	0	4	22	6	3	35
2	North Western	0	7	10	0	0	17
3	Western	1	8	8	0	0	17
4	Delta	10	9	1	0	0	20
5	Southern	10	18	8	0	0	36
6	All	21	46	49	6	3	125

Source: Same as Table 5.9.

The low level of development of groundwater irrigation in *talukas* of Ramanathapuram District despite the apparently high potential is also noteworthy. One would expect the productivity impact of irrigation to be particularly high in this region. Some recent studies suggest that the productivity difference between irrigated and rainfed land in this district is less than the state average. But this may simply reflect the fact that much of irrigation here is from tanks whose water supply is low and precarious. Water quality may also be a limitation. Recent studies in the area report brackishness in several locations (Janakarajan and Vaidyanathan, 1997). The possibility that potential availability and its reliability may be overestimated cannot be ruled out either.

Most *talukas* are served by both surface and groundwater, but in varying degrees. In 31 *talukas* surface sources of irrigation accounted for over 75 per cent of NIA; groundwater was the predominant source in 37 *talukas*. In another 33 *talukas* groundwater was more important than surface sources but the latter was sizeable (see Table 5.11). Groundwater-dominated irrigation is characteristic of the North Western zone and to a lesser degree Western zone. The Delta zone predominantly depends on surface water, as does the Southern zone.

Table 5.11

Frequency Distribution of Talukas with Dominant Source of Irrigation by Agro-Climatic Zone, 1986-1988

Sl. No.	*Zone*	*Surface*				*Surface with Groundwater**		*Groundwater with Surface***		
		Canal alone	*Tank alone*	*Canal and tank*	*Tank and canal*	*Canal and wells*	*Tank and wells*	*Well and canal*	*Wells and tanks*	*Wells alone*
1	N.E	0	1	0	0	2	1	6	6	19
2	N.W	0	0	0	0	1	1	2	2	9
3	West	0	0	0	0	4	0	7	4	4
4	Delta	13	1	1	0	3	0	1	0	1
5	South	1	9	1	4	1	11	0	5	4
6	All	14	11	2	4	11	13	16	17	37

Note: N.E = North Eastern zone, N.W = North Western Zone; West=Western zone, Delta=Delta zone, South = Southern zone.

* In this combination, surface water is the dominant source supplemented with groundwater.

** In this combination, groundwater is the dominant source supplemented by surface water.

Source: Same as Table 5.10.

Table 5.12

Frequency Distribution of Talukas by Dominant Source of Irrigation by Agro-Climatic Zone

Year	*Zone*	*Canal alone*	*Tank alone*	*Well alone*	*Canal+ tank*	*Canal+ well*	*Tank+ canal*	*Tank+ well*	*Well+ canal*	*Well+ tank*	*Total*
1970-71	N. East	0	3	1	1	0	0	17	1	12	35
	West	0	0	4	0	5	0	0	7	1	17
	N. West	0	0	7	0	0	1	3	3	3	17
	Delta	15	1	1	0	1	1	0	1	0	20
	South	0	12	4	1	0	4	9	0	6	36
	Total	15	16	17	2	6	6	29	22	12	125
1985-86	N. East	0	1	8	0	1	0	11	2	12	35
	West	0	0	7	0	1	0	0	8	1	17
	N. West	0	0	9	0	1	0	1	3	3	17
	Delta	14	1	1	1	1	1	0	1	0	20
	South	0	11	7	0	1	4	13	0	0	36
	Total	14	13	32	1	5	5	25	14	16	125

Source: Same as Table 5.11.

Impact of Different Sources of Irrigation

Irrigation raises productivity per unit of land by increasing cropping intensity, changing crop patterns and raising crop yields. The nature and magnitude of these changes depend on the additional volume of water provided by irrigation, its reliability and seasonal distribution. These differ between different sources of irrigation. Our concern here is to explore the differences in these respects under groundwater irrigation compared to other sources. Our analysis is limited by the fact that available information needed for this purpose is scanty.

A special National Sample Survey of irrigation conducted in 1976-77 gives some estimates, at the state level of crop patterns under three major sources of irrigation. The estimates relating to Tamil Nadu (presented in Table 5.13) highlight these differences. Paddy, which is hardly raised under rainfed conditions in this state, is the dominant crop under all types of irrigation accounting for 96 per cent of area irrigated by tanks, 93 per cent under canals and 56 per cent under wells. The other striking feature is that well-irrigated lands grow a wider range of crops (including other cereals, pulses, oil seeds, cotton and sugarcane) than those under surface irrigation. Altogether, areas irrigated by groundwater are cultivated more intensively and have a far more diversified crop pattern than those under surface irrigation. In both respects, tanks and wells present the sharpest contrast.

Table 5.13

Source-Wise Cropping Pattern in Tamil Nadu

	Area in 00 ha				*Percentage*			
Crops	*Canal*	*Tank*	*Wells*	*Total*	*Canal*	*Tank*	*Wells*	*Total*
Paddy	6538	4361	7778	18677	92.6	96.1	55.5	72.9
Jowar	56	5	938	999	0.8	0.1	6.7	3.9
All cereals	6683	4446	10217	21346	94.7	97.9	72.9	83.4
All pulses	7	8	87	102	0.1	0.2	0.6	0.4
All oil seeds	219	21	1373	1613	3.1	0.5	9.8	6.3
Sugarcane	52	7	509	568	0.7	0.2	3.6	2.2
Cotton	54	6	453	513	0.8	0.1	3.2	2.0
Condiments	38	22	907	967	0.5	0.5	6.5	.8
All other crops	6	30	463	499	0.1	0.7	3.3	1.9
All crops	7059	4540	14009	25608	100	100	100	100

Source: *Sarvekshana*.

Data on crop patterns in different types of irrigated land are very scarce. However the quinquennial Agricultural Census provides a more detailed categorisation of area and crop pattern under different dominant irrigation sources at the *taluka* level. It distinguishes three broad categories of irrigation sources: (1) those where groundwater accounts for over 75 per cent of NIA; (2) those where groundwater along with canal or tanks constitutes the dominant source; and (3) those where surface water sources are dominant. Under each of them, it provides estimates of crop patterns in area irrigated using different combinations of canal, tank and groundwater irrigation. Table 5.14 presents the state level picture of this aspect for two points of time: 1970-71 and 1985-86.

Paddy is the dominant crop accounting for the predominant share among crops in *talukas* where canals, tanks or a combination of the two are the main source of irrigation. Paddy is also the major crop in *talukas* that depend on both surface and groundwater but its importance is considerably less compared to the first category. Paddy is a minor crop in predominantly groundwater-dependent *talukas*. These have the most diversified crop patterns with a higher proportion of area devoted to high value crops like sugarcane, vegetables and orchards and coconut compared to the other two categories especially those solely dependent on surface water.[2]

Table 5.14

Cropping Pattern by Dominant Sources of Irrigation

	Dominant	*Year*	*Paddy*	*Other Cereals and Pulses*	*Vegetables etc.*	*Oil Seeds*	*Cotton*	*Sugar-cane*	*Coconut and Orchards*	*Others*
	Well dominant	1970-71	33.3	25.8	8.6	4.7	10.9	5.8	3.2	7.5
		1985-86	41.7	9.5	4.8	8.7	5.8	7.5	2.9	16.6
All	Well and Surface dominant	1970-71	63.5	13.2	4.1	8.8	2.9	3.9	1.9	1.4
		1985-86	60.3	10.2	1.4	8.5	2.6	3.7	2.7	10.3
	Surface dominant	1970-71	91.6	2.4	1.3	1.9	0.09	0.99	1.04	0.41
		1985-86	76.3	5.5	2.9	2.8	1.4	2.4	1.1	7.3

Source: Same as Table 5.12.

There have been significant changes in all these respects between 1970-71 and 1985-86 which is evident from the above table. While the differences between the three broad source categories in 1970-71 and 1985-86 are more or less similar, the pattern of change within each of these categories shows significant differences. Predominantly surface irrigated *talukas* show a steep reduction in the share of area under paddy to total, accompanied by an increase in practically all other categories (including coarse grains and pulses). By contrast, in areas solely dependent on groundwater, the share of paddy and oil seeds, and 'other crops' in

2. More detailed tabulations (not shown here) suggest that there are significant differences within each of these categories depending on which of the three sources—canal, tanks and wells—is more dominant. Thus in the areas depending on surface water, the importance of paddy is higher in *talukas* where canals are the dominant source compared to those where the dominant source is tanks. Since canal provides more assured supply for a longer duration than tanks, one would expect cropping intensity to be higher and crop pattern to be more diversified. In the case of tanks, there is a considerable difference between system and non-system tanks—the former being better placed in terms of reliability and, in some cases, duration of supplies than non-system tanks depending wholly on local rainfall. Areas where both surface and groundwater are used and where surface sources are dominant tend to have more paddy and less diversified patterns compared to *talukas* where groundwater is the more important source.

irrigated area show a sizeable increase accompanied by reduction in the share of area allocated to other non-paddy crops. In *talukas* using both surface and groundwater, the importance of paddy has come down marginally accompanied by some changes in the distribution of area under different non-paddy crops. Overall, irrigated crop patterns in 1985-86 are considerably more diversified than in 1970-71. The main shift away from paddy to relatively low-water-consuming seasonal crops could be interpreted as an attempt to economise on water. There is also a shift towards commercial crops meant for the market. One would need to know more about the composition of 'other' crops, and also the extent to which the conditions of rainfall in the two years may have affected the pattern before the significance of these changes and the extent to which they reflect long-term trends can be inferred.

That crop patterns under comparable irrigation sources as well as the patterns under different sources vary greatly across agro-climatic regions which is evident from Table 5.15. In all regions, paddy was the largest single crop in *talukas* where the bulk of irrigation is from surface sources, but its share in total irrigated crop area in 1970-71 varied from 91 per cent in the Delta to 79 per cent in the North East. Very little area is devoted to long duration crops or vegetables, condiments and spices under surface irrigation in these regions. The regional differences in the predominantly groundwater-dependent *talukas* are much more striking: paddy accounts for the major part of gross irrigated area (GIA) in this category of *talukas* in the North East, North West and Delta Regions, but for a much smaller fraction in the southern and western zones (18 and 11%, respectively). Being relatively low rainfall areas, cultivation of paddy, a very water-intensive crop, in these tracts with limited groundwater supplies is risky. Evidently, soil and climate in these tracts offer a wide range of other, more profitable, irrigated crops. On the other hand, sugarcane, coconut and orchards, which accounted for nearly 23 per cent of GIA in the groundwater dominant areas of North East and 10-11 per cent in the West in 1970-71, are relatively unimportant in the Delta and in the South. The Southern zone uses its groundwater to grow seasonal vegetables and related crops. In 1970-71, vegetables were grown in 29 per cent of total area compared to 5 per cent in the West and 1.4 per cent in the North-East. The well/tank combination *talukas* falls generally in between the groundwater-dominant

Table 5.15

Crop Patterns under Comparable Irrigation Sources

	Dominant Source	*Year*	*Paddy*	*Other Cereals and Pulses*	*Vegetables etc.*	*Oil Seeds*	*Cotton*	*Sugar-cane*	*Coconut and Orchards*	*Others*
North-East	Well alone	1970-71	66.8	6.9	1.4	1.2	0.8	16.2	6.7	0.8
		1985-86	60.7	8.4	1.1	9.2	0.04	9.1	0.11	11
	Well and surface	1970-71	73.2	7.6	1.7	13.2	0.1	3.7	0.4	0.1
		1985-86	71.3	6.9	0.5	9.7	1.1	4	0.51	5.7
	Surface	1970-71	78.7	10.7	1.5	6.5	0	1.4	0.1	1.1
		1985-86	62.4	29	0.13	3.9	0.01	2.3	0	1.9
North-West	Well alone	1970-71	57.4	14.9	3.6	3.8	1.8	4.8	2.3	12.1
		1985-86	22.9	13.8	1.2	1.3	13.7	12.3	2.5	32.3
	Well and surface	1970-71	58.6	15.9	4.5	4.9	3.3	5.5	3.1	4.3
		1985-86	51.7	11.9	3.1	4.7	3.11	2.6	4.3	19.3
West*	Well alone	1970-71	11.2	34.3	5.3	3.6	28.2	7.2	3.3	7
		1985-86	24.6	6.5	7.1	9.1	8.2	11.9	17.9	14.2
	Well and surface	1970-71	32	30.3	8.3	4.3	10.2	7.4	4.4	3.1
		1985-86	27.3	21.2	2.1	10.3	7.3	4.7	11	15.6
Delta*	Well alone	1970-71	257.4	13.9	7.4	16.8	0.1	0.8	2.3	1.3
		1985-86	47.7	1.8	3.7	12.8	0	1.4	0.5	7.7
	Well and surface	1970-71	58.2	16.3	4.9	5.8	1.2	5.4	6	2.2
		1985-86	41.1	7.2	4.8	8.4	0.16	3.9	2.5	31.6
	Surface	1970-71	90.9	1.2	0.7	1.7	0.1	0.8	1.1	0.4
		1985-86	88.1	1.4	0.3	2.7	0.3	2.6	0.05	4.4
Southern	Well alone	1970-71	18.4	41.1	29.2	2.9	4.5	0.2	1.6	2.1
		1985-86	50.6	19.2	2.9	3.1	2.9	2.8	3.3	7.6
	Well and surface	1970-71	51.2	15.2	9	13.5	5.2	0.8	4	7.8
		1985-86	61.2	10.1	3.9	3.9	3.3	1.8	1.4	14.7
	Surface	1970-71	87.8	5	2.5	0.4	0.3	1.1	1.2	0.2
		1985-86	66.5	8.6	5.3	2.5	2.9	2.9	0.6	10.5

Note: * North-West and Western zone, there are no surface source dominant *talukas*.

Source: Same as Table 5.14.

areas in all regions. In most regions, the cropping intensity is highest in the groundwater *talukas* and the least in the surface-water-dependent *talukas*.

The patterns have changed since 1970-71 but in varying degrees across different categories. Among *talukas* with predominantly groundwater-based irrigation, the share of paddy has declined steeply in the North-East but less so in the Delta and in the North-West. Paddy has become a much more important crop in this category of *talukas* in the West and, even more in the South. In the West this shift has been mainly at the expense of other cereals and pulses and cotton; while in the South the share of cereals and pulses and chillies and cotton has recorded a steep decline. The west and south have also recorded significant increases in long-duration crops even as the North-East and North-West report significant decline. The share of others has increased everywhere. Except in the Delta, irrigated crop patterns in the groundwater dominant tracts in 1985-86 are more diversified than in 1970-71. This tendency is most striking in the Western zone.

In *talukas* where the bulk of irrigated area is under canal or tanks, the share of paddy has fallen and the decline is steepest in the South. The North-East has shifted in a big way to coarse cereals and the south to a lesser extent. While there is a tendency towards greater diversification in all three zones, their crop patterns continue to be paddy dominated.

The groundwater–canal/tank combination in all regions, except South, reported a marginal shift away from paddy and other cereals and pulses. The share of long duration crops has not changed much (in fact it has declined somewhat) in all regions except the North-West. Overall diversification of irrigated crop patterns in this category of *talukas* is strikingly evident in the Western zone (already the most diversified), much less so in the North-East and marginally the North-West. There is by contrast greater concentration in the crop pattern of the Delta and the Southern zone.

Productivity

The combined impact of irrigation on crop intensities, crop patterns and individual crop yields is reflected in higher output per unit of irrigated land compared to rainfed land. While this is widely recognised, quantifying the magnitude of the impact on overall productivity and the contributions of different elements to it is rendered extremely difficult by paucity of data.

Estimates of irrigated and unirrigated areas under major crops are available for states and districts. But there are doubts about the reliability of data on irrigated crop areas. Also information on area sown with 'minor' crops which occupy small areas—but high value productivity, e.g. vegetables and flowers—is not available. Separate yield estimates for irrigated and unirrigated areas based on crop cutting experiments are available for only a few major crops (major cereals, oilseeds and cotton). In some case like sugarcane and banana—which are predominantly irrigated—one can take the overall crop yield estimates while for most other crops there is a weak basis. In any case, separate estimates are not available for irrigated area. Because of this, estimates for production and productivity of irrigated areas cannot be comprehensive in scope. Vaidyanathan *et al.* (1994) found that only 21 crops could be covered at the state level.

At the district level, yield estimates are not always based on scientifically designed crop cutting surveys, and even where they are, the estimates are subject to large margins of errors. The crop coverage is also more limited: we have been able to cover only 11 major crops for estimating productivity of irrigated areas. In some cases, they cover as much as 90 per cent of total gross irrigated area but they account for as little as 70 per cent in some districts in recent years. The proportion of area covered by theses crops has also been changing.

Table 5.16

Irrigated Area of Crop Coverage of 11 Crops

(Percentage)

Districts	*1971-72*	*1975-76*	*1981-82*	*1985-86*	*1990-91*
Chengalpattu	98.9	98.3	98.1	97.3	97.1
South Arcot	98.3	97.2	96.3	95.7	92.7
North Arcot	97.8	96.2	93.7	94.7	88.9
Salem	84.1	89.2	81.6	75.9	76.6
Coimbatore	88.4	86.2	81.1	80.3	83.3
Trichy	93.9	83.7	89.7	88.6	83.7
Thanjavur	98.3	98.2	98.7	98.8	97.1
Madurai	92.9	91.2	90.2	85.6	84.6
Ramanathapuram	96.3	95.3	95.8	92.7	92.8
Tirunelveli	89.9	90.7	89.1	89.7	84.4
State	91.9	83.7	82.5	80.4	80.5

Source: GoTN, *Season and Crop Reports*, various issues.

The fact is that the proportion of GIA under the selected crop varies across space and time (Table 5.16). As one cannot get any direct assessment of productivity levels or change under different sources of irrigation, the best that can be done, pending improvement in the quality and design of data collection to permit much analysis, is to see how far the variations in productivity between regions and over time are associated systematically and consistently with relative importance of different irrigation sources. The results, we need hardly emphasise, are highly tentative and must be interpreted with much caution.

During the 1980s, output per irrigated crop hectare in the state average of ₹ 9749 was lowest in Ramanathapuram at ₹ 4997 and Tirunelveli at ₹ 7307 and highest in Coimbatore at ₹ 15835. Output per ha of NIA as well as the difference between productivity of irrigated and rainfed lands are naturally much higher. For reasons mentioned earlier, the estimates understate the differential between the productivity of these two classes of land.

Table 5.17

Value of Irrigated and Unirrigated Productivity per ha across Districts of Tamil Nadu

Districts	*Irrigated*					*Unirrigated*				
	1971-72	*1975-76*	*1981-82*	*1985-86*	*1990-91*	*1971-72*	*1975-76*	*1981-82*	*1985-86*	*1990-91*
Chengalpattu	4819	6413	5996	7888	9124	4158	6017	5216	5601	7775
South Arcot	7884	9147	13179	13230	16755	4670	5161	3478	5907	4501
North Arcot	7052	8044	10214	7304	12387	5740	6796	7243	6532	7224
Salem	8031	8219	8435	14580	14403	4979	4440	5002	3598	6073
Coimbatore	12488	13143	15030	15838	16932	3904	4674	3518	2892	4345
Trichy	6423	5803	7425	10709	9130	3609	3641	4214	5317	6689
Thanjavur	4823	4787	5849	5720	9130	3203	2350	3405	3603	4670
Madurai	7832	8445	9975	12107	11660	7355	6929	6850	8348	6726
Ramanathapuram	4934	5386	6510	4997	9409	3261	2109	3340	4246	7043
Tirunelveli	5869	5791	6592	7307	10551	2955	1557	3081	1705	6106
State	6826	7332	8912	9749	11986	4383	4367	4535	4774	6115

Source: Computed from Annexure 4. Tamil Nadu Agricultural University, 1985.

Productivity of irrigated areas has a rising trend in all districts, and in most districts that of unirrigated crops shows no significant trend during

1970-1990. They fluctuate around a more or less stagnant average. Based on the extent of deviations from the estimated long-term trend, it is seen that irrigated crop yields are not only growing, but also liable to smaller fluctuations around the trend, compared to productivity per unirrigated crop ha. The latter is liable to a much larger fluctuation and near stagnant trend.

Table 5.18

Relationship between Productivity and Various Factors across Districts of Tamil Nadu

Output/GIA *RF*	*NIA*	*NIAgw/NIA*	*RF*	*WIA*	*NIAgw/NIA*	*NIAtank/NIA*
1.21**	-28.3**	79**	0.88	23.3	70.3**	-41.4**

Note: ** t value more than 2. (RF: rainfall); WIA: well irrigated area.

Source: Same as Table 5.17..

As noted earlier, it is not possible with this data to assess the differences in productivity between land irrigated by different sources and the contributions of cropping intensity, crop patterns and individual crop yields in accounting for the differences. All that we can do is to see whether and to what extent spatial and temporal variations in productivity of irrigated areas are related to variation in the importance of groundwater as a source of irrigation. Since importance of groundwater irrigation is not the only factor affecting productivity of irrigated land, it is necessary to control for other factors influencing the outcome. These include rainfall and its seasonal distribution, as well as the extent of dependence on tanks. The role of rainfall needs no explanation. The composition of irrigation sources is important inasmuch as the quantum, reliability and extent of flexibility of irrigation supply differ between canals, tanks and groundwater. Groundwater irrigated areas are expected to do much better than surface irrigation, especially tanks. The expectation is that the higher the proportion of NIA under groundwater, the higher will be the productivity of land (keeping other factors constant). Similarly the higher the proportion of tank irrigation in total irrigated area, the lower is likely to be the average productivity of all irrigated land.

Thus irrigated productivity is viewed as a function of total rainfall, its seasonal concentration (measured by the proportion of total falling in the North-East monsoon), the percentage of net irrigated area under groundwater and under tanks. This function, assumed to be linear, is estimated by using standard multiple regression technique applied to: (1) pooled data for all 10 districts for all 20 years; (2) pooled district cross-section for 1971-1973, 1984-1986 and 1988-1990; and (3) data for districts in each of the five major agro-climatic zones pooled for all 20 years.

Table 5.19

Factors Affecting Variations in Productivity of Irrigated Areas: All Districts and Zonal Levels

All Districts	*Output/GIA*				*Output/NIA*			
	RF	*NE %*	*NIAgw/NIA*	*NIAt/NIA*	*RF*	*NE %*	*NIAgw/NIA*	*NIAt/NIA*
1971-73	-3.44**	-6.9**	29.8*	-28.1**	-3.79	-26.7	3.07	31.66**
1988-90	-0.29	-28.7	51.6**	-52.1	-4.04**	80.1	63.9**	5.39
				Zonal Level Time Series				
North East	-0.73	31.45	10.9	-111.5**	0.75	12.63	-3.79	-43.9**
North West	4.85**	-.56	202.6**	-267.7	2.66**	5.14	96.6*	-100.4
West	1.98*	-12.75	45.7	-245.4**	1.04	22.06	40.3	-178.8**
Delta	0.48	-28.6	194.3**	130.5**	1.02	32.29*	178.3**	-109.7**
Southern	2.05	-0.08	-26.8	-59.95**	3.20**	7.14	70.86*	-47.1*

Note: NE: Northeast; NIAE: net irrigated area to total.

Source: Same as Table 5.18.

The estimates for the district level data (Table 5.19) for all years from 1971 to 1990 show that: (1) there is a negative but non-significant relation between total rainfall and irrigated productivity; (2) the coefficient for the index of seasonal concentration is significantly positive (suggesting that higher the seasonal concentration, the higher the productivity of irrigated land); (3) the groundwater ratio coefficient is significant and positive even as that of tanks is significantly negative. This means the productivity of irrigated areas tends to be higher in areas where the proportion of total rainfall occurring in the North-East monsoon and when the proportion of net area irrigated under groundwater are both relatively high. On the other hand, the higher the dependence on tanks, the lower is likely to be the overall output per ha of irrigated land.

Inter-district variations in irrigated productivity during 1971-1973 follow the same pattern as above. But in 1988-1990, only groundwater irrigation has a significant positive coefficient. At the zonal level, the rainfall variables turn out to be mostly non-significant (except in the Western and Southern zones where total rainfall has a significant positive effect on irrigated yield), but in all cases, the ratio of tank irrigated to total irrigated area has a significant negative co-efficient; the coefficient for groundwater is significant and positive in three out of the five zones.

Regression based on time series for individual districts shows total rainfall to be significant in Salem, Madurai, Ramanathapuram and Tirunelveli—all low-rainfall areas. Greater dependence on tanks is associated with lower irrigated productivity in five districts—including North Arcot, Salem, Ramanathapuram, Coimbatore and Thanjavur. Groundwater irrigation coefficient is positive and significant only in four cases (South Arcot, Salem, Tiruchi and Tirunelveli) and is in fact significantly negative in Ramanathapuram. The results are substantially similar when we look at the productivity per ha of NIA. The results thus confirm that, other things given, groundwater irrigation makes a significant improvement in productivity of irrigated areas.

References

Janakarajan, S. and A. Vaidyanathan (1997). *Conditions and Characteristics of Groundwater Irrigation*. MIDS

Vaidyanathan, A. (1996). "Depletion of Groundwater: Some Issues", *Indian Journal of Agricultural Economics*, January-June

Vaidyanathan, A. and S.Janakarajan (1989). *Management of Irrigation and its Effect on Productivity under Different Environmental Technical Conditions*. MIDS.

Vaidyanathan, A., Asha Kumar, A. Rajagopal and D. Varatharajan (1994). "Impact of Irrigation on Productivity of Land", *Journal of the Indian School of Political Economy* 6(4): 601-45, October-December.

6 Changes in Amaravathi Basin with Special Reference to Karur Region

S. Neelakantan

Characteristics of Amaravati Basin

Amaravathi River rises in the Western Ghats, is a tributary of Cauvery and flows entirely within the territory of Tamil Nadu. The river flows at first through the dense forests in the Anamalai Hills and then later through the reserve forests in Coimbatore District. From its origin, the river flows along a length of 192 km before it merges with the Cauvery at the border of Karur and Kulithalai *talukas*. The catchment area of Amaravathi lies in the eastern side of Western Ghats in Anamalai-Valparai-Munnar area. Besides four main tributaries, several other smaller streams flow into the river.

The river receives water both from north-east and south-west monsoons. Both monsoons supply almost equal quantity of water to the river. However the north-east monsoon confers relatively more benefit on the farmers in the basin. In pre-independence days, the river had water flowing for most of the year. Even during the dry season, some water continued to flow even if in a trickle. The river along its course had substantial and deep sand cover below Chinnadharapuram. A part of the river flow was absorbed and stored under the river in the sand bed. The volume of water held in the sand cover was large and this was regenerated gradually through the year as surface flow downstream. All along the river bed, depending on the depth of the sand cover, substantial amounts of water were available in sub-surface aquifers. There were deep pools along the river especially where small streams and *velladharais*—watercourses carrying rainwater—merged with the river. The traditional, centuries old, irrigation system thus had abundant and assured water supplies.

The traditional irrigation system consisted of 15 masonry structures across the river, one temporary dam ('Kattida korambu') and six temporary sand dams ('Korambu') constructed annually across the river situated at different places between Udumalapet where the river enters the plains and Karur at the tail end before its confluence with the Cauvery. The names of the 18 anicuts and Korumbus and canals that were in use in 1950, the capacity of the canals that drew water from them and the estimated area irrigated by each are shown in Table 6.1. All these dams were devices to divert available flows in the river through open-head canals for irrigating the area under their respective commands. Drainage water from these canals and the old *ayacut* flowed back to the main river. These canals were all unlined. The lands irrigated by them, which formed a narrow strip along both the banks of the river, were classified as two paddy crop wetlands (Iru Bogha Nanjai). The total extent of land irrigated by the system is estimated to be around 29000 acres, half of which was served by 11 canals on the left bank of the river and the other half by 14 canals on the right bank (Table 6.1).

In the 1950s, the traditional system had ample and assured supplies of water throughout the year. Water started flowing in the river following the onset of south-west monsoon in June. The north-east monsoon in October-November again brought fresh water. This enabled two crops to be raised in wetlands between June and March. The situation began to change after the construction of Amaravathi reservoir and Amaravathi Main Canal (AMC hereafter) in 1958 diverting much larger volumes of water than envisaged in the original design. This led to a reduction in the volume, duration and reliability of river flow and supplies for *ayacuts* in the lower reaches of the traditional system. The cultivation of high-value annual crop, Korai, which depended on the near perennial flow in the river, declined and eventually disappeared when the flow declined substantially. River flow started only in July and stopped in January-February. Farmers still managed to raise two crops between July and February taking advantage of new shorter duration varieties introduced in the 1960s. In critical years, the meagre supply in the river together with the regenerated water was diverted to canals and was used for irrigating the crops, especially when they had matured and needed only one or two irrigations. The Vaikal Maniagar would ration the water among the *ayacutdars* on those special occasions.

Table 6.1

Total Land Irrigated by Canals

No.	Name of Channel	Dam Length in Feet	Cusecs	Length in Miles	Irrigation in Acres
1	Ramakulam	Within dam	3 0	6.1.44	1384
2	Kallapuram	At the dam	3 0	7.0.23	1450
3	Kallapuram	672.00	40.00	9.6.00	1259
4	Kallapuram	300.00	20.00	7.1.00	661
5	Sarkar Kannadiputhur	720.00	27.00	4.2.00	580
6	Cholamadevi	748.00	55,00	7.2.00	11 7 1
7	Kadathur	580.00	17.32	5.0.00	3 9 0
8	Kaniyoor	Natural rock	37.00	7.6.00	6 2 5
9	Karatholuvu	750.00	50.75	7.0.00	1054
10	Alangiyam	440.00	50.00	7.0.22	9 3 2
11	Dalavaipattinam	650.00	105.00	15.0.0	2417
12	Dharapuram	1283.00	130.00	10.5.0, 4.5.0, 6.1.33, 13.1	3227
13	Kolinjivadi	779.00	18.50	4.5.640	4 9 4
14	Nanjai Thalayur	1468.00	70.00	6.2.390	1878
15	Chinnadharapuram	743.00	10.80	16.6.330	2 9 2
16	Sundakkapalayam	910.00	20.00	10.4.000	3 9 6
17	Nanjaikalakurichi	1830.00	110.00	9.7.000	3623
18	Pallapalayam	Korambu	30.00	5.0.210	9 11
19	Thirumanilayoor	Korambu	35.00	7.5.380	1093
20	Karurpalambapuram	Korambu	20.00	5.1.530	4 6 4
21	Sanappiratti	Korambu	45.00	6.7.165	1370
22	PuliyurKoyampalli	Korambu	30.00	6.0.000	9 4 6
23	Kattalai	Korambu	60.00	4.5.330	1755
24	Manavasi	Korambu	20.00		5 7 7
25	Mayanur	Korambu	15.00		4 1 5
	Total		1076.37	201.1.235	29364

Source: An undated pamphlet published by Karur farmers C. 1990.

For the most part, these irrigated lands raised two crops of paddy. In the lower part of the system, farmers in head reaches of canals would raise annual crops such as banana or 9-10 month crops such as turmeric. In wetlands close to the head reaches of canals that had access to more abundant and assured supply of river flow, a profitable annual crop of reeds—Korai—was cultivated. These long-duration crops made use of regenerated water from the river in summer seasons. Tracts irrigated by the old system were marked by an intensive, highly productive and prosperous agriculture.

Lands at a higher elevation than the canal could be irrigated by lifting water from canals. Water could be lifted only by devices operated with the animal or human muscle power. (Though energised pumps had been introduced in the state from the 1920s, they did not spread in this region till much later.) The volume and the height over which water could be lifted with these devices were quite limited. Lifting water from canals was illegal. It was subject to government approval which was limited to no more than two *'kavalais'* per *pattadar*. Violations were strictly monitored and severely punished by local *Vaikal Maniyagar* and *Neerkandis*. Because of these factors, the extent of upland areas irrigated by these lifts was quite small and confined to within a short distance (about 100 meters) from the canal.

Conditions—in terms of water availability, irrigation, agriculture and socioeconomic profile—in the area served by the traditional system as well as the basin as a whole have undergone dramatic and far-reaching transformations during the post-independence period following the construction of a reservoir-based canal system at the head reach of the river in the 1950s and subsequently by large-scale pumping of water from the riverbed to irrigate extensive areas in the rainfed upland tracts located in the proximity of the river. These developments led to the growth in the demand for access to and use of the river's water outstripping available supplies, forcing difficult and painful adjustments for different claimants and increasing tensions between users in different segments of the basin. The growing scarcity of water was exacerbated by growth in the demand for non-agricultural uses resulting from urbanisation and industrial expansion, and widespread mining of sand in the riverbed compounded by deterioration of water quality due to industrial pollution. This paper traces these developments, the responses of various users and stakeholders (including institutions of governance and the political class) to cope with the emerging trends.

The Advent of Reservoir

Construction of a reservoir on Amaravathi near Udumalpet was proposed as early as 1901. A scheme prepared in 1905 was also considered by Government but abandoned on the ground that it would be "expensive both due to heavy compensation and the necessity for providing for large surplus discharges." Another proposal based on a fresh investigation in 1918 was also not pursued because the estimated return was considered too low.

A severe famine in Udumalpet, Palladam and Dharapuram *talukas* in 1938-39 caused revival of interest in the project. A government investigation in 1946 suggested constructing a reservoir and a main canal to irrigate 15000 acres in Udumalpet and Dharapuram *talukas*. A fresh investigation, in response to representations from farmers of the region led to a modification of the proposal by extending the length of the canal from 35 miles to 40 miles to irrigate 7500 acres of wet crops and 7500 of irrigated dry crops. The reservoir construction began in 1953 and was completed in 1958.

Opposition to the Reservoir Proposal

The proposal was opposed by farmers in the lower reaches of the river. Farmers in Karur *taluka* contended that water supply in Amaravathi canals on which they depended was already insufficient and that the construction of a reservoir and digging of a new canal at the upper reaches would reduce the water flow to the tail-end canals. The Government's approval for replacement of traditional animal-operated lifts with diesel engines to lift canal water in one of the villages aggravated their concerns.

Several leading figures got together and formed the Karur Division Amaravathi *Ayacut* Agriculturists Association to safeguard their traditional rights. In 1950, a delegation of the lower *ayacutdars* of Amaravathi River met the then Minister for Public Works. They protested against the decision to construct the reservoir even as the Government had failed to consider several proposals that had been made to ensure adequate water supplies to the canals in the lower *ayacuts* by constructing a channel to bring water from the Cauvery; draining surplus of Lower Bhavani project into the lower Amaravati *ayacut*; and constructing a reservoir across one of its main tributaries and raising the Anaipalayam regulator to conserve more water for utilisation in the drought season. They sought an assurance that their established riparian right to have top priority of the tail-end *ayacuts* to Amaravathi waters would be protected. And further they should be entitled to have first preference over the proposed additional *ayacut* to water during drought. Such an assurance was given formally by the district collector and reportedly by the then Chief Minister in the state legislature.

Not satisfied, they insisted on knowing details of "the design and plan under which the present scheme has been chalked out and how and on what basis the water is going to be let out from the reservoir to our Ayacut" and measures to check the tendency for unauthorised drawing of "... water from Amaravathi by means of oil engines and bailing stands to irrigate Punjai lands...." In response to persistent appeals and agitations by ayacutdars of the lower reaches of the basin to secure their traditional entitlements to water, the Government gave a commitment to: (1) ensure that only 20 per cent of the direct *ayacut* would be permitted to grow wet crops and that 80 per cent of the area should grow only dry crops and that too only in one season by limiting the opening of the AMC to 6 months (between August and January); (2) construct separate sluices in the dam dedicated to supply water to the traditional *ayacut*; and (3) implement a turn system for releasing water from the dam to the new and old *ayacut* whereby the latter would get 500 cusecs of water to ensure adequate supplies to all its canals. The expectation then was that with normal rains, the reservoir would fill up three times a year. The excess natural flows in the river over and above the requirements of the old *ayacut* were to be impounded in the reservoir. Whenever the natural flows in the river were inadequate to meet the irrigation requirements of the old system, supplemental irrigation supply was to be given to the old *ayacut* from the impounded water.

Impact of the Reservoir

In the very first year in which supplies were released from the reservoir, the fears of the lower *ayacutdars* that there might not be enough water in the reservoir for both new and old *ayacutdars* to share proved to be correct. The north-east monsoon failed that year, and the reservoir did not fill up. Crops in the Karur area began to wilt. *Ayacutdars* of the lower segments of the traditional system sought an *ad hoc* increase in the release for their lands from 400 cusecs to 500 cusecs a day for a couple of days. But Karur and Kultihalai *talukas* at the tail end complained that this was inadequate to ensure the maturing of crops already sown in the area. This led to formal proposals for introduction of a turn (*'murai'*) system for release of water for different canals of the river in times of drought.

The commitments made by the Government to ensure adequate supplies of water to the traditional system after commissioning the AMC were not fulfilled. The Government did not enforce the cropping pattern restrictions on areas under direct irrigation from the reservoir. The proportion of area growing water-intensive and long-duration crops in the direct *ayacut* was allowed to increase far beyond the limits specified in the regulations. Proposed arrangements for ensuring the traditional entitlements of the old system for water from the river through dedicated sluices at the dam at all times and for introduction of a turn system to ensure priority access in times of drought were not implemented.

As a result, the quantum of water used by them was allowed to increase much beyond the design. This resulted in a progressive reduction in the volume, duration and reliability of water supplies to the old system downstream of the river. Complaints of inadequacy of water supply and inequitable distribution of available supplies especially at the tail end increased even in normal times and more so in times of inadequate rainfall. When the storage position in the reservoir was relatively low, there was a struggle for water between the upper and lower riparians. The lower riparians felt aggrieved. Their appeals and agitations for fair and equitable distribution of available water were of no avail.

The turn system, which was meant to ensure that entitlements of the old *ayacut* were given priority, was not implemented. The Public Works Department (PWD) authorities had considerable discretionary authority to decide when and how much water would be released to the AMC and for the old *ayacut*. They determined whether to open the canal gates all of which were located at the dam or to keep them closed till water reached the tail end before opening the gates of the canals feeding the direct AMC *ayacut*. Whenever water flowed to the tail end, the canals in the upper reaches also received water. But when water was released in small quantities, only the canals in upper reaches would get the benefit, while the tail-end *ayacutdars* were deprived. Whether releases to the old *ayacut* would reach the tail end in sufficiently large quantities was also depended on the decision of the authorities.

The old system, particularly its tail end, could not get adequate redress partly because of disadvantageous location and the inability to pressure the bureaucracy or invoke political influence. Members of the Legislative Assembly (MLAs) of tail reaches of the basin (Aravakurichi—Karur belt) were relatively powerless in the party hierarchies. Farmers in the lower region attempted to form a single association to redress their grievances. Unfortunately, there were clashes among different groups who had lands in different canals, and, therefore, no single association was formed to represent the grievances of the lower riparians. In all these respects, the upper regions were far better placed.

Farmers of the head reach on the other hand were able not only to violate crop pattern restrictions with impunity but also succeeded in getting the government to extend the canal by another 5 miles, increase the direct *ayacut* from the original 15000 acres to 21500 acres and implement improvements to the canal by lining it. Restrictions on crop pattern were eventually removed. Nothing was done to check the spread of direct pumping of water from the river downstream of the reservoir to irrigate lands outside the *ayacut*. During 1980s, the farmers along the main canal had formed an association which collected considerable financial resources to be used for getting water along the main canal. It so happened that, right from 1970s till now, the Udumalpet-Pollachi belt had an influential cabinet minister in both Dravida Munnetra Kazhagam (DMK) and Anna Dravida Munnetra Kazhagam (ADMK) Governments. Using their political influence and organisational strength, the farmers in the upper reaches managed to obtain more wettings than they were entitled to.

Direct Extraction of Water from the Riverbed

Simultaneously, in the region below the reservoir, water began to be pumped directly from the river to the fields and the area irrigated by that source increased considerably. The AMC runs parallel to the river for more than 50 km. Most farmers with lands close to the river but who did not get water from the AMC began to draw water directly from the river using energised pumps which by then were spreading rapidly. Politically powerful people in these tracts are reported to have invested large amounts of resources and used their influence to pump river water to their freshly acquired lands adjacent to the river. As a result, the flow of the river downstream began to fall.

Even before independence, it was not uncommon for farmers in lands adjacent to the river to draw water from the river as a supplemental source of irrigation in critical times to save a crop which had almost matured. Though water in the traditional canals flowed only for a few months, their *ayacutdars* could tap abundant spring water from the riverbed throughout the year to sustain two wet crops. Farmers whose lands were not close to the river could use manual or animal-operated lifts from the canals to irrigate them when needed. But this was limited in scale. The traditional system of Vaikal Maniagars and Kudimaramath (community maintenance) monitored direct tapping of river water for irrigation to lands which were not directly located on the river or canal banks to check violations of water rights. Unauthorised use of water was punished by levying penalties which were usually multiples of '*kist*' or land tax. The village munsiff collected this water rate along with *kist*. Since they could use only muscle or animal power to lift water in those days, the land thus irrigated was small in extent and the 'water rate' generally twice or three times the *kist*.

After the commissioning of the AMC, supplies to the canals of the old system, especially in the lower segments, got smaller and more unreliable. The area for which water was lifted or pumped from the old *ayacut* canals declined. In the late 1950s, some farmers began to use energised pumps to tap water from the ditches in the riverbed by laying pipelines in the wetlands between the old canal and river to bring river water into their open wells. Many farmers constructed narrow ditches to divert river flow into tiny 9-12 feet diameter '*vattai*' wells on their patta land adjacent to the river which was then directly pumped into the siphon system to irrigate dry land located at a higher elevation across the canal. This was not legal. There was no Vaikal Maniagar to monitor such activities after 1949. Since this system did not involve direct extraction of canal water, villagers in the lower sections of the canal did not immediately complain. Nor did PWD authorities intervene to prevent the practice.

The siphon system was an inefficient and costly mechanism to pipe water over long distances. In the Cauvery basin, farmers began adopting a direct pumping system since 1950s which used high horsepower pumps to lift larger quantities of water over greater heights than was possible with traditional lifting devices and low horsepower pumps. The water from the direct pumping system was then distributed through cement pipelines to irrigate a much larger extent of dry lands at higher elevations and outside the canal commands. This direct pumping system was adopted in the Amaravathi belt in the early 1960s. In the early days, bringing upland rainfed lands under cultivation of wet crops was a tough job. The advent of tractors and earthmovers made it easier and cheaper to prepare the dry uplands for irrigated farming. The emergence and spread of hiring services for short periods made it possible even for small farmers to use machinery to prepare their lands for irrigated cultivation. The combined effect of these developments vastly increased the potential for using water pumped from river and canals for irrigating lands located at a higher elevation and at a considerable distance from the river.

This led to a surge in the use of pumps to tap water from the riverbed. Farmers adopted ingenious devices to increase the volume of water from both surface flows and from under the riverbed to their wells and to convey them over longer distances. Those who wanted to irrigate their dry lands used their owned or acquired plots adjacent to the river to locate their pumping stations there. Lands adjacent to the river began to be coveted more and commanded a premium. In the British days, the lands on both banks of the river were maintained as *Purambokku* lands. They were known as *'Kuttukadu'* where small timber naturally grew. The *Kuttukadu* strengthened the banks and prevented their erosion during the floods. From the beginning of this century, and especially in the 1950s and 1960s, the Kuttukadu lands were encroached upon by landowners who owned adjacent lands or in rare cases, by service castes. When prohibition was introduced, *Kuttukadus* happened to be places with enough vegetation cover to carry on illicit brewing of liquor. The local villagers did not protest too much against the encroachment of *Kuttukadus* by adjacent landowners. Political influence and corruption played a major role. Both along the Amaravathi and Cauvery belts, the *Kuttukadus* simply disappeared.

Farmers using owned or encroached lands in the old *Kuttukadu* areas and owned *patta* lands adjacent to the river bank were the first to divert river water to their dry lands located at a distance from the river. Later, many private parties started laying pipelines to their lands from the riverbed. They would purchase a small plot of *patta* land—about 5 to 20 cents—on the river bank, dig a well, install a diesel pump, link it to a pipeline traversing under the canal, align it along the hamlet's roads, *'velladharais'* and other *poramboke* lands to take water to their fields. A shallow well or *'vattai'* well was dug in these plots and a pipeline would be laid from the well to their dry lands. Then river water would be let into the well by a connecting link—a little ditch or by a pipeline. An electricity connection would then be applied for, and, after many formalities were completed, would be received, to pump 'well' water to their fields at higher elevations.

Tapping water from the canal or river was illegal. Since the Government was neither willing nor able to prevent this, the additional area under unauthorised irrigation was levied penalties. The village officials were required to record such areas in a special account (called account 6) in revenue records as unauthorised and subject to penal rates to determine the quantum of penal rates. Though the prescribed maximum penal rate was around 20 times the normal *kist* rate, village *munsiffs* could be, and were, persuaded to use their discretion to mitigate the 'illegality' in several ways: charging lower penal rates on a selective basis; understating the unauthorised irrigated area, and recording the area as growing short-term dry crops when in fact such lands were used to grow water-intensive, long-duration crops. These practices significantly reduced the real cost of unauthorised use to farmers. However, insofar as account 6 recorded the unauthorised irrigated land, it provided the basis on which their owners could approach the revenue authorities for issue of permits to regularise their illegal extraction of water after paying penalties.

Getting electrical connections to the pump sets for wells situated within 50 meters from the river, required a 'No Objection Certificate' (NOC hereafter) from both the revenue and PWD officials. Theoretically the NOC is meant only for pumping the well water percolating into the well or deep bore well in the *patta* lands located near the river. But in practice, once the NOC was issued and the electricity connection was established, the farmer would dig a little ditch or lay a pipeline directly from the river to the well and draw river water freely. All the concerned officials knew that the intention of the farmer applicant for electricity connection was to pump river water. However they pretended as if this was not known. This gave enormous discretionary power to the Village *Munsiff* (now Village Administrative Officer), Revenue Officials, PWD Officials and the Electricity Department Officials to permit irrigation rights to fresh lands. Any farmer with the right political connections and willing to spend the expected amount of cash could get the NOCs and the electricity connection for drawing river water to his lands. The amount of corruption involved was mind-boggling.

Initially, only influential farmers with large holdings could afford the investments. As technological change made these investments attractive, more and more farmers in the basin as a whole got interested in direct tapping of water from the river. Dwindling and increasingly unreliable supplies in canal water was an additional factor that induced ayacutdars to do so. They adopted a variety of stratagems to overcome these constraints including the formation of irrigation 'co-operatives', using political influence and exerting organised political pressure through their MLAs for legitimizing such extension of irrigation. The Government is reported to have regularised all electricity connections of those who had extended their irrigation up to 1971. Efforts of farmers along the Amaravathi River to get MLAs to use their political influence for regularisation of their unauthorised irrigation up to 1980s were however unsuccessful.

Growth of Irrigation and its Impact

The processes described above occurred mostly during the 1970s and 1980s but continued in subsequent years as well. As a result, the total area drawing water from the river is estimated to have increased to more than 100000 acres which is nearly three times the *ayacut* of the traditional system. Part of the difference is accounted by the authorised direct *ayacut* of the AMC of 21500 acres. Based on the extent of area recorded in village revenue records as liable to pay penalties for unauthorised irrigation (account 6), the additional area drawing water from the river is estimated at 55000 acres: 30000 acres in the upper reaches of the basin and 25000 acres in the lower reaches. This is likely to be an underestimate because a large amount of area with unauthorised irrigation is left out of the No. 6 account.

The problems arising from the expansion of irrigated area and volume of water usage much beyond the original design became increasingly manifest over the years. Upper reaches of river and rainfed uplands outside canal commands were the principal beneficiaries of this expansion. Prescribed restrictions on crop patterns were extensively violated. Both the direct ayacut and its unauthorised extension used water to raise wet crops for two seasons or annual crops especially sugarcane and coconut. The impact of this on the quantum and reliability of downstream water supplies was severe and was borne by farmers in the lower reaches.

Those served by the traditional system, especially in its tail end, being unable to get any redress from officials or the Government to protect their traditional entitlements, were forced to adapt to reduced and uncertain supplies in their canals and dwindling river flows. The tail-enders had to give up growing high-value long-duration crops like sugarcane and bananas. In years with normal rainfall, they could still manage to raise two crops of paddy within the short duration when river water flowed by using the new short-duration varieties. But increasingly they had to resort to various ways to augment water supplies by using diesel engines to lift water from canals and tapping groundwater. Farmers attempted to deepen the ditches in the riverbed to augment water available for pumping from their wells. Success depended on the depth of the sand cover, and with the extensive mining of the sand, this method ultimately became ineffective. Competitive digging of bore wells to supplement river water irrigation became a widespread practice in the entire basin after 1980s. However, along with the depleting sand cover, the groundwater table itself began to fall and the volume of water from many bore wells fell/ran dry in the late 1990s and early 2000s. They had also to shift to less water-intensive crops and use water saving methods like drip irrigation.

Before water pumped from the river became available, uplands grew mostly rainfed short-duration crops like groundnut, hybrid *cholam, cumbu* and cotton. With the spread of the pump set-pipeline technology, they initially preferred to raise high-value water-intensive crops like sugarcane, paddy, banana, turmeric and flowers. This helped speedy recovery of the high investment costs of using modern technology. But with declining supplies, they too were forced to resort to more elaborate devices to tap the water from under the riverbed. But given the decline in river flow and storage of water under its bed, the upland irrigators were also forced to shift to less water-intensive crop patterns.

These tendencies became progressively more widespread through the 1970s and 1980s. They have since been further intensified for several reasons: the growth in demand for water for domestic and industrial uses; diminution in the underground storages and springs in the riverbed as the result of mining of sand; and the growing pollution of water sources from untreated effluents of a rapidly growing dyeing industry in the region. The unravelling of these complex and inter-related trends in an anarchic manner resulted in further deterioration of water supply in the river and its quality and attendant ecological, social and economic consequences.

Spread of Sand Mining

Before the construction of the reservoir and the spread of pumping of river water, the riverbed along most of its course had a deep sand cover which absorbed and stored a large volume of water during the seasons when the river was in full flow. Water stored in the sand bed was the source of regenerated flows which helped maintain the flow of water downstream of the river even during the dry season. In the summer months there was also regeneration of water in the river which was earlier used to irrigate the lands along the banks in the higher elevation. The stored water in the sand bed was the main source of supplies for extending irrigation to rainfed uplands using high energy pumps and pipelines. Till the 1980s it was possible for all the pump set-pipeline farmers to use these methods to irrigate their lands, raising annual crops such as sugar cane, banana or turmeric.

Sand was mined from the riverbeds routinely for construction purposes for a very long time. It was done on a small-scale and localised in the vicinity of major towns along the rivers of Tamil Nadu. Commercial mining by contractors required permits from the Collector and was subject to conditions stipulated by the law. In the Amaravati, the scale was small and what was taken out got replenished during the next flood. The scale of sand extraction from the river began increasing around the mid-1970s to meet the rapid growth of construction activity as a result of growing urbanisation and industrial development in the region. The acceleration of this process led to further growth in demand for sand for construction of factories, roads and all types of residential and non-residential buildings. The scale of demand was far too large to be met by traditional methods. It required specialised equipment and organisation for extraction and transport of huge volumes involving large investments. Such commercial operations became highly profitable as market prices for sand rose to unprecedented levels. This began to attract numerous contractors. However, it was not easy to locate places where sand deposits were large enough to be mined economically and had access to roads for transporting the material. Moreover, they had to have a valid permit.

In the early days, the revenue department stuck to the rules and did not permit deep level sand mining. However, when the price of sand became high and continued to rise, contractors began to use extra legal methods and political influence to overcome opposition from local communities to secure mining permits from officials. Over time, heavy machinery for mining and big trucks for hauling sand were brought into the operation. Illegal mining, transport and public sale of sand became brazen and widespread. Many abuses of power came to be noticed for obtaining mining permits. Mining without permits and transporting sand by trucks with forged permits became common. The government machinery was not only ill-equipped to cope with extensive violations, but also was induced to turn a blind eye to them by regular 'mamools' paid to officials at various levels.

Numerous protests and agitations by communities close to the river against mining of river sand in their vicinity went unheeded by the officials. Contractors were undeterred by them. They used different stratagems—bribing protestors, co-opting locally influential groups and use of muscle power—to establish and continue illegal mining. Over the years the close links they forged with influential politicians in all parties and at all levels gave them additional protection from penalties and prosecution. Sand mining became an unholy combination of politicians, bureaucrats and mining contractors who were so influential that the illegal mining spread and flourished with impunity.

In response to sustained campaigns in the media and public forums highlighting the damage being caused by unregulated sand mining to water supply for essential uses and to the ecology of rivers, an attempt was made in the late 1990s to amend the law giving the local bodies the right to regulate and lease the sand deposits within their territorial limits. Contractors however got the High Court to stay its implementation. A public enquiry in 2002, organised by civil society groups and chaired by Justice V.R. Krishna Iyer, underscored the gravity of the problem and recommended total prohibition of sand mining till a new set of regulations were enacted and implemented. But such is the clout of the sand contractors and builders that sand mining has continued with unabated vigour.

In September 2006, a contractor obtained a permit to mine sand along a stretch of about 10 km south of Karur town. The farmers along the river bank in that area filed a writ petition against the award in the Madurai Bench of the Madras High Court and sought an immediate injunction. The contractor resorted to delaying tactics. However, the injunction was granted in December 2006. In the interregnum, in a period of about two and a half months, more than 60000 truckloads of sand were mined and transported out of the riverbed employing heavy earth moving machinery. Now the rocks in the bottom of the river are visible in the belt, since all the sand in the upper reaches which normally would have flowed down to cover the holes have also been mined. The *panchayats* in that region lost their source of drinking water, which benefit they had enjoyed from time immemorial.

Growth in Water Requirements for Non-agricultural Uses

The loss of sand cover caused further reduction in the supply of surface water available for *ayacut* for the traditional as well as for the pump set-pipeline systems. This continued even after channels that drew water from the riverbed to wells from which water was pumped uplands were lengthened and deepened. Dependence on groundwater for irrigation and drinking water increased. More and more wells were constructed to irrigate lands near the river. At the same time, *Panchayat* Unions and Municipalities in the region had put up public water supply systems. In all the riverside villages, wells were dug in the river and water from the well was piped to overhead tanks in those villages. Piped water supply came to most of the villages by the mid-1980s. Faced with declining water levels in wells along the river and in the riverbed, deepening of wells became widespread but it was not sufficient to meet the growing demand. By the 1990s, the supply of water from all these wells became inadequate to meet the irrigation requirements of crops and of drinking water during summer. The situation worsened progressively and water scarcity became increasingly widespread and intense.

This led many of the village communities and towns along the river to opt for getting supplies from the Cauvery. By the turn of the past century, Amaravathi was not supplying drinking water to the most populous town along its entire route, namely Karur. Not all villages had the resources to implement water supply schemes obtaining water from Cauvery. They continued to depend on Amaravathi. The drinking water position in those villages adjacent to the river became more and more critical with every passing year. Even as the capacity of the wells to supply water declined, the requirement of water for dyeing from the Karur dyeing factories began to multiply. They began to dig new wells along the river. As a result, fierce competition emerged among the farmers, dyers and the *panchayats* for available supply of spring water in the riverbed. Access to water became a source of increasing tension between uses, users and user communities in the region.

The Problem of Pollution

In the 1960s, the Karur area emerged as an exporter of textile fabrics. A major factor that attracted the industry to this town was its proximity to the river with abundant supplies of water. During the 1960s and 1970s, its expansion was largely in and around the town. As the number of units and the scale of their operations in the town and its vicinity increased, the volume of water used from the river and local canals also grew rapidly. The used water containing a variety of toxic chemicals was discharged without any treatment back into the canals or river. Up to 1980, pollution was not seen as a major problem, because the volume of flow of canal water was large relative to that of effluents. Thereafter, the Municipality became concerned about the increasing concentration of effluents in local water sources and its impact on public health, agriculture and other end uses. As demand for cleaning up of the pollutants and limiting the growth of the industry in the town grew, dyeing factories began to spread out to numerous villages around the city along or in the vicinity of the river.

Initially, the growth of the dyeing industry and the unprecedented boom that it generated in the regional economy was widely welcomed by all sections. Several of the substantial land owners and businessmen of the region entered the industry. Villages competed with each other to attract entrepreneurs to set up units. The units needed land preferably close to sources of water. This forced up the prices of land. Land adjacent to the river banks began to fetch very high prices. Landowners were naturally attracted by this prospect. Non-landowners welcomed the substantial additional avenues for employment generated by the factories. As a result, the industry spread rapidly into villages along the canals and the river in the Karur region. With it, the problems caused by the impact of their growing water use on its availability and quality for irrigation and domestic use also became increasingly pervasive. Their intensity also increased with the progressive decline in the overall water supply from the river and from underground.

Dyeing factories were established in 1980s in the lands adjacent to the two canals flowing along both banks of Amaravathi. They let the effluents to flow along open drains which ultimately flowed into, spread and accumulated upstream and downstream of both banks of the river. Gradually the effluents began to affect the subsoil water in several stretches of different canals leading to the contamination of groundwater, making it unfit for drinking by humans and animals, and even the tender coconut water from the trees irrigated with that water became unpotable. Large diameter drinking water wells (*Vattais*) in the riverbed constructed between thc 1960s and 1980s by several riverside villages had to be abandoned because of contamination by dyeing factory effluents.

The increasing use of water by dyeing factories even as supplies in the river and canals were declining and contamination of water sources by their effluents gravely affected individuals and communities in the Karur region. They attempted to get dyeing units to desist from dumping the effluents into their canals, river and cultivated lands through protests, agitations and in some cases through third party mediation. A couple of local agitations in the mid-1990s to prevent pollutants from being discharged led units to cover their open drains with pipelines and closure of some units for a few days. But this proved temporary: the units resumed operations after a while. Several *panchayats* passed formal resolutions for this purpose and, lacking the authority to enforce compliance, they appealed to Panchayat Unions, district officials and sometimes even to government for action but to little avail. These were mostly village specific. Affected villages did not come together for mounting a collective campaign to get redress.

The government did not address the problem seriously. Dyeing units and other polluting industries were obliged by the law to ensure that they did not discharge untreated effluents into water sources. Standards of permissible quality of effluents had also been laid down. But there was no regular monitoring of effluent discharges and their quality even after specific complaints from communities. Hardly any effort was made to levy penalties for violations and to ensure compliance with the law. It took a long time before official sources admitted that the effluents from the dyeing units had made the water in their region unfit for human consumption.

Resort to courts has not solved the problem. In November 1997, the gravity of the situation was brought before the Supreme Court. Their judgment prohibiting all dyeing factories in and around Karur discharging their effluents either in the canals or in the Amaravathi river led to their closure but only for a few days. Its adverse effect on Karur's economy was sought to be mitigated by allowing them, after negotiations, to open on condition that Common Effluent Treatment Plants (CETPs) would be constructed within a period of 6 months which was extended by another term.

In 1997-98, a total of eight CETPs hereafter were established around Karur. More than 300 dyeing units joined as members of those eight CETPs. Unfortunately, the technology employed in those CETPs was outmoded and could not remove all the pollutants from the effluent water of the member units. The removed pollutants were stored as solid waste in the premises of CETPs. No one knew how that solid hazardous waste could be disposed of. CETPs did not fulfil the purposes for which they were established. The members rightly complained that the Pollution Control Board had misled them to invest heavily on white elephants.

As problems of scarcity and contamination of drinking water continued to worsen, and the clamour for effective action from the Government intensified, the District Collector, officials of pollution control and water supply departments as well as the local MLA were forced to intervene. Getting parties involved to agree on a solution through peace committees of officials, affected panchayats and dyeing industry representatives ran into problems. Getting an agreement was difficult. But even when one was agreed to by all parties [requiring all units to switch to a superior technology: Reverse Osmosis (RO hereafter)] with the active mediation of the MLA, it could not be implemented because of conflicts between villages and because units which did not wish to comply with the conditions of the new agreement raised unreasonable demands to be met during the interregnum before the new RO plants could be constructed and activated. A stronger intervention by the District Collector ordering all units in a designated belt to switch to RO plants for treating effluents met with a similar fate: the units were unwilling to make the investment and threatened closure of all units in the area if forced to do so. The state was on the horns of a dilemma.

As the initial enthusiastic welcome to the expansion of the industry in the region began to wane once its adverse impact on availability and quality of water became manifest, the industry started to attract opposition. For a while, they were not worried because villages were competing to attract the industry. Protests and opposition being limited, they could be managed by offering bribes to protestors, getting the support of influential local persons and use of muscle power. As dissatisfaction increased, they chose to spend huge sums of money to purchase political influence and also for bribing the officials to avert government pressure for corrective measures. But more important is the fact that the adverse effects of their operations on water supply was borne by agriculturists depending on irrigation; the benefits of increased employment accrued mostly to landless labour groups. The adverse health impact of inadequate and contaminated water supply for domestic use of course affected both segments. But, given divergent interests of major groups, it was difficult to mobilize and sustain a unified opposition to prevent or discipline the dyeing units in individual communities. Whenever some persons tried to organise protests against the pollution by dyeing units, the dyers paid their labourers and those under their protection to sabotage them.

The dyeing industry is primarily responsible for the acute scarcity of water for human use and the unacceptable levels of its contamination. It has been able to resist all pressures to take corrective action partly by exploiting the differences within the community between agricultural classes and those who are employed in these units with the threat of closure. Added to this is the fact that affected communities are competing with each other to access available supplies to meet their individual needs and cannot come together and exert concerted pressure for corrective action. Under these conditions, the government remains a helpless bystander powerless to exercise its power to provide adequate potable water supply of acceptable quality. The impasse continues and conflicts over water sharing have become more and more intense and complicated.

In 2011, the Madurai Bench of the Madras High Court had ordered that the Government should monitor and ensure zero emission of pollutants in the discharged effluent water of the dyeing factories. Consequently most of the dyeing factories in the Karur belt which had not installed RO treatment were ordered to be closed. Factories which attempted to operate clandestinely were exposed by rival groups. A large number of labourers remain unemployed. The future of the dyeing industry remains uncertain.

Tensions between lower and upper reaches of the river over the sharing of the river's water, which predate construction of the Amaravati reservoir, grew as upper riparians managed to appropriate larger volumes than their entitlements specified in the original design. The resulting reduction in downstream flows, compounded by expansion of direct pumping from the riverbed and subsequently by sand mining, led to more frequent complaints of inadequate and unreliable supplies from the lower *ayacut* even in 'normal' years. Reduced water availability for agriculture and domestic use in the lower reaches due to the spread of dyeing units created a new axis of conflict between agriculturists and dyeing industry especially in the tail end of the basin. As supplies of water in the lower reaches became more and more precarious and contaminated, protecting access to drinking water at the village level has become a source of inter-village conflicts. All these conflicts and resulting tensions have grown in scale and intensity. So have protests, agitations and litigation to secure redress, which, as recent experience shows, become particularly severe in times of drought.

The basic cause of the current water crisis in the basin is the gross overexploitation of the water resources of the basin and the mismanagement of its distribution. The primary responsibility for both lies with the government. Irrigation increases crop yields much above levels realizable with rainfed cultivation. This naturally generates huge demand for spread of irrigation. To be sustainable, the scale of expansion in any river basin must be consistent with its utilizable water potential. The investigations before approving the construction of the reservoir clearly established that adequate water was available to sustain the proposed design. However the subsequent decisions to allow expansion of the command area of the project and for the massive expansion of downstream irrigation by direct pumping of water from the river were largely in response to political compulsions to meet the growing ground level pressures for expansion of irrigation facilities. The large-scale expansion of irrigation in areas outside the authorised command and of area under water-intensive crops much beyond stipulated levels was clearly illegal. Despite growing evidence of overuse of water and attendant conflicts, the Government did not undertake any assessment of the implications of these decisions on water utilisation. Nor was there any monitoring of the impact.

The Government and institutions of governance not only failed to take note of these violations but also allowed them to continue without effective enforcement of penalties. They, in fact, regularised the violations after some time. Taking firm corrective action would be politically costly to whichever party happened to be in power. Moreover the upper riparians were better organised and happened to command greater influence with the Government than the lower riparians. These governance failures and asymmetric distribution of political power affected the lower riparians to a much greater extent.

Complaints from the old *ayacut* about the failure of the Government to honour its commitments to protect their prior rights, dwindling supplies and growing water scarcity from downstream areas were not addressed seriously. Government orders regarding management of water releases from the reservoir to meet entitlements of the old *ayacut* on a priority basis and implementing a turn system to ensure equitable distribution in times of shortage were not honoured. Appeals and agitations did not have much effect. In recent years, when a series of droughts and consequent distress led to intensified agitations and court cases by the lower riparians, the Government had to intervene more forcefully to give them relief by stricter enforcement of rules of operation of releases from the reservoir and turn systems for water distribution to upper and lower segments. But these were inadequate and in any case, their implementation was thwarted by upper riparians.

Government's record in tackling the problem of pollution and sand mining leaves even more to be desired. It did not take any initiative to check the emergence of pollution as a major problem in the lower reaches. Limited and hesitant interventions came only at a late stage when the problem had assumed serious dimensions and that too in response to agitations over shortage and contamination of drinking water. Here again the Government did not and could not take effective remedial action. There was great reluctance to enforce penalties on polluting units sanctioned by the law. Solutions sought to be forged through negotiations and mediation with concerned parties were not always successful and none could be implemented. Even on the few occasions when stronger measures were announced, the polluters were in a position to thwart implementation by threatening closure. Governments, irrespective of political colour, could not handle the political consequences of large-scale unemployment that would ensue from such closure.

Much the same is true of sand mining. It is supposed to be regulated. But the regulations and their enforcement are so weak that most of the mining is illegal. It is sustained and grows by massive corruption that extends to officials at all levels and also to the political class. Sand mining is extraordinarily profitable thanks to the boom in the construction activity and shortage of supplies. Sand miners and the building industry have forged close connections with the local and higher level politicians of all parties. This gives them formidable political clout to flout regulations with impunity. The failure of governments to handle these problems thus cannot be attributed to any inherent incapacity. Their willingness and ability to devise and implement strict regulations for dealing with matters that affect diverse and conflicting interest groups is constrained by the unequal capacity of different groups to press their claims on institutions of governance and in the political space.

Note: This paper is based on my paper entitled 'Changes in the Amaravati Basin with Special Reference to Karur' which provides a detailed account of the development of water resources in the Amaravati basin, changing patterns of their use across its different segments, their impact on economy and society in the lower portions of the basin, emerging problems and how they have been managed. Partly due to limitations of length for contributions to this collection, it has been abridged and edited by Professor A. Vaidyanathan with his own additional inputs to highlight the problems of ensuring sustainable, efficient and equitable use of water resources in the light of the Amaravati experience. Thanks are due to him as well as Professor Natraj. This experience is typical of much of water resource planning and management in the country. MIDS Working Paper No.182, "A Gossipmonger's Revisit to Chettipalayam" (2003) by the author provides a more detailed elucidation of the Amaravati experience.

Industry

7 Industrial Development in Tamil Nadu

Vinish Kathuria

Introduction

Tamil Nadu (TN) is the second most industrialised state after Maharashtra accounting for over 11 per cent of India's industrial output. The post-1991 era has witnessed significant investment in the state—both domestic and foreign.[1] The industrial profile of the state indicates that her strength lies not only in traditional industries but also in several modern industries. In other words, the state has a dual industrial structure. TN accounts for nearly 21 per cent in cars, 26 per cent in motorcycles and mopeds, over 27 per cent in heavy commercial vehicles, 30 per cent in auto components, 49 per cent in railway coaches and nearly 50 per cent in power driven pumps of the all-India (AI) output in these segments. All of these are modern and capital intensive. On the other hand, the important traditional industries, where TN has a sizeable share and which also provide significant employment, are cotton yarn (32%), leather products (70%), safety matches (90%)[2] and textiles. Apart from this, TN is number two in software accounting for a 14 per cent share. The two main features of TN industrialisation are: (1) well spread out resources unlike other states like Gujarat, Maharashtra, where they are concentrated in small areas[3] and (2) large number of industries being export-oriented. For instance in 2004-05, TN exported one-third of its industrial output valued at US$ 6.5 billion.[4]

1. In terms of foreign direct investment (FDI), the state is number three after Maharashtra and Delhi (*Source*: *http://www.intamm.com/ industry/business/business.htm*, accessed on May 12, 2006).
2. *Source*: Ibid.
3. *Source*: *www.en.wikipedia.org/wiki/Tamil_Nadu* accessed on May 12, 2006.
4. *Source*: "Tamil Nadu Welcomes Japanese Investors" (*www.tidco.com/tn_policies/slide_show/slideshow.ppt* acccessed December 2006).

However, despite widespread industrialisation, the share of manufacturing is continuously on the decline. Not only is manufacturing's share falling, the organised sector employment is also on the wane. The last few years have witnessed declining performance of some of the traditional sectors also. For instance, cotton textiles and food products registered a negative growth during 2000-2005.

Under this backdrop, this paper looks into the following:

1) The trend of industrialisation in TN in the past two to three decades and contribution of industries to the overall development of the State.
2) Since industrial development does not occur in a vacuum, a well-intentioned policy direction is imperative; the paper then looks into what important policy decisions were taken in the past that navigated the state's industrial development.
3) The next part scrutinises the performance of various vital industries and investigates if there is any change in the pattern of industrialisation since 1991?
4) The late 1990s has also witnessed increasing globalisation; the paper looks into the opportunities and perils of globalisation the state's vital industries face.
5) As indicated above, the state has a dual industrial structure with both labour- and capital-intensive industries contributing their share. The last section investigates what needs to be done so as to cope with globalisation in the newer World Trade Organization (WTO) regime.

Before moving further, it needs to be mentioned that the term 'Industry' generally refers to a number of activities and includes mining, manufacturing, electricity generation and construction. Our analysis, however, is confined mainly to manufacturing activity.

Industrialisation in Tamil Nadu: A Trend

Defining industrialisation is often a daunting task, as many a time competing indicators do not reflect the true impact. For instance, an increase in the number of factories and value of output of manufacturing

Figure 7.1

Gross Value of Output (Current and Constant Prices), No. of Factories and Employment since 1979-80: A Trend

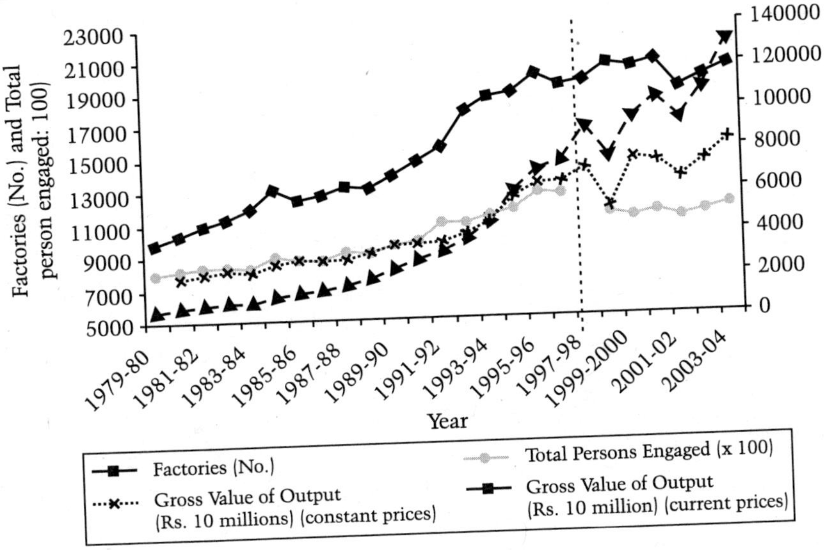

sector is often termed as increased industrialisation. However, if the share of manufacturing sector in the state domestic product (SDP) has increased but with fall in employment in manufacturing, can we still suggest that the state is industrialising? For a state or a country having full employment, this is an example of labour saving industrialisation. However, for any Indian state which has a high unemployment rate, one of the aims of industrialisation should be to reduce unemployment. This is true for TN also, because in 2002-03, the unemployment rate in TN was the third highest in the country.[5] The data indicates that in 1999-2000, TN had an unemployment rate of 12.05 per cent against AI average of 7.32 per cent (Bindhumadhavan, 2004). Keeping all these issues in mind, this section looks into the trend in value of output, employment and share of manufacturing in SDP for TN since 1981-82. Figure 7.1 gives the trend in gross value of output (GVO) (at current and constant prices) and number of factories and persons engaged in these factories since 1980. From the

5. *Source*: Lok Sabha Debates Part II Proceedings other than Questions and Answers (XIII Lok Sabha) *(164.100.24.208/debate/debtext.asp?slno=5804&ser=&smode=)* accessed December 2006.

Table 7.1

Shares of Agriculture, Manufacturing and Services in SDP since 1981 at Constant Prices

Year	*GSDP (₹ Billion)*	*Agriculture Share (%)*	*Industry Share (%)*	*Manufacturing Share (%)*	*Services Share (%)*
1980-81	282.4	26.24	37.91	31.11	35.84
1981-82	312.13	29.39	35.82	29.07	34.78
1982-83	298.99	24.28	38.99	32.32	36.73
1983-84	316.94	27.04	37.31	30.84	35.64
1984-85	355.69	28.14	37.72	31.80	34.14
1985-86	372.4	24.98	36.54	30.36	38.47
1986-87	370.04	25.39	35.50	29.69	39.11
1987-88	393.69	24.10	34.75	28.35	41.15
1988-89	425.11	22.76	38.95	31.17	38.29
1989-90	454.55	23.76	35.11	28.14	41.13
1990-91	487.89	23.03	37.35	28.53	39.62
1991-92	502.29	24.80	33.89	25.65	41.31
1992-93	529.12	24.09	34.51	26.11	41.40
1993-94	574.86	24.12	34.51	26.30	41.37
1994-95	643.63	23.91	35.66	27.29	40.43
1995-96	670.02	19.99	37.53	29.04	42.48
1996-97	703.83	18.85	36.42	27.68	44.74
1997-98	788.93	19.59	33.31	23.46	47.10
1998-99	812.92	20.05	28.93	20.04	51.02
1999-00	844.44	18.23	34.50	24.87	47.27
2000-01	910.11	17.23	34.13	24.25	48.64
2001-02	890.11	17.62	31.62	22.71	50.76
2002-03	917.03	13.35	33.53	23.18	53.12
2003-04	949.60	12.55	31.75	22.09	55.70
2004-05	1032.48	13.28	30.68	21.49	56.04

Notes: Industry comprises: (a) Manufacturing (Registered and unregistered); (b) Mining and Quarrying, (c) Construction; and (d) Electricity, Gas and Water Supply.

GSDP: gross state domestic product.

Source: Central Statistical Organisation (CSO), different years.

Figure, one can see that the gross value of output, number of factories, and total persons engaged in manufacturing had an almost steady growth until 1996-97. However, after that there seems to be a structural change in manufacturing. The (organised sector) employment and the number of

Figure 7.2

Declining Share of Industry and Manufacturing in GSDP in TN

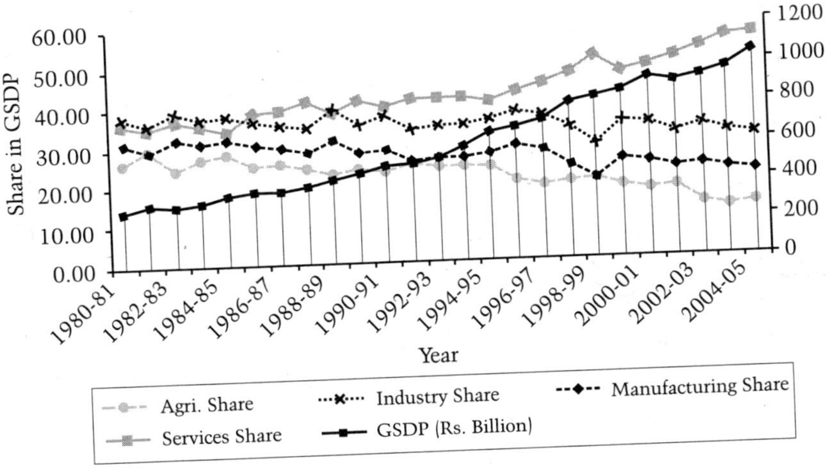

factories have not increased, whereas the GVO at constant 1993-94 prices has shown a wavering pattern.

This declining GVO and almost stagnant number of factories are a pointer towards declining share of manufacturing. Table 7.1 and Figure 7.2 give the share of manufacturing (and agriculture and services) in SDP since 1981. It is evident that the share of manufacturing is on the decline since 1996-97. The TN economy seems to have softened up from 2000-01 onwards with the share of services crossing one-half mark. In the year 2004-05, services contributed nearly 56 per cent to SDP as compared to merely 13 per cent by agriculture and the remaining 31 per cent by industry (of which manufacturing contributed just 22%).

The declining role of industry is apparent from Table 7.2 also, which gives the average annual growth rate of different sectors in the past 24 years (i.e., since 1980) *vis-à-vis* that of GSDP. From the table, it can be seen that of these 24 years, industry and agriculture had a negative growth in 6 and 7 years, respectively, whereas only once services had a negative growth. Figure 7.3, which gives the annual growth rate of different sectors, indicates that barring a 6-year period of 1992-93 to 1998-99, the growth rate of

Table 7.2

Growth Summary of Various Sectors vis-à-vis GSDP since 1981 at Constant Prices

	GSDP	*Agriculture and Allied Services*	*Industry*	*Services*
Annual Average Growth rate	5.6	3.3	5.0	7.7
Years having negative growth	3	7	6	1
Years having negative growth during 1981 to 1990 (first 10 years)	2	2	2	0
Years having negative growth during 1991 to 2000 (next 10 years)	0	3	2	1
Years having negative growth during 2001 to 2005 (last 4 years)	1	2	2	0

Source: Own compilation from CSO.

Table 7.3

Employment in Different Sectors: Agriculture, Manufacturing and Services

	2000 June	*2001 March*	*2004 March*	*2004 December*	*% Change*
Primary sector/Agriculture, Forestry, Fishing, etc.	88,310 (3.5)	87,027 (3.5)	90,300 (4.0)	81,131 (3.6)	-8.1
Secondary/Industry	858,330 (34.2)	860,240 (34.3)	675,240 (29.6)	666,517 (29.5)	-22.3
Manufacturing	687,950 (27.4)	693,850 (27.7)	521,280 (22.8)	519,723 (23.0)	-24.5
Tertiary/Services	1,560,960 (62,2)	1,558,370 (62.2)	1,516,130 (66.4)	1,513,908 (66.9)	-3.0
Total	2,507,590	2,505,637	2,281,670	2,261,556	-9.8

Source: *Quarterly Employment Review*: various quarters (*http://dget.nic.in/publications/welcome.html*).

manufacturing sector has often been of the vacillating type with any rapid increase in growth punctuated by a negative or rapid decline in growth in the following period.

The nearly stagnant gross value of output (Figure 7.1) and declining share of manufacturing (and agriculture) can have a justification if the service sector absorbs most of the labour. Table 7.3 gives the extent of employment in the three sectors in the organised segment since 2000. The

Figure 7.3

Annual Growth in Different Sectors since 1981-82

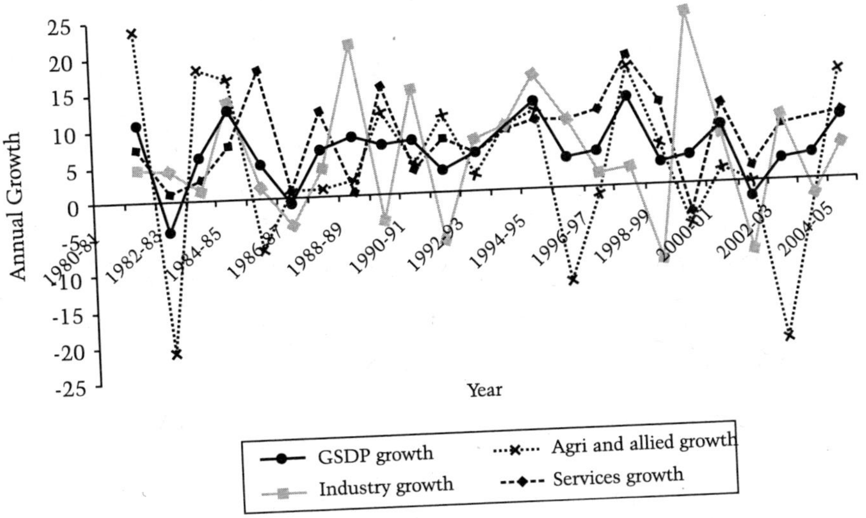

table indicates a very dismal picture as the organised sector employment has fallen in all the three sectors—primary, secondary and tertiary. However, the fall is the maximum in manufacturing sector amounting to nearly one-fourth of the decline. Together with Tables 7.1 and 7.3, it can be easily concluded that of late though the state's income is on the rise contributed mainly by service growth, it is accompanied by a decline in employment in the organised sector.

The following analysis also reinforces the conjecture that the recent increase in the state's income is not from manufacturing output. The correlation between SDP and the value of manufacturing output, which was 0.96 for the period 1981-82 to 1990-91 fell to 0.85 for the next 10 years (i.e., 1991-92 to 2000-01). On the other hand, the correlation between the two has slumped to only 0.61 for the last 10 years (i.e., 1995-96 to 2004-05).

This implies that the contribution has not come from manufacturing and has not resulted in organised sector employment either, but mainly from the unorganised sector employment in services. The only silver lining is that the increased GSDP has also led to increased per capita income

Figure 7.4

PCI versus Gross Value of Manufacturing Output (Constant Prices) since 1981

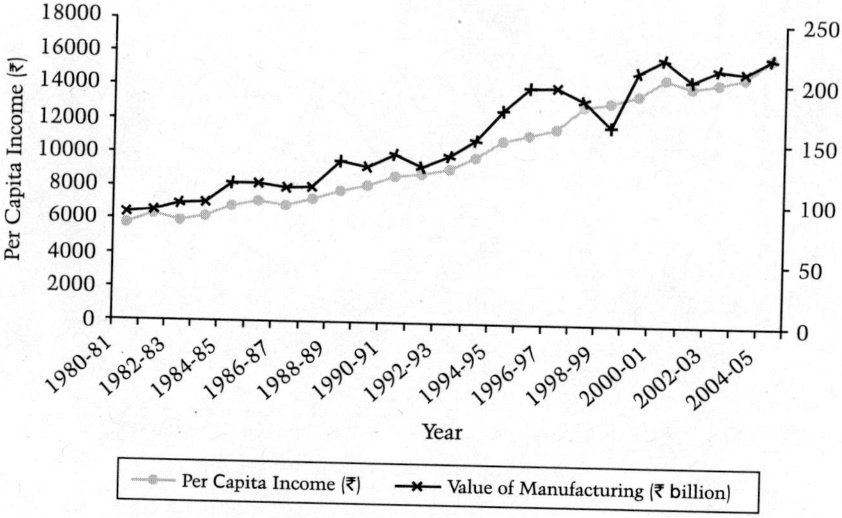

(PCI) as indicated in Figure 7.4. However, if the state is industrialised, for it to have a positive influence on the lives of people, the Gini coefficient, which is a measure of spread of income—a higher value indicating more inequality, should show a declining trend. The data show that the Gini index which was highest in TN in 1983 (37.1) is still highest in 1999 (36.6) with a marginal fall of -1.4 per cent during the 16-year period. Though the inequality has fallen in rural areas, from 36.6 to 28.4 (by 25.4%) during the period, it has increased in the urban areas, from 35.2 to 38.8 (by 9.7%) during the period.[6] In fact, TN has the highest internal inequalities in terms of per capita consumption expenditure for both the periods.[7]

6. *Source: www.tn.gov.in/spc/annualplan/ap2004-05/ch1_1.pdf* accessed December 2006.

7. According to National Sample Survey (NSS) estimates, the two states with the highest Gini coefficients for per capita consumption are TN (with a Gini ratio of 0.398 in 1999-2000) and Maharashtra (with a Gini ratio of 0.345). Incidentally, these two states have the highest per capita SDP in the country (*Source: www.macroscan.com/fet/aug03/fet100803SDP _1.htm* accessed October 10, 2006).

Figure 7.5

PCI and Change in Inter-district PCI at Constant 1993-94 Prices

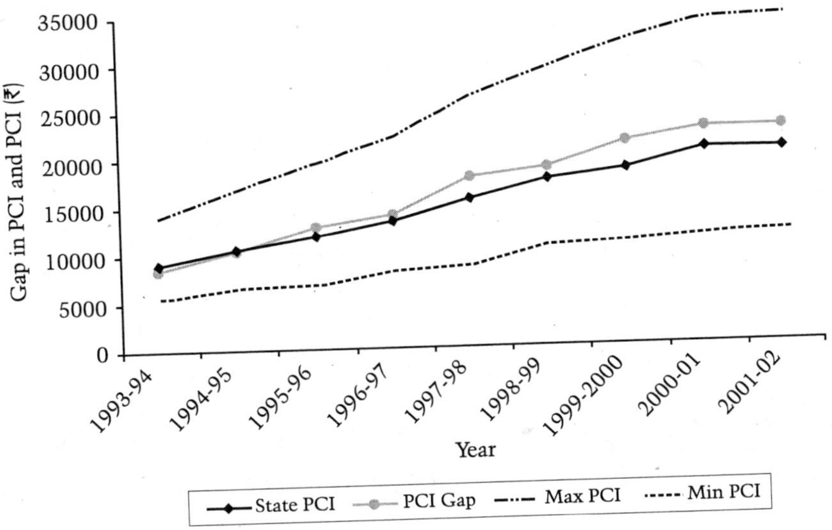

Thus, the higher PCI needs to be viewed with caution. Moreover, if the industrialisation or increased income has impacted the state equally, the inter-district income disparity should show a declining trend. Figure 7.5 gives the PCI gap across districts—i.e., between the maximum and minimum PCI and the average PCI of the state during 1993-94 to 2000-01. From the figure, it can easily be inferred that the inter-district gap is increasing despite increase in PCI implying that the disparities are on the rise. Chennai which had highest PCI in 1993-94, in 2000-01 also, maintains the first position, whereas Villupuram remains the poorest district of the state in these 8 years. In fact, more than two-thirds of the districts are below the state average and their number has increased from 19 to 20 during this period.

Vital Industries and Policy Directions

Policy directions can be of two types: (1) on the broad policy changes like reducing corporate tax or sales tax or allowing FDI and (2) industry specific e.g., for textiles/tanneries/for information technology, etc. These industry-specific policies are often formulated keeping in view the overall importance of the industry for the growth of the state. An industry can be considered vital if it fulfils any of the six conditions: (1) it has widespread linkages; (2) it is viable given the natural resource base; (3) it is feasible given the human capital base; (4) has significant employment generation potential; (5) carries a high weight in the index of state's industrial production (IIP); and (6) generates high exports. It is to be noted that these conditions are not mutually exclusive.

There are a number of industries fulfilling one or more of these conditions. Historically, TN's position has been *numero uno* in leather and cotton textile sectors. Both have generated significant export earnings and facilitated widespread linkages. Of late, in the last 10 years or so, software and automobile industries have spread their wings in the state. Software has gained importance due to the presence of a large number of technical institutes resulting in ready availability of skilled workforce. Similarly, automobile industry could get a foothold in the state due to (1) presence of world class suppliers such as Sundaram Fasteners, Rane Brake Linings, etc., and (2) the available skilled pool of labour. These factors are in addition to relatively better road, power and other infrastructure in the state. The data indicates that in 2001, TN had an infrastructure index of 144 against AI average of 100 and was only third after Punjab and Kerala.[8]

Table 7.4 gives the list of vital industries for TN based on these six conditions. From the table, it is clear that industries like textile, leather, biotechnology, etc., not only have high linkages but have a potential to generate significant employment. Table 7.5 gives the contribution of these industries to exports. These vital industries contribute over 75 per cent of exports from the state. Table 7.6 gives the location of these industries and the linkages generated by these industries. An interesting aspect of TN industrialisation is that many of the industries are in clusters. Table 7.7 indicates that there are 27 major clusters spread out in 13 districts. Chennai, Coimbatore and Virudhunagar house 60 per cent (i.e., 16) of these 27 clusters. Table 7.8 gives characteristics of these clusters in terms of exports, employment, turnover, etc.

---

8. Centre for Monitoring Indian Economy (CMIE) computed the index for different states based on 11 parameters (*Source*: Tamil Nadu Profile *www.small industryindia.com/publications/traderep/sptnadu.pdf* accessed December 2006.

Table 7.4

List of Vital Industries for Tamil Nadu

	Industry Potential (F, B)	Linkages	Feasible for Resource Base	Feasible for Human Capital	Employment Generation Potential	High Weight in IIP	Export Potential	Industry Type
1	Textiles	B	Y	Y	Y	Y	Y	T
2	Leather	B	Y	Y	Y	Y	Y	T
3	Automobiles	B		Y	Y		Y	M
4	IT	F		Y			Y	M
5	Biotechnology	B	Y	Y	Y		Y	M
6	Safety Matches				Y	Y		T
7	Cement		Y					M
8	Pump and Motor cluster	B, F		Y	Y			M
9	Food products	B			Y	Y		T

Notes: IT: Information Technology; Y: Yes; F: Forward, B: Backward; T: Traditional; M: Modern.

Source: Own compilation.

Table 7.5

Exports of Major Products during 1994-95, 1999-2000 and 2000-01

(₹ *Million)*

	Product	*1994-95*	*1999-2000*	*2000-01*
1	Engineering goods	773 (6.2)	2208 (9.2)	2412.3 (7.9)
2	Readymade garments	2881 (23.1)	5425.59 (22.7)	6188.14 (20.2)
3	Leather Products	2477 (19.9)	6952.06 (29.0)	9004.32 (29.4)
4	Plastic Products		199.64 (0.8)	208.89 (0.7)
5	Cotton Textiles	1800 (14.5)	2450 (10.2)	2965.64 (9.7)
6	Marine Products	780 (6.3)	312.58 (1.3)	393.75 (1.3)
7	Software	12 (0.1)	1914 (8.0)	3116 (10.2)
8	Handloom	540 (4.3)		
9	Granites	360 (2.9)		
10	Miscellaneous	2835 (22.8)	4655.13 (19.4)	6346.96 (20.7)
	Total	12454	23937	30636

Notes: Figure in parenthesis gives the exports in percentage. During 1995-96, TN exported US$ 4.6 billion which accounted for 15.7 per cent of AI exports and 63 per cent of the southern region export.

Source: 10th Plan document, Chapter 10 on Tamil Nadu and *www.tidco.com/tn_policies/slide_show / slideshow.ppt* accessed December 2006. For 1994-95 *www.intamm.com/industry/business/ business.htm* accessed December 2006.

Table 7.6

Districts where Vital Industries are Housed

	Industry	Linkages	District
1	Textiles	Cotton Growers	Coimbatore, Chennai,
2	Leather		Chennai, Vellore
3	Automobiles	Auto ancillaries	Chennai, Kanchipuram
4	IT	Manufacturing, Services	Chennai
5	Biotechnology	Pharmaceuticals, Pesticides, Environment	Chennai
6	Safety Matches		Tuticorin, Virudhunagar
7	Cement	Construction	Salem
8	Pump and Motor cluster	Machine tool manufacturer, Component manufacturer	Coimbatore
9	Food products	Agriculture	

Source: Own compilation.

Table 7.7

TN Industrialisation: Number of Clusters by Districts

S. No.	District	Number of Clusters	Clusters
1	Chennai	4	Auto components, Leather Products, Electroplating, Software
2	Coimbatore	7	Diesel Engines, Agricultural Implements, Hosiery, Machine Tools, Castings and Forgings, Power loom, Wet grinding machines
3	Cuddalore	1	Pharmaceuticals
4	Erode	1	PowerBook
5	Karur	1	PowerBook
6	Madurai	3	Readymade Garments, Rice Mills, Dal Mills
7	Namakkal	1	Rigs
8	Salem	2	Starch and Sago
9	Thanjavur	1	Rice Mills
10	Tiruchirappalli	2	Engineering Equipment, Artificial Diamonds
11	Tuticorin	1	Safety Matches
12	Vellore	1	Leather Tanning
13	Virudhunagar	5	Cotton Mills, Tin Container, Printing, Safety Matches and Fire Works, Toilet Soap

Source: Compiled from *http://web5.laghu-udyog.com/clusters/clus/smelist.htm#clus* and other sources.

Table 7.8

Various Clusters in TN (Nov. 2003): Location and Other Characteristics

	District	Location	Product	Large Unit Centred—Vertical/ Horizontal/Both*	Potential for Technology Upgradation	Export Potential	No. of Units in the Cluster@	Employment#	Annual Turnover (₹ Crore)$
1	Chennai	Chennai	Software	B	Medium	High	C	B	A
2	Chennai	Chennai	Auto Components	B	Medium	Medium	D	C	B
3	Chennai	Chennai	Leather Products	B	Medium	High	C	B	A
4	Chennai	Chennai	Electroplating	Vrt	Medium	Low	B	B	A
5	Coimbatore	Coimbatore	Diesel Engines	Hz	Medium	Medium			B
6	Coimbatore	Coimbatore	Agricultural Implements	Hz	Medium	Medium	B		A
7	Coimbatore	Tiruppur	Hosiery	Hz	Medium	High	B	B	A
8	Coimbatore	Coimbatore	Machine Tools	Hz	Medium	High			
9	Coimbatore	Coimbatore	Casting and Forging	Vrt	Medium	Low	D	C	B
10	Coimbatore	Coimbatore, Palladam, Kannam, Palayam	Power loom	Hz	Medium	Medium	C	A	B
11	Coimbatore	Coimbatore	Wet Grinding Machines	Hz	Medium	Medium	D	C	
12	Cuddalore	Cuddalore	Pharmaceuticals	Hz	Medium	High	D	C	B
13	Erode	Surampatti	Power Loom	Hz	Medium	Medium			
14	Karur	Karur	Power Loom	Hz	Medium	Medium			
15	Madurai	Madurai	Readymade Garments	Hz	Medium	Medium			A
16	Madurai	Madurai	Rice Mills	Hz	Medium	Medium	D	C	B
17	Madurai	Madurai	Dal Mills	Hz	Medium	High			
18	Namakkal	Thiruchengode	Rigs	Hz	Medium	Medium			C

contd...

...*contd*...

	District	*Location*	*Product*	*Large Unit Centred—Vertical/ Horizontal/Both**	*Potential for Technology Upgradation*	*Export Potential*	*No. of Units in the Cluster@*	*Employment#*	*Annual Turnover (₹ Crores)$*
19	Salem	Salem	Readymade Garments	B	Medium	High			A
20	Salem	Salem	Starch & Sago	Hz	Medium	Medium	C	A	C
21	Thanjavur	Thanjavur	Rice Mills	Hz	Medium	Medium			C
22	Tiruchirappalli	Tiruchirappalli	Engg. Equipment	B	Medium	Medium			C
23	Tiruchirappalli	Tiruchirappalli (Rural)	Artificial Diamonds	Hz	Medium	High			C
24	Tuticorin	Kovilpathi	Safety Matches	Vrt	Medium	Medium			C
25	Vellore	Ambur, Vaniyambadi, Pallar Valley	Leather Tanning	B	Medium	High	C (Pallar Valley)		
26	Virdhunagar	Rajapalayam	Cotton Mills (Gauge Cloth)	Hz	Medium	Medium	D	B	C
27	Virudhunagar	Virudhunagar	Tin Container	Hz	Medium	Low	D	C	B
28	Virudhunagar	Sivakasi	Printing	Hz	Medium	Low	D		D
29	Virudhunagar	Sivakasi	Safety Matches & Fire Works	B	Medium	Low	C	B	B
30	Virudhunagar	Srivilliputhur	Toilet Soap	Hz	Medium	Low			

Notes: $: Annual Turnover - A: > ₹ 1000 crores; B: 100-1000 crores; C: 10-100 crores; D: <10 crores. # - Level of employment - A: > 100,000; B: 10,000-100,000; C: 1,000-10,000; D: < 1000; @ - Number of Units - A: > 10,000; B: 1,000-10,000; C: 500-1,000; D: 100-500; E: < 100; * - B: Both, Hz: Horizontal, V: Vertical.

Source: *http://web5.laghu-udyog.com/clusters/clus/smelist.htm#clus* and other sources.

Table 7.9

Change in Weights for Different Industries in the IIP Over Time

NIC Code	*Industry*	*1970 base*	*1981-82 base*	*1993-94 base*
23	Cotton Textiles	18.765	13.075	18.4
20-21	Food Products	7.263	10.552	12.406
35-36	M/cry and Equipment other than Transport equipment	17.260	12.863	9.494
31	Rubber, Plastic, Petroleum and Coal products	4.873	17.419	9.404
30	Chemicals and Chemical products	4.366	7.718	8.695
37	Transport Equipment and Parts	12.415	10.939	6.294
29	Leather Products	0	3.379	5.025
26	Textile products other than mills	0	1.348	4.59
	Total for top 8 industries	64.942	77.293	74.308
	Total Manufacturing	81.025	90.426	92.013

Note: NIC - National Industrial Classification.

The above discussion reflects the presence of a strong engineering base in the state involving products ranging from automobiles, bicycles, castings and forgings, to textile machines, electrical and non-electrical machinery, pumps and transportation equipment, engineering ancillary industries. Most of these are concentrated in Chennai (Madras), Coimbatore, Salem and Tiruchi. The strong engineering base consists of a network of nearly 3000 units, employing a skilled workforce of more than 2.5 lakh workers.[9]

As mentioned earlier, the relevance of an industry can also be gauged from the weight it has in the manufacturing sector. Though the weight of different industries has changed often, the 1993-94 base indicates that Textiles (23), Food Products (20-21), Machinery and Equipment other than Transport Equipment (35-36), Rubber, Plastic, Petroleum and Coal Products (31) are the top five industries in the index of production. Table 7.9 indicates the change in the weights over time for the top eight industries with 1993-94 as the base.

Tables 7.4-7.6 indicate that there are a number of important industries facilitating the growth of TN. Barring IT, all are manufacturing industries.

9. *Source: www.tntdpc.com/Tsmes/index.php* accessed December 2006.

A number of policy changes have been introduced in these vital industries. Tables 7.10, 7.11, 7.16, 7.17 and 7.20 summarise these policy changes in the context of Biotechnology, IT, Textile and Leather. Appendix Table A-7.1 gives the policy changes in general. The discussion below gives the background and current status of these industries.

Biotechnology Industry[10]

With 5000 species of flowering plants, 22,500 sq.km of forest cover and a coastline of 1000 km, TN is exceptionally rich in biodiversity. It is estimated that TN accounts for 30 per cent of total bio-resources in India. Pichavaram in Nagapattinam district is one of the three mangrove forests of the country, which are very vital for marine biology. The extensive coral reef systems across TN's southern coastline are often compared with the tropical rainforests in terms of wealth of biodiversity.[11] In order to put this wealth into sustainable use, especially since the market for biotechnology products in the country is expected to double to ₹ 15,000 crores in the next 5 years, an active policy has been formulated.

Table 7.10 gives various policy initiatives taken for the biotechnology industry. TN is the first state to have a Biotechnology policy and has already given an industry status to biotechnology. The state's initiatives have also led to setting up of Biovalleys[12] in TN—i.e., a number of biotechnology parks. These include Biotechnology Incubator Park in Chennai, Women's Biotechnology Park Siruseri (Kelambakkam) near Chennai, Medicinal Plants Biotechnology Park in Madurai (Hill Biotech park), Marine Biotechnology Park in Mandapam and Bioinformatics and Genomics Centre (BGC) in Chennai.

For different biotechnology projects to be commercially feasible, the requirement is for a strong networking of state and global research institutions that would cross-utilise the facilities and avoid 're-inventing the wheel'. This is all the more important for biotechnology industry as the industry is highly capital and knowledge intensive. The collaboration with

---

10. This subsection builds on the 10th Plan chapter on TN (*www.tn.gov.in/spc/tenthplan/CH_10_1.PDF* accessed December 2006).
11. *Source*: Ibid.
12. Biovalley is a term used to indicate formation of clusters to attract biotechnology industry.

Table 7.10

Summary of Policy Changes in Biotechnology Industry

GO and Date	*Policy Pronouncement*
G.O.(2D).No. 30 Dated: 27.5.2005	Tamil Nadu Industrial Investment Corporation (TIIC)—Part II Scheme for the year 2005-06—Financial support to TIIC for conducting seminars/training/Buyer—seller meets in the field of Biotechnology—Orders—Issued.
Nov 2004	TNEB has extended to TICEL the power tariff applicable to R&D institution to promote growth of biotechnology R&D in TN.
Nov. 2004	TICEL Bio Park Ltd (biotechnology incubator park), world class bio-technology park in technical collaboration with Cornell University, USA, at Chennai at a cost of ₹ 625 million, the completed lab space for biotech activities. (TICEL—a hub for Biotech R&D industry in medical biotechnology, nutraceuticals, agriculture biotechnology and bioinformatics.
G.O.Ms.No. 65 Dated: 7.10.2004	Land Acquisition—Kanchipuram District—Chengalpattu *Talukas*—Siruseri Village—S.No.230 etc.—Extent—15.95.5 hectares and Egattur Village-S.No. 85/2 etc. Extent - 4.84.5 hectares of lands proposed to be acquired for SIPCOT-TACID under Section 2 of Section 4 of the Tamil Nadu Industrial Purposes Act 10/99—Form 'E'—Approved and Forwarded.
G.O.Ms.No. 58 Dated: 2.9.2004	Industries—Capital subsidy to New Industrial Units and New Units located in Government promoted industrial parks and approved private industrial parks in terms of the Tamil Nadu New Industrial Policy, 2003—Orders—Issued.
May 2001$	First Biotechnology park exclusively for Women established at Sirsuri near Chennai inside SIPCOT, IT park. Being in Notified Backward Area, all units in the park eligible for Capital Subsidy from TN Government and Central Government.
2000	TN Biotechnology Board a technical-cum-advisory body constituted by Government with Dr M.S. Swaminathan and, eminent scientists and policy planners of state/central Governments to streamline the biotech activities in the state and also formulate/make amendments in the state biotechnology policies from time to time.
G.O.Ms.No.318 Dated: 12.09.2000	Biotechnology Policy of Tamil Nadu 2000—Issued.
1999	₹ 67 million women's biotechnology park created at Chennai in 20 acres.

Source: *http://www.ticelbiopark.com/aboutus.html*; and $: *www.biospectrumindia.com/content/BioSpecial/10508161.asp.*

Cornell University for Biotechnology Incubator Park in Chennai is a step in this direction.

The State Government has already committed a ₹ 30 crore venture fund to provide the single-window clearance facility from the various

Central Government Agencies, such as the Recombinant DNA Advisory Committee, the Institutional Biosafety Committee, the Review Committee on Genetic Manipulation and the Genetic Engineering Approval Committee, and to establish biotechnology enterprises. A Biotechnology Board has already been created, under the chairmanship of an expert, consisting of senior government officials, scientists and industrialists. The Board has constituted standing advisory committees to identify and attract investments, mobilise resources, work out guidelines and set up a regulatory framework for the use of bio-resources. Schemes are being worked out to protect and develop various biosphere resources, such as the Gulf of Mannar off Rameswaram, the Pichavaram mangroves in Nagapattinam district and Muthupettai in Tiruvarur district. In this context, it is important to note that the Global Environmental Facility (GEF) has announced an assistance of $7.85 million to protect the Gulf of Mannar.

Unfortunately, industrial activity has so far been confined largely to first generation biotechnology enterprises such as fermentation of antibiotics. To broaden the industrial base, a large number of plant tissue culture units are being set up besides efforts to promote the production of food and industrial enzymes, classical fermentation products (antibiotics and immuno-modulators), bio-energy and bio-polymers, and other such activities.

According to the policy document, all efforts are directed towards the creation of a critical mass of industrial activity in biotechnology. The policy document has emphasised the need to evolve a two-pronged strategy so as to encourage modern processes in the areas of agriculture, industry and medical and veterinary sciences together with focusing on traditional biotechnology products, especially industrial and food enzymes. There is also a move to encourage commercial enterprises to develop recombinant DNA (deoxyribonucleic acid)—based products and bioinformatics.

In the field of medical biotechnology (the state accounts for 11 per cent of the market in the country), the focus is on such areas as diagnostics, vaccines (hepatitis-C and malaria), therapeutics (interferon and insulin) and veterinary drugs. In the field of agriculture, the Government plans to work with the germplasm data available with the Tamil Nadu Agricultural University and the M.S. Swaminathan Research Foundation

Table 7.11

Summary of Policy Changes for IT Industry

Year	*Policy Announcement*
G.O 11 Dated 25-10-2005	Information Technology Enabled Services (ITES) Policy of Tamil Nadu 2005—Orders issued (all incentives offered in IT Policy 2002 shall be applicable to ITES sector also).
G.O 6 Dated 29-06-2005	Information Technology Act, 2000 (Central Act 21 of 2000)—Computers, Systems and Networks—Declared as a protected system - Orders issued.
G.O 15, 29-04-2005	Coimbatore IT Park—Constitution of District Executive Committee to oversee the further Development of Coimbatore IT Park—Orders issued.
G.O 14, 19-04-2005	Constitution of State Apex Committee, State e-Governance Group (SEG) and Department e-Governance Group (DEG) to Implement National e-Governance Action Plan (NeGAP)—Orders issued.
G.O 4, 18-04-2005	Establishment of Knowledge Data Centre at Anna University in Collaboration with M/s. Sun Microsystems and 50 engineering colleges—Administrative Sanction—issued.
G.O (2D) 13, 27-12-2004	Guidelines for availing 30% subsidy to SMEs on stall rent for participation in international/national exhibitions—Orders issued.
G.O 18, 05-11-2004	IT Policy of Tamil Nadu 2002—Date of effect of IT Policy—Orders issued.
G.O (D) 2, 03-02-2004	Appointment of an International consultant for Positioning in Chennai/TN as the most preferred state for IT investments—refloating the tender—Orders issued.
G.O 39, 23-12-2003	Setting up of Software Technology Park (STP) at Hosur—Conduct of feasibility study—Appointment of Consultant—Sanction of ₹ 4.00 lakhs—Orders issued.
G.O 31, 18-11-2003	Setting up of Tamil Nadu State Wide Area Network (TNSWAN)—Orders issued.
G.O (D) 10, 29-11-2002	Formation of Expert Committee for evaluating options between Open Source Software or Proprietary Source Software—Orders issued.
19-09-2002	IT Policy 2002.
G.O 13, 16-08-2002	Designation of Electronics Corporation of TN (ELCOT) as Certifying Authority for utilising additional Floor Space Index (FSI) Permission from CMDA—Orders issued.
G.O 12, 31-07-2002	Electronic Delivery of Services (EDS) – Constitution of Steering Committee for implementation of EDS Project—Orders issued.
G.O 03, 06-06-2002	Permission to provide Optic Fibre Cable connectivity network within the premises and the buildings under the control of Government Offices—Orders issued.
G.O 2, 01-04-2002	Setting up of Base Transreceiver Station Towers and installation of equipment for tele-communication networks—Leasing of space in govt. offices on a non-exclusive basis to any licensed telecom company on certain prescribed terms and conditions—Orders issued.
G.O 16, 16-08-2001	ELCOT—Works done by ELCOT in respect of Tamil in Information Technology—Transfer to Tamil Virtual University (TVU)—Orders issued.

contd...

...contd...

Year	*Policy Announcement*
G.O 14, 24-07-2001	State IT Task Force and its Sub-Committee—Disbanded—Setting up of a State Level TN IT Council and an Executive Committee of TN IT Council—Orders.
G.O 30, 27-03-2001	GO of Planning and Development Department on Geographic Information System (GIS).
G.O 7, 12-02-2001	Communication Infrastructure—Use of public right of way for laying optic fibre cables—Consolidated policy guidelines for grant of permission issued.
G.O 24, 20-09-2000	Establishment—IT Department—sanction of a temporary post of Adviser to the Chief Minister on IT and e-Governance and appointment to the post—Orders issued.
July 2000	Establishment of Software Technology Park (TIDL) at Taramani, near Chennai.
G.O 10, 04-05-2000	Use of Public right of way for laying optic fibre cables—guidelines for grant of permission.
24-04-2000	Grant of exemption to the Software Industries in TN from the provisions of Chapter II of the TN shops and Establishments Act, 1947.
G.O 35, 29-10-1999	Allotment of Land to Electronics Corporation of Tamil Nadu Limited for promoting the growth of IT Industries in Tamil Nadu.
Letter No 2267, 06-07-1999	Software companies (including services and training) in TN are assured of uninterrupted power supply, and exempted from Pollution Control regulations, Factories Act and Chapter II of the TN Shops and Establishment Act (*www.elcot.com/sinotification.htm*).
G.O 20, 21-06-1999	Grant of Stamp Duty Concessions to units in the private Sector IT Parks.
G.O 48, 01-03-1999	G.O—Revision of Tariff on supply of Energy for IT Industries.
18.02.1999	Exemption in Stamp Duty for IT Parks and STPs.
G.O 160, 25-05-1998	Development of land and building for the purposes to accelerate the growth of IT.
1997	Comprehensive IT policy announced.
03.11.1997	Continuous Power supply for IT industries.

Source: * *http://www.tn.gov.in/gorders/IT/default.htm*

to develop biopesticides and biofertilisers, natural health care products, animal feed, transgenics and diagnostics. The Government has already created quarantine facilities and sanitary/phytosanitary measures as per the WTO agreements for biological items.

Information Technology

TN has put special emphasis on IT industry and that too mainly on the software sector as indicated in Table 7.11. This is primarily because of two reasons: (1) the state distinctly enjoying a large pool of highly skilled technical manpower[13] and (2) of late Bangalore losing its sheen due to (i) increased costs and infrastructure bottlenecks and (ii) high attrition rates. As of now, TN is the number two IT exporting state in the country. The state has experienced a 25 per cent growth in software and hardware exports during 2004-05 crossing for the first time the ₹ 10,000 crores mark against ₹ 7,622 crores in 2003-04 and has contributed to 17 per cent of the country's IT exports. The item-wise exports indicate that application and system software has topped the list at 60 per cent, next were consultancy services at 28 per cent and ITES at 8 per cent.

It is to be noted that IT has three distinctive components—software, hardware and ITES. ITES include medical transcription, legal database processing, back office operations, call centres, business process outsourcing, insurance claim processing, etc. In October 2005, the state came up with ITES policy (Table 7.11), and the Hardware Policy is still in preparation.

Learning from the bottleneck and infrastructural needs of the industry and example of Bangalore, an interesting aspect of TN IT and ITES policy is spreading the opportunities and employment to Tier II cities like Coimbatore, Hosur, Madurai, Tirunelveli, etc. The spreading is showing dividends as in 2003-04, Coimbatore exported software and IT-related services to the value of ₹ 100 crores.

Since IT and Biotechnology are idea-driven industries and entail high risk and return, entrepreneurs often lack resources to put these ideas into practice. To fill this gap of finance and felt need, earlier the Tamil Nadu Industrial Development Corporation Ltd. (TIDCO) in association with Infrastructure Leasing & Finance Services (IL&FS) set up venture capital funds, namely 'Tamil Nadu Infotech Fund' and assisted seven units.[14]

Automobile Industry

TN is the home of major automobile companies and is called the Detroit of South Asia. The state has a number of mother automobile plants like Ashok Leyland, Tractors and Farm Equipment (TAFE), Heavy Vehicle

---

13. It is estimated that the state churns out nearly 79,000 engineers and 58,500 diploma holders every year in different engineering fields (*Source*: *Economic Appraisal, Tamil Nadu 2003-04: 67*).

14. *Source*: *www.tn.gov.in/policynotes/archives/policy2004-05/ind2004-05-2.htm* accessed December 2006.

Table 7.12

Component-wise Production Capacity Share (%) in India

Share	*Items (No.)*	*Components*
>50%	19	Inlet and exhaust valves, valve guides, valve tappets, fuel pumps (petrol), oil pump assembly, thermostat, timing chain, water pump assembly, starter motors, alternators, camshafts, oil seals, brake linings, wiper motors, air brake assembly, engines
30–50%	17	Fuel pump nozzle holders, voltage regulators, flywheel magnetos, steering gears (mechanical and power), wheel rims, electric horns, dashboard instruments
10–30%	10	Fuel pump nozzle and elements, delivery valves, crankshafts, bi-metal bearings, fuel injection pumps, radiators, clutch assembly, clutch plates, shock absorbers, automotive tyres and seats
<10%	7	

Source: *www.tidco.com/tn_policies/slide_show/slideshow. ppt*, accessed December 2006.

Table 7.13

Major Cement Plants, Location and their Installed Capacity in Million Tonnes (2004-05)

Sl. No.	*Name of Cement Company*	*Location*	*Installed Capacity*
1	ACC Ltd.	Madukkarai	0.96
2	Grasim Industries Ltd.	Reddipalayam	1.03
3	The India Cements Ltd.	Tulaiyuth	1.55
4	The India Cements Ltd.	Sankaridurg	0.72
5	The India Cements Ltd.	Trichy	1.30
6	The India Cements Ltd.	Alangulam	0.40
7	Tamil Nadu Cements Corp. Ltd.	Ariyalur	0.50
8	Madras Cements Ltd.	R.S. Raja Nagar	0.75
9	Madras Cements Ltd.	Alathiyur	3.12
10	Chettinad Cement Corporation Ltd.	Karur	0.60
11	Chettinad Cement Corporation Ltd.	Karikalli	1.20
12	Dalmia Cements (B) Ltd.	Dalmiapuram	1.23
13	UltraTech Cement Ltd. (G)	Arakonam	1.20
		Total	14.56

Source: *http://www.cmaindia.org/industry.html*, accessed December 2006.

Factory, Integral Coach Factory, Enfield, TVS, etc., each of them supporting a large number of auto ancillaries in small and medium enterprises (SME) sector. With the setting up of three car projects by Ford, Hyundai and HM-Mitsubishi and with expansion of TAFE and Ashok Leyland, TN's position has been strengthened as a major hub. A large number of new ancillaries with foreign collaborations have also come up as a result of these projects. Consequently, a significant 35 per cent of India's auto component production comes from nearly 110 ancillaries in Chennai. TN's current annual output in the automotive sector is estimated to be $3-3.5 billion with an estimated share of 25 per cent in the Indian automotive industry and its contribution to the state's GSDP is 7-8 per cent. The share of TN in manufacturing of car, heavy commercial vehicles, auto components and railway coaches was 21 per cent, 33 per cent, 35 per cent and 50 per cent, respectively, in 2001.[15]

For a number of auto components, the contribution of Chennai auto industry is more than half. Table 7.12 gives the share of the component industry for different items. Visteon is the largest component manufacturer of India located in Chennai. The data show that over 50 per cent of the component manufacturers have International Organization for Standardization (ISO) certification and more than one-fourth (26%) are Quality Service (QS) certified. The quality of these component manufacturers is reinforced from the following facts. Sundaram Clayton is one of the five firms outside Japan that has won Deming Prize for quality. Similarly, Sundaram Fasteners has won General Motors (GM) Supplier of the Year award for the 5th consecutive time in 2004-05.

The State Government intends to transform the state into one of the top three manufacturing hubs for automotive and auto ancillary in Asia by 2015. According to a recent Confederation of Indian Industry (CII) report, the sector has a potential to generate an additional 5 lakh jobs in the next 10 years. On the basis of this report, the state is aiming to achieve an output of $18 billion in automotives with an employment of 6 lakh people by 2015. As of now, the sector employs 80,000 people. To achieve this growth, TN needs investments of $5 billion in the automotive sector in

---

15. *Source*: ACMA (Automotive, Components Manufacturers' Association) and CMIE as referred in *www.tn.gov.in/spc/tenthplan/CH_10_1.PDF—10th Plan chapter on TN accessed* December 17, 2006.

the next 10 years to expand the existing capacities; the CII reports indicate that 60-70 per cent of this would have to be from global multinational companies (MNCs) and the balance from Indian companies (CII, 2005). In fact, part of the investment can be obtained from venture funds. Earlier also TIDCO in collaboration with IL&FS assisted eight units by creating 'India Auto Ancillary Fund'.

Cement Industry

Cement is one of the main industries in TN and is ranked 4th in India. The state is endowed with good limestone deposits—the main raw material for cement manufacture. The prospects for the industry are high, especially in the next 5-10 years, due to: (1) ongoing work on the golden quadrilateral project joining the four metros through road; (2) spur in construction activities caused by the entry of MNCs; and (3) the fall in input costs due to recent policy promulgations of mandating utilisation of fly ash in cement manufacture.

TN produced 12.29 million tonnes (mt) of cement in 2003-04 which was 10.46 per cent of total cement produced in the country. The capacity of the cement industry was 14.56 mt in 2003-04, which is 9.95 per cent of the entire cement industry capacity of India. In terms of cement consumption, TN consumed 9.10 mt of cement in 2003-04. There are 13 major cement firms in the state. Table 7.13 gives the location of these plants and the installed capacity for the year 2004-05.

Table 7.14

Difference in Processes and Raw Material Use in Various Textile Segments

	Mill	*Power loom*	*Hosiery/Knitwear*	*Handloom*
1 Intensity of Operation	Capital	Semi-capital	Semi-labour	Labour
2 Nature of operation	Centralised	Decentralised	Decentralised	Decentralised as household unit
3 Raw material	Natural and Man-made fibre	Cotton and non-cotton yarn	Cotton and non-cotton yarn	All natural fibres
4 Predominant Process	Spinning	Weaving	Knitting	Hand weaving
5 Technique	Spindles, looms, shuttle looms	Shuttle looms	Knitting machine	Hand looms
6 Operation for	Spinning and weaving	Fabric requirement	Inner garments	

Source: Adapted from *www.unido.org/file-storage/download/?file_id=41692*, accessed January 2007.

Table 7.15

Textile Sector of Tamil Nadu and All India (AI): A Comparison

Sector	No. of Units		Output/ Production		Employment (lakh)	
	TN	AI	TN	AI	TN	AI
1 Handloom	2.11 lakhs$		108.326 mn meter		11.64	120
2 Power loom	4 lakh	16.66 lakh	103.72 mn meter			
3 Textile Mills	1729#	2939	1164.80 mn kg. spun yarn	3065.26 mn kg spun yarn	2.21	
4 Garment and Hosiery Sector	2900*	6000			1.5	36
5 Processing	2500 hand & 757 power processing@					

Notes: $: 2.11 lakh handlooms functioning in 1247 handloom weavers co-operative societies—1169 are cotton weavers societies and 78 silk weavers societies. Handloom weavers co-operative societies mostly exist in rural and semi-urban areas, where there is large concentration of handloom weavers; #: This includes 18 co-operative spinning mills, 13 national textile corporation mills and 20 composite mills; *: Located in Tiruppur; @: Of these 757 power processing units, 531 units, are processing knitted fabrics.

Source: Tamil Nadu (2005), Census of Handlooms (1995-96).

Textile Industry

Textile industry since the advent of industrialisation in India is holding a prominent place in the economy. Indian textile industry employs 35 million people[16] and accounts for nearly one-quarter of the country's exports. The industry is relevant for TN economy because of three important reasons: (1) its contribution to industrial output—cotton textiles and textile products together account for nearly 23 per cent weight; (2) employment generation—together with handloom and power loom sector, the employment provided by the industry is to the tune of nearly 1.4 million; and lastly (3) the top-most earner of foreign exchange (Table 5).

The industry has four pillars: (1) mill or spinning segment, (2) handloom segment, (3) power loom and (4) garment segment. TN is the leading producer of cotton, spun and non-cotton yarn in the country and provides large-scale employment to rural population, second only to agriculture. More importantly, the industry provides employment to women. Of the four pillars, handloom is responsible for the bulk of employment. Power loom industry in the state meets the clothing needs of

16. Of these, 12.4 million are in handloom segment (Tadaka, 2005).

Table 7.16

Summary of Policy Changes in Textiles Industry

GO No. and Date	*Abstract*
	Technology Upgradation Fund Scheme (TUFS) for Textile and Jute industries extended up to end of 10th Five-Year Plan (FYP), i.e., 31.03.2007. Main feature of this scheme is reimbursement of 5 per cent point on interest charged by lending agency on a project of technology upgradation.
2004-05	Textile cluster at Tiruppur granted by GOI at a project cost of 143.50 crores with central assistance of 50.00 crore.
	Establishment of Power loom service centre—a one-stop shop for training to weavers, testing facilities, design development, technical consultancy and dissemination of information about modernisation of looms.
G.O.Ms.No.47, Dated 31.7.2003	Handloom Industry—Low Cost Sarees and Dhoties Scheme, fixation of procurement rate and selling price of sarees, dhoties and salwar kameez sets
G.O.Ms.No.127, Dated 27.11.2002	Handloom Industry—Low Cost Sarees and Dhoties Scheme to give alternative employment to 15000 handloom weavers—Orders issued
G.O.Ms.No.74, Dated 30.07.2002	Handloom Industry—Distribution of Dhoties and Sarees Scheme for the year 2001-2002 and 2002-2003—Distribution of dhoties and sarees—Alternative employment to the weavers under the Scheme—Orders issued
G.O.Ms.No.72, Dated 27.04.2000	Weavers Cooperative Societies—TN Cooperative Handloom Weavers Savings and Security (TNCHWSS) Scheme—Enhancement of Insurance coverage from ₹ 40,000 to ₹ 50,000.
G.O.Ms.No.73, Dated 27.04.2000	Handloom Industry—TNCHWSS Scheme—Enhancement of Pension to the weaver members from ₹ 150 to ₹ 200 per month.
G.O.Ms.No.79, Dated 19.04.1999	Weavers Cooperative Societies—TN Cooperative Handloom Weavers Savings and Security Scheme—Enhancement of Insurance coverage from ₹ 35,000 to ₹ 40,000.
G.O.Ms.No.153, Dated 16.06.1998	Handlooms—Development of Handloom Industries—Constitution of State Level Advisory Committee.
G.O.Ms.No.114, Dated 02.06.1998	Weavers Cooperative Societies—TN Cooperative Handloom Weavers Insurance Scheme—Implementation of 'Self Insurance Scheme'—Enhancement of Insurance coverage from ₹ 25,000 to ₹ 35,000.
No.92, 12.05.1998	Handloom Industry—Rebate Scheme—Revised Orders.
No.35, 17.03.1998	Textile Policy of Tamil Nadu 1998.

Source: *http://www.tn.gov.in/hhtk/dht/dht-schemes.htm*, accessed October 25, 2006, and *http:// www.tn. gov.in/hhtk/handloom-textiles-2002-03.htm* and *http://www.unido.org/file-storage/download/?file_id=41692, accessed* January 2007.

the people by producing a wide variety of cloth—both grey and processed. The sector along with handloom and garment segments also contributes significantly to the export earnings of the country. Table 7.14 gives the share of these four pillars in the total output of the country, and Table 7.15

tabulates the basic differences in the raw material use and process involved for these pillars. Table 7.16 lists some of the policy initiatives in the textile industry.

Mill Segment

Out of 2049 large and medium textile mills in India, 893 (44%) mills are located in TN. Similarly, out of 1146 small units in India, 904 (79%) are located in TN. Thus, out of 3195 large, medium and small spinning mills in India, 2039 (64%) are located in TN. The spinning capacity of the state is 15.66 million spindles with a labour force of about 2.21 lakhs.[17] The state produces over 1164 million kg of spun yarn per annum, which amounts to over one-third of the total production of spun yarn (3081.37 million kg) in the country. The comparison at AI level shows that TN during 2003-04 accounted for 46.47 per cent of total textile mills, 41.14 per cent of installed spinning capacity, 38.42 per cent of yarn production and 19.96 per cent of workers employed, but only 7.73 per cent of looms installed and 4.68 per cent of cloth produced. This implies that the mills in TN are more geared towards the raw material, not the finished clothes.

The state contributes more than 22 per cent of the country's exports of cotton yarn and fabrics. The cotton textile export (including ready-made garments, RMG) in 2000-01 was US$ 2.2 billion.[18] The two main textile centres are Tiruppur and Chennai. The USA, the UK, France and Germany are among the principal buyers of cotton textiles from TN. Tiruppur housing 700 odd job working units (in knitting cloth and post-knitting operations) has emerged strongly as a major industrial township. As a consequence, several important spin-off industries have emerged in neighbouring regions—the textile machinery industry is one such offshoot.

The 893 large and medium textile mills include 18 co-operative Spinning Mills, 17 National Textile Corporation Mills and 23 composite mills.[19] Thus, most textile mills are managed by the private sector. The 18 co-operative spinning mills were started between 1958 and 1985 with the

---

17. *Source: http://www.tn.gov.in/hhtk/dht/dht-textile.htm accessed* in October 2006.
18. *Source*: *10th Plan*, chapter 10 (*www.tn.gov.in/spc/tenthplan/CH_10_1.PDF accessed* in October 2006).
19. *Source*: Same as 17.

objective of providing uninterrupted supply of quality hank yarn to the co-operative handloom weavers at reasonable rates. The installed capacity of 4.69 lakhs spindles has since been downsized to 2.86 lakhs spindles.

Handloom Segment

Handloom sector is the single largest cottage industry of the state providing employment to a large number next only to agriculture and facilitating in foreign exchange earnings. The data indicate that the segment and its related economic activities provide employment to over 4.29 lakhs weaver households and 11.64 lakhs weavers.

The exact number of working handlooms in TN is difficult to specify, as different estimates exist. The 1987 Handloom Census puts the figure as 4.27 lakhs handlooms. According to Roy (1999), there were 1.5 lakh handlooms at work around late 1990s. The TN Government official website puts the number at 2.83 lakhs. These handloom owners are members of about 1354 handloom weavers co-operative societies in the state and most of these societies are affiliated to the Apex Level (TN) Handloom Weavers' Co-operative Society Ltd. popularly known as Co-Optex.[20]

The average annual production of various handloom products through the handloom weavers is around ₹ 500 crores. Out of this, 35 per cent is being procured by Co-Optex through its various showrooms in the country and the rest about 65 per cent is being sold by weavers' societies through other means. Recently 'Loom World' came into existence to strengthen the marketing of handloom products in the state by establishing a few showrooms at Chennai, Erode and Coimbatore.

To protect handloom weavers and the handloom industry from the power looms, the Government of India (GoI) has enacted Handlooms (Reservation of Articles for Production) Act 1985 and Hank Yarn Obligation Act (1985) for implementation by all the states in the country. According to these acts, GoI reserved 22 items exclusively for Small Scale Industry (SSI) and specified that spinning mills have to provide 50 per cent of their yarn at reasonable prices for handloom production. In 1996, the GoI reduced

20. *Source: http://www.tn.gov.in/hhtk/dht/dht-handloom.htm* accessed October 2006.

Table 7.17

Handloom Development Schemes Implemented by the Department

	Scheme	*Activity*
1	Rebate Subsidy	20% rebate is provided by the Govt. of TN on the sale of handloom cloth throughout the year
2	Free Supply of Uniform to school children from Std I to Std VIII in the state under Noon Meal Programme	'Co-optex' implements this scheme with the help of handloom weavers' societies by producing and procuring material.
3	Deen Dayal Hathkargha Protsahan Yojana (Scheme) (GoI)	Subsidy is given by both Central and State Governments towards margin money assistance, supply of new looms and accessories, providing infrastructure facilities, training, designs, publicity and marketing incentive or rebate.
4	Enforcement of Handloom (Reservation of Articles for Production) Act, 1985	To protect the interest of the Handloom weavers, a separate Enforcement Wing with headquarters at Chennai and 5 field level offices at Madurai, Salem, Tiruchengode, Erode and Tiruppur established.*
5	Interest Subsidy Scheme	Under the Scheme, the Primary Weavers Cooperative societies are provided with Working Capital finance at normal rate of interest with the interest subsidy of 3 per cent being directly paid by the Government to the Primary Weavers Cooperative Societies.
6	90 per cent Loss Guarantee Scheme	GoI introduced '90% Loss Guarantee Scheme' in 1956 to provide guarantee cover to Cooperative Central Banks and to offset the losses arising out of non-recovery of loans (working capital loan) advanced by them to Handloom Weavers Cooperative Societies under Reserve Bank of India (RBI) Handloom Finance Scheme.
		The claims under the scheme are in sequence to the guarantee given by the TN Government in respect of Cash Credit sanctioned to the Primary Weavers Cooperative Societies and Co-optex.

Note: * During the year 2001-02, 42,366 power looms were inspected.

Source: Same as in Table 7.16.

the number of items reserved to 11.[21] These include: (1) sarees, (2) *dhoties*, (3) towel, *gamcha* and *angavastram* (4) *lungi*, (5) *khes*, bedsheet, bedcover, counterpane, Furnishing (including tapestry, upholstery), (6) *jamakkalam durry* or *durret*, (7) dress materials, (8) barrack blankets, *kambal* or

21. Studies indicate that this measure and measures such as the Hank Yarn Obligation Act (1985) had limited success. See for example, Mazumdar (2005) as referred in Action Aid (2005).

Kamblies, (9) shawl, *loi*, muffler, *pankhi*, etc., (10) wollen tweed and (11) *chaddar*, *mekhala/phanek*. Table 7.17 provides information on some of these policy initiatives.

Power Loom Segment[22]

Power Looms are small-scale weaving factories with 10-20 looms each that not only weave but also perform spinning and processing in the same premises. The small economies of scale and hence the absence of indivisible inputs make them labour intensive. The power loom industry in TN dates back to 1960s with cotton greys, but the real growth along with high exports took place in early 1990s. They are the main suppliers of fabrics to garment exporters. According to SITRA (South Indian Textile Research Association), 38 per cent of looms employ grey cotton and the remaining 62 per cent coloured cotton. Grey cotton cloth is an intermediate good which can be used for a variety of uses after processing—garment for local and export markets and fabric for local and export markets. Coloured garments are primarily for home market with a fringe for exporting.

It is to be noted that the region specializes in cotton weaving because it has a strong advantage in the main raw material, i.e., cotton yarn. Apart from availability of cotton yarn, acute scarcity of water and consequent limited scale of processing are other reasons for high proportion of cotton weaving in the state. Though there are a few large process-houses in the state, those that exist were set up mainly by spinning mills and are located where water is relatively easily available—Erode on the Kaveri and Madurai on the Vaigai. With such constraints, only about 30-40 per cent of fabric is processed locally. The rest is either grey fabrics sold as grey or designed by means of the drop-box, dobby or jacquard. Grey cotton is mainly purchased by merchants from Northern or Western India who process it in their states.

TN has a quarter of the total number of power looms in India and possibly over half of them are engaged in cotton (Roy, 1999). Unlike the number of handlooms, the exact number of power looms in TN is less contentious. According to Roy (1999), the number of power looms in mid-1990s was around 4-4.5 lakhs. Recent survey-based estimates put the

---

22. This section builds on Roy (1999) and *www.texmin.nic.in/tnpl.pdf*, accessed on December 20, 2006.

number of registered power looms in the state at 4.37 lakhs as on August 2002 with an estimated employment of 7 lakh people, of which 5.5 lakhs are involved in weaving alone.[23] An important aspect of power looms in TN is their role in vitalizing the rural economy as they are distributed in 15 districts and six major urban-rural clusters. Of these six clusters, the two largest are near the nodal towns—Coimbatore and Erode, with each of these clusters containing nearly 1.5 lakhs looms. The three other smaller clusters are around Karur, Salem and Rajapalayam towns with each containing 30-50,000 looms. Table 7.18 gives the estimated number of power looms from different sources. Due to recession in the late 1990s, the recent estimates indicate mortality in the segment with the number in registered power looms declining only to 3.20 lakh (Roy, 1999).

There are 142 Power Loom Weavers Co-operative Societies covering 24,000 looms. The annual turnover of these societies is around ₹ 20.00 crore. These societies produce all types of grey bleached dyed gadas, printed sarees, lungies, bedsheets, furnishings, pillow covers, blended dhothies and sarees etc.

Garment or Knitwear segment

Tiruppur also called the T-city or Banian (local term for vest) city is the town in TN that has been a centre for knitwear and the largest exporter of cotton knitwear from the country. The total export turnover from Tiruppur, according to Tiruppur Exporters Association's data, is to the tune of US$ 500 million per year which accounts for about 85 per cent of cotton knitwear exports from India (Neetha, 2002). The first unit in Tiruppur was set up in 1925, but the growth of the industry was slow until independence. In 1942, 34 units were engaged in production of knitwear (Manthagini, 1983 as referred in Neetha, 2002). All these units were composite mills and the production was carried out in the same unit. By 1961, the number of units rose to 230 and till early 1970s, the industry catered only to the domestic market. These units were mostly composite mills without any subcontracting systems of production. It was in the mid-1980s, that the GoI specifically targeted the segment for export promotion (Jha, 2005). Along with the expansion of the export market, the composite mill-based

23. *Source: texmin.nic.in/tnpl_exe_sum.pdf*, accessed on December 20, 2006.

Table 7.18

Number of Power Looms in Different Clusters in Tamil Nadu in Mid-1990s and 2001

	Power Loom Cluster	*Power Looms (No. in lakhs)*		*Type of Cloth Processed*	*Sub-clusters*	*District of Sub-cluster*
		Mid-1990s	*2001$*			
1	Coimbatore	1.50	1.40	Greys	Palladam, Tiruppur, Somanur and Avanashi	Coimbatore
2	Erode	1.50	1.07	Coloured goods	Bhavani, Komarapalayam, Pallipalayam and Chennimalai	Erode, Namakkal, Dharmapuri
3	Karur	0.3-0.5	0.28	Finishing cloth with woven designs (home textile products)	Vellakovil/Kangeyam Mulanur/Muthur	Karur/Erode
4	Salem	0.3-0.5	1.17	Yarn dyed fabrics	Elampillai, Omalur, Vembadithalam, Jalakantapuram, Tharamangalam, Edapdi, Attayampatti, Rasipuram, Tiruchengode	Salem, Tiruchengode
5	Rajapalayam/ Madurai	0.3-0.5	0.23	Exportable gauge cloth	Sankarankovil, Rajapalayam, Virudhunagar, Jakkampatti	Madurai, Ramnad, Virudhunagar, Tirunelveli
6	Chennai	@	0.23	Dyed *Lungi*, Saree, Shirting	Thiruvallur, Kancheepuram, Kurinjipadi, Prodatturpet Chennai, Thiruvallur, Kancheepuram, North Arcot	

Note: @ – Not available.

Source: Roy (1999) and $: *http://texmin.nic.in/tnpl_exe_sum.pdf.*

Table 7.19

Number of Units across Various Operations in Tiruppur

Operations	*Number of Units in 1998*
Knitting/stitching units	2500
Dyeing and bleaching	750
Fabric printing	350
Embroidery	150
Other ancillary units	250
Compacting and Calendaring	200
Total	4200

Source: South Indian Hosiery Manufactures Association, Bulletin (1998) as referred in Neetha (2002).

production structure of the industry also has undergone significant changes after mid- 1980s.

By 1980, there were about 400 composite units, 200 fabricators knitting units and 250 finishing or making up units (Manthagini, 1983, as referred in Neetha, 2002) and there has been a phenomenal growth in the number of small units during the 1980s and 1990s. According to Swaminathan and Jeyaranjan (1994) in early 1990s, there were 2500 knitting and manufacturing units, 600 processing units and 100 embroidery units. A 1998, estimation of the total number of registered units as provided by Employers' Association puts the figure at 4200 units (Table 7.19). The number has not changed much in the past few years, and the Wikipedia on Tiruppur also indicates the same number.[24]

Though no global estimates of the size of the labour force in the industry are available, according to trade union leaders and workers, there are 2-3 lakh workers in the cluster (Neetha, 2002). An important feature of the cluster is that roughly over 50 per cent of the workers are women and children (Jeyaranjan, 2000). The 1990s witnessed informalisation and feminisation of the work force in Tiruppur. According to the Chief Inspectorate of Factories, the proportion of female workers in the garment making units has increased from 7.51 per cent in 1990 to 33.23 per cent in 1998. A survey by Neetha (2002) finds that the feminisation of labour has been more in processes which are highly labour intensive and supposedly

24. Kindly refer *http://en.wikipedia.org/wiki/Textile_valley_of_India* that gives almost the same number of units for different categories in Tirupur in 2006.

Table 7.20

Summary of Policy Changes in Leather Industry

Policy	*Policy Pronouncement*
June 2005	Policies to facilitate modernisation/upgradation: a US$ 64 million 'modernising scheme' called the 'Integrated Leather Development Programme' initiated by GoI, All leather tanning and product units' eligible for modernisation assistance. The assistance includes 30 per cent of project cost for SSI units and 20 per cent for non-SSI units, subject to a ceiling of US$ 110 thousand per unit.
2004-05	Ambur cluster for leather industry granted by the GoI at project cost of 67.34 crores with central assistance of 43.94 crores.
	De-licensing of integrated tanneries that convert raw hides and skins into finished leather.
Notification No. SO 603(E) dated 29 June, 2001	11 items dereserved—semi-finished hides and skins, leather shoes, leather washers and laces, moulded rubber soles and heels for footwear, flexible polyurethane foam, polyurethane shoe soles, shoe-tacks and eyelets and leather pickers and other leather accessories for leather industry, vide.
	No Industrial Licence needed for most items of the leather industry. The location of industrial projects will, however, be subject to central or state.
	Free import and export of raw hides and skins, semi-finished and finished leather and leather products.
	Concessional duty on imported machinery and chemicals.
	Setting up of leather parks: An outlay of US$ 24.5 million for setting up five leather parks—two in Chennai and one each in Nellore, Agra and Kolkata. CLE (The Council for Leather Exports) estimated that this scheme would generate a total investment of US$ 267 million in about 3 years.
	Establishment of 'design centres' at individual manufacturing units, to facilitate improvement in design capabilities: Under this scheme, 25 per cent of the project cost is provided to the units under the market access initiative scheme of the Ministry of Commerce and Industry. Several individual units have come forward to establish their own design centres.

Notes: Items like leather shoe uppers (closed), leather sandals and *chappals*, leather garments, industrial leather gloves, leather suitcases and travel goods, leather purses and handbags, fancy leather goods and novelty items, watch straps and leather straps of all types are still reserved for exclusive manufacture by the small-scale sector unless firm meets an export obligation of 50 per cent of the production each year.

Source: Compiled from the *Compendium of Textile Statistics 2003*, Office of the Textile Commissioner, Ministry of Textiles, GoI.

less skilled but require more dexterity like damage checking, over locking, arranging, trimming, folding, flat locking and helper.

Leather-based industries

TN has a dominant presence in leather and leather-based industries. The tanning industry in India has a total installed capacity of 225 million pieces of hide and skins of which TN alone contributes as much as 70 per cent (CII-PriceWaterhouse 2000 referred to in Tewari, 2003). The state enjoys a leading position with 40 per cent share in India's exports. The main features of the leather industry in India including TN are the following: employment to 2.5 million persons; a large part (nearly 60-65%) of the production coming from the small and cottage sector in products such as shoe uppers, shoes, garments and so on; annual export value of nearly US$ 2 billion; and lastly, endowed with 10 per cent of the world's raw material, export constitutes about 2 per cent of the world trade. The leather industry comprises tanning, footwear, leather garments and leather goods. To encourage leather industry, the state government offers a special capital subsidy. Table 7.20 contains some of the key policy initiatives for the sector.

Tanning Sector: In TN, most of the tanneries (or firms that process leather and skins) are concentrated in a handful of locations mainly Palar valley in Vellore district and the Cauvery river basin. Finished leather and leather goods production is centered in and around Chennai. TN has over 9000 registered small and medium firms in the leather sector, about 70 large firms and nearly 40 composite firms that are vertically integrated and have their own tanneries and finished goods production (CLE, 2000). It is estimated that 35 large firms account for 60 per cent export base of the country (Tewari, 2003), whereas a large number of smaller firms cater mainly to the domestic market.

Tanneries have been compelled to become environmentally sensitive to some extent. Also due to changing fashions in the importing countries, the industry has had to remain in a state of advanced preparedness. The colour shade card for the world is now made in Chennai. Recognising the need and importance of modernisation of tanneries in India, the GoI has commissioned a Tannery Modernisation Scheme. The scheme provides investment grants for enabling the small and medium enterprises to readjust quickly to the changed circumstances of the WTO regime.

Footwear Sector: The footwear industry in TN is export driven. The installed capacity of closed shoes manufacturing is estimated at 71 million pairs as of 1999, which represents nearly 50 per cent of the installed capacity of the country. Some high quality brands of shoes are made in the state. Interestingly, the technology absorption in footwear factories in Vellore district during 1985-95 has led to the generation of more than 50,000 jobs for women.

The unit-value realisation from export footwear industry in TN is higher than in many other states. Though this facilitates dynamism in the segment, it also engenders a state of vulnerability in global leather trade. Since the non-leather footwear component industry is not developed adequately in the state or in adjoining states, there is an excessive dependence on imports of components adding to inventory costs and time delays in supply.

The national policy of reservation of footwear industry for the small-scale sector has led to the emergence of a large number of small footwear enterprises in the state. These units though do not enjoy economies of scale for supplying the large volume, but are more suited to the markets where the economy of scope and small volume supply are advantageous.

Leather Garments and Leather Goods: TN enjoys a strong position in the export trade of leather garments. It is strong in the manufacture of leathers from goat and sheepskins suited for leather garments. The manufacture of small leather goods like wallets, dress gloves and bags has registered a significant increase in India during 1995-2000. TN has kept up with the pace of national growth in the leather goods sector so far.

Pump Manufacturing

Coimbatore is known for pump and motor manufacturing units since the 1920s. Subsequent to the first FYP, a lot of emphasis was placed on modernising agriculture and rural electrification which led to an astonishing growth of the pump industry in Coimbatore. There are different estimates of the number of units and contribution of the cluster. The Coimbatore district industrial centre's directory puts the total number of producing units registered around 737 as on 1995-96 (Mohanan Pillai, 2000: 4208). UNIDO's (2001) study mentions that the cluster has over 1100 units[25] accounting for around ₹ 2000 crores i.e., 40 per cent to 50 per cent of the value produced in the country. According to another estimate,

25. It is interesting that the same document on pages 4 and 8 gives two different figures. On page 4, it mentions that there are about 1670 registered and more than 500 unregistered units situated in the district, whereas on page 8 the number changes to 803.

the region with over 1000 pump set and motor manufacturing units (including 500 units in the organised sector) had an annual turnover of around ₹ 1200 crores in 2002-03.[26] This amounted to nearly 48 per cent of the countrywide sales. The export of pumps and motors from this region was around ₹ 30 crores in 2002-03.

The pump industry can be divided into three broad categories: Category 1: Medium-scale industries (Composite), Category 2: SSI (Large) Composite/Sub contracting and Category 3: SSI (Small) Assemblers. Table 7.21 gives the contribution of these categories to total output as per UNIDO (2001). To supply these firms, there are nearly 1700 vendors in different categories. These include 1000 machinery components suppliers, 613 castings (motor body) suppliers, 30 rotor die casting and stator supplier, 1 copper wire supplier and 26 other suppliers.

Table 7.21

Estimated Number of Units and Value of Output in Pump Cluster

	Category	*Firms in the Cluster (approx.)*	*Value of Production in ₹ Crores (%)*
1	SSI (Assemblers)	600	100 (4.7%)
2	SSI (Large)	500	1600 (74.4%)
3	Medium	3	1450 (20.9%)
	Total	1103	2150

Source: UNIDO (2001).

An interesting aspect of pump clusters in Coimbatore is that throughout its development phases, the industry has remained largely in the small-scale sector. One reason for this is the GOI policy of reserving centrifugal pumps up to 10 x 9 cm size used in irrigation and most categories of electric motors, for exclusive manufacturing in SSIs. Though this reservation entailed free entry and consequent high mortality, it has had a long-term implication for quality and efficiency. Another factor that detrimentally affected the dynamic efficiency and technical change in the sector was the policy of giving subsidised power to the farmers. Since

26. *Source: The Hindu*, "Proposal for pump and motors submitted", Feb. 01, 2004.

Table 7.22

Annual Growth of Eight Top Industries (in Terms of Share in IIP) since 1993-94

Industry	*Cotton Textiles (23)$*	*Food Products (20-21)$*	*M/cry & Eqpmt other than Transport Equipment (35-36)#*	*Rubber, Plastic, Petroleum & Coal Products (31)#*	*Chemicals & Chemical Products (30)#*	*Transport Eqpmt & Parts (37)#*	*Leather Products (29)$*	*Textile Products Other than mills (26)$*
Weight	18.4	12.406	9.494	9.404	8.695	6.294	5.025	4.59
1994-95	-1.2	12.1	5.0	17.9	13.9	4.9	-13.7	-4.7
1995-96	0.1	4.5	41.6	-19.1	-8.4	34.1	7.0	3.6
1996-97	0.7	-7.7	-11.6	15.8	-5.2	9.4	0.5	-0.2
1997-98	3.4	-15.6	-3.6	-3.7	3.5	1.4	-16.3	36.5
1998-99	-21.8	8.1	-10.0	-15.1	14.3	-3.0	21.6	8.8
1999-2000	41.4	26.8	-5.1	1.0	3.1	-1.2	37.6	8.2
2000-01	-1.1	8.6	-6.7	-5.0	0.2	8.8	22.9	-35.2
2001-02	-2.8	1.3	-6.7	-3.9	2.6	-7.5	9.8	16.7
2002-03	3.1	-6.1	9.0	2.8	-16.5	4.3	-8.4	31.9
2003-04	-2.1	-7.4	11.3	6.3	9.8	16.7	-8.0	-7.3
2004-05	-5.2	4.3	41.3	27.3	12.8	11.9	14.3	-37.4
Av. Growth								
Period 1 (1994-95 to 1999-2000)	3.1	5.3	1.4	-1.2	3.0	7.8	8.5	2.4
Period 2 (2000-01 to 2004-05)	-1.7	-2.0	13.7	8.1	2.2	6.3	1.9	1.0

Note : $: Traditional, #: Modern

energy was highly subsidised, neither producers nor users gave emphasis to quality, efficiency and standardisation. Only in the 1980s, the concept of energy-efficient pumps spread after the introduction of quality standard IS-9097 and National Bank for Agriculture and Rural Development (NABARD) notification offering finance to efficient pump systems that conform to this standard (Mohanan Pillai, 2000: 4209).

Pattern of Industrialisation in the Post-1991 Era

The above section (Tables 7.10, 7.11, 7.16, 7.17 and 7.20) illustrates that the state and the GoI are very active in promoting new industries as they promulgated a number of policy changes to stimulate the growth of these industries. This section looks into the effect of policy changes on the performance of these industries. The section starts with the performance of those industries having a high share in the IIP in Table 7.22. The last two rows of the table give the average performance in two time periods—period 1 from 1994-95 to 1999-00 and period 2 from 2000-01 to 2004-05. Of the eight industries, four are traditional and four are modern. The traditional industries are more labour intensive with high impact on employment generation, whereas modern industries are more capital intensive having high value added, but less impact on employment. Moreover, nature of employment also differs across the two categories. Modern industries require more skilled workers, whereas traditional industries require unskilled and semi-skilled labour.

It can be seen from the table that the traditional industries like cotton textiles (23), food products (20-21), leather (29) and textile products other than mills (26) have done poorly in period 2. In fact, the two most important industries, having the highest share in IIP—cotton textiles and food products, had a negative growth from 2000-01 to 2004-05. Given their high share in IIP, this seems to have directly impacted manufacturing output from 2000 onwards. On the other hand, machinery and equipment other than transport (35-36) and rubber, plastics, petroleum and coal products (31), which were not doing well in period 1, have shown commendable growth in period 2. For transport equipment and parts (37), the growth, quite high, is slightly lower in the second period. Lastly, chemical and chemical products (30) had a poor growth in both the periods. The

Figure 7.6

Performance of Software and Hardware Industry since 1993-94

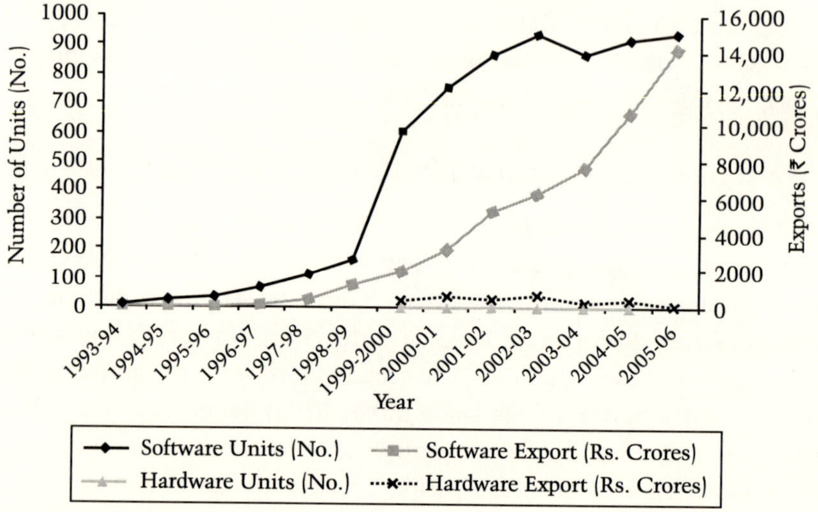

remaining section looks into the performance of some of these industries individually.

Performance of IT Industry

The previous section indicates that TN has put special emphasis on the IT industry and that too mainly on the software sector. As a result of these efforts, Chennai has become a preferred destination for software companies. Starting with a modest 10 software firms in 1993-94, the number has increased to over 935, whereas exports have increased by a whopping 381 times in the last 10 years to ₹ 14,115 crores in 2005-06. Against a share of 4 per cent in India's software exports in 1995-96, it has increased to 14 per cent in 2005-06. Figure 7.6 gives the growth of software firms and exports from TN. Since the state is yet to come up with a hardware policy, this delay is getting reflected in the not so spectacular performance of the hardware sector *vis-à-vis* the software sector (Figure 7.6). Though the sector is growing, one disturbing feature is that the exports are primarily in the low end segments as indicated in Table 7.23. For instance, of the total software exports of ₹ 5219 crores in 2001-02, less than 0.4 per cent was in product exports and over 76 per cent was in application or on-site consultancy services. The situation has hardly changed in 2004-05. Despite over 100 per cent increases in software exports to 10,703 crores, the product exports have reached barely 3 per cent (Table 7.22).

Performance of Textile Industry

Table 7.22, using Annual Survey of Industries (ASI) data, has already indicated that the performance of the sector as measured by growth in output is lacklustre. Since the industry has four pillars: (1) mill or spinning segment; (2) handloom segment; (3) power loom; and (4) garment segment, this subsection looks at the performance of each segment separately.

Mill Segment

As indicated in the previous section, the textile industry in the state is predominantly spinning oriented with spinning mills occupying 97.3 per cent share of the total 835 mills. Table 7.24 gives the growth of different

Table 7.23

Nature of Software Exports from India

	Area of Expertise	*2001-02 No. of Units**	*2001-02 Export Value*	*2004-05 Export Value*
1	Application Software	257 (49.9)	2259.41 (43.3)	6528.83 (61)
2	On-site consultancy services	36 (7.0)	1716.71 (32.9)	
3	System software	33 (6.4)	702.02 (13.5)	1284.36 (12)
4	IT enabled services	114 (22.1)	340.01 (6.5)	1070.3 (10)
5	Web Applications	60 (11.7)	184.93 (3.5)	
6	Product/Packages	15 (2.9)	16.84 (0.3)	321.09 (3)
7	BPO			535.15 (5)
8	Others			963.27 (9)
	Total	515	5219.92	10,703.00

Notes: Figures in parentheses are the percentage in that category; a unit may be dealing in more than one category.

BPO: Business Process Outsourcing.

Source: Software Technology Parks of India, Chennai (*www.chennai.stpi.in/perform_software.htm*).

Table 7.24

Performance of Textile Mill Segment: 1995-96 to 2003-04

	Parameter	*1995-96*	*2003-04*	*% Change*
1	Number of Textile Mills	717	834	16.3
2	Installed Spinning Capacity (lakh spindles)	108.6	154.58	42.3
3	Number of Looms installed (x10 numbers)	637	687	7.8
4	Yarn Production (million kgs)	777	1172.38	50.9
5	Cloth Production (million sq. metres)	136	67.16	-50.6
6	Number of workers (lakh numbers)	1.91	1.95	2.1
7	Cloth production per worker (in sq. meter)	712.0	344.4	-51.6
8	Yarn Production per worker (in kg)	4068.1	6012.2	47.8

Figure 7.7

Performance of Textile Mills Segment since 1995-96: Key Indicators

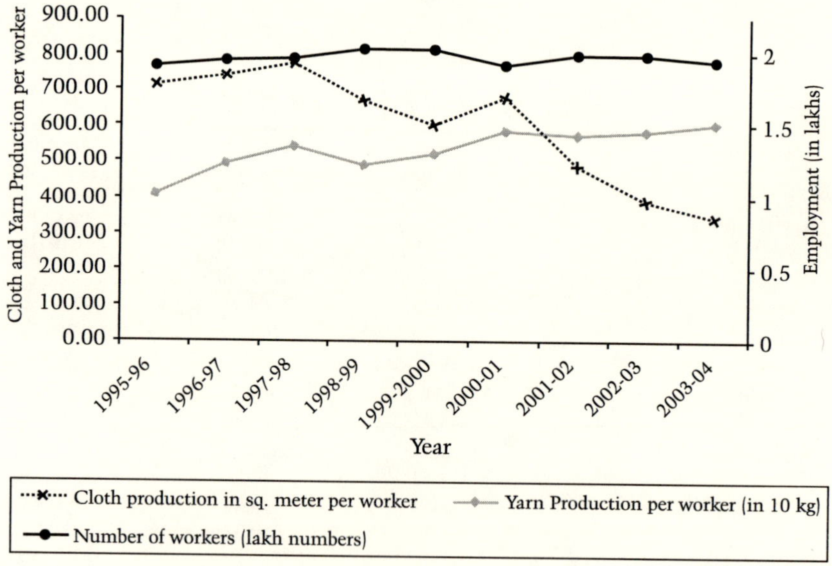

parameters for the mill segment for the period 1995-96 to 2003-04. From the table, it can be seen that there is a modest increase in number of mills, looms installed and the labour employed. However, yarn and cloth production has shown a contrasting pattern. The yarn production in these 8 years has increased by over 50 per cent, whereas the cloth production has fallen by the same margin. Figure 7.7 gives details.

From Figure 7.7, it is apparent that the employment in organised mills segment has remained more or less static in the last 8 years. However, the cloth production per worker is declining over time, whereas the yarn production per worker is showing an upward trend. The increased yarn production per worker indicates increased productivity of labour, which has a good implication for competition.[27] The stagnant employment and increased number of mills also indicate that there would be a decline in workers per factory. Against 128 workers per textile factory in 1980-81, the value was 111 in 1989-90 and fell to 90 in 1997-98 (Bhaumik *et al.*, 2005).

Handloom Segment

The partial liberalisation in the segment has led to declining performance of the handloom sector in the country in the past 10-15 years. Between 2000 and 2005, the average annual growth rate has been -6.99 per cent. Since TN specialises in cotton handloom weaving, the segment has been specially hit. Following the 1991 liberalisation, several export restrictions on cotton and cotton yarn have been eased. This has led to a significant growth in cotton exports. From a paltry 40.38 million kg cotton exports in 1988-89, they grew more than 10 times to 486.78 million kg in 1998-99.[28] These developments have hit cotton weavers hard, because 70 per cent of the input cost in handloom weaving is the cost of yarn. The situation has worsened since 2002 with the removal of remaining restrictions on export of cotton and cotton yarn.[29] As a result of the increase in input costs, there is a widespread closure of handloom weaving units. The Compendium of Textile Statistics (2000) indicates that by 2000, the number of idle looms had risen by nearly 3.5 times to 66,835 from 19,285 in 1985.

Power Loom Segment

The early 1990s were the glorious period for power looms. For instance, in 1995, there used to be a six-month waiting period for a new

27. However, one needs to find out whether this increase has not been caused by labour-capital substitution.

28. Source: GoI, Ministry of Textiles (1999). *Report of Expert Committee on Textile Policy.*

29. *Source: http://dgftcom.nic.in/exim/2000/pn/pn01/pn5901.htm* accessed December 2006.

loom. When export of cotton cloth surged in the early 1990s, the power loom industry of the state had two impacts. In the case of indirect exports, which consisted mainly of greys processed out-of-state, the effect was an expansion of loomage without much qualitative change in organisation or technology. But, in the case of direct exports, which consist of both grey and coloured cloth of non-traditional types, it resulted in technological and organisational changes (Roy, 1999). The situation changed after 1995 due to recession in the industry and by November 1997, only 30-40 per cent of the looms were at work (Roy, 1999). This was due to fierce international competition. Pakistan's fabrics as well as Indonesia's were of better quality and as they used uncontaminated cotton, they drove Indian goods out of similar markets (Ibid.).

Garment or Knitwear Segment

The value of India's garment exports has grown significantly since the early 1990s. In 2003, the sector constituted 16 per cent of total manufacturing exports and 12.5 per cent of total exports from India. Against exports of US$ 0.2 billion in 1976, they have increased to US$ 6.6 billion in 2003 (Tewari, 2005). The credit goes to Tiruppur, since it constitutes 85 per cent of garment exports. Because of this, Tiruppur is sometimes referred to as Textile Valley of India. In 2004, the export turnover from the town was more than ₹ 50,000 million ($1100 million).[30] The Export Import Policy of 2002-2007 has specifically acknowledged Tiruppur for its contribution to the export efforts.

The increased exports have a number of effects. Since the early 1990s, the employment in the segment has increased by 165 per cent (Jha, 2005). However, increased employment and export growth of the segment is a result of casualisation of labour, which led to declining share of wages in total manufacturing costs. Wages as a share of total manufacturing costs in the garment segment have fallen from 26.86 per cent in 1973 to 17.07 per cent in 2000 (Jha, 2005). This implies that the employment terms and conditions in the segment may have worsened in the post-liberalisation regime. According to one estimate, today more than 90 per cent of the workers are considered informal or unorganised.

---

30. *Source*: "Economy of Tamil Nadu"—*Wikipedia* (*http://en.wikipedia.org/wiki/Economy_of_Tamil_Nadu*, accessed December 2006).

Next to Tiruppur, the town of Karur generates around $300 million a year in foreign exchange through home textile exports such as bed linens, kitchen linens, toilet linens, table linens and wall hangings.

Performance of Pump Manufacturing

The period between 1970s and early 1990s can be considered the golden era for the pump industry particularly for Coimbatore. During the period 1981-1992, the pump industry in Coimbatore and in India grew at a compounded annual growth rate of 5 per cent with demand coming from agriculture. From 1991 to 1995, the pump industry again grew at about 5 per cent per annum but the factors fuelling this growth were different. The liberalisation measures initiated in 1991 resulted in boom in industries and urbanisation; as a consequence, there was a structural shift in the demand pattern (UNIDO, 2001). The proportion of the domestic user segment increased, whereas the proportion of agricultural user segment decreased.

The 1990s with the opening up of the economy, removal of subsidy in pumps to farmers and a skewed duty structure led to declining profitability and recession in the industry. The cluster suffered most as its share fell from around 60 per cent in 1980s to 40 per cent in 1990s. This is well supported by Mohan Pillai (2000) in his study of Coimbatore pump cluster who found evidence of falling sales, reduced employment, declining capacity utilisation and reduced profit during late 1990s.

Performance of Auto Industry

Table 7.22 indicates that transport equipment and parts have maintained an overall growth of over 6 per cent since 1994-95. The average growth rate during the 11-year period is 7.2 per cent. The automobile industry in the state accounts for nearly 50 per cent of the AI export market. Engineering products exports from TN are around ₹ 14.50 billion (US$ 320 million) of which automobile ancillaries alone contribute around US$ 150 million. Auto component industry is one of the key industries in TN. The industry having 110 key players is housed mainly around Chennai and has invested about ₹ 36,000 million (i.e., US$ 800 million). These units produced an output of US$ 1.2 billion in 2001-02, of which nearly 12 per cent (140 million) was exported.

Table 7.25

Export Performance of Leather and Leather Products: Share of Tamil Nadu

	1992-93	*1993-94*	*1994-95*	*1995-96*	*1996-97*
Total (US$ million)	420.8	514	609.8	687.9	644.4
Finished leather	170.5 (40.5)	164.4 (32)	231.3 (38)	234.2 (34)	191.1 (29.7)
Leather footwear	55.9 (13.3)	74.1 (14.4)	79.0 (13)	100.2 (14.6)	109.2 (16.9)
Footwear Components	87.4 (20.8)	116.0 (22.6)	123.7 (20.3)	153.8 (22.4)	153.3 (23.8)
Leather Garments	79.3 (18.8)	118.0 (22.9)	130.1 (21.3)	148.2 (21.5)	135.1 (21)
Leather Goods	27.7 (6.6)	41.4 (8.1)	45.7 (7.5)	51.5 (7.5)	55.7 (8.6)
TN's Exports (US$ million) and share in India's exports	228.3 (45.5)	249.2 (50.43)	236.9 (48.24)	245.2 (46.9)	243.2 (46.4)
Finished leather	83.89	77.57	77.02	75.44	71.59
Leather footwear	47.01	46.29	33.33	35.21	35.87
Footwear Components	49.09	58.36	63.72	75.69	76.88
Leather Garments	33.63	43.95	42.86	42.83	35.89
Leather Goods	14.68	23.06	19.96	16.03	22.94

Note: Figures in parentheses are percentages.

Source: Pillai (2000) as referred to in Tewari (2003).

Performance of Leather Industry

A crucial turnaround in the Indian leather industry came with the implementation of the recommendations of the Seetharamaiah Committee in 1973, which banned the export of raw and semi-tanned leather and made it mandatory to export finished and dyed leather i.e., value added leather. As a consequence of this implementation, the value of finished leather exports from India increased by 18 times in 7 years from a paltry ₹ 140 million in 1973-74 to ₹ 2660 million in 1980 (Usha, 1984, as referred to in Sujatha, 2002). Since TN was a major hub for the leather industry, there was a corresponding increase in the share of finished leather good exports. The exports increased from ₹ 86.04 million in 1973-74 to nearly ₹ 1000 million in 1980, an increase over 10 times.

The trend in the 1990s however was different as indicated in Table 7.25. Two important events affected the performance of the industry drastically. In 1989-90, the largest leather importer, Germany, banned the import of leather items containing more than 5 mg/kg of pentachlorophenol (PCP). This was followed by a ban in import of leather (and textiles) treated with azo dyes (benzidine) in 1994. The other event was in 1995 when, adjudicating on a public interest litigation (PIL) about groundwater polluted by tannery effluents, the Supreme Court of India ordered closure of tanneries that were not treating their effluents in accordance with pollution control norms. The partial closure and then gestation period of building of common and individual effluent treatment plants affected the performance of the sector. From Table 7.25, it can be seen that though TN has contributed nearly 45-50 per cent of India's leather exports in the mid-1990s, in dollar terms, the exports did not increase. The finished leather and leather footwear exports from TN declined during the period. The footwear components and leather goods exports from the state, however, partially increased (Table 7.25).

The 1990s trade liberalisation has also affected the industry. Since 75 per cent of production in the sector is by small-scale, cottage and artisan units, these units which primarily cater to the domestic market have faced increased hardship as a consequence of tariff liberalisation and abolition of import restrictions in late 1990s. For instance, in the footwear segment, the policy change has resulted in increased entry of Chinese shoes. Import of ready-made sports shoes from China increased from 468,000 pairs in March 1999 to 570,000 pairs in October 2000, and as a consequence, production level in the domestic shoe industry fell by 11.24 per cent.[31] The small-scale shoemakers have also suffered because of increased scarcity of raw materials, i.e., raw hides, leading to increased raw material prices caused by change in government policy of allowing exports of raw hides. The exports of leather hide increased by 147 per cent from 1999 to 2005,[32] after the GoI under pressure from European Union (EU) abandoned measures that effectively banned the export of leather hides throughout 1990s (Action Aid, 2005).

Performance of Cement Industry

Table 7.26 and Figure 7.8 describe the performance of the cement industry since 1993-94. The last two rows of the table give the annual

31. *Source: http://commerce.nic.in/ad_pre02.htm* accessed December 2006.

32. Same as above.

Figure 7.8

Performance of Cement Industry since 1994-95

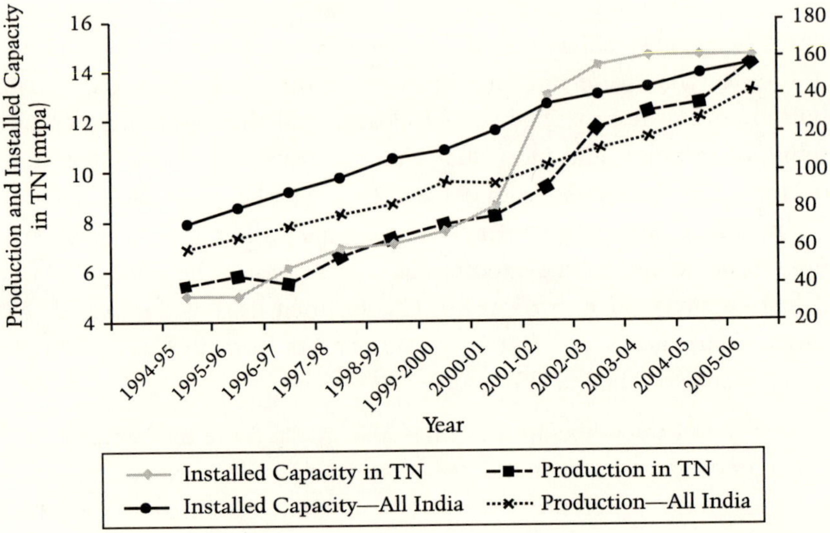

growth of the production and installed capacity for TN *vis-à-vis* AI. From the table, one can infer that the performance of TN's cement industry was inferior to AI both in terms of production and installed capacity during the period 1993-94 to 1999-2000. However, starting from 2000-01, TN's cement industry has done much better, as the growth in production is over 15 per cent compared to 10 per cent at the AI level. Similarly, the capacity addition growth is close to 14 per cent against 6 per cent at the AI level. Of the 36 million ton of capacity added during 2000-01 to 2005-06, TN's contribution is nearly one-sixth, i.e., over 16.5 per cent. The table and the figure indicate that the performance of the industry is quite commendable. The main causes for this improved performance are increased construction activity due to Golden Quadrilateral project and increased foreign direct investment (FDI) in the state and lastly, more use of fly ash as a raw material for cement production. Apart from this, the switch from wet to dry process has also aided in reducing input costs.

Based on the above discussion, one can see that the more modern and skill-intensive industries like IT, automobile and cement industry have

Table 7.26

Performance of Cement Industry in Tamil Nadu vis-à-vis All India

Year	*Tamil Nadu (Refers to 8 Major Firms)*			*All India*		
	Installed Capacity (mtpa) (1)	*Production (mtpa) (2)*	*Capacity Utilisation (%) (3)*	*Installed Capacity (mtpa) (4)*	*Production (mtpa) (5)*	*Capacity Utilisation (6)*
1993-94	5.0	5.05 (9.3)	101	65.69	54.09	85
1994-95	5.0	5.5 (9.4)	110	71.25	58.35	85
1995-96	5.0	5.75 (8.9)	115	80.72	64.53	82
1996-97	6.11	5.52 (7.9)	90.3	88.60	69.98	81
1997-98	6.86	6.55 (8.5)	95.48	96.64	76.74	82
1998-99	7.08	7.29 (8.9)	102.07	106.63	81.65	76.6
1999-2000	7.59#	7.86 (8.4)	103.60	107.47/111	94.01	87.5
2000-01*	8.6#	8.16 (8.8)	94.9	121	93.06	76.9
2001-02	12.91#	9.31 (9.1)	72.1	135	102.4	75.9
2002-03	14.16$	11.67 (10.5)	82.4	140	111.4	79.6
2003-04	14.56$	12.29 (10.5)	84.4	144	117.5	81.6
2004-05	14.56$	12.60 (9.9)	86.5	151	127.6	84.5
2005-06	14.56$	14.29 (10.1)	98.1	157	141.8	90.3
Annual Growth: 1993-94 to 1999-2000	8.63	9.27		11.5	12.3	
Annual Growth: 2000-01 to 2005-06	13.86	15.02		5.95	10.47	

Notes: #: 0.9 million tons in public sector units; *: From 2000-01 for All India—ICRA (2006) *http://icra.in/recentrel/ Cement-200607.pdf*; $: *http://www.cmaindia.org/industry.html*.

Source: Tamil Nadu Cement Corporation Ltd. (*www.tidco.com/tn_policies/tninfo/cement.asp*, accessed December 22, 2006) .

performed well in the last 7-8 years. Traditional industries like textile, handloom, and even pump manufacturing are not doing well for want of modernisation and the kind of policies pursued. The performance clearly indicates that the trend is towards those industries which have relatively less employment generation potential or where the employment potential is more skilled in nature. This has an important implication for the human capital formation in the state. The next section looks into the opportunities and challenges faced by these industries in the era of globalisation.

Challenges in the Post-WTO Regime

There is no denying that not all industries are affected equally because of globalisation and the new WTO regime. Still, the macroeconomic impact of government policy of increasing liberalisation will have micro repercussions and will be felt by all the industries, due to widespread linkages. There is no doubt that after liberalisation, some sectors like IT and services have done exceedingly well, whereas sectors such as textiles and leather have struggled to survive the impact. This has resulted in widespread closure, declining incomes and job losses (Action Aid, 2005). This section looks into the impact of WTO on different industries. In order to see the impact and future prospects of these industries, it is imperative to understand the key elements of WTO negotiations.

Negotiations on non-agricultural market access (NAMA) under WTO have three key elements: (1) increasing the amount of bound tariffs (i.e., setting ceilings on tariff rates for at least 95 per cent of manufacturing product lines); (2) reducing tariffs under some formula; and (3) making big reductions or eliminating tariffs in specific sectors (Action Aid, 2005). It is the third element that will have the biggest impact, because the sectors specified are India's labour-intensive traditional sectors such as textiles, clothing, footwear and leather.[33] Deep tariff cuts would expose these traditional industries to international competition and the impact could be disastrous especially from the employment point of view.

Power Loom Segment[34]

The contrast between the two main power loom regions of the country, the Western states of Maharashtra and Gujarat, and TN in the South indicates that growth in the latter will continue. The West is primarily, though not exclusively, a man-made fibre weaving region with the typical output as polyester shirting or rayon sarees. On the other hand, the South is almost exclusively a cotton region. The South started late but grew more rapidly in the 1990s. The growth of the South was assisted by cotton exports. Given the increasing demand for cotton or blended cotton,

33. However, the bargaining power of the developing countries would decide whether the cut would be voluntary or involve some mandatory commitments.

34. This subsection builds on Roy (1999).

the South has greater potential to benefit from the abolition of the quota regime.

With globalisation, consumers tend to become wiser and begin choosing better quality goods. As a consequence, the worst hit would be the smaller firms or the ones that are traditional and produce poorly finished cloth. It is important to note that many importers in North America prefer buying Indian cloth in grey state because Indian processing is usually of poor quality (Roy, 1999). Thus, ordinary grey cotton cloth or the generic coloured goods will be more affected than the more sophisticated checked shirting or grey cloth made in modern facilities. This differential impact, in fact, indicates the critical supply side problems. The power looms in developing countries including TN have always been plagued by three shortages: power, capital and quality. In TN, power is relatively abundant, but costlier than elsewhere, especially *vis-à-vis* Maharashtra.[35] The scarcity of term-credit has forced most power looms to operate at low level of technology. Even in normal conditions, the formal sector banks and power looms have a history of avoiding each another (Roy, 1999). SSIs including power looms have apprehensions about the procedures of banks and fear asymmetric information problems that affect their directed credit operations. The quality aspect is manifested in (a) low technological capability of an average firm; (b) inefficiency of decentralised weaving; and (c) low technological capability of the average industrial complex.

In the past, decentralised production has engendered the moral hazard problem. It is a common complaint of foreign buyers that Indians cannot be trusted to deliver sustained good quality punctually. As a result, most export business from India involves orders that are individually small. Given the small-scale and remoteness of the average producer, too many intermediaries are involved. There is, thus, a sustained tendency on the part of the trade to squeeze rates and a response from the producer to adjust by compromising on quality. Since no trader has complete control over quality and supervision and communication are imperfect, the contracts are mostly terminable and few producers expect repeated transactions. Even if contracts are renewed, quality tends to fall. There is relatively small

35. *Source: http://texmin.nic.in/tnpl_chap9.pdf accessed* December 2006.

usage of advances and letters of credit and thus of firm commitments (Roy, 1999).

Easy to set up and low wages are the strengths of power looms in SSIs *vis-à-vis* mill weaving. But the functioning of these small power looms is highly inefficient, because they lack training, quality control and the ability to diversify quickly. The small scale and size confer other disadvantages too. Given India's reputation in the world market for poor quality control and chaotic delivery, many foreign buyers prefer to deal with the more visible, efficient and reliable suppliers (which are often big in size) (Roy, 1999). Such contracts imply that the supplier must have close supervision of the firms under subcontract or must itself have a relatively advanced production facility. To be able to muster large fixed (or variable) capital, the supplier must have the financial capacity to pay high interest rates, which is not easy for everyone, especially during recession. As happened in the past during the quota regime, many firms preferred to sell quotas so as to tide over the crises. This benefited large firms who bought these quotas. Finally, direct contracting requires the ability to make frequent trips abroad and possibly considerable education, which small firms often lack. Many of these problems can be countered effectively if small firms cooperate among themselves.

As for capability of industrial complexes, the standard of cloth processing has remained backward in India compared to Asian standards. This situation is largely due to adverse policy. In a bid to protect the handloom industry, the current excise policy makes a distinction between cloth processed in manual and mechanised units. The former is taxed at a lower rate. Consequently, a significant quantity of power loom cloth gets declared as manually processed, though in reality, it is mechanically processed. This excise policy has on the one hand discriminated against the integrated mills, which cannot misreport processing method, and on the other has had a detrimental impact on technological improvement in the power loom segment. In most power loom towns, to avoid attention, units have not modernised themselves despite having capabilities (Roy, 1999).

Knitwear Segment

For many industries, high dependence on SSIs for their performance would induce them to informalise and casualise. Tiruppur knitwear industry in the 1990s is a classic example of this. Widespread evidence exists that this informalisation has a direct bearing on the earning of the labour class, which in most cases belongs to the lower strata of society and this may lead to increased disparity. For instance, a survey by Neetha (2002) in Tiruppur finds that nearly 50-60 per cent workers belong to backward castes or are Scheduled Caste (SC). Since of late, there is a push for export-oriented growth with abolishing of MFA, there is greater opportunity to export and hence more pressure to casualise.[36] The challenge to the policy makers would be how exports can be sustained without informalising the production chain.

Handloom Segment

Reduction in tariffs on cotton fabric import under WTO may prove disastrous for cotton handloom weavers if it leads to increase in imports.[37] On the other hand, further liberalisation of tariffs on cotton yarn as a result of WTO's NAMA may lead to greater exports of cotton yarn from India as found by Jha (2005) in a general equilibrium analysis. This may have an adverse implication for the handloom segment, which has to depend on affordable and adequate supply of cotton yarn for their survival. In fact, even the power loom segment is complaining that as better spinning mills have switched to yarn exports, there is a scarcity of premium quality yarn.[38] This implies that handloom (and power loom) segments would be adversely affected due to increase in yarn exports and prices and increased imports of handloom fabric.

---

36. The Bulletins of the South Indian Hosiery Manufacturer's Association (SHIMA) have mentioned though not directly that the export market was dominated by countries like Taiwan, Hong Kong, Pakistan, and South Korea where the prices of knitwear items were 10 per cent less than that of Tiruppur. Thus there is a need to informalize labour relations so as to spur the export growth, as this would lead to reduced wages and thus increased competitiveness in the export market (Neetha, 2002).
37. The apprehension is not unfounded as the tariff reduction from 35 per cent to 20 per cent in the last four years (2000-01 to 2004-05) led to phenomenal increase in another handloom segment import i.e., silk (Action Aid, 2005). This has affected the silk weavers in Varanasi (Check: *http://commerce.nic.in/eidb/ecomq.asp*)
38. *Source: http://texmin.nic.in/tnpl_chap9.pdf* accessed December 2006.

Tanneries

Tanneries in China and other major competing countries have already invested significantly in modernisation. This indicates urgency in the tannery sector to modernise. Apart from this, the three critical challenges the leather sector is facing in the new WTO regime are the growing emphasis on environmental and pollution control standards (phyto-sanitary standards), greater scrutiny over labour practices of local firms and increased tendency towards casualisation. It is the smaller firms that are likely to suffer the most.

Globally, the trend seems to be that the economies of scale improve the industry's productivity, but at the same time, recent experiences by firms like the Tata group and others point to other options. They have succeed in achieving profitability and increasing productivity despite the government's employment focus by adopting innovative practices that involve the upgrading and close mentoring of small suppliers by large firms. Others have improved productivity by nurturing high end niches and the production of finished leather products. All these would be a greater challenge if India has to increase its share from a mere 2.5 per cent to 5 per cent.

Leather Garment Segment

Since the leather garment units in the state do not any longer enjoy cost competitive advantages with respect to the leather garment manufacturing units in other states, it is becoming necessary for the sector to specialise in some select markets. The main markets for the leather products of TN have been in Western Europe. These markets are sensitive to the technical and non-trade barriers including environmental and social audit norms. The leather garment units in TN may need to prepare themselves for exacting demands of the market.

Biotechnology Industry

As of now, the focus of the industry is mainly on biopharma. Other areas which need to be strengthened are diagnostics, therapeutics, pharmacogenomics, bioinformatics, agricultural biotechnology, industrial biotechnology, inputs to the industry (hardware suppliers—instrumentation and chemicals), marine biotechnology and forest and environment-focused biotechnology. If fact, there is a pressing need for contract research in all areas of biotechnology. Since the industry is idea driven and capital intensive, venture funds need to play a bigger role. The existing evidence however indicates that the most of venture capital funding has gone to the existing firms, but not to the start-up firms that require the funding most (Kathuria and Tewari, 2007). For existing firms, other formal channels of funding like banks, etc., are available, but for start-up firms, it is primarily the venture capital that can convert these ideas into practice.

Pump Industry

The 1990s liberalisation made the pump and motor cluster in Coimbatore increasingly vulnerable. On the one hand, drastic cuts in investment in minor irrigation and reduced subsidies for buying pumps resulted in reduced farmers' demand. The situation was worsened by the power shortages in several states leading to a ban on new power connections for pumps, which in turn affected their off-take. The decline in production affected downstream industries, like casting, component manufacturing, machine tools and subcontracting. On the supply side, gradual reduction in import duty on pumps encouraged import of pumps from China and hence greater external competition (Mohanan Pillai, 2000: 4214).[39] Thus, in pump clusters in Coimbatore, the problem is one of Government's withdrawal of subsidies and opening up of the economy for international competition. The two other major constraints faced by the pump manufacturers in Coimbatore hampering the expansion of their market share are: (1) finding newer applications for the pumps and (2) use of improved materials to meet environmental regulations for exports. Nearly 99 per cent of the pumps produced in the region are used for water lifting and the foreign buyers insist that the pumps should not contain parts made of metals such as zinc. To meet such environmental considerations, the pumps would have to contain mainly stainless steel parts, which would be expensive and beyond the means of most small producers. However, the ongoing upgradation envisages changing construction material and

39. The import duty was 22 per cent in 2000 against 35 per cent in 1991. The ability to compete was further undermined by skewed import policy where import duty on important raw materials such as silicon, pig iron, copper and steel increased to 40 per cent in late 1990s (Mohanan Pillai, 2000).

upgrading technical know-how, which would help address these issues and enable Coimbatore pumps to be used in the food products and petroleum industries. Once the modernisation project is implemented, the value of export of pumps from the region is expected to go up from ₹ 33 crores (in 2003) to ₹ 400 crores by 2010 (Narayanan, 2005).

Even though the GoI has sanctioned a scheme for the upgradation of the cluster (Table 7.7), the dynamic efficiency may still elude the manufacturers and their ability to compete successfully with Chinese pumps or to export will not materialise in the long run. This is because of two reasons: (1) small size of the firms producing pumps and (2) pumping systems having a very low efficiency to the tune of 30 per cent as indicated by studies (see for example, Rehman, 1991). The drive to improve efficiency and grow bigger may still be missing. The prime reason is the fact that electricity (energy) is highly subsidised for agriculture which does not give any incentive either to the user or to the producer to improve the quality and efficiency of pump sets. Another factor that may hamper pursuit of efficiency is lack of standardisation.

The discussion shows that the impact of globalisation and problems of different industries are not identical. Traditional industries seem to be the most affected, whereas in industries like power looms, pump manufacturing, etc., the prime issue is technical upgradation. Segments like handloom and power looms may experience high input costs and dwindling share, whereas segments like footwear, knitwear, etc., may experience more casualisation.

Future Directions

The above section shows that not all industries are affected equally and the impact would be diverse. However, the preparation for weathering the impact involves efforts at two levels: (1) at the level of government (state and/or central) and (2) at the firm level. Before moving further, it is to be noted that for many of the industries, low wages are not the advantage of TN. It is the historical involvement (e.g., in power looms or tanneries) or availability of skilled manpower (as in the case of IT and automobile) that has led to the growth of the sector. These advantages have been utilised and sustained over time. The future directions need to be looked keeping these features in mind.

Infrastructure: Focus Shift

The growth and development of many industrial towns in TN is because of two factors: (1) labour, mainly peaceful, and (2) well-developed infrastructure. For instance, textile labour is known to be relatively peaceful and well-trained in textile regions and the road-rail-port network functions better in TN than in Northern and Eastern India. Road transportation, specifically, is very well-developed in the textile regions[40] (Roy, 1999). Inter-city commuting of workers and traders in the Coimbatore or Erode cluster is easy which, to an extent, is unthinkable for the Eastern or Northern region. In fact, that is why nodes have developed in the marketing of cloth, despite the production remaining fairly dispersed. Another advantage of TN in textile is the extensive and fairly secure handloom weaving tradition that made local knowledge in weaving dispersed and widely available. Traders utilised these local resources, having no inclination to travel or remove themselves from local roots. However, these strengths of the past are not easy to access now in other regions due to IT diffusion and spread of infrastructure, namely, power and roads. Of late, in the post-WTO regime, the infrastructure needed is different.

Ports and environmental infrastructure are the two key components in this export-led industrialisation. For instance, in the footwear market, the demand has become fashion oriented with the supply of each consignment limited and is effected quickly. It is estimated that three to four different consignments need to be shipped within 3-4 months of a season. The cost competitiveness of the footwear market can be ensured if there are port facilities with an infrastructure for adjusting to the quick turnover. Similarly, environmental regulations under WTO require modernisation of CETP and efforts to build the capacity of textile dyeing units and tanneries to comply with the Total Dissolved Solids (TDS) norm of 2100 mg/litre. Though the state is endowed better than any other state in India with respect to port facilities, it still lacks good environmental infrastructure. The voluntary postponement of production by nearly 700 textile dyeing/

---

40. An important enabling factor for power looms is the concentration of cotton spinning, textile engineering and handloom weaving activities.

bleaching units since January 1, 2007, for want of treatment is testimony to this limited environmental infrastructure.[41]

Modernisation: Broader Definition Needed

Modernisation is often interpreted rather narrowly in policy making. For instance, in power loom segment, modernisation is seen as an issue of supplying better looms to small firms at cheap credit. In the new WTO regime, looms represent a problem for two reasons: (1) existing shuttle looms are inadequate in terms of quality of weave, electricity consumption and speed and (2) the automatic and shuttleless looms that are fast, consume less power, do not need winding and supply a spotless fabric[42] but they are very expensive even when bought second-hand. The 1997 price ratio between a new local plain loom and a new Sulzer was 1:24 and that between a plain loom and a second-hand automatic shuttle loom 1:4-6. It will be next to impossible to replace all shuttle looms with shuttleless looms in India,[43] but as an intermediate first step, a faster shuttle loom with some key features of an automatic loom needs to be promoted. It is estimated that machine-specific defects decrease by half in automatic looms (13%) compared to power looms (25%), whereas the reduction from power looms to shuttleless loom (3%) is 9 times. Thus, huge investment is needed in textile processing. Similarly, in pump manufacturing, modernisation means use of newer materials like steel, etc., so that pumps can be used in other applications.

Modernisation also encompasses improvement in capability at the shopfloor, especially for small-scale units. For instance, in power looms,

41. The Madras High Court has given these units an option to continue operating provided they pay a fine of ₹ 0.06 per litre for discharging untreated effluent in Noyyal river. This amounts to nearly ₹ 8 million as a fine per day. The units have declined to exercise this option (The Hindu, 2007) and have suspended production.

42. For instance, the maximum speed of a narrow width shuttle loom that would be needed to produce a prosthesis is about 200 picks/minute (Taws, 2003, as referred to in Anderson, 2004). In comparison, shuttleless looms can run at speeds ranging 900-1800 picks/minute. Mechanical problems concerning acceleration and decelartion of large mass are the prime reasons that loom speeds are slow compared to shuttleless looms.

43. The data indicates that of the 1.7 million shuttle looms in 1996, nearly 90 per cent (i.e., 1.5 million) were in India and remaining 0.2 million in Pakistan (*Source: http://www.tco.gov.pk/Webs/Material%20For%20Website/Reports/ Report%20Textile%20Vision%202005.PDF* accessed January 2007).

training required is primarily in the operation of automatic looms, managing and maintaining looms, avoiding faults, operation of dobby and drop-box, etc. There is at present very little formal training facility available. An earlier study by Roy (1999) has concluded that the Government's power loom service centres have inadequate facility for teaching loom operation. In fact, existing technical colleges set up by some of the textile firms in the region teach students, not weavers. The Indian Institute of Handloom Technology has a small power loom section, but is inadequate and backward. Similarly, the existing industry bodies such as the Power Loom Development and Export Promotion Council furnish information on markets, but not on technology (Ibid.). Neetha (2002) based on her study in Tiruppur has also found the lack of any formal knitwear training institute in Tiruppur and that most of the training being imparted is on-the-job.

Policy Changes: Long-Term Vision

Several problems affecting vital industries are policy induced. In many industries, there is a lack of a rational policy that motivates firms to strive for dynamic efficiency. Apart from modernisation, a bigger policy change required is to rationalise electricity tariffs at the national level. Similarly, the excise policy needs to be fine tuned so as to give disincentives for power looms to not underreport their output.

Of late, a problem encountered by many of the industries is non-availability of suitable skilled persons. The growth of IT industry has led to unprecedented demand of IT professionals. Estimates exist that there is a huge shortfall of software trained professionals. This has led to two adverse impacts on all other industries. Firstly, due to the highly skilled and export-intensive nature of the industry, a software engineer commands a premium over an engineer from other industry. This premium is sufficient for companies to attract and recruit engineers from other fields like electronics or electrical engineering and so on.[44] Secondly, with the tremendous growth of the software sector, the demand for other branches has come down drastically. Such a scenario has wide repercussions on the industrialisation

44. To give an example, Verizon Ltd., a US firm, recruited nearly 400 engineers to work in their software unit in Chennai and Hyderabad. Of these 400 engineers, impressive numbers belong to electrical and electronics branch and electrical engineering (Source: Discussion with an engineer working with Verizon Ltd.).

and growth of the state. Since a state, which is highly diverse, cannot survive only on software, this implies that there is an urgent need for a policy at two fronts: (1) the demand for software professionals is met and (2) there should not be any shortfall for engineers in other fields. However, this may require bridging of the salary gap between software and other branches.

Policy initiative in one sector often has an unintended effect on other areas. To give an example, the competitiveness of the textile garment sector depends, among other things, on quality of knitting. Reducing import duty on knitting machinery can facilitate their wide diffusion leading to better finish, quality and productivity. However this may have a detrimental impact on the indigenous textile machinery industry. In fact, this is what happened to textile machinery industry of Coimbatore in the recent past. With the reduction of duty and allowing free import of knitting machinery, within a few years, about 250 garment manufacturers in Tiruppur imported nearly 10,000 machines. This led to immediate collapse of the local textile machinery industry in Coimbatore.[45]

Institutional Linkages

With the ongoing integration with the world economy and consequent liberalisation of imports, several sectors will face cost competition and stress. Infrastructure assistance to reduce incidence of fixed cost and common facilities, cheaper credit and flexibility of labour laws to reduce variable costs will become increasingly necessary. There may be a need for institutional linkages between different segments. For instance, growth of power loom sector depends to a great deal on how garment exporters perform. Since the power looms are small in size and have short production run, this constitutes a significant advantage over the mills from the point of view of fashion-oriented apparel manufacturers. With the abolition of MFA, there would be need for flexibility, specialisation and frequent product diversification for apparel exporters and one of the ways apparel

45. There is a caveat. This will happen if domestic industry is technically inferior. In the above example, an imported knitting machine costs between ₹ 15 lakhs and ₹ 75 lakhs as against an Indian machine, which is available for ₹ 75,000. However, the imported machines, with computerised jacquards, offer productivity levels several times higher than those of Indian machines, thereby justifying the price difference (Source: Industrial Economist, 2005).

manufacturers can achieve better product differentiation is by having close ties with power looms. This implies close linkages between the power loom and knitwear segments.

Change in Product Mix

Though firms take signals from the market to alter their product mix, many a time, suitable incentives are needed for smoother and faster transition. Sometimes, the lack of information with the producer brings rigidity in the path-dependency and the ongoing product mix is continued. The returns are higher if the product mix is altered. For instance, in leather, emphasis should be on finished products rather than exporting raw hides or finished leather. This is because the average value addition on raw hides and skins worth ₹ 100 amounts to ₹ 345 for finished products against ₹ 86 on finished leather as found by Sankar (2001). Even in finished products, the emphasis should be more on footwear production due to India's clear labour cost advantage among all footwear producing countries. The data indicate that in 1998 for the segment, the labour cost was US$ 0.2/hr against 7.2 for Korea, 5.9 for Taiwan, 5.3 for Portugal, 0.7 for Indonesia and 0.6 for China.[46] Similarly, in pump manufacturing, the aim should be to produce pumps for other uses.

Strengthening of Human Resources Pool

Since many industries are skill intensive (e.g., IT, automobile, biotechnology, etc.), strengthening of the human resource pool is essential. The evidence shows that in Coimbatore, the existence of a large number of engineering and training institutions set up by the Central and the State Government and the local bodies[47] have facilitated access to technical services. This has led to identification of the required needs of the industry, which then facilitated technology adaptation in pump manufacturing (Pillai, 2000: 4213) and textile clusters. In biotechnology, however, efforts are needed to facilitate greater interaction between scientists in various

46. *Source: http://www.factbook.net/leather_patterns.php* accessed December 2006.

47. In 2000, in and around Coimbatore, there were 80 engineering colleges, more than 10 polytechnics and a large number of industrial training institutes (ITIs) to support the industrialisation (Mohanan Pillai, 2000: 4213).

universities and representatives of industries including users of the various Biotechnology Parks.

The industries which are skill intensive require greater attention. For instance, in biotechnology industry, human resource initiatives need to consist of the following: (1) suitably changing the procedures in existing state-supported universities and institutions to facilitate better interaction with the business community and encourage the production of scientist/ technologist entrepreneurs; (2) initiating the creation of new, short-duration technician-oriented courses in universities in specific areas (post B.Sc./M. Sc.); (3) increasing the intake of students in biotechnology courses currently offered; and (4) the thrust areas in environmental biotechnology courses should be those concerning traditional industries facing waste management problems—leather and textiles.

To conclude, there are several avenues for government intervention that can solve the problem of scarce resources such as capital, technology and training affecting several major industries in TN. However, no simple or known forms of intervention can solve the organisational problems that lead to bad practice or unreliable contracting. The industry itself has to find its way out of these problems through more internal collaboration, by seeking the help of relatively larger units, etc.[48] Moreover, the policy intervention can be called effective and judicious if different clusters develop as industrial districts and generate more linkages and employment potential, with commensurate reduction in inequality, which at the moment is not happening.

References

Action Aid (2005). "Looming Crises: The Threat of Industrial Trade Liberalisation Negotiations at the WTO on India's Textile and Leather Industries (*www.actionaid.org/wps/content_document.asp?doc_id=376*, accessed Dec. 2006).

Anderson, Kim (2004). "Seamless Textiles with Inherent Shape", Unpublished Dissertation, Textile Technology Management, North Carolina State University, Raleigh (*http://www.lib.ncsu.edu/theses/ available/etd-01212005-110651/unrestricted/etd.pdf*, accessed January 2007).

48. At present, the state of formal organisation within some industries that might serve some of these objectives is weak and undeveloped. For instance, in power loom segment, associations are more concerned with wresting government concessions than facilitating co-operation among power loom firms (Roy, 1999).

Bhaumik, S.K., S. Gangopadhyay and S. Krishnan (2005). "Policy, Economic Federalism and Product Market Entry: The Indian Experience" (*www.idfresearch.org/ EntryBookChapter_14Dec2005.pdf*).

Bindhumadhavan, P.R. (2004). "Human Development", *http://www.tn.gov.in/spc/ workshop/MS_paper-HD.pdf*, accessed December 2006.

CII (2005). "Industry Monitor: Tamil Nadu" (*www.ciionline.org/southern/images/TNIM.pdf*, accessed December 2006).

CLE (2000). *Leathers*. A publication of the Council for Leather Exports, Chennai.

Industrial Economist (2005). "Promising Performance", August, Chennai (*www. indeconomist.com/ 300805_cover.html*, accessed December 2006).

Jeyaranjan, J. (2000). "Child Labour in Tiruppur Knitwear Industry", Unpublished *mimeo*, Noida: V V Giri National Labour Institute.

Jha, V. (2005). *Trade Adjustment Study: India Case Study*. UNCTAD Conference. January. (*http://www.unctad.info/upload/TAB/docs/TechCooperation/india_ study.pdf* accessed in 2007).

Kathuria, V. and V. Tewari (2007). "Venture Capitalist's role in Choosing Entrepreneurs: A Study of Indian Biotechnology Industry", in D. Audretsch, Max Keilbach and J. Tamvada (eds.), *Entrepreneurship and Innovation Studies on Germany and India*, Kluwer Publications (Forthcoming).

Manthagini, B. (1983). "The History of Knitwear Industry at Tiruppur", Unpublished M Phil Dissertation. Erode: Department of History, Vellalar College for Women.

Mazumdar, I. (2005). Approach Paper: Vulnerabilities of Women Home Based Workers. Delhi: Centre for Women's Development Studies, p.13.

Mohanan Pillai, P. (2000). "Industrial Clusters under Duress: Coimbatore Pump Manufacturers and Liberalisation", *Economic and Political Weekly*, November, 25.

Narayanan (2005). "Centre Approves Coimbatore Industrial Cluster Proposal", *Business Line*, April 15.

Neetha, N. (2002). "Flexible Production, Feminisation and Disorganisation: Evidence from Tiruppur Knitwear Industry", *Economic and Political Weekly*, May 25.

Pillai, P. (2000). "The State and Collective Action: Successful Adjustment by the Tamil Nadu Leather Clusters to German Environmental Standards". Unpublished Masters Thesis, Cambridge, MA: Massachusetts Institute of Technology.

Rehman, K.A. (1991). "Free Electric Power Supply for Agro Pump Sets: How Long, Small Industries". Coimbatore: Testing and Research Centre. Referred in Mohanan Pillai, P. 2000).

Roy, T. (1999). "Growth and Recession in Small-Scale Industry: A Study of Tamil Nadu Powerlooms", *Economic and Political Weekly*, Oct. 30.

Sankar, U. (2001). *Economic Analysis of Environmental Problems in Tanneries and Textile Bleaching and Dyeing Units and Suggestions for Policy Action*. New Delhi: Allied Publishers Ltd.

South Indian Hoisery Manufacturers Association (various issues). *SIHMA Bulletin*, Tiruppur.

Sujatha, V. (2002). "Leather Processing: Role of Indigenous Technology-Tamil Nadu", *Economic and Political Weekly*, November 23.

Tadaka, Yadagiri (2005). *Globalisation and Rural Industries: A Study of Handlooms*. Hyderabad: Department for Political Sciences, Nizam College. Referred in *http:// www.actionaid.org.uk/sites/default/files/doc_lib/ 59_ 1_looming_crisis_report.pdf* accessed in 2007)

Taws, John (2003). Personal interview of Kim Anderson, Fletcher Industries", Southern Pines, NC. September.

Tewari, M. (2003). *Engaging the Dragon: The Emerging Dynamics of Inter-regional Trade and Investment between India and China*. Draft paper prepared for the South Asia Program, Columbia University's Earth Institute and the Ministry of Commerce, India. July.

———. (2005). *Post MFA Adjustments in India's Textile and Apparel Industry: Emerging Issues and Trends*. New Delhi: ICRIER.

Textile Vision 2005. *http://www.tco.gov.pk/Webs/Material%20For%20Website/Reports/Report% 20Textile%20Vision%202005.PDF*, accessed January 2007.

The Hindu (2007). Dyeing Units Cease Production, *The Hindu*, January 2, Chennai.

UNIDO (2001). Diagnostic Study: Motors and Pumps Cluster. Coimbatore, Tamil Nadu. *www.msmefoundation.org/folder/Diagnostic/110.pdf*. Accessed in June 2007)

Usha, P. (1984). "Leather Industry of Tamil Nadu: Study of Structural Change with Special Reference to the 1973 Export Trade Control Policy", Unpublished PhD thesis submitted at Madras Institute of Development Studies, Chennai.

Websites

http://164.100.24.208/ls/CommitteeR/Communication/5rep.pdf (Standing committee on IT 2004-05, Lok Sabha).

http://commerce.nic.in/pr_archive.htm

http://www.tidco.com/tn_policies/tn_policies/bio_technology_policy1.asp

http://www.tn.gov.in/department/industries.htm

http://www.intamm.com/ industry/business/business.htm accessed on May 12, 2006.

http://www.en.wikipedia.org/wiki/Tamil_Nadu accessed on May 12, 2006.

http://www.tidco.com/tn_policies/slide_show/slideshow.ppt accessed December 2006.

Appendix Table A-7.1

Policy Initiatives (G.Os.) Pertaining to Different Industries

G.O.	*Policy Pronouncement*
G.O.MS.No. 91 Dated : 18.7.2005	Industries: New Industrial Policy, 2003, Framing of guidelines for sanction of Structured Assistance Package-Guidelines framed-Orders-Issued.
May 11, 2005	GoI approved upgradation of facilities at Pump, Motor and Foundry cluster at Coimbatore at a cost of ₹ 66.39 crores within 24 months under Industrial Infrastructure Upgradation Scheme (IIUS). Central Grant—₹ 39.22 crores. Remaining from State Govt, users and lending agencies.
2004-05	Auto Ancillary cluster at Chennai granted by GoI at project cost of 47.20 crores with central assistance of 35.00 crores.
G.O.Ms.No. 41 Dated : 28.3.2005	Industries—TN Industrial Investment Corporation Limited (TNIICL)—State Capital Subsidy of ₹ 11,71,37,777 for the year 2004-2005 sanctioned.
G.O.Ms.No. 34 Dated : 14.3.2005	Industries - INIICL—State Capital Subsidy of ₹ 5,91,600 for the year 2004-2005 sanctioned.
G.O.Ms.No.6 Dated : 10.1.2005	TN Relief Undertakings (Special Provision) Act, 1969 (TN Act 21 of 1969) Tvl. Southern Structurals Ltd.—Notification Issued.
G.O.Ms.No. 5 Dated : 10.1.2005	TN Relief Undertakings (Special Provision) Act, 1969 (TN Act 21 of 1969) Tvl. Southern Structurals Limited, Chennai—Declaration as a Relief Undertaking-Notification Issued.
No. 69, 15.10.2004	Industries: TNIICL—State Capital Subsidy of ₹ 2,270,623/- for 2004-05 sanctioned.
G.O.(3D).No.72 Dated : 13.7.2004	Industries: TN Steels Ltd., Arakkonam—Recovery of House Building Advance from the employees by adjusting the Fixed Deposit (FD) with TN Transport Development Finance Corporation Limited (TDFC)—Discharging the FD of the individuals whose principal and interest is less than the FD amount and to refund surplus amount to them—Orders Issued.
G.O.Ms.No.19 Dated : 19.4.2004	Mines and Quarries: Minor Minerals—TN Minor Mineral Concession Rules, 1959—Use of machinery for quarrying of sand in river beds—Further amendments to Rule 36-A of TN Minor Mineral Concession Rules, 1959—Issued.
No.16, 31.3.2004	The TNIICL—State Capital subsidy of ₹ 5,66,08,879 for the year 2003-2004—Sanctioned.
G.O.Ms.No.12 Dated : 18.3.2004	Industries: Subsidy to small, medium and large scale industries—Grant of subsidy to the eligible pipeline cases—Orders Issued.
G.O.Ms.No.11 Dated : 17.3.2004	Public Services: TN Agricultural Extension Services—Creation of one post of Deputy Director (Technical) in the office of the Commissioner of Sugar—Framing of *ad hoc* Rules for the post—Orders Issued.
No.8, 2.3.2004	Industries: TNIIC Ltd.—State Capital Subsidy of ₹ 58,44,724 for 2003-2004—Sanctioned.

contd...

...contd...

G.O.	*Policy Pronouncement*
Lr..Ms.No.112 Dated : 25.11.2003	TIDCO - Formation of a Special Purpose Vehicle to implement the Ennore SEZ project—Proposals Approved.
No. 103, 20.10.2003	Industries: TNIIC Ltd.—State Capital Subsidy of ₹ 75,07,208 for 2003-2004—Sanctioned.
G.O.Ms.No.95 Dated : 1.10.2003	Mines and Quarries: Minor Minerals—TN Minor Mineral Concession Rules, 1959—Introduction of Rule—38A Amendment to TN Minor Mineral Concession Rules, 1959—Notification Issued.
G.O.Ms.No.83 Dated : 14.8.2003	Industries: TNIICL—State Capital Subsidy of ₹ 3.00 crores for the year 2003-2004—Sanctioned.
G.O.(2D).No.23 Dated : 13.6.2003	Industries: Part II Scheme for 2003-2004—Mines and Minerals —Scheme for Geographic Information System (GIS) in Geology and Mining Department—Orders Issued.
G.O.(2D).No.22 Dated : 13.6.2003	Industries—Part II Scheme for 2003-2004—Mines and Minerals - Scheme for reappraised of limestone deposit in Southern and Western districts of Tamil Nadu—Orders Issued.
GSR 328(E) Dated. 17.4.2003	Mineral Conservation and Development (2nd Amendment) Rules, 2003, 17-04-2003 (GoI Notification)
329(E), 10.4.2003	Mineral Concession (Amendment) Rules, 2003, 10-04-2003 (GoI Notification)
GSR 330(E) Dated: 10.4.2003	Mineral Conservation and Development (Amendment) Rules, 2003. dated 10-04-2003 (GoI Notification)
G.O.Ms.No.31 Dated : 6.2.2003	Industries-Incentives-Extension of Interest Free Sale Tax Deferral Concessions for the change of Management and Diversification of the Unit—Orders Issued.
G.O.(2D).No.4 Dated : 4.2.2003	Industries: Individual Family Satisfaction Team (IFST) Waiver/ Deferral Scheme—Plant and Machinery acquired under hire purchase—Eligibility for consideration under the IFST Waiver/Deferral scheme—Cancelled.
No.38, 1.4.2002	M.G.R. KNOWLEDGE PARK within the M.G.R. Film city—Formation—Orders issued.
G.O.Ms.No.127 Dated : 22.3.2000	Industries: Sales Tax-based incentives to Industries by way of Deferral and Waiver Schemes–Phasing out the deferral and waiver schemes—Orders Issued.

Source: http://www.tn.gov.in/gorders/industries/default.htm, dipp.nic.in/iius/Approval-%Coimbatore_Engg.pdf; www.finmin.nic.in/the_ministry/dept_expenditure/outbud/ob/INDUSTRIAL_POLICY_PROMOTION.pdf.

8 IT Industry in Tamil Nadu

Meenakshi Rajeev

Introduction

Services sector has shown enormous potential as a growth driver for many developing countries and India is prominent among them. With the development of information technology (IT), trade in services was born again in an entirely new 'avatar'. The traditional definition of services as something non-storable, non-tradable and intangible appears to be too narrow today. With the development of IT-enabled services (ITES), service goods, which are traditionally thought to be non-tradable, have increasingly been taking up a sizable share of international trade. Some Indian states notably Tamil Nadu (TN), Karnataka, Andhra Pradesh (AP) and Maharashtra are active players in this segment.

International Monetary Fund (IMF) provides data on imports and exports of services by different countries, but it is difficult to segregate clearly the volume of IT-ITES sector from such balance of payments (BoP) statistics, as these services are not separately accounted. As per IMF classification,[1] 'a' category, *viz.*, 'other business services', includes management fees, professional, technical and consultancy services, legal services, market research agencies and research and development (R&D). Exports and imports under this category and the 'computer and information services' category would together constitute IT and ITES (see Amiti and Wei, 2004; Chanda, 2002; Prasad and Kapoor, 1996).

If we examine the *share of other business plus computer and information services* in the total imports of Organisation for Economic Co-operation and Development (OECD) countries under these two heads, it can be seen that over 80 per cent of trade in other business services are confined

1. "Balance of Payments Statistics", Part 2 and 3, *IMF. Year Book 2003*, pp.296, 410, 443.

to the OECD countries only (in the year 1990). India's share was only about 2 per cent and China's around 1 per cent. The shares of some of the other competing countries in the IT and ITES segments are presented in Table 8.1.

Table 8.1

Country-wise Break-up of Other Business and Computer and Information Services Exports in OECD's Imports of these Services

Countries	*1990*	*2002*
Australia	1.22	0.76
Canada	6.09	3.41
China	0.73	3.40
India	1.57	5.73
Indonesia	0.21	0.00
Ireland	0.61	4.74
Malaysia	0.71	0.72
Mexico	0.32	0.08
Netherlands	7.25	6.62
Philippines	1.73	0.08
Singapore	4.59	4.01
Thailand	0.50	1.11

Source: Compiled from the *Balance of Payments Statistics Year Book, IMF.*

From Table 8.1, it can be seen that subsequently, i.e., after 1990, the export shares changed considerably for India; it increased to 6 per cent in the global market in 2002. During the same period, the shares of Ireland and China too increased to 5 per cent and 3 per cent, respectively, from about 0.61 per cent and 0.73 per cent, while that of Philippines on the other hand declined and become almost negligible. A look at India's relative comparative advantage (RCA)[2] ratios in IT and ITES sector *vis-à-vis* the above countries confirms the position (Table 8.2).

A closer examination of India's export of services at a disaggregated level reveals the growing importance of this sector in the country's trade in services. Figure 8.1 shows that while the share of this sector was about 42 per cent in the year 1990 (Figure 8.1), it increased to a much higher level of 76 per cent in 2002 (see Rajeev and Vani, 2006; 2007). It further increased

2. RCA_{India}={India's export of other services/World's export of other services}/{India's total export of services/World's total export of services}

in 2006 but a slight decline observed during 2011 may be due to global recession.

Table 8.2

RCA (Computer and Information and Other Business Services) of India vis-à-vis Other Selected Nations

Year	*India*	*Mexico*	*Philippines*	*Singapore*	*Canada*	*Ireland*	*China*	Australia
1990	3.1	0.4	4.8	3.3	2.9	1.6	1.1	1.1
2000	4.6	0.3	0.7	2.7	2.2	3.4	1.8	0.8
2001	5.1	0.2	0.5	3.0	2.2	4.0	1.9	0.9
2002	5.5	0.1	0.6	3.2	2.2	4.0	2.0	1.1

Source: BoP Statistics, IMF.

Figure 8.1

Shares of Different Sub-sectors of Services Sector Exports to Total Services Export of India[3]

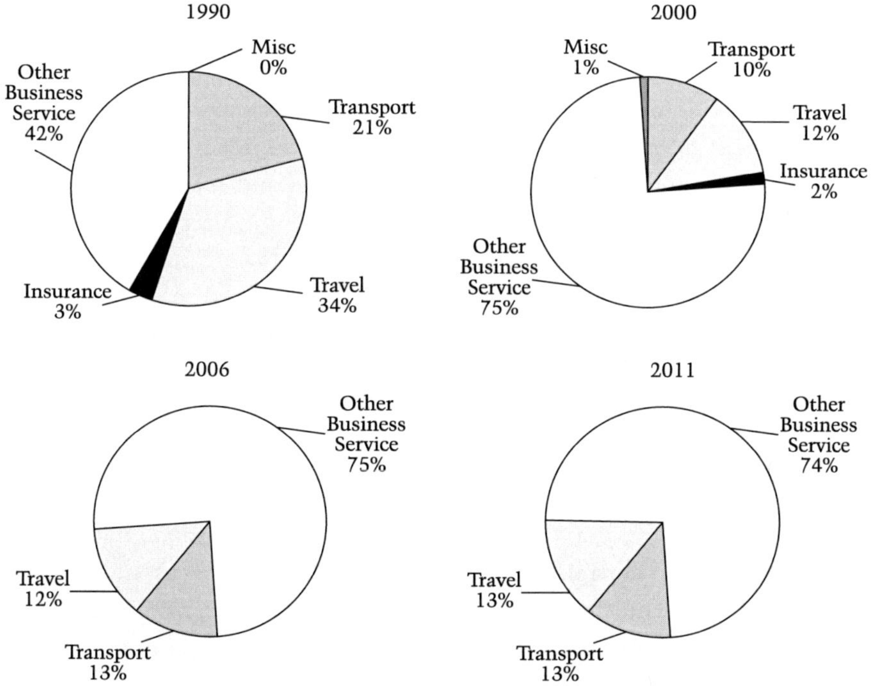

Source: Compiled from the *Balance of Payments Statistics Year Book*, IMF.

3. See also the Reserve Bank of India (RBI) *Monthly Bulletin* various issues.

Within the country however, not all regions have developed IT/ ITES industry equally. In this respect, South India has always been in the forefront and is often termed as the 'dynamic south'. The US ambassador to India, Richard Celeste, mentioned that the 'Silicon Triangle' in South India (with Chennai, Bangalore and Hyderabad as its vertices) rivalled the Silicon Valley in California. The contributions of these three states are considerable as far as India's export revenue from this sector is concerned. Though in software exports, Karnataka has been ahead of TN, in recent years, the latter has been catching up fast, and its growth of IT exports has increased from about 25 per cent in 2002-03 to 31.54 per cent in 2005-06.[4]

The availability of educated manpower, high standard of educational institutions, sound infrastructure, low costs of operation, disciplined labour force, presence of international airports and a major sea port are some of the factors which have made TN in general and Chennai in particular the prime destination for IT industry. Further, the state has taken substantial steps through the Software Technology Parks of India (STPI) to develop the industry.

Export promotion is only one dimension of the IT industry (see NASSCOM, 2002a; 2002b; 2005). With the development of the industry and the resulting penetration of IT knowledge, the technology has come to be harnessed for various development purposes and sociopolitical goals, and the Government of TN has been at the forefront in this pursuit as well. Furthermore, IT industry in India is generally concentrated in a few selected metros. This spatial concentration not only has induced migration of job seekers to these locations from all over the world, but in turn has also put considerable pressure on the infrastructure of these metros. Bangalore is a glaring example of this phenomenon. With a view to easing the pressure on current IT hubs and disperse benefits of IT revolution widely in the state, Tamil Nadu has initiated steps to develop two- and three-tier cities.

This paper looks at the IT sector of TN with special focus on its export earning capabilities. Use of IT for development purposes is also looked into and further potentials identified. The paper considers the policies and programmes taken up by the TN government for the

4. This growth rate is observed in data from the Chennai Centre of STPI; *Source*: Electronics Corporation of Tamil Nadu (ELCOT).

development of IT sector and discusses the further steps needed in this regard. Given this thematic sequence, the paper is arranged as follows. In view of the centrality of state government's proactive measures in shaping the industry in TN, the paper commences with a discussion of such measures. The next section discusses impact of such measures in terms of development of the industry base, its export growth and other indicators. A comparison of TN with other southern states is also taken up in this section. Application of IT for development purposes needs attention in the Indian context. Therefore, some of the noteworthy steps taken by the TN government in this direction are examined in the penultimate section (see also Ramachandran and Goebel, 2002). The last section speculates on the options available to the state for strengthening and extending the application of IT for development and change in the future. The paper is mainly based on secondary information. However, we have also had an opportunity to discuss the status of the industry with industry leaders, CEOs of a number of both small and large firms as well as officials of the government and organised bodies like Confederation of Indian Industry (CII). Secondary information has been supplemented with findings from such primary level discussions.

State Initiatives: The Crucial Factor

Tamil Nadu is a state with a strong industrial base (see Figure A-8.1 in the Appendix). Possibly, given the flourishing manufacturing sector with wide ranging activities that the state enjoys, it did not feel the urgency to pursue vigorously the development of the IT sector. For example, in the year 1990-91 itself, Karnataka had exported software worth about $2 million. In 1997-98 Karnataka's software export increased to $478 million, in which year Tamil Nadu's export was only $138 million. Next year (1998-99) Karnataka increased its software exports to $833 million, while that from TN was around $311 million.

However, after observing the success of a few other states especially that of Karnataka, the TN government began to introduce appropriate policy measures to develop this emerging industry in the state.[5] It is also observed that the state is one of the largest producers of engineering

5. As revealed during our discussions with the state government officials.

graduates in IT, but human resource from the state was moving to other states like Karnataka, Maharashtra or AP in search of better job opportunities. At this juncture, it was felt by the state that it was necessary to develop the IT industry if it were to retain the talent pool. The urge to develop the sector became stronger after the emergence of the ITES/ business process outsourcing (BPO) industry segment which promised large-scale job opportunities to the youth even with moderate educational qualifications. Furthermore, the state realized that if network facilitates were made available, the industry would develop in the two- or three-tier cities too, which could lead to more balanced regional development. Given the possibility of such multiple benefits, the state government began taking a number of measures to develop the IT industry.

Tamil Nadu was the first state to come out with an IT policy. The state's IT policy was first promulgated on 3rd November, 1997 (*www.elcot.com/policy.htm*); it was revised in 2002 (19th September) and an appropriate ITES policy was announced on 25th October, 2002. The pioneering concepts of the policy like Right Of Way (ROW) and computer education in schools have found emulation all over the country. The major thrust of the state's policy objectives is on two aspects: (1) development of IT industry for commercial purposes, i.e., to generate revenue and create employment, and (2) facilitate use of IT specifically for development purposes. While the first objective would be eminently served by firmly establishing Tamil Nadu as a major investment destination, the stated objective of the policy document, *viz.*, to have a strong R&D base is intended to help both commercial and developmental endeavours. The latter can be achieved if, for example, software is developed to cater to local needs like use of local language in computers or through hardware-related advancements such as making computers available at an affordable price. The other major objectives mentioned in the policy document are upgrading of quality of life for the citizens through e-governance and IT application in the government, empowering people in the rural areas so as to bridge the digital divide, promoting use of Tamil in IT and directly engender promotion of IT for domestic and development purposes.

More recent IT policy 2008 of the state envisages transforming Tamil Nadu as the information and communications technology (ICT) hub of South Asia by creating a "knowledge driven ecosystem, leveraging entrepreneurship and promoting socially inclusive growth to achieve a 25 per cent production share of the Indian ICT industry" (ICT Policy Document, 2008). If this target is reached, the sector would be able to create substantial employment opportunities for the youth of the state both directly and indirectly. It is estimated that a total of 0.8 million direct jobs will be created in the ICT sector. By the year 2011, ICT was estimated to employ around 0.7 million people and ICT manufacturing close to 0.1 million people. It was further estimated that 2.2 million indirect jobs would be generated by 2011. Thus, this policy aims at the creation of approximately 3 million additional jobs in the sector on its full implementation. The actual and estimated employment in the ICT sector in the country and in TN is given in Figure 8.2.

Figure 8.2

Current and Potential ICT Employment (in million) in Tamil Nadu and in India

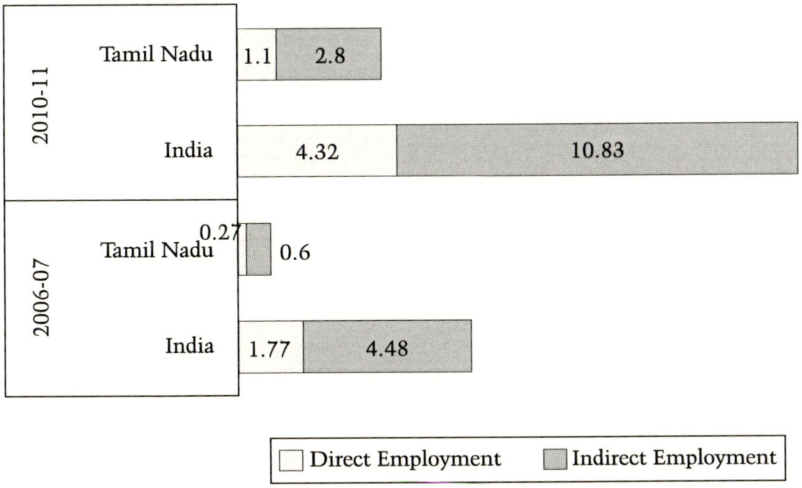

Source: ICRA analysis, NASSCOM Mckinsey report 2005, FICCI CEHA presentation and Data Quest; KPMG Estimates.

Further, the State Government has plans to establish an ICT Academy in TN to train the trainers for further dissemination of IT related expertise in the state. The ICT Academy is mandated to upgrade curriculum and enhance skills of the faculty engaged in teaching ICT-related disciplines. Several other initiatives are spelt out in the ICT policy 2008.

With these objectives in mind, a number of proactive measures have been introduced by the state with a view to capturing at least 25 per cent of the market. While some of them are direct measures in the form of fiscal initiatives, others are more facilitating in nature. For example, capital subsidies are provided to units according to their level of investments. Additional fiscal incentives are ensured to the firms having more than 40 per cent women employees or to those employing physically challenged persons.

Measures to Attract Investment and Improve Exports

With a view to reducing bureaucratic hassles, it was decided to permit the IT companies to self-certify that they are maintaining the registers and forms as contemplated under various employment acts, including Tamil Nadu Shops and Establishment Act, Payment of Wages Act, etc. This self-certification by the companies is regarded as sufficient compliance with the law.

The major factors for a company to locate in a particular region are appropriate infrastructure and availability of resources. In the case of IT and ITES sectors, these are relate to communication network, real estate and human resources. On all these three fronts government has taken appropriate supply side policy initiatives.

The state has a sizeable number of engineering colleges turning out graduates in large numbers. Further, government has decided to provide basic training in computers in all schools. To make the process complete, training for the teachers is also provided. In the telecommunication sector, under government initiative, optical fibre cable network with a bandwidth of 8.4 Tbps has been laid. This is the world's biggest and India's first private submarine optical fibre cable project. This project connects Chennai and Singapore by submarine cable. Government is also trying to provide uninterrupted quality power supply to the ITES sector at competitive rates. With these initiatives, the state's power situation improved slightly compared to other states but only for a while and has deteriorated in the recent past.

In addition government is also creating infrastructure for investors through software technology parks. Creation of IT Parks in the two-tier cities has been encouraged and supported by the government. Private participation is prominent in all these endeavours. A separate entity, *viz.*, ELCOT, has been created as the certifying authority for issuing 'No Objection Certificate' for IT buildings.

One of the major problems facing smaller IT firms is the dearth of market for their products. To overcome this handicap, government (through ELCOT) participates in various national and international IT-related events to promote the state as an investment destination and create a distinct TN brand.

Hardware Segment: Incentives for Manufacture of Computers

Although India has a well-developed IT industry, the achievements in the hardware segment lag behind those in software. The indigenous development of computers is crucial for reducing the digital divide. In order to upgrade expertise and capability in this area, the state has announced several concessions for establishing factories for the manufacture of computers. These concessions would operate for a period of 10 years from the year of commencement of commercial production.

Initiatives of the Government for ITES Segment

In general, the state is well known for its investment friendly policies and ambition to become a global leader in industrialisation. The World Bank as well as other global institutions has their back offices in the state. Over the years, the government has simplified its bureaucratic procedures and has accorded priority sector status to the ITES segment for loans from financial institutions and for creating venture capital funds.

To supply much needed human resources to the ITES industry, several steps are being taken to enhance computer literacy. Further English has been made a compulsory language in school/college curriculum to improve English language skills.

Development of Second Tier Cities/IT Parks

In most Indian states, IT and ITES industries are concentrated in one major metro only. This has not only created congestion but also led to migration and regional disparity. TN has several 2 and 3 tier cities with well-developed infrastructure and a flourishing manufacturing sector.

Taking advantage of this, the government is trying to develop these locations as IT/BPO hubs. Knowledge Industry townships are created in some of these cities through private-public partnership programmes to foster IT skills, and various large software parks like Tidel parks etc., are established in the state in order to provide necessary infrastructure in 2-tier and 3-tier cities.

Among the major IT parks developed in the state, the following deserve particular mention. The 1,00,000 sq ft Texcity Park in Coimbatore is the first state-of-the-art IT Park, complete with reliable high quality infrastructure and supporting amenities. During 2010, the TIDEL Park, initially built in Chennai, was replicated in Coimbatore at a cost of ₹ 380 crore. The IT Park at Siruseri was developed by the State Industries Promotion Corporation of Tamil Nadu (SIPCOT), a state government undertaking. This park has all basic infrastructure facilities like separate sub-stations for power supply, separate Telecom Exchange and High Speed Data Connectivity. Several IT companies have already booked land in this location.

IT policy 2008 clearly spells out incentives like capital subsidy and electricity tax exemption for the development of the industry in the two and three-tier cities.

TIDEL Park

TIDEL Park jointly promoted by TIDCO and ELCOT in 2000 is within the city limits of Chennai and is only 12 km from the International Airport. The park is equipped with high speed data connectivity, 100 per cent power back-up, video conferencing facilities and 24 x 7 services to the occupants. Most of the space in this park is occupied by multinational companies and over 12,000 software professionals are employed in the park. Later TIDEL Park II and III came up nearby.

Elnet Technologies Limited

Elnet Technologies Ltd. is a joint sector company under the aegis of M/s ELCOT. The company was established with the objective of constructing and maintaining the first ever private sector software technology park. The software technology park at Taramani is a part of the cyber corridor being developed by the Government.

In Pondicherry too, the government is trying to develop 1 lakh sq km space as IT and electronic parks under phase 1 and another 3 lakh sq. km under phase 2. STPI-Trichy/Madurai as well as Tirunelveli provide high speed data-communication (HSDC) services to software exporters under the cap of SoftNET, but local loop connectivity is provided through microwave communications or BSNL. Though the total footprint of IT and ITES endeavours in smaller cities is not substantial now, with the ongoing ITES movement, the tier 2 and 3 cities are expected to come up fast and reduce the congestion faced by the metros.

Rise of IT Industry in Tamil Nadu

Notwithstanding the preponderance of Karnataka in terms of most indicators relating to the IT industry in the country, Tamil Nadu has shown considerable growth in recent times. The role of STPI has been considerable in this. Established in 1991, STPI was registered as an Autonomous Society under the Department of Information Technology, Ministry of Communications and Information Technology. It was set up to implement STP Schemes and to promote software exports by providing infrastructure facilities including HSDC links. It is also executing the Electronics Hardware Technology Park (EHTP) Scheme.

According to STPI records, the number of companies increased enormously from 166 in 1998-99 to 601 in 1999-2000, showing a spectacular growth rate of 265 per cent (Figure 8.3). Though the number of STPI units has been declining in the last couple of years, the number of units outside STPI has been increasing. More importantly, there was 200 per cent increase in the total revenue from software exports between 2003 and 2005. The ITES–BPO segment has also been bringing in considerable export revenue.[6]

6. STPI units recorded software exports of over ₹ 37,176 crore during 2002-03. This was nearly 80 per cent of the country's total software exports.

Figure 8.3

Software Industry Growth in Tamil Nadu

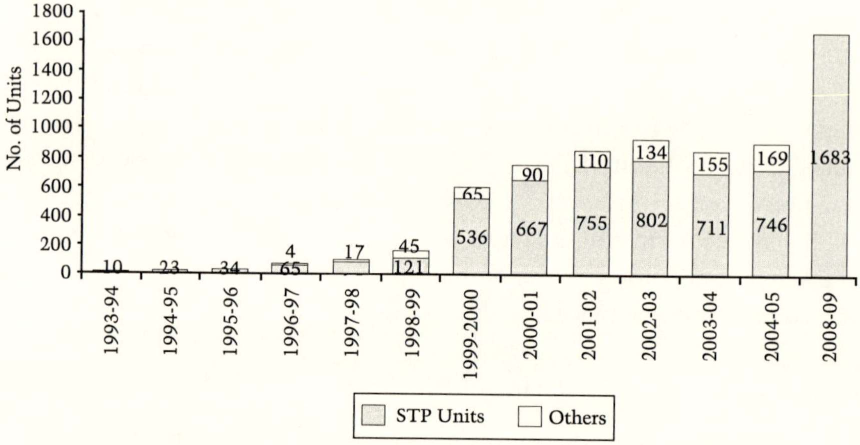

Source: *www.stpc.soft.net.*

It is noteworthy that the significant growth of the industry has brought about a situation where there are a large number of units in the small and medium enterprises (SME) segment operating parallel with larger units (Table 8.3).

Table 8.3

Number of Units according to Export Level Software Export Growth Performance of Tamil Nadu

Software Export Growth Performance of Tamil Nadu							
Sl. No.	*Software Export Turnover (in ₹)*	*No. of Units*					
		1999-2000	*2000-01*	*2001-02*	*2002-03*	*2003-04*	*2004-05*
1	Above 500	-	-	1	2	3	5
2	100-500	4	6	7	8	6	14
3	50-100	2	1	4	9	7	14
4	Oct-50	17	18	32	52	53	63
5	10-Jan	70	97	112	144	153	169
6	Up to 1 cr.		136	180	244	260	179

Source: STPI, Chennai.

A breakdown of the STPI units with respect to export turnover (Table 8.3) shows that the number of companies involved in export activities is increasing, indicating that the industry is not concentrated in the hands of a few. While expectedly at the very top level, there are only a few companies, the number of IT firms with turnover level below 50 crores is increasing rapidly.

Table 8.4 shows that TN has a fair mix of multinational companies and indigenous ones, and that the state has been able to attract foreign direct investment in this sector. In case of exports, one of the noteworthy features is that the share of SME units is over 50 per cent. It is clear, therefore, that the industry is not overly concentrated geographically and that export market is not captured entirely by the multinationals. It is also evident that IT industry is attracting investment from indigenous entrepreneurs.

Table 8.4

Structure (Ownership) of the Industry, 2005-06

MNC and JVs Presence	
No. of Wholly owned subsidiary/MNCs	153
JV companies	24
MNCs/WOS Share of Exports (05-06)	₹ 6223.36 crore
JVs Share of Exports (05-06)	₹ 131.80 crore
SMEs Share of Exports (05-06)	₹ 7637.76 crore

Note: MNC: multinational companies; JV: joint venture.
Source: STPI, Chennai.

Figure 8.4 shows the composition of different segments of IT–ITES industry in the total export basket of TN from which it is clear that there is a good mix of various components and presence of higher end services.

The major achievements cited above have become possible due to the proactive measures that the state has taken for the development of IT and ITES sectors. Our discussions with the industry personnel revealed their satisfaction with respect to state initiatives. They have acknowledged that the administrative procedures adopted by the state are sufficiently investor friendly.

Figure 8.4

Segment-wise Disaggregated Picture of Export of IT and ITES Products, 2010-11

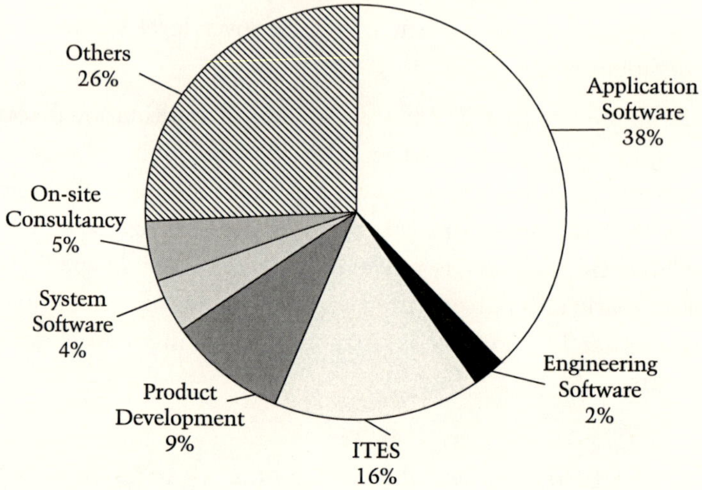

Source: Computed using STPI data.

Export Growth

The aggressive push of the Government has resulted in significant growth not only of IT and ITES firms but also in export earnings. While software industry is the major export earner, ITES segment is also catching up fast as is clear from the fact that while software export was worth a mere ₹ 57 crore in 1995-96, it increased to ₹ 10,703 crore, in the next 9 years (in 2004-05) showing an annual average increment of 20 per cent. At present, the software export level stands at ₹ 42210.65 crore as against ₹ 36765.53 crore in 2009-10. This indicates an annual average growth of 15 per cent for the period 2009-10 to 2010-11 (Figure 8.5).

The major export destination for TN (as for the rest of the country) is the US (Figure 8.6). The share of exports to the US is 58 per cent followed by the UK with 12 per cent. However the state has been exporting to other European countries as well. Diversification of export destinations is good for risk diversification as well.

Figure 8.5

Growth of Export Earnings through Software Industry:
Tamil Nadu and Pondicherry

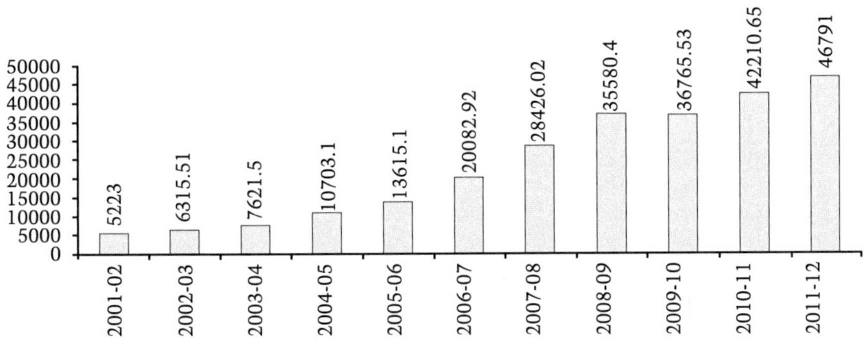

Source: STPI, Chennai.

Figure 8.6

Country-wise Software Exports from Tamil Nadu and Pondicherry (2008-09)

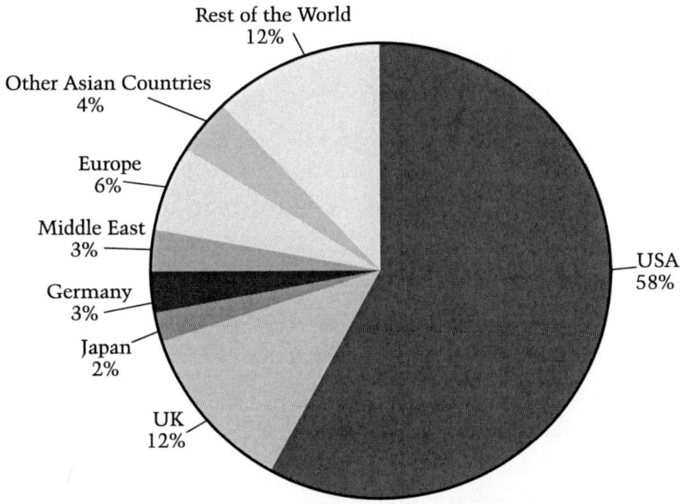

Source: STPI, Chennai.

While India's major strength is in the software segment, there have been some efforts to develop hardware industry too. TN is taking certain measures towards this end. During 2004-05, hardware exports amounted to ₹ 211 crores which came down drastically to ₹ 101 crores in the next couple of years but increased again and remained stagnant till 2010-11 after which we see an increase in exports (Figure 8.7).

Figure 8.7

EHTP Units and Hardware Exports

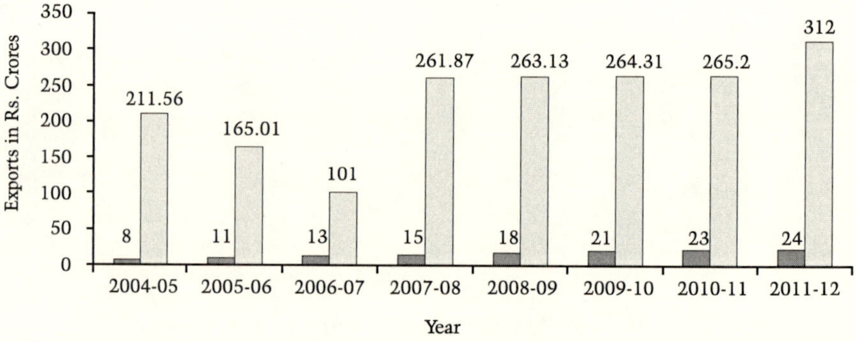

Source: STPI, Chennai.

The ITES sector in TN has been able to register an export growth of 63 per cent between 2003-04 and 2004-05. An important feature of the TN ITES segment, as revealed during our discussions with the ITES firms, is their capability to deliver higher-end services. As can be noted from Table 8.5, TN firms are operating in diversified areas including higher-end areas like computer-aided design-computer-aided manufacturing (CAD-CAM), e-learning and so on (Table 8.5) and not concentrating on call centres alone, and export earnings from all these segments are registering increase. It is a positive trend that the state is earning considerable revenue from the data-processing segment as well. Data-processing segment does not necessarily require its employees to work in night shifts like firms in the customer care segment. This has the added advantage of reducing not only human resources (HR)-related problems but also certain social ones. Further, competition from other countries is less in this segment and opportunities to move up the value chain are also available.

Table 8.5

ITES Industry in Tamil Nadu

Area of Expertise	*2003-04*		*2004-05*	
	Export ₹ *Cr.*	%	*Export* ₹ *Cr.*	%
IT enabled services (total)	(1000.34)	(13.09)	(1636.06)	(15)
Data Processing/Data Entry	399.82		443.85	
Medical Transcription and Medical Billing	71.25		91.26	
CAD/CAM	71.13		69.14	
BPO	304.64		567.02	
Call Center	153.50		162.95	
Web Applications (Multimedia/Internet/E-Commerce)	39.37	0.52	93.2.1	9
Product/Packages	8.63	0.11	341.66	3

Note: On-site Consultancy services are also included.

Source: STPI, Chennai.

Tamil Nadu in Comparative Perspective

Software exports

Even though Karnataka began developing its IT industry much earlier than TN, the latter is fast catching up and has already attained the second position. The state's share in the nation's total export earning however has remained more or less the same at around 17 per cent since 2001-2003. As can be seen from Table 8.6, the highest exports by STPI registered units were from Karnataka (₹ 12350 cr), followed by TN (₹ 6305 cr) and Maharashtra (₹ 5508 cr).

A quick comparison with Karnataka reveals the following. In the year 2003-04, total export of software services from Karnataka was $4000 million as against $1955 million of TN. Software exports increased to $6270 and $2677 million in 2004-05 for Karnataka and TN, respectively. As far as the number of companies is concerned, Karnataka still retains its leading position; it had about 1322 companies in 2003-04 which increased to 1520 by 2004-05. In contrast, increase in the total number of companies in TN was from 866 in 2003-04 to 915 in 2004-05.

Table 8.6

Software Exports: Tamil Nadu versus Other States (STP Units)

(Rs crores)

Name of the State	*Exports in FY 2001-2002*	*Exports in FY 2002-2003*	*Growth Rate (%)*	*Exports in FY 2009-2010*	*Exports in FY 2010-2011*	*Growth Rate (%)*
Karnataka	9904	12350	25	67100	70240.93	5
Tamil Nadu	5014	6305	26	26363.51	28289.75	7
Maharashtra	4603	5508	20	45709.34	49873.78	9
Andhra Pradesh	2805	3638	30	27665.85	28674.57	4
Uttar Pradesh	2000	2541	27	10590	10945	3
Delhi	1750	2065	18	1892.49	1541.2	-19
West Bengal	604	1200	99	5441	5665	4
Orissa	213	260	22	1116.83	1253.29	12
Kerala	159	165	4	1956.45	2071.67	6

Source: Ministry of Communications and Information Technology, Government of India (GoI), Press Release, 22nd May, 2003, *http://pib.nic.in/archieve.*

Table 8.6 also provides figures of exports in fiscal year (FY) 2009-10 and 2010-11. In FY 2009-10, the growth rate in almost all the states were very encouraging, but in the subsequent period (2010-11), there has not been much growth primarily due to global recession. Although the value of exports has been increasing, the rate of increase is not very satisfactory. While states like Delhi experienced a decline in export performance in year 2010 compared to 2009-10, the growth of southern region states like Karnataka, TN and Kerala was in the range of 5-7 per cent during the period.

Hardware Industry in Tamil Nadu

Similar to STP units, the exports from the hardware segment given by EHTP units have been the highest from Karnataka (₹ 1404 cr), followed by TN (₹ 718 cr) and Maharashtra (₹ 113 cr) (Table 8.7).

ITES Segment

Of late, companies engaged in ITES activities have been increasingly locating themselves in TN. In particular, Bangalore's deteriorating infrastructure has led to this trend. Though AP and Karnataka are ahead of TN, more and more high end BPOs are shifting to or establishing in TN cities which is a welcome trend from the state's perspective.

Table 8.7

State-wise (Hardware) Exports by EHTP Registered Units

Name of the State	*Exports in FY 2001-2002*	*Exports in FY 2002-2003*	*Growth Rate (%)*
Karnataka	829	1404	69
Tamil Nadu	461	718	56
Maharashtra	91	113	24
Others	97	141	46
Total	1478	2376	61

Source: Ministry of Communications and Information Technology, GoI, Press Release, 22nd May, 2003, *http://pib.nic.in/archieve/*.

Table 8.8

ITES Segment: Comparison of Tamil Nadu with Other States, 2002-03

State	*Revenues*	*Comments*
Andhra Pradesh	₹ 1411 crore	Andhra Pradesh already gets a hefty 40 per cent of its IT revenues from ITES.
Karnataka	₹ 988 crore	The number of approved ITES companies increased from 28 to 41 in fiscal 2002-03. Revenues earned by them also grew to ₹ 988 crores, which is 8 per cent of the overall exports of ₹ 12,350 crores earned by the state.
Tamil Nadu	₹ 523 crore	ITES earnings have jumped 8.3 per cent to ₹ 523 crores last fiscal from ₹ 340 crore the year 2001-02.
Kerala	Not available	The number of ITES companies in Kerala which is pushing very hard to be among the preferred ITES destinations is said to be below 10.

Source: Ministry of Communications and Information Technology, GoI, Press Release, 22nd May, 2003, *http://pib.nic.in/archieve/*

A comparison of the performance of TN with Karnataka in the ITES segment reveals that in the recent years, ITES exports from Karnataka amounted to $486 million in 2003-04 while that of Tamil Nadu was $250 million. By the year 2004-05, export earnings of Karnataka reached $805 million while that of TN stood at $409 million. Thus it appears that Karnataka still retains the first mover's advantage (Table 8.8).

Employment Share and Human Resources in Tamil Nadu[7]

Added to other advantages, TN has the best technical and higher education infrastructure with 25 universities and 252 engineering colleges. A key advantage lies in the highly skilled software professionals of TN who make up a considerable proportion of current army of software professionals in the country. Nearly 60,000 engineering students graduate from the engineering institutions of the state annually, and this number keeps growing year after year. Of the 60,000 engineers who graduate every year from TN, 35,000 are from IT-related disciplines and are products of premier institutions of excellence such as IIT, Anna University, Chennai and others of repute. With over 33,000 professionals presently working, TN has one of the largest pools of software professionals in the country.

According to TN government estimates, TN software industry employs around 145,000 professionals (*http://www.tn.gov.in/department/IT.htm*). There were also attempts to estimate the total number of professionals employed in the state on the basis of the state's export shares in the total exports of the country. NASSCOM Strategic Review, 2007, estimates the total export of IT and ITES services (see Appendix Table A-8.2) at $12.9 billion for 2004-05, Tamil Nadu's share in that being $3.08 billion.[8] Thus the state's share turns out to be 23 per cent in total exports. NASSCOM Strategic Review, 2007, also provides figures of total employment in export and domestic segments (see Appendix Table A-8.2) separately. Taking an identical per cent of the total employees involved in export segment in the country as a whole, total employment strength in TN can be computed as approximately 117,760 in 2004-05. Similarly, we estimate total employment in TN IT–ITES export segment at 190620, as the share of Tamil Nadu's exports is approximately 26.6 per cent of the total national export (Table 8.9).

7. *www.tidelpark.com*

8. Assuming $1 = ₹ 40.

Table 8.9

Estimate of Employment in the IT-ITES Export Segment in Tamil Nadu

Year	*2004-05*	*2005-06*
Total IT/ITES export in India (in $ billion)	17.7	23.6
Tamil Nadu's share	23%	27%
Estimate of Tamil Nadu's employment	117760	190620

Source: The Author's Estimate.

However, the recent IDC-Dataquest survey (see Arora, 2005) shows that the share of the southern states has been declining and of late, Maharashtra has emerged as the biggest producer of IT professionals. According to an IDC-Dataquest survey done in 2005, the four southern states of AP, TN, Kerala and Karnataka dominated the manpower market with the highest contribution to the needs of the industry; however, the overall proportion of their contributions came down from 48.7 per cent in 2004 to 45.3 per cent in 2005[9]. Interestingly, Bangalore had to give up its *numero uno* position as Maharashtra took its place as the biggest source of IT professionals. Maharashtra has made significant strides in the last 2 years, taking its contribution from 5.9 per cent in 2003 to 15.8 per cent in 2005, while Karnataka's share came down to 12 per cent in 2005. India's Silicon Valley even failed to make it to the 2nd position as the contribution of Andhra Pradesh to the industry outstripped that of Karnataka. However, Tamil Nadu saw a significant drop in its supply of manpower during the year 2003, but by 2004 its share had improved to 13 per cent and to 14 per cent by 2005. Another interesting trend is the narrowing of the gap between the top-most state and those in lower positions, which is indicative of the success of the latter's effort to measure up to the better performing states.

Given the highly uneven performance of the industry across states, as revealed by the various indicators, it is of interest to look at some of the factors that seem to have impacted upon the performance of certain states. It is hoped that such an exercise would point out the shortcomings and also suggest policy initiatives needed to overcome these limitations.

9. The DQ-IDC (International Data Corporation) India: Salary Survey '05, over 2850 employees across 32 IT companies surveyed, Dataquest, September 11, 2005.

Perception of Attractiveness of Major Locations: A Survey-Based Analysis

Public perception about the prospects of the industry plays an important role in bringing investment to a region. This area, therefore, needs meticulous attention. Though governments of the respective states have been making some efforts to develop smaller cities as IT hubs, IT and ITES industries are still mainly concentrated in major metros. In order to assess the charm of various metros as investment destinations, we have conducted a survey of mainly the ITES firms in the major metros with the aid of some indicators. Of late, ITES segment has been showing considerable growth and increasingly capturing a larger share in the entire IT-ITES industry and hence our focus on this emerging area. A survey was conducted with a sample consisting of 70 firms spread across India, wherein the perceptions of the top managements of these firms were elicited through personally canvassed structured questionnaires. The respondent firms were requested to rank different cities in terms of selected indicators pertaining to the IT and ITES industry, and modal rank was used to represent a location with respect to that particular indicator. Five metros are compared in this exercise, *viz.*, Hyderabad, Chennai, Bangalore, Mumbai-Pune area and Delhi-Gurgaon area. In some cases, respondents have also brought in Kolkata.

General City Infrastructure: With respect to general city infrastructure, which mainly is a feedback of the respondents on the condition of roads and traffic, Bangalore appears to be the least attractive city (Figure 8.8). As per the rankings given by the industry circle, Chennai is considered better than even Hyderabad.

Attractiveness with respect to Wages

In terms of availability of skilled personnel at a cost effective rates, Kolkata stands first and is closely followed by Hyderabad. Bangalore and Chennai are ranked equally by the respondents (Figure 8.9).

Attractiveness with Respect to Government Incentives: Governments in the respective states should play a proactive role in developing the industry and this has been done by the governments of almost all states. This involves putting in place an entrepreneur friendly bureaucracy and

Figure 8.8

Attractiveness with respect to City Infrastructure

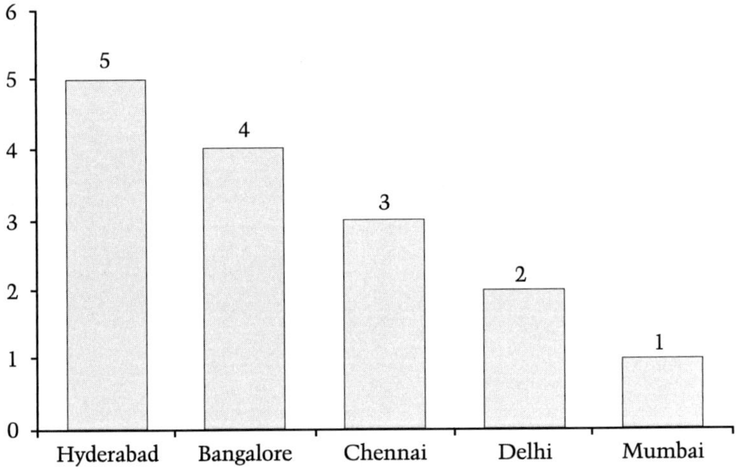

Figure 8.9

Attractiveness with respect to Wages

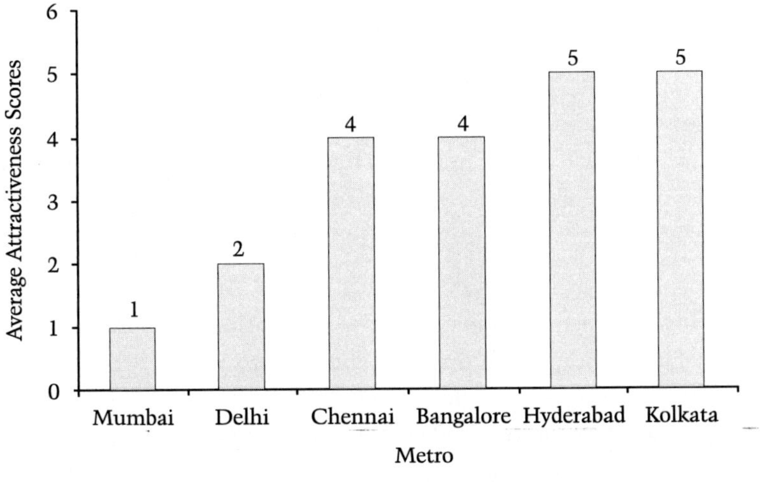

Source: Field Survey.

providing fiscal and other incentives to attract foreign direct investment. With respect to government initiatives, AP stands first, followed by both TN and Karnataka (Figure 8.10).

Figure 8.10

Attractiveness with respect to State Initiatives

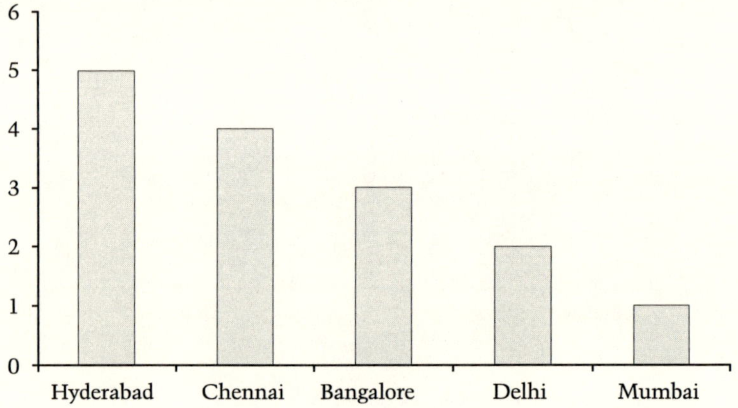

Source: Field Survey.

An Overall Index: In terms of the index constructed by us incorporating all the indicators and giving equal weights, it appears that in an overall sense, Hyderabad is the emerging location while Bangalore still remains attractive in spite of its unsatisfactory urban infrastructure, but is closely followed by Chennai. However, it is important to note that all the five metros are quite close to each other with respect to the overall attractiveness and would continue to lure investors (Figure 8.11).

It was during our survey of the IT-ITES firms in Tamil Nadu that we were able to secure a look into the perception problem that the state seems to face. Though Chennai is superior to many other locations in matters of both talent pool and investor friendly bureaucracy, the city is not yet perceived as the most ideal location by many prospective investors/entrepreneurs. This is partly due, as the industry circles put it during our survey, to "Chennai not being a promoted brand". It has been suggested by many professionals that government should work towards removing such a perception, portray a cosmopolitan image of Chennai and build a TN brand.

Figure 8.11

Ranking of Metros on the Basis of an Over All Attractiveness Index

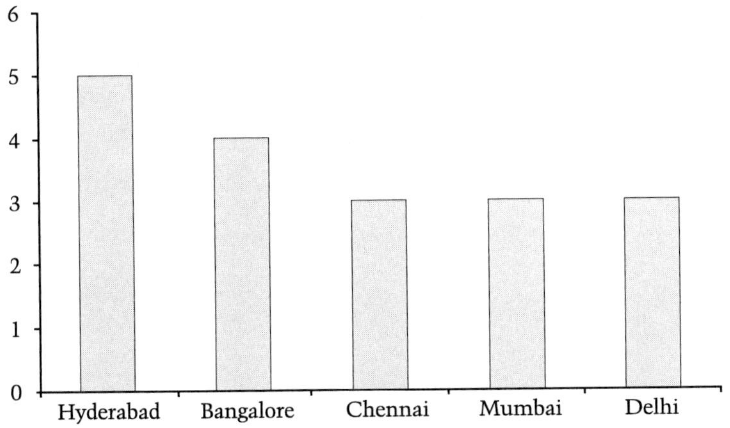

Source: Computed by the author using field survey data.

It is also useful to take stock of the ground reality. An effort to change the perceptions would be successful only if ground reality also supports it. In this context while it is difficult to quantify and compare indicators like state initiatives, it is possible to compare the availability of physical infrastructure facilities across states.

Physical Infrastructure: Tamil Nadu and Other States

The above indicators are based on the perceptions of selected practitioners in the industry. However, there are also data available on certain indicators concerning the status of physical infrastructure across states in India. In order to compare TN with the major states of India, we have considered 15 major states and focused on a few relevant indicators in each state to represent the physical infrastructure. The indicators selected are as follows:[10] road length per square km of geographical area (measured in km), railway length per square km of area (measured in km), number of post offices per capita, number of telephone exchanges per capita, number of registered motor vehicles per capita and installed electricity generating capacity per capita (in MW), intake of engineering colleges (per

10. These data have been taken from the *Statistical Abstracts*, GoI, various issues.

lakh population) and volume of air traffic, domestic and international (per thousand population). The position of each state with respect of the above indicators is shown in Figures 8.12 and 8.13 (see also Appendix Table A-8.1). Data on the number of telephone exchanges per population in 2000-01 show Punjab and TN well placed. It is clear therefore that Tamil Nadu's telephone infrastructure in terms of reach is far better than of many competitors in the IT-BPO segment (see Figure 8.12).

Figure 8.12

Telephone Exchanges per Population

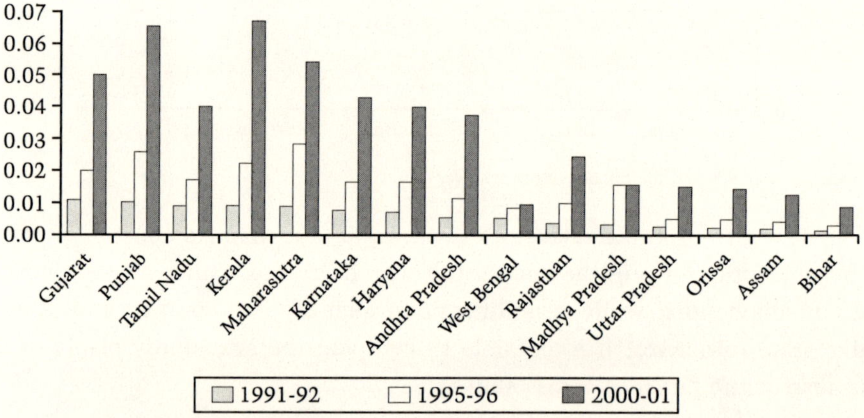

Source: Computed by the author using data from Economic Survey, GoI, different Issues and indiastat.com.

Our survey indicates that availability of quality power is a major concern of the sector. Tamil Nadu's position in this indicator too is better than its southern rivals, despite the severe power crunch that the state has witnessed in recent times (see Figure 8.13). Power supply data for 2000-01 reveal that Punjab, Gujarat and Haryana are at the top, followed by Maharashtra and TN.

In terms of other indicators that capture the status of infrastructure facilities, Tamil Nadu's position is ahead of most of its rivals. With respect to road length per person, Kerala tops the list and Maharashtra and Punjab are ahead of TN. In terms of number of post offices, which indicates connectivity, Maharashtra, Punjab and AP are ahead of TN. When all these indices are aggregated with equal weights, Tamil Nadu's position becomes higher than the other states that have sizeable presence of IT and ITES sector (Figure 8.14).

Figure 8.13

Installed Capacity per Population

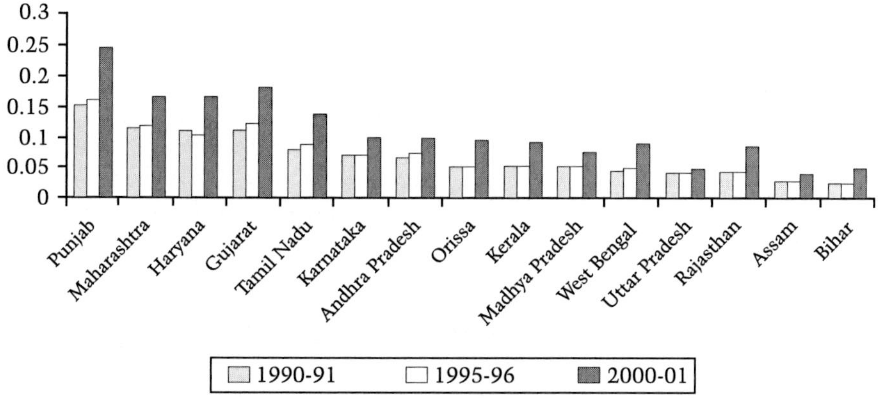

Source: Computed by the author using data from Economic Survey, GoI, different Issues and indiastat.com.

Figure 8.14

Combined Infrastructure Indices

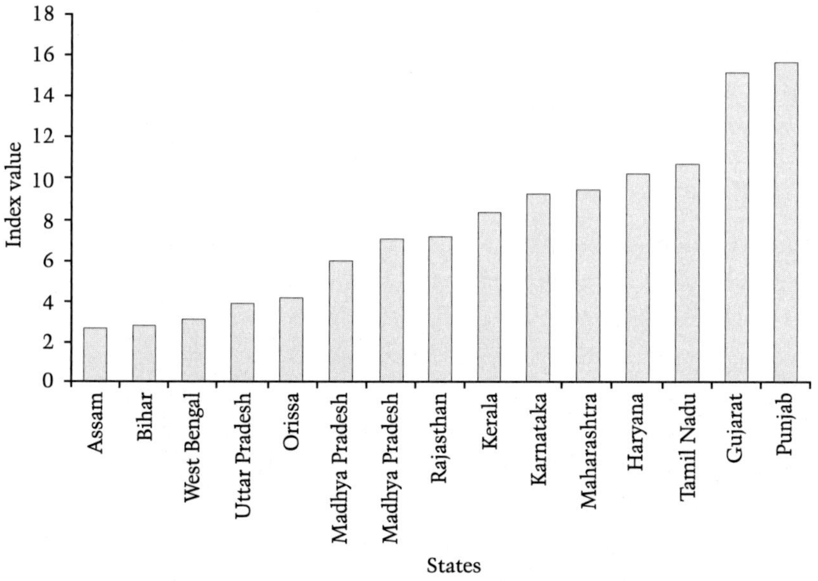

Source: Same as the Figure 8.13.

Both the perception indices and the indicators on the status of physical infrastructure show a comfortable position for Tamil Nadu. Naturally the state has been able to attract sufficient investment due to these factors. However, the important question that remains is how does the development of the industry benefit the country at large and the state in particular? Export earnings through the industry are naturally a major contribution to the current account of India's balance of payments. However, it is well recognised that ICT is a powerful tool for carrying out a number of development activities. Success of any state in India in the field of IT should be judged by the domestic use of the technology. In India, we observe that domestic demand for IT is minimal. This is true across states as well and to its credit the Government of Tamil Nadu has already taken up substantial steps to set this right.

Generating Domestic Demand for IT

To create domestic demand for computer services and to bring about better governance by ensuring transparency, the state has taken a number of initiatives which include using IT for sociopolitical development purposes. Government has initiated e-governance programmes and is trying to reduce the digital divide by providing computer education in the rural areas. The state is making efforts to create a data base in Tamil and increase the penetration of personal computers (PC) in the rural areas. This policy is aimed at removing computer illiteracy and promoting use of technology, especially in the rural areas.

Use of IT for Development

Information and communication technology (ICT) can be a powerful tool in achieving development goals. However, for this to happen, ICT needs to be closely connected to the development strategies. For example, it has to be appropriately linked to the agriculture sector to stimulate production, raise productivity and assist in marketing of products. ICT can also be used as a valuable tool in providing essential health information to the weak and marginalised sections (Cecchini and Scott, 2003). In the field of education, ICT can offset remoteness, help alleviate shortages of teachers and can expand distance-learning opportunities (Roy, 2005). In politics and governance, e-governance can bring in transparency, the lack of which is the root cause of many corrupt practices (Sangita and Dash, 2005). Small and medium enterprises can be helped enormously through ICT by providing the necessary marketing- and technology-related information (Moyi, 2003; Qureshi, 2005). Thus, to sum up in the words of Cohen and co-workers "ICT could be a 'revolution'... as it could be considered akin to diffusion of a 'general purpose technology'...with applicability across a broad range of uses" (Cohen *et al.,* 2004). The most crucial component of ICT is that it has a powerful communication component (Qureshi, 2005).

It has been argued by some scholars (see Bajpai and Radjou, 2000) that Indian IT development strategies have mostly focused on attracting foreign investment into the local IT industry and exploring market opportunities in the western hemisphere. Such export-led strategies have tended to neglect the domestic market. This requires to be remedied.

Directorate of e-Governance

Tamil Nadu is committed to harnessing e-governance as an enabler for ushering in a new era of digital governance, where services will be delivered to the citizens through convenient and easily accessible delivery channels. The Directorate of e-governance will be instrumental in helping the other departments in providing better accountability, enforceability, transparency and increased efficiency in service delivery to the citizens. In order to do so, as a first step, 12 *'Mission Mode Departments'* have been selected, which include (1) land records, (2) commercial taxes, (3) registration, (4) agriculture, (5) food and civil supplies, (6) health, (7) *panchayats*, (8) education, (9) treasuries, (10) municipalities, (11) transport and (12) employment. Priority will be given to matters that fall within these departments in making services available to the citizens. In order to empower the people in the rural areas to bridge the digital divide, a framework for rural service delivery through Village Resources and Service Centre (VRSC) is being formulated. The key objective of this project is to "Provide hassle free one-stop solution to the citizen." This will minimise multiple interaction points for the citizen and hence reduce the wastage of valuable time. This will ensure better turnaround time in receipt, processing and issue of services. It will increase access to government services by providing them at the doorstep of the common man.

The Village Resources and Service Centre (VRSC) initiative aims to leverage the *panchayats* as access points for service delivery and centres of knowledge and information dissemination. The venture aims at providing complete financial, technical training and hand holding support to the self-help groups operating the kiosks.

The State Government is taking all possible measures for spread of e-governance throughout the state, covering all the sectors with a view to providing hassle-free, transparent and efficient service to the common man (both in urban and rural areas). Towards this end, computerisation of Regional Transport Offices (RTOs), registration departments and other departments which have direct contact with the citizens has already begun.

The Government has decided to set up an e-governance training academy.

Computer Education in Government Higher Secondary Schools and Colleges

The Government has entrusted the work of implementation of the Computer Education Project in 1197 Government Higher Secondary and Corporation Schools to ELCOT. The Government has also entrusted the implementation of computer education in 60 Government Arts, Science Colleges, 5 Law Colleges and 12 Medical Colleges to ELCOT. It has been announced that all schools will be provided with computers in a phased manner.

Tamil Virtual University

The Government of Tamil Nadu has established the Tamil Virtual University (TVU) as a registered society, for providing Internet-based educational resources and opportunities to the Tamil communities living in different parts of the globe as well as the others interested in learning Tamil and acquiring knowledge of the history, art, literature and culture of the Tamils. This is a unique institution—the first of its kind in India. The TVU offers certificate courses at three levels (Basic, Intermediate and Advanced) and B.A. programme in Tamil. So far, nearly 12.62 lakh people have visited the TVU website. About 2249 students from 58 countries have registered for the certificate programme, and 2613 students for the B.A. (Tamil) degree. It has 16 coordinating centres spread over 12 countries.

E-Learning Infrastructure

The teaching/learning methodology adopted for the academic programme is e-learning through Internet-based lessons with multimedia support. To further strengthen and augment TVU's web-based virtual education programme, a state-of-the-art e-learning methodology through virtual class room, video conferencing equipment along with a streaming server and high-speed Internet connectivity is being established in the TVU.

Study Centres

TVU has opened four study centres, one each in Australia, France, Myanmar and South Africa to be coordinated respectively by Tamil e-learning, Arts and Literature Academy of Australia, Association for South Indian Studies, France, Cholia Muslim Religious Fund Trust-Myanmar and Ramamurthy Center for Tamil Propagation in South Africa. This is in addition to the 12 established centres in the USA, Sri Lanka, Malaysia, Mauritius, Canada, Germany and Switzerland. It is planned to establish three more study centres shortly.

The Road Ahead

TN has made considerable progress in the IT field in a short span of time. However, certain areas still need attention. The first relates to the smaller companies; our survey has revealed that even though there are a large number of small companies in both IT and BPO segments, they seldom receive adequate governmental support. Though software parks developed by the state provide several facilities, their user charges are quite exorbitant. Small companies often find this unaffordable and often have to locate themselves in areas with grossly inadequate facilities. Financial support for these companies is also not easy to come by. Smaller BPOs face the problem of marketing their services also.

The second aspect is related to development of smaller cities. TN has taken several significant steps to develop a large number of two- and three-tier cities. Coimbatore, Tiruchi, Madurai and Tirunelveli are now being developed as possible IT/BPO locations through public-private participation (PPP) model whereby infrastructure is built and provided through technology parks. The state also promotes the generation of adequate human resources from these locations. However, these locations are yet to attract investors in a big way. It is worth noting that, for bigger companies to move, connectivity preferably through air is a necessary prerequisite. In this regard, locations like Tiruchi and Tirunelveli need further attention.[11] Lack of proper infrastructure in the new locations would tempt IT firms to concentrate in existing metros like Chennai. It is to be borne in mind that development of small towns is crucial to spread development across regions and to check the undesirable growth of rural urban migration. Most states have plans in this regard but actual development continues to occur in the metros. This is one area that needs more focused attention and long-term planning.

Thirdly, there is the use of IT for domestic and development purposes. Though every state government has ambitious proposals for this area, in practice, little has been done. Digital divide still remains stark in all states of India and penetration of IT as a tool to provide necessary information to the farmers or to the small-scale industries sector is very low. Tamil Nadu may be comparatively better than other states, but much more needs to be done in this front.

Finally the 'perception factor' needs to be changed with concerted efforts to build the 'Tamil Nadu brand' as has been done for Bangalore. The fruition of these efforts will ensure a bright future for this segment in Tamil Nadu.

11. As revealed during our discussions with NASSCOM, Chennai office.

References

Amiti, Mary and Shang Jin Wei (2004). "Demystifying Outsourcing", *Finance and Development*. 41: 36-39. A quarterly magazine of IMF. December.

Arora, Shopra (2005). "The DQ-IDC India: Salary Survey '05", Dataquest, Sept. 12, 2005.

Bajpai, Nirupam and Navi Radjou (2000). "Raising Global Competitiveness of Tamil Nadu's IT Industry", *Economic and Political Weekly*, February 5.

Bhide, Shashank, B.P. Vani and Meenakshi Rajeev (2005). "Outsourcing of Business Processes: The Indian Experience as an Offshore location", Paper Presented at the, 30th FEFA Conference, Manila, Philippines.

Cecchini, Simone and Christopher Scott (2003). "Can Information and Communications Technology Applications Contribute to Poverty Reduction? Lessons from Rural India", *Information Technology for Development* 10: 73-84

Chanda, Rupa (2002). *Globalisation of Services, India's Opportunities and Constraints*. New Delhi: Oxford University Press.

Cohen, Daniel, P. Garibaldi and S. Scarpetta (eds.) (2004). *The ICT Revolution: Productivity Differences and the Digital Divide*. New York: Oxford University Press.

Government of India, *Economic Survey*, Various Issues.

Government of Tamil Nadu (2002). *IT Policy Document*. New Delhi: Information Technology Department.

————. (2002a). *Draft ITES Policy Document*. New Delhi: Information Technology Department.

India Brand Equity Foundation (2004). *Indian States Economy and Business*. Tamil Nadu: India Brand Equity Foundation.

International Monetary Fund. *Balance of Payments Statistics Yearbook* (different Issues), Washington, DC: IMF.

Moyi, E.D. (2003). Networks, Information and Small Enterprises: New Technologies and the Ambiguities of Empowerment, *Information Technology for Development*, 10: 221-232.

NASSCOM (2002a). *NASSCOM McKinsey Report*. New Delhi: NASSCOM.

————. (2002b). *NASSCOM Handbook of IT enabled services*. New Delhi: NASSCOM.

————. (2005). *Strategic Review*. New Delhi: NASSCOM.

Prasad, H.A.C. and R. Kapoor (1996). *Trade in Invisibles*. New Delhi: Commonwealth Publishers.

Qureshi, Sajda (2005). "How does Information Technology Effect Development? Integrating Theory and Practice into a Process Model", Americas Conference on Information Systems. Retrieved from *http://aisel.isworld.org/article_by_author.asp?Author_ID=5984*.

Rajeev, Meenakshi and B.P. Vani (2006). "India's Export of Selected BPO Services, Understanding Strengths and Weaknesses", Project No. Eco/76, ISEC. Bangalore.

———. (2007). "Direct and Indirect Benefits of Business Process Outsourcing on Indian Economy", *Journal of Information Technology Impact* 72: 159-80

Ramachandran, Vijaya and J. Goebel (2002). Linkages between the Information Technology Sector and Traditional Sectors in Tamil Nadu, A Report of the consultants from Centre for International Development, Harvard University, Retrieved from *www.cid.harvard.edu/india/papers.htm*.

Reserve Bank of India, *Monthly Bulletin, RBI*, Various Issues.

Roy, Sumit (2005). *Globalisation, ICT and Developing Nations: Challenges in the Information Age*. New Delhi: Sage Publication.

Sangita, S.N. and Bikash Chandra Dash (2005). "Electronic Governance and Service Delivery in India: Theory and Practice", Working paper no. 165, Institute for Social and Economic Change, Bangalore, India.

Websites Used:

www.itparkchennai.com

www.tidco.com

www.stpc.soft.net

www.elcot.com

Appendix Table A-8.1

Cost of Living Ranking in India

City	Cost of Living Rankings Rank		
	2004	*2003*	*2002*
Mumbai	1	1	1
Delhi	2	2	2
Ahmedabad	3	7	6
Kolkata	4	5	7
Pune	5	4	4
Chennai	6	3	5
Bangalore	7	6	3
Lucknow	8	-	-
Kochi	9	-	-
Patna	10	-	-
Jaipur	11	-	-
Hyderabad	12	8	8

Source: Bpoindia.org.

Appendix Table A-8.2

Indian IT Industry: Export and Employment

	Indian IT Industry by Sector			
USD billion	*FY 2004*	*FY 2005*	*FY 2006*	*FY 2007E*
IT Services	10.4	13.5	17.8	23.7
Exports	7.3	10.0	13.3	18.1
Domestic	3.1	3.5	4.5	5.6
ITES-BPO	3.4	5.2	7.2	9.5
Exports	3.1	4.6	6.3	8.3
Domestic	0.3	0.6	0.9	1.2
Engineering Services and R&D, Software Products	2.9	3.9	5.3	6.5
Exports	2.5	3.1	4.0	4.9
Domestic	0.4	0.8	1.3	1.6
Total Software and Services Revenues	16.7	22.6	30.3	39.7
Of which, exports	12.9	17.7	23.6	31.3
Hardware	5.0	5.9	7.0	8.2
Total IT Industry (including Hardware)	21.6	28.4	37.4	47.8

Source: NASSCOM Strategic Review 2007.

Appendix Table A-8.3

Employment: Indian Software and Services Sector

Sector	*FY 2004*	*FY 2005*	*FY 2006*	*FY 2007E*
IT Services	215000	297000	398000	562000
ITES-BPO	216000	316000	415000	545000
Engineering Services and R&D, Software Products	81000	93000	115000	144000
Domestic Market (including user organisations)	318000	352000	365000	378000
Total*	830,000	1,058,000	1,293,000	1,630,000

Source: NASSCOM Strategic Review, 2007.

Appendix Figure A-8.1

Tamil Nadu's Share in India's Output in Various Industries (in per cent) (2000-01)

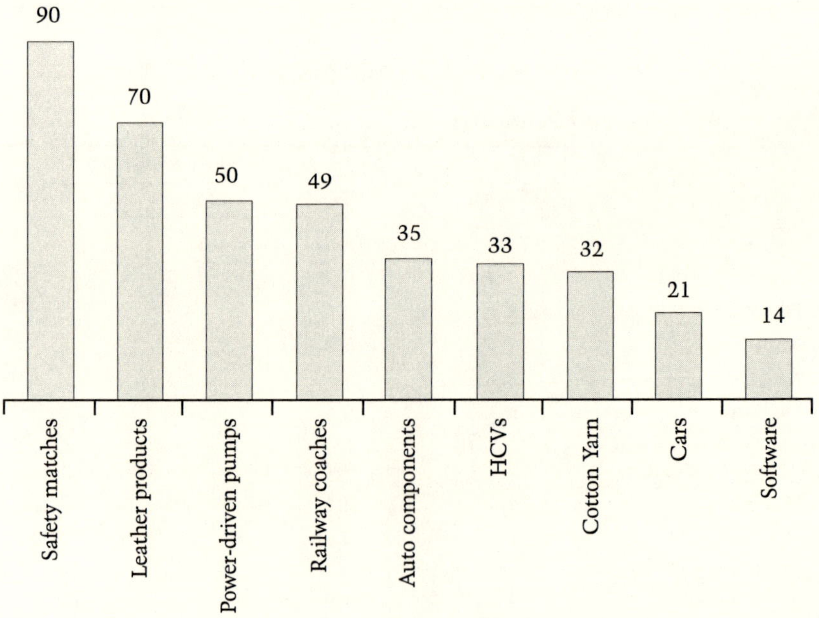

9 Business Establishments in Tamil Nadu

Exploratory Findings from Economic Census Surveys 1990, 1998 and 2005

R. Srinivasan

Introduction

The decennial population censuses are the most widely used source of data on employment. They collect detailed information on the number of workers by gender, their education level, the sectors in which they are employed and nature of occupations from all households. Published tabulations give the number of male and female workers by sector of employment and occupation in great detail. Estimates of total workers are also published for all villages and towns and town wards. But sectoral employment estimates are available only for three or four broad groups (cultivators, agricultural labour, household industry and others); they are an inadequate basis to obtain information relating to the kinds of activities that comprise these different sectors, the nature of enterprises that are engaged in them and their variations across regions and over time. These are however available from the successive Economic Census surveys conducted by the Central Statistical Organisation (CSO) since 1976. The latest census was in 2005.

So far, five Economic Census surveys have been conducted in 1977, 1980, 1990, 1998 and 2005. The Economic Census is a complete enumeration of all establishments in the country. It collects information about every establishment relating to: (1) location, (2) with or without premises, (3) perennial or non-perennial, (4) with or without hired labour, (5) classification of activity as per National Industrial Classification (NIC) 4-digit Code, (6) sources of funds, (vii) social and gender classification of ownership, (viii) classification of workers by sex, type of establishment, sector and location and (ix) registration of establishment under various Acts. The primary data on these characteristics are available in digitized form for each village, town and ward. The unit level data are presented with reference to the location of each establishment up to revenue village or urban ward. This database is useful for spatial land use planning and to analyse evolution of industrial clusters.

The CSO primarily uses the economic census as a sample frame and carries out several follow-up surveys to estimate National Income from the unorganised sector. But the Economic Census data are amenable to several cross-tabulations that reveal the pattern of economic diversification in terms of location, organisational type, size of establishment, activities and size of employment. Besides the decennial population census and quinquennial National Sample Survey Organisation (NSSO) surveys on employment and unemployment, the Economic Census is one more data source on employment. This paper presents a broad picture of selected key features of economic establishments in rural and urban areas for Tamil Nadu as a whole and for some of these aspects at the district level in 2005 and the changes that have occurred between 1990 and 2005.

Concepts and Definitions

The basic unit for data collection is called an establishment. Till the 4th Economic Census (1998) the basic unit was called an enterprise defined as "an undertaking in production and/or distribution of goods and services not for the sole purpose of own consumption." As this definition was vague giving rise to many queries from the field workers, it was changed to Establishment in the 5th Economic Census (2005). "Establishment is defined as an enterprise or part of an enterprise that is situated in a single location in which one or more predominantly one kind of economic activity (sic) is carried out. It is an economic unit under a single legal entity." According to the new definition, if there are two factories under a single management in two buildings with separate entrances, then each factory is counted as one establishment.

The establishments are basically classified as own account enterprise (OAE) and establishment (ESTT). The OAEs are establishments without hired labour, for example self-employed and household production units which do not utilise hired labour. An ESTT has at least one hired labour. The ESTTs are further classified as Directory ESTT with six or more total workers with at least one hired worker and non-directory ESTT with five or less than five workers with at least one hired labour.

Establishments are also classified as agricultural and non-agricultural. An agricultural establishment is "engaged in livestock production, agricultural services, hunting, trapping and game propagation, forestry and logging and fishing. All agricultural activities except those involved in crop production and plantation are covered under agricultural establishments. All other establishments, that is, those not engaged in crop production, plantation and other agricultural activities as defined above, are classified as non-agricultural establishments." All the establishments also grouped under 14 to 17 major categories in the non-agricultural division and 3 categories in the agricultural division.

Employment data are solicited by asking for the number of usually working persons in an establishment, classified as child labour and adult labour and by gender. Here the definition of the 'usually working person' is not given and is left to the discretion of the field staff. This survey does not explicitly define employment as is being done in the decennial population census and in the NSSO's sample surveys. To that extent, the data source becomes unreliable and mostly underestimates total employment. In a similar fashion, it classifies ownership of establishments by gender and social classes, which are meaningful only for sole-proprietorship establishments. Classification of establishments by location, use of different sources of power, sources of finance and registration under different Acts are interesting facts to highlight the changes in the pattern of establishments in terms of these characteristics.

A Snapshot of Tamil Nadu in 2005

In 2005, there were nearly 4.5 million establishments in the state employing around 10 million workers. In terms of numbers, more than 60 per cent of the establishments were OAEs but they accounted for barely 35 per cent of the workers, that is, the ESTTs accounted for 40 per cent of total establishments and 65 per cent of total employment. Non-agricultural establishments were on the average larger in terms of employment per establishment. Around two-thirds of the establishments were engaged in non-agricultural activities and they accounted for about 80 per cent of workers (Table 9.1).

Table 9.1

Salient Features of Establishments in Tamil Nadu, 2005

Particulars	*Number of Establishments (in Million)*					*Number of Employment (in Million)*				
	Total	*Agri*	*Non-agri*	*OAE*	*ESTT*	*Total*	*Agri*	*Non-agri*	*OAE*	*ESTT*
State	4.43	1.09	3.34	2.74	1.69	10.06	1.59	8.47	3.53	6.53
Rural	2.72	1.04	1.69	1.91	0.82	5.31	1.51	3.80	2.52	2.79
Urban	1.71	0.05	1.65	0.83	0.87	4.75	0.08	4.67	1.01	3.74

About 60 per cent of all establishments and a little over a half of their total employment were in rural areas; agricultural establishments were predominantly rural in terms of both numbers and employment. Non-agricultural establishments were more evenly distributed between the two areas. Rural and urban areas had roughly the same number of non-agricultural establishments but in terms of employment the share of rural areas was much smaller at 30 per cent compared to urban areas (70 per cent). On the average, a non-agricultural establishment had more workers than an agricultural establishment. The differences in this respect were much more pronounced in urban areas, where the average non-agricultural establishment was 3-4 times as large as an agricultural establishment and twice as large as its rural counterpart.

There are also striking rural-urban differences in the relative importance of own account enterprises and establishments. Roughly 70 per cent of OAEs and employment therein were in rural areas, that is, OAEs were predominantly rural in character. In the case of ESTTs, they were equally distributed between rural and urban areas, but urban ESTTs accounted for 57 per cent of employment. On the average, OAEs were much smaller than ESTTs in both rural and urban areas. The average size of OAEs was more or less the same in rural and urban areas; urban ESTTs were somewhat larger than their rural counterparts.

If we measure size of establishments by employment per establishment, then most establishments are very small. In 2005, 96 per cent of establishments had less than five workers and accounted for more than two-thirds of the total workforce. Those employing 6-50 workers account for 4.3 per cent of establishments and had one-sixth of workers. Larger units (with more than 50 workers) constituted less than 0.5 per cent of all establishments in numbers but they accounted for 15 per cent of workers (Table 9.2).

As we move from the smallest to the higher sizes of establishments, the share of employment in each category declines up to establishments with employment in the range 25-49 and then the share of employment increases with the size of enterprises. Thus, tiny establishments on one side and large establishments on the other side are the larger providers of employment. This raises the question about the employment potential in small and medium enterprises, which needs further probing.

Table 9.2

Distribution of Establishments and Employment by Size of Units

Employment Size	*2005 ('000)*	
	Estb.	*Empl.*
1-5	4237.2 (95.6)	6822.8 (67.8)
6-9	128.1 (2.9)	917.0 (9.1)
10-14	29.3 (0.7)	341.7 (3.4)
15-19	12.5 (0.3)	204.4 (2.0)
20-24	7.0 (0.2)	148.8 (1.5)
25-49	3.8 (0.1)	99.4 (1.0)
50-99	12.0 (0.3)	57.6 (5.7)
100-199	2.0 (0.0)	266.2 (2.6)
200-499	1.2 (0.0)	342.6 (3.4)
>500	0.4 (0.0)	342.5 (3.4)
Total	4433.4 (100)	10063.0 (100)

Trends in Growth of Enterprises since 1990

The total number of establishments has more than doubled, whereas employment has increased only by 61 per cent between 1990 and 2005; much of this increase has been between 1998 and 2005. Compared to urban areas, the rural areas had a larger number of establishments in 1990, 1998 and 2005. It is interesting to find that the employment in rural establishments was lower than in urban establishments in 1990, but this was reversed in 2005. In 2005, the rural establishments had 0.56 million more workers than the urban establishments whereas employment in it was lower than the urban employment in 1990 but gradually increased to 5.31 million in 2005, which is nearly 0.56 million more than the urban employment. Between 1990 and 2005, the number of establishments increased in rural and urban areas by 132 per cent and 82 per cent respectively, whereas the number of workers in rural and urban establishments increased by 83 and 41 per cent respectively (Table 9.3).

Table 9.3

Growth of Establishments and Employment: 1990 to 2005

Particulars	*Establishments (Millions)*			*Employment (Millions)*			*Employment per Establishment*		
	1990	*1998*	*2005*	*1990*	*1998*	*2005*	*1990*	*1998*	*2005*
Total	2.11	2.51	4.43	6.24	7.19	10.06	2.96	2.86	2.27
Rural	1.17	1.41	2.72	2.88	3.58	5.31	2.46	2.53	1.95
Urban	0.94	1.12	1.71	3.35	3.61	4.75	3.56	3.22	2.78
Agri	0.18	0.30	1.09	0.33	0.56	1.59	1.83	1.87	1.46
Non-agri	1.93	2.21	3.34	5.91	6.63	8.47	3.06	3.00	2.53
OAE	1.38	1.42	2.74	2.10	2.24	3.53	1.52	1.58	1.29
ESTT	0.73	1.09	1.69	4.14	4.96	6.53	5.67	4.55	3.86

Agricultural establishments accounted for about two-fifths of the increase in the number of establishments as well as their total employment. Practically all of this increase has been in rural areas. There is hardly any change in both aspects in urban areas. Non-agricultural establishments have also grown both in rural and urban areas. The pace of growth has been much faster in rural areas, the increment in both number of enterprises and employment has been more or less of the same magnitude as in urban areas.

On the whole, the employment per establishment has consistently declined between 1990 and 2005. We find that in three categories, the employment per establishment increased in 1998, but only to decline below the 1990 level in 2005, namely, agricultural, rural and OAEs. Obviously there is a lot of overlapping between these categories. In all the other categories, that is, in non-agricultural, urban and ESTTs, the employment per establishment declined gradually from 1990 through 1998 to 2005.

Another notable feature of recent trends is that OAEs have grown faster than ESTTs both in numbers and in employment. The bulk of this increase has been in rural areas. The ESTT segment has also grown faster in rural areas in both numbers and employment and accounted for nearly half of the overall increment in this sector. There is thus a pronounced trend towards greater ruralisation of establishments in general. Much of this growth has occurred in the latter half of the period, that is, in 1998-2005 (Table 9.4).

Table 9.4

Growth of OAEs and ESTTs in Rural and Urban Areas of Tamil Nadu, 1990-2005

Type of Estb	*Year*	*State*		*Rural*		*Urban*	
		Estb (Million)	*Empl (Million)*	*Estb (Million)*	*Empl (Million)*	*Estb (Million)*	*Empl (Million)*
ALL	1990	2.12	6.20	1.17	2.90	0.95	3.31
	1998	2.52	7.20	1.41	3.60	1.11	3.56
	2005	4.42	10.00	2.72	5.30	1.71	4.71
OAE	1990	1.39	2.10	0.84	1.30	0.55	0.81
	1998	1.43	2.26	0.92	1.50	0.51	6.71
	2005	2.74	3.50	1.90	2.50	0.84	1.01
ESTT	1990	0.73	4.10	0.33	1.60	0.40	2.50
	1998	1.09	4.90	0.49	2.10	0.60	2.80
	2005	1.68	6.50	0.82	2.80	0.87	3.70

If establishments are classified by size of employment, we find from Table 9.5 that generally the proportion of establishments declines with increase in size of employment. In 1990, nearly 79 per cent of establishments were in the 1-5 employment range and this proportion increased to 95 per cent in 2005. In total employment, these smallest establishments increased their share in employment from 34 per cent in 1990 to 68 per cent in 2005. Between 1990 and 2005, though the percentage of establishments declined by eight percentage points in the 6-10 employment category, the percentage of employment in this category has declined only marginally. As the size of establishments increased from 6-9, the proportion of establishments declined gradually. However the proportion of employment declined as size of establishment (defined by employment size) reached 20-24 or 25-49, thereafter the proportion of employment increased with size of establishment. This indicates that employment was generated on a large scale either by very small or very large establishments. The medium size establishments generated very little employment.

Table 9.5

Distribution of Establishments and Employment by Size of Units

Employment Size	*1990 ('000)*		*1998 ('000)*		*2005 ('000)*	
	Estb	*Empl*	*Estb*	*Empl*	*Estb*	*Empl*
1-5	577.5 (79.4)	142.5 (34.4)	2329.7 (92.7)	4409.3 (61.3)	4237.2 (95.6)	6822.8 (67.8)
6-9	74.5 (10.2)	525.8 (12.7)	101.2 (4.0)	702.4 (9.8)	128.1 (2.9)	917.0 (9.1)
10-14	35.3 (4.8)	402.1 (9.7)	45.9 (1.8)	583.3 (8.1)	29.3 (0.7)	341.7 (3.4)
15-19	14.1 (1.9)	231.6 (5.6)	13.6 (0.5)	222.6 (3.1)	12.5 (0.3)	204.4 (2.0)
20-24	8.1 (1.1)	173.7 (4.2)	7.8 (0.3)	165.0 (2.3)	7.0 (0.2)	148.8 (1.5)
25-49	11.5 (1.6)	377.4 (9.1)	10.2 (0.4)	330.7 (4.6)	3.8 (0.1)	99.4 (1.0)
50-99	4.0 (0.6)	264.2 (6.4)	3.8 (0.2)	249.2 (3.5)	12.0 (0.3)	57.6 (5.7)
100-199	1.4 (0.2)	190.6 (4.6)	1.0 (0.0)	137.8 (1.9)	2.0 (0.0)	266.2 (2.6)
200-499	0.9 (0.1)	250.0 (6.0)	0.5 (0.0)	160.8 (2.2)	1.2 (0.0)	342.6 (3.4)
> 500	0.3 (0.01)	299.5 (7.2)	0.2 (0.0)	223.4 (3.1)	0.4 (0.0)	342.5 (3.4)
Total	727.6 (100)	4139.7 (100)	2514.1 (100)	7191.0 (100)	4433.4 (100)	10063.0 (100)

In all segments, the average size of units (in terms of workers per establishment) has declined. This trend is largely a reflection of rapid increase in the small sized units. Even in 1990, 70 per cent of the units employed 5 or fewer workers and nearly 90 per cent had less than 10 workers. Together they accounted for less than half of the total employment of all enterprises. Those having more than 50 workers comprised less than 1 per cent of enterprises but accounted for nearly a quarter of employment. By 2005, the number of enterprises with 5 or fewer workers had increased more than sevenfold and their work force increased nearly by five times. They now account for 96 per cent of all enterprises by number and more than two-thirds of total employment. Nearly 60 per cent of the increase in employment between 1990 and 2005 has come from this category of enterprises. At the other extreme, the share of enterprises employing more than 50 workers has declined progressively from around 1 per cent in terms of numbers and 24 per cent in terms of workers to less than 0.5 per cent and 15 per cent respectively (Table 9.5).

The factors that have contributed to these trends—the spurt in growth after 1998, the marked shift towards very small establishments, the rapid growth of agricultural establishments and own account workers in rural areas and the relatively slower pace of expansion in larger-sized enterprises—deserve closer study.

Table 9.6 shows the distribution of all non-agricultural establishments and employment by 10 major sectors. In 1990, the wholesale and retail trade sector had 34 per cent of establishments and 22 per cent of employment, and in 2005, this sector continued to increase its share both in terms of number of establishments and employment to 35 per cent and 26 per cent respectively (see Annexure 9.1 for a detailed analysis). Manufacturing and repairing sector had only 29 per cent of establishments but a higher proportion of employment of 38.5 per cent and both these ratios increased to 32.7 and 36.7 per cent respectively in 2005. Apart from these two major sectors, communications and financial services sectors registered substantial growth in establishment and employment during this period. All other major sectors remained stagnant retaining the same proportions of establishments and employment between 1990 and 2005.

Table 9.6

Distribution of Non-agricultural Establishments and Employment by Major Sectors

Sectors	*1990 ('000)*		*1998 ('000)*		*2005 ('000)*		*1990-2005 Growth Rate*	
	Estb	*Empl*	*Estb*	*Empl*	*Estb*	*Empl*	*Estb*	*Empl*
Mining and Quarrying	3.3 (0.2)	16.0 (0.3)	1.9 (0.1)	12.6 (0.2)	8.1 (0.2)	42.4 (0.5)	145	62
Manufacturing and Repairing	583.4 (29.2)	2257.3 (38.5)	565.7 (25.6)	2328.0 (36.2)	1086.9 (32.7)	3112.2 (36.7)	86	38
Elec., Gas and Water	2.6 (0.1)	21.3 (0.4)	4.6 (0.2)	17.8 (0.3)	13.5 (0.4)	43.6 (0.5)	419	105
Construction	21.0 (1.1)	35.1 (0.6)	16.5 (0.7)	52.1 (0.8)	32.5 (1.0)	77.8 (0.9)	55	122
Wholesale and Retail Trade	653.2 (33.8)	1264.0 (21.5)	865.9 (39.2)	1825.3 (28.4)	1176.0 (35.4)	2229.8 (26.3)	80	76
Hotels and Restaurants	122.2 (6.3)	307.2 (5.2)	144.3 (6.5)	367.1 (5.7)	196.7 (5.9)	452.1 (5.3)	61	47
Transport and Storage	39.5 (2.0)	126.3 (2.2)	35.0 (1.6)	3.4 (0.1)	77.9 (2.3)	190.1 (2.2)	97	64
Communication	10.0 (0.5)	58.4 (1.0)	17.5 (0.8)	55.1 (0.9)	75.5 (2.3)	165.4 (2.0)	655	183
Financial Services	70.4 (3.6)	190.7 (3.2)	93.4 (4.2)	302.4 (4.7)	143.2 (4.3)	418.4 (4.9)	103	228
Community and Personal Services	445.0 (23.0)	1538.1 (27.0)	466.4 (21.1)	1470.2 (22.8)	509.2 (15.3)	1740.5 (20.5)	14	13
Total	1931.8	5868.3	2211.1	6434.0	3319.8	8472.7	72	44

Note: Figures in brackets are percentages to column total.

Spatial Patterns: Inter-district Variations

The distribution of enterprises and workers as well as their time trajectories of change is uneven. This is evident from Table 9.7 which gives the share of each of 21 districts in the number of enterprises and their employment in the state at three points of time. In 2005, there are 11 districts[1] whose individual share in total establishments is more than 5 per cent in terms of number and more than 6 per cent in terms of employment. Together they account for nearly four-fifths of the state total in both

1. Chennai, Kancheepuram, Vellore, South Arcot, Salem, Erode, Coimbatore, Tiruchirappalli, Thanjavur, Madurai and Tirunelveli.

respects. Each of the remaining 10 districts[2] has less than 3 per cent of establishments and less than 4-4.5 per cent of employment.

Table 9.7

Distribution of Establishments and Employment by Districts (in %)

Sectors	*1990 ('000)*		*1998 ('000)*		*2005 ('000)*	
	Estb.	*Empl.*	*Estb.*	*Empl.*	*Estb.*	*Empl.*
Chennai	6.1	9.8	5.9	8.6	6.2	8.4
Kancheepuram	7.1	7.5	7.3	7.8	6.3	8.0
Vellore	6.1	5.6	6.4	5.2	5.0	4.0
Dharmapuri	3.1	2.7	3.2	2.9	3.9	4.3
Thiruvannamalai	4.0	3.2	4.1	2.9	4.2	3.1
South Arcot (Cuddalore+Villupuram)	6.4	4.9	6.9	5.7	7.1	5.7
Salem	7.6	8.5	7.9	8.6	9.2	9.8
Erode	5.5	5.8	5.5	5.6	5.4	6.0
The Nilgris	0.8	1.0	0.8	0.9	0.7	0.8
Coimbatore	7.3	9.6	7.0	9.6	8.5	10.3
Dindigul	3.1	2.7	3.0	2.8	3.1	2.9
Tiruchirappalli	6.5	6.5	6.3	6.0	7.2	5.7
Thanjavur	7.8	6.0	7.2	5.7	5.4	4.7
Pudukottai	1.9	1.7	1.8	1.6	1.5	1.5
Sivagangai	1.7	1.5	1.5	1.3	0.9	1.0
Madurai	5.4	5.3	5.7	5.9	5.2	5.1
Virudhunagar	3.4	4.6	3.4	4.7	3.0	4.1
Ramanathapuram	1.9	1.5	2.0	1.3	1.2	1.1
Thoothukudi	3.4	3.1	3.2	3.7	3.8	3.0
Tirunelveli	7.8	5.6	7.7	6.2	7.0	5.7
Kanniyakumari	3.1	3.0	3.0	3.0	2.0	2.7

The majority of districts in the first category (most of them are in the northern and western parts of the state) have increased their share in the total number of establishments and workers in the state between 1990 and 2005. Six districts had a lower share in establishments and four districts a lower share in employment. With a few significant exceptions (notably Dharmapuri), these shares have declined in most of the remaining

2. Dharmapuri, Thiruvannamalai, The Nilgiris, Dindigul, Pudukottai, Sivagangai, Virudhunagar, Ramanathapuram, Thoothukudi and Kanniyakumari.

10 districts. There is, thus, an increase in the spatial concentration of establishments and employment over the period.

More detailed analysis of differences in composition of establishments in terms of sector, nature of enterprise and rural-urban distributions as well as their underlying factors is necessary to understand the reasons for these variations. Such detailed analysis is beyond the scope of this paper but is clearly an important and fruitful area for further research.

The Caveat

We have already noted that the term 'usually employed' is not precisely defined; hence, there could be underestimation of employment in establishments by Economic Census surveys. Table 9.8 gives a comparison of non-agricultural employment between NSSO's estimates and Economic Census' estimates for the period 1987-88 to 2004-05.

We find from this table that the Economic Surveys have consistently underestimated the employment size compared to the NSSO's surveys. The underestimation is in the range of 45 to 53 per cent. Therefore, there is need for caution in interpreting the employment data emanating from the Economic Census surveys. It is also essential that the follow-up surveys correct the underestimation of employment while calculating the contribution of labour to national income.

Table 9.8

Distribution of Non-agricultural Employment by Sectors: Comparison between NSSO's and Economic Census' Estimates

Sectors	*NSSO Survey 1987-88*	*Economic Survey 1990*	*NSSO Survey 1993-94*	*Economic Survey 1999*	*NSSO Survey 1999-2000*	*NSSO Survey 2004-05*	*Economic Survey 2005*
Mining	0.11	0.01	0.10	0.01	0.14	0.10	0.04
Manufacturing	4.94	2.26	5.05	2.33	5.30	6.49	2.90
Electricity	0.09	0.02	0.11	0.02	0.10	0.08	0.04
Construction	0.92	0.03	1.08	0.05	1.45	1.93	0.08
Trade, etc.	3.20	1.76	3.57	2.40	4.67	5.52	2.89
Services	2.85	1.83	3.32	2.32	2.88	3.92	2.51
Total	12.11	6.24	13.23	7.13	21.67	18.04	8.46

To Recapitulate

This is an exploratory note on the Economic Census surveys carried out in Tamil Nadu in 1990, 1998 and 2005. The Economic Census surveys are carried out to create a sample frame for sample studies on the unorganised sector and to estimate its contribution to the National Income. Nevertheless, simple tabulations of this survey data show the composition of the non-farm units by size of employment, type of activity and location. The establishments are classified by location, size of employment, activity as rural/urban, OAE/ESTT and agricultural/non-agricultural establishments.

- The number of establishments (OAE+ESTT) has been higher in rural areas in all the three surveys, whereas the number of persons employed has been higher in rural areas only in 2005. The growth rates of both establishments and employment have been higher in rural areas in all the three surveys.
- In terms of agricultural and non-agricultural activities, both in absolute numbers and growth rates, the rural areas have larger numbers of both agricultural and non-agricultural establishments. But, in terms of employment, the urban non-agricultural offered more employment.
- The OAE establishments are larger in size, in terms of both the number of establishments and the aggregate employment. The ESTT are predominant in urban areas. Generally, ESTTs have larger employment per unit because of the use of hired labour.
- Between the two time periods, 1990-98 and 1998-2005, the first period showed clear decline in the growth rates of both establishments and employment across all categories, and the growth rates increased in the second period.
- Of the 10 major categories in the non-agricultural activities, nearly 90 per cent of the establishments and employment are concentrated in five categories, namely, manufacturing and repair, wholesale and retail trade, hotels and restaurants, financial services, and community and personal services. In all the five categories, the ratio of OAE to ESTT has been declining.

- Of the 21 districts in the state, nearly 75 per cent of the establishments and employment are concentrated in 10 districts.
- Segregating the establishments by size of employment and the amount of employment generated in each category reveals that both establishments and employment are concentrated in smaller size units, which employ up to 20 labourers.
- There is a decline in the total employment generated as the size of unit increases up to 20-50 workers: after this the employment generation increases with the size of the establishment.

All told, this data set generates interesting patterns in the non-farm sector by activities, size and location. There are many other socioeconomic patterns that could be generated from this data set. For instance, the following can be noticed: the social category of ownership of units (see Annexure A-9.2), labourers employed and the type of units registered under different Acts. It is also possible to compare the growth of units of various sizes in a specific activity by location, so that we can see the changing character of the co-existence of small and large units in a location, and to discern industrial clusters (see Annexure A-9.2).

Annexure A-9.1

Trends in the Growth of Establishments in Retail Sector in Urban Tamil Nadu 1990-2005

The wholesale and retail trade is the largest sector in terms of number of establishments and employment generation and within this category, the retail sector is larger. It consists of retail businesses from vegetables to petroleum products and steel.

Table A-9.1

Trend in Growth of OAE and ESTT in Retail Sector in Urban Tamil Nadu 1990-2005

Particulars	*No of Enterprises*			*Number of Enterprises per 1000 Population*		
	1990	*1998*	*2005*	*1990*	*1998*	*2005*
OAE	201434 (66)	216236 (49)	340770 (55)	10.73	8.66	10.57
ESTT	101934 (33)	220444 (51)	274791 (45)	5.43	8.83	8.52
OAE Non-perennial	4601 (81)	12962 (47)	4203 (70)	0.25	0.52	0.13
ESTT Non-perennial	1061 (19)	14683 (53)	1776 (30)	0.06	0.59	0.06
OAE without premises	39977 (93)	40299 (95)	69149 (74)	2.13	1.61	2.14
ESTT without premises	3054 (07)	20006 (05)	24697 (26)	0.16	0.80	0.77
OAE without power	194485 (67)	199840 (51)	292409 (58)	10.36	8.01	9.07
ESTT without power	94510 (33)	194051 (49)	214087 (42)	5.04	7.77	6.64
OAE Perennial	196833 (66)	203274 (50)	336567 (55)	10.49	8.14	10.43
ESTT Perennial	100873 (34)	205761 (50)	273015 (45)	5.38	8.24	8.46
OAE with premises	161457 (62)	175937 (47)	271621 (52)	8.60	7.05	8.42
ESTT with premises	98880 (38)	200438 (53)	250094 (48)	5.27	8.03	7.75
OAE with power	6949 (48)	16396 (38)	48361 (44)	0.37	0.66	1.50
ESTT with power	7424 (52)	26393 (62)	60704 (56)	0.40	1.06	1.88

The Annexure Table A-9.1 gives the distribution of OAE and ESTT and the three sub-categories in each of these two broad categories in the retail sector in urban Tamil Nadu during 1990-2005. Though there was a steady increase in the total number of establishments, the percentage of OAE has declined from 66 per cent in 1990 to 49 per cent in 1998 and then marginally increased to 55 in 2005. We also find from the table that the number of establishments per 1000 population increased from 5.43 to 8.52 for ESTT, whereas for OAE, it declined from 10.73 to 10.57 between 1990 and 2005. On an average, the growth of ESTT (wherein at least one hired labour is employed) has substantially displaced the OAE (wherein no hired labour is employed).

Both the OAE and ESTT are classified into non-perennial/perennial, with/without premises and with/without use of power. Generally the establishments which are non-perennial or without premises or without use of power could be considered as smaller and mostly unorganised compared to establishments which are perennial or with premises or with use of power. If we compare the proportions of OAEs and ESTTs in these three categories, we find that the decline in the proportions of OAEs is substantially in every category. The OAEs which are non-perennial, without premises and without power have registered 9, 19 and 9 percentage points decline, compared to 10, 10 and 4 percentage points decline in perennial, with premises and with power categories. Thus the decline of OAEs in all the categories establishes that they are being edged out by the growth of ESTTs in these categories.

If we compare the number of establishments per 1000 population for the above mentioned six categories between OAE and ESTT, we see some interesting trends. In non-perennial, without premises and without use of power categories, the number of OAE per 1000 population did not decline substantially, so too the ESTT per 1000 population did not increase substantially. Next, consider the perennial, with premises and with use of power categories. In the perennial and with premises categories, the number of OAE per 1000 population declined very marginally and number of ESTT per 1000 population increased substantially. In the category 'with use of power,' the number of OAE and ESTT per 1000 population increased. Thus, the growth of ESTT has substantially displaced OAE in the categories of 'perennial' and 'with use of power.' This is an interesting result because, with increasing number of ESTT in retail of perishable commodities like fruits, vegetables, fish and meat and household consumption items like groceries and textiles, there is a general belief among traders that they displace OAEs and smaller establishments. This hypothesis could be tested if we analyse the growth rates of ESTT and OAEs, size of establishments by employment, organisation of establishments such as private, public limited, cooperative and government and classification of establishment activities by 4-digit NIC code in specific locations.

For an illustration, we take retail business in cereals and pulses, tea, coffee, spices, flour, vegetables and fruits, meat and fish, bakery, dairy and poultry products, aerated water, soft drinks, ice creams, *pan*, *bidi*, cigarette, wine, liquor and intoxicants. The 1987 NIC 4-digit codes have eight different classifications for these business activities, which were used in Economic Census surveys 1990 and 1998. In the 2005 Economic Census survey, this classification was completely changed; hence, we have not included it in this analysis. We analyse by classifying establishments as OAEs and ESTTs and the total employment generated in these categories. We confine our analysis to urban Tamil Nadu.

Table A-9.2

Retail Trade in Food and Food Articles

NIC Code	*Commodities*	*OAEs/100 ESTTs*		*Estb/1000 Persons*		*Empl/1000 Persons*	
		1990	*1998*	*1990*	*1998*	*1990*	*1998*
6500	Cereals, pulses, tea, coffee, spices, flour	185	105	2.3	2.9	4.7	6.6
6510	Veg and fruits	452	183	1.1	1.6	1.7	3.1
6520	Meat, fish, poultry	399	147	0.5	0.6	0.8	1.1
6530	Sweatmeat, bakery and dairy products, egg	207	89	0.5	0.8	1.1	1.9
6540	Aerated water, soft drinks, ice creams	181	110	0.2	0.3	0.5	0.8
6550	Pan, *bidi*, cigarette	756	238	2.0	2.1	2.8	3.7
6560	Wine, liqour	55	43	0.1	0.1	0.2	0.4
6590	Food, food articles, beverages, tobacco, intoxicants	335	137	0.4	0.5	0.7	0.6
	Total	312	140	7.1	8.9	12.4	18.2

The total number of establishments has increased by nearly 70 per cent from 1.33 lakhs to 2.22 lakhs and the total employment increased by 49 per cent from 2.33 lakhs to 4.55 lakhs between 1990 and 1998 in the retail sector. Much of the increase in the number of establishments and employment ought to have been in ESTT category. We find across all the eight categories that the number of OAEs per 100 ESTT has declined, indicating that the growth in ESTT has been larger than the growth in OAEs. Thus the ESTTs have virtually displaced the OAEs. Nearly 50 per cent of the establishments are in NIC codes 6500 and 6510, that is, retail trade in groceries and vegetables and fruits and in these categories, we find a sharp decline in the OAEs per 100 ESTTs. But the number of establishments per 1000 persons increased in both these categories. It is necessary to remember that the ESTT has hired labour, hence higher capability to create more employment per unit than OAE. Consequently the number of employment per 1000 persons also increased substantially in these two categories. The fact is that the OAEs are being replaced by ESTTs at the same time creating a large number of employment opportunities in all the eight categories mentioned in the Annexure Table A-9.2; but only a detailed study with more information will throw light on the distributional impact of this development.

Annexure A-9.2

Ownership of Establishments: Social Classes

The Economic Census identifies the ownership of establishment by four categories: (1) private establishments, which is further sub-divided as sole proprietor and partnership firms, (2) public limited companies, (3) cooperative societies and (4) public sector undertakings. In the case of sole proprietor and partnership firms, the social class of owners is classified as Scheduled Castes (SC), Scheduled Tribes (ST) and others. In the latest survey of 2005, backward classes are also included in this classification. The proportion of establishments owned by ST has nearly doubled from 0.9 per cent in 1990 to 1.5 per cent in 2005. Similarly the proportion of establishments owned by SC has increased by 60 per cent from 5.6 to 9 per cent. This signifies the social broadening in the ownership of establishments. Nevertheless, if we divide the establishments into OAE and ESTT, then some questions need to be raised. The participation in ownership of OAE by ST increased marginally from 0.5 to 0.9 in 1998 and then doubled to 1.7 in 2005, whereas the proportion of ownership of ESTT by ST increased marginally from 0.3 to 0.8 and then to 1.1 in this period. Thus much of the substantial increase in the ownership of establishments by ST is attributable to increase in ownership of OAE than of ESTT. This is the same story with regard to ownership by SC. Therefore, increases in the proportion of establishments owned by SC and ST are mainly due to increase in ownership of OAE by people of these deprived groups. The increase in the number of establishments by SCs and STs may be regarded as signifying some economic empowerment of the SCs and STs, but the increase mainly in the ownership of OAE can be seen as signifying the marginalisation of these groups in the production sector. Further analyses of the size, location and sectoral classification of enterprises owned by SCs and STs would reveal some more interesting trends about changing social character of the production economy.

Table A-9.3

Ownership of Establishments: Social Classes

Category	*1990*			*1998*			*2005*		
	OAE	*Estt*	*Total*	*OAE*	*Estt*	*Total*	*OAE*	*Estt*	*Total*
ST	7283	1871	9154	13504	9127	22631	46948	18708	65656
	0.5	0.3	0.7	0.9	0.8	0.9	1.7	1.1	1.5
SC	100910	17954	118864	78914	49333	128247	295331	102075	397406
	7.3	2.5	5.6	5.5	4.5	5.1	10.8	6.0	9.0
Total	1383469	727561	2111030	1424923	1089201	2514124	2744576	1688815	4433391

Social Sectors

10 Inequities in Health in Tamil Nadu

A Study of Dharmapuri District

T.K. Sundari Ravindran,
P. Balasubramanian and G.K. Mini

Inequities in Health

In public health, the concept of health inequity is often used to describe inequalities in health that are perceived to be *avoidable, unnecessary and unfair* (Daniels *et al.*, 1999). Equity—the absence of particularly unfair differences—is different from equality—the absence of differences in general. The use of equity rather than equality when assessing the nature of differentials in health arises from the recognition that there are bound to be differences in the health status of individuals, and for a number of reasons, many of these are random or biological and hence unavoidable.

There is sufficient evidence now from across the globe to show that differences in health status across social groups are not just the result of genetic endowments or life style differences but that socially and economically disadvantaged groups get more sick more often and have less access to health services as compared to their more privileged counterparts even within the same country or region. Most of these differences originate in inequities in access to social and economic resources and living conditions essential for leading a healthy life.[1]

The use of the concept of health equity may appear to be in conflict with health equality, as viewed from a human rights perspective, but this is not the case. Equity, which embodies a dimension of justice, indicates

---

1. Marmot *et al.*, 1987; Pappas *et al.*, 1993; Lynch *et al.*,1998; Muntaner, 1999; Muntaner and Lynch, 1991; Kreiger *et al.*, 1993; Willams, 1996.

that change should be in the direction that is fair and just even if it means preferential treatment of disadvantaged groups over others.

Pursuing equity in health means trying to reduce social disadvantages or their health effects among disadvantaged groups; it thus requires selectively focusing on disadvantaged groups. Yet, health policies and programmes continue to remain focused on disease-specific interventions and outcomes. Inadequate attention paid to addressing social determinants of health has contributed to a widening of the gaps in health status between and across countries (Legge, n.d.).

Health Inequities in India

Most of the studies in India on differences in health across social groups have looked at either self-reported morbidity as a proxy for health status, or at extent and nature of utilisation of health care services as a proxy for access to health care services. Few studies go beyond observing the extent and direction of differences to probing the pathways in terms of association with health differences with unequal access to resources that are necessary for good health. Also, studies that examine more than one source of social disadvantage, caste, class or gender, are rare to come by.

Differentials in Health Status

Reports from studies examining differentials in health status across social groups provide conflicting findings. There seem to be as many studies indicating poorer health status in disadvantaged groups as those that find the social advantaged sections reporting poorer health status.

Caste

The National Council for Applied Economic Research (NCAER) 1994 survey data of India showed that those belonging to the Scheduled Castes (SCs) and Scheduled Tribes (STs) had higher levels of morbidity (Duraisamy, 2001). On the other hand, using National Sample Survey Organisation (NSSO) 52nd round data of West Bengal, one recent paper (2004) reported that the prevalence of morbidity among the ST population was lower (38 per 1000 population) than other castes groups (68) (Ghose, 2004). Another study in rural Karnataka (1994) also highlighted that the morbidity was the lowest among SC and ST populations (Deshpande, 1998).

Income/Standard of Living

Rates of prevalence of morbidity by economic status are also reported in some studies to be positively associated (the higher the status, the higher the morbidity rate) and in others, to be negatively associated. Iyer and Sen (2000) reported that morbidity rates in the top Monthly Per Capita Expenditure fractile (MPCE) were 1.5 to two times higher than the rates in the lowest fractile in rural and urban areas of India. Similarly, Duggal and Amin (1989) found the prevalence of both acute and chronic diseases to be higher in upper classes than in lower classes. It is also observed that the poor report less ill health than the rich even though the poor have higher mortality rates. For example, the incidence of self-reported morbidity was much higher in the state of Kerala than in Bihar despite higher education levels and greater longevity in Kerala (Sen, 1999).

However, other studies observe the prevalence of morbidity to be highest for those with the lowest standard of living (Deshpande, 1998) and that both acute and chronic illness prevalence rates decrease with an improvement in socio-economic status (Sen, 1999).

Gender

Gender differentials in reported morbidity are evident in a number of micro level and large-scale studies. Most of the studies show that the prevalence of illness was higher for females than males (Ghose, 2004; Kannan *et al.*, 1991; Mishra and Dilip, 2004). However, one study analysing 1986-87 data for Tamil Nadu indicates that the males reported significantly higher morbidities than females (Duraisamy, 1998). Madhiwalla *et al.* (2000) found that morbidity rates were consistently higher among disadvantaged groups of women, migrants, SCs and minorities in rural areas of Maharashtra.

Place of Residence

Most studies examining rural/urban differentials in levels of morbidity have shown that morbidity rates are higher in rural areas than in urban areas.[2] Other studies reported that morbidity rates are higher in urban areas than in rural areas (Duraisamy, 1998; Madhiwala *et al.*, 2000; NCAER,

2. Duggal and Amin, 1989; NCAER, 1992; National Sample Survey Organisation, 1998; Sundar, 1995.

1992). One recent study in the year 2003 reported that acute illnesses were more prevalent in rural households, whereas chronic illnesses were more common in the urban population (National Sample Survey Organisation, 1998).

Age

A considerable number of studies have found 'J' and 'U' shaped relationships between age and morbidity, an indication that elders and children are more susceptible to illnesses as compared to other age groups.[3]

Differentials in Utilisation of Health Care

Of studies examining differentials in health care seeking behaviour, most examine variations across socioeconomic class groups and a small number examine variations across other attributes such as gender and place of residence.

Caste

Vaguet *et al.* (1995) examined differential access to health providers by caste. The study observed that patients of any physician were of two different spatial groups: those who went to him because they belonged to the same caste and lived among that caste and those who attended his practice because it was in their quarter. The ex-untouchable castes never visited the physician or the public hospital (Ibid.).

Income/Economic Status

Large-scale surveys have observed that a high percentage of the poor do not seek care when ill. An analysis of NSS 52nd round survey indicates that about 24 per cent of the poorest quintile do not seek care, compared to 9 per cent of the richest quintile (Gupta, 2003). And according to National Family Health Survey (NFHS) 2 data of Indian states, a person from the poorest quintile of the population despite more health problems was six times less likely to access hospitalisation than a person from the richest quintile (International Institute for Population Sciences [IIPS] and ORC Macro, 2001a). The socially less privileged were unable to access health

3. Duraisamy, 2001; Ghose, 2004; Deshpande, 1998; National Sample Survey Organisation, 1998.

care due to geographical, social, economical or gender related distances (Deogaonkar, 2004).

Not much seems to have changed over time in terms of improved access to treatment for those from low-income groups. Sen *et al.* (2002) based on NSS data observed that in India, untreated illness among poor had increased over a period of time (1986-1996). Inequality by economic class appeared to have worsened and the divide between rich and poor in terms of untreated ailments and expenditure on health care services had grown (Ibid.).

In a study by Rao and Richard (1984) in Tamil Nadu, 90 per cent of respondents with lower incomes preferred home treatment for common ailments in the initial stages when compared to 56 per cent of those with higher incomes.

Gender

Gender differences within poor households in access to health care have also been observed by Gita Sen. Her study based on NSS data 2002 found that members from poor households were less likely to get their illness treated and these differences by household economic class status were more acute among women than among men (Sen, 2001). Another study in India indicated that the proportion seeking care for common childhood illness in India was higher for boys than girls (Ghose, 2004).

Education

A 1984 study from Tamil Nadu found that the proportion who said they would approach a physician even during the initial stages of ailments increased significantly with education and the proportion whose first choice was a government hospital declined as education increased (Rao and Richard, 1984).

Place of Residence

There appear to be some differences by rural-urban residence in reasons for not seeking treatment, with financial difficulties and lack of medical facilities being a more common reason in the former. The NSSO 42nd round survey (1986-87) highlighted that in rural areas, the major causes for not seeking treatment were that the ailments were not considered serious (75%) financial difficulties (15%) and no medical facility (3%). In urban areas, the major causes for not seeking treatment were that the ailments were not considered serious (81%) financial difficulties (10%) and no medical facility (less than 1%) (Bandewar and Saha, 2000).

Studies looking into source of treatment for various morbidities reveal that private hospitals are mostly used. An all-India morbidity study conducted by the NCAER in 1992 reported that in 55 per cent of illness episodes, treatment was sought from private facilities, whereas for 33 to 39 per cent, it was sought from government facilities (NCAER, 1992). A more recent study in 2003 reported that an overwhelming majority of patients still prefer to use private facilities for hospitalisation in India. The percentage of individuals visiting a private facility in the urban areas was about 65 per cent, whereas this number was about 55 per cent in the rural areas (Gupta, 2003). There appears to have been a steady move towards seeking health care in the private sector during the 1990s.

However, even now, government services may be the main source of health care for the less privileged groups. NSS data shows that as late as in 2003, those from SCs and STs had a higher probability of seeking care in the government facility. Education also seems to be positively influencing seeking care in the government sector (Gupta, 2003).

Overall, while caste, class, gender, educational status and place of residence emerge as social determinants of health status, the evidence on the direction of relationship is inconclusive even among studies which have all relied on self-reporting of morbidity. On the other hand, a more privileged status by caste, class or gender does increase utilisation of health care.

The study presented in this paper attempts to address some of the gaps in our understanding of inequities in health in India by gender, caste and class. The study examined inequities in prevalence and utilisation of health care services for acute, chronic and reproductive morbidity. The study was carried out in Dharmapuri district of Tamil Nadu in 2004. The present study was undertaken by the Rural Women's Social Education Centre in Tamil Nadu (RUWSEC), an organisation working in the Kancheepuram district for more than two decades in the area of health, including community-based work and research.

The structure of this paper is as follows. Following this introductory section on the literature of health equity in India, the second section describes the objectives, study area and methodology, and characteristics of the study populations. Sections three, four and five examine the prevalence and health seeking behaviour for acute, chronic and reproductive morbidity respectively. Each section describes the prevalence and patterns of treatment seeking, analyses their correlates and examines differentials by gender, caste and class in factors associated with acute, chronic and reproductive morbidity respectively. Section six summarises the findings and discusses their implications.

The Present Study

Objectives

The overall objective of the study is to assess inequities in health by caste, class and gender.

- To examine differences by caste, class and gender in prevalence and in correlates of morbidity;
- To examine differences by caste, class and gender in rates and in correlates of treatment seeking for morbidity.

Study Area

The choice of Tamil Nadu for a study examining inequities in health was to some extent influenced by the state's unique position in terms of health achievements. Tamil Nadu witnessed a rapid decline in fertility since the early 1980s and reached close to replacement levels in the mid-1990s. All sections of the population have experienced large fertility declines, desire fairly low family sizes and have low fertility (IIPS and ORC Macro, 2001b) (Also see K. Nagaraj's paper in this volume). Maternal health care initiatives including tetanus immunisation for pregnant women have been highly successful in Tamil Nadu, with near complete coverage by antenatal care (98%) and immunisation (89%), high levels of contraceptive prevalence (52%) and proportion of deliveries attended by skilled personnel (84%) (Ibid.). To what extent do these successes mask inequities in health? This was the question that motivated the study.

The district chosen for the study was Dharmapuri which is known for its comparatively disadvantaged position in terms of social and economic development among all districts of the state. The population of Dharmapuri district as per the census of 2001 constituted 4.6 per cent of the state's population. The district's overall sex ratio of was 938 females per 1000 males in the year 2001 (Census of India, 2001). The district literacy rates were 69 and 49 per cent for males and females respectively, far below the average for Tamil Nadu as a whole (Directorate of Census, 2001). According to the 2001 Census, nearly 70 per cent of Dharmapuri's workforce was dependent on agriculture and allied activities (Government of Tamil Nadu, 2000). The district is one among the most backward and drought-prone areas in the state.

According to Sample Registration System (SRS) estimates by the year 2000, the district recorded the highest birth rate in Tamil Nadu, 21.9 per 1000 population. Of the 30 districts in the state, Dharmapuri recorded the highest infant mortality rate of 67 per 1000 live births (Government of Tamil Nadu, 2000). The child sex ratio (0-6 years) in the district is very low, 860 and 923 girls per 1000 boys in rural and urban areas respectively (Government of Tamil Nadu, 2000). It is very important to mention here that Dharmapuri is one of the districts in Tamil Nadu where female infanticide has been found to be prevalent. A district level survey in 1996 found female infanticide accounted for more than half (59%) of all female infant deaths in Dharmapuri District (Visaria, n.d.).

According to Reproductive and Child Health II project (RCH-II), female age at marriage is very low with about 34 per cent of currently married women in the 15-44 years age group married before 18 years of age. Utilisation of maternal and child health services, although showing high averages, is also marked by inequalities by social groups. About 98 per cent of pregnancies received some form of antenatal care (ANC) and 65.5 per cent received ANC at home from a health worker. During 1995-1999, only 63 per cent of deliveries were institutional and 27 per cent were reported as 'not safe' (home deliveries assisted by neighbours and relatives). The survey also highlighted that 45 per cent of the deliveries of women belonging to SCs and STs were unsafe. The district recorded the highest sexually transmitted and other reproductive tract infections (STI/RTI) prevalence in Tamil Nadu, with about half of the women (48.4%) in 15-44 years age group reporting one or more symptoms of STI/RTI (Population Research Centre *et al.*, 2001).

Methodology

Sample Selection and Data Collection

Based on the need to stratify by caste, class and gender, as well as resource availability, the sample size was fixed as 2500 households. In order to capture disparities, three blocks, Uttangarai, Morapur and Harur that had moderate socioeconomic and health indicators and a higher than district average proportion of SC population (in order to ensure an adequate sample size of this group), in Dharmapuri district were selected for the study. Fifty villages were selected randomly with probability proportion to size, and a systematic sample of 50 households was selected after carrying out house-listing in the sample villages.

A structured questionnaire was used to gather information on characteristics of the household and its members. Information on acute, chronic and reproductive morbidity and on health seeking behaviour as reported by the person affected (or the mother, in case of children below 15 years) was collected. Field investigators consisted of trained social workers who had experience working with rural communities and prior experience in collecting data for health surveys. An intensive four-day training including piloting the questionnaire was implemented in preparation for this study. There was close field-based supervision and daily checking of the data gathered, to ensure data quality. The field survey period was March-May 2004. Of the 2500 households selected, interviews were completed in 2475 households. The remaining households were absent for an extended period. The overall response rate was 99 per cent.

Dependent and Independent Variables

Dependent Variables

Dependent variables included:

- *Prevalence of acute morbidity*: Proportion of those reporting symptoms of an acute morbidity that they had or have been experiencing at any time during the period starting 30 days prior to the survey and including the day of the survey, excluding acute episodes of chronic morbidity (for example, flaring up of wheezing in an asthmatic person, or of joint pains in a person suffering from rheumatism) and excluding any symptoms of morbidity of the reproductive system for a list of symptoms included.

- *Prevalence of chronic morbidity:* Proportion of those reporting symptoms of a chronic health condition that they have been suffering from and/or have been taking treatment for, of which they had or have been experiencing an acute episode at any time during the period starting 30 days prior to the survey and including the day of the survey and excluding any symptoms of morbidity of the reproductive system.
- *Prevalence of reproductive morbidity:* Proportion of ever-married women between 15-49 years of age who report any morbidity related to their reproductive system at any time during the period starting 3 months prior to the survey and including the day of the survey for a list of symptoms included.
- *Proportion seeking treatment:* Those seeking any treatment (other than self-treatment) from a health provider, whether government or private, qualified or unqualified, as a proportion of those reporting any morbidity. This was calculated for those reporting acute, chronic or reproductive morbidity.
- *Proportion seeking treatment from government and private health facilities/providers:* Private health providers included both qualified and less-than qualified providers.

Independent Variables

Independent variables were divided into two groups. One set of variables were what we considered 'proximate' determinants of health status and/or health seeking behaviour. The other set included caste, class and gender, which we view as variables that would have a modifying effect on the proximate determinants.

Proximate determinants chosen included:

- *Age:* Less than 15 years, 15-34 years, 35-59 years and 60 years and older.
- *Literacy status:* Illiterate and literate.
- *Occupation:* Labourers, those in salaried employment, self-employed and those engaged in unremunerated work including domestic tasks usually performed by housewives.
- *Housing conditions:* This included type of house (*kutcha*, semi-*pucca* or *pucca*); number of rooms; nature of cooking fuel; existence and nature of toilet facility; nature of sanitation; and source of drinking water. Scores were given to each of these attributes using the same scoring pattern as in NFHS-2 and observations classified as below average and above average.

In the case of prevalence and health seeking for reproductive morbidity, the following additional independent variables were included:

- *Contraceptive use:* Current use of a reversible or permanent method of contraception by the woman concerned. A number of studies have found association between contraceptive use and reproductive morbidity, especially in the case of female sterilisation.
- *Parity:* Association may be expected between number of pregnancies and reproductive morbidity, which in turn may influence treatment seeking behaviour.
- *Type of family:* Nuclear and other, and an indicator of a woman's ability to make decisions about her health or to access health care. We expect 'belonging to a nuclear family' to be associated with lower prevalence of reproductive morbidity. As for utilisation of health services for reproductive morbidity, the relationship could go either way. Utilisation of health care for those belonging to a nuclear family may be expected to be higher because they have greater decision-making power as compared to those in joint families or lower because they may not have the social support necessary to seek health care outside the home.

Inequality variables:

- *Gender*: Male and female.
- *Caste*: Three categories were considered: SCs or STs; most backward castes (MBC); and other castes.
- *Ownership of Assets* (as a proxy for class): Included ownership of a wide range of durable goods, house property, cultivable land (all land and irrigated land) and livestock. Scores were given to each of these attributes using the same scoring pattern as in NFHS-2 and observations classified as below average and above average.

Statistical Analysis

For each of the dependent variables, associations were examined using bivariate analysis with independent variables: sex, caste and asset-ownership, as well as age, education, occupation and housing conditions. In the case of reproductive morbidity, associations with type of family, parity and contraceptive use were also analysed.

Subsequently, stratified analysis by sex, caste and asset ownership of the association of 'proximate determinants' of morbidity and treatment seeking was carried out. This was in order to understand whether the influence of proximate determinants on morbidity and health seeking differed significantly by sex, caste or asset ownership.

Characteristics of Sample Households and Population

Household Characteristics

The study covered 2475 households, of which 94 per cent lived in rural areas. Table 10.1 presents characteristics of the sample households.

Demographic Characteristics

More than 95 per cent of the households were Hindu, about 3 per cent were Muslim and the remaining Christian. Over all, a third (32.3%) of the households belonged to the socially deprived group of SCs or STs. Thirty-one per cent belonged to the 'most-backward' caste groups, 33 per cent to backward castes and 3 per cent to forward castes. About two-third (64.5%) of the households were nuclear families and 35.5 per cent were extended or joint families.

Table 10.1*

Characteristics of Sample Households

	Variables	*Frequency*
Place of residence		
	Rural	2326 (94.0)
	Urban	149 (6.0)
Religion		
	Hindu	2361 (95.4)
	Christian	34 (1.4)
	Muslim	80 (3.2)
Type of family		
	Nuclear family	1596 (64.5)
	Joint/extended family	879 (35.5)
Housing conditions		
House type		
	Kutcha	552 (22.3)
	Semi-*pucca*	1375 (55.6)
	Pucca	548 (22.1)
Separate kitchen		
	Yes	709 (28.7)
	No	1766 (71.4)
Smoke outlet		
	Yes	324 (13.1)
	No	2151 (86.9)
Source of drinking water		
	Public tap	1213 (49.0)
	Public well/borewell	545 (22.0)
	Own house well/tap	588 (24.8)
	Others	129 (5.2)
Toilet facilities		
	Yes	249 (10.1)
	No	2226 (89.9)
Assets		
Land:	Land owned	1145 (46.3)
	Landless	1330 (53.7)
Livestock:	Owned	767 (31.0)
	Not owned	1708 (69.0)
Standard of Living		
	Low	916 (37.0)
	Medium	927 (37.5)
	High	632 (25.5)
Total		2475 (100.0)

Note: * Source for all tables in this paper: Primary Survey conducted by the Rural Women's Social Education Centre, Dharmapuri district.

Housing Conditions

Overall 22 per cent of households lived in *kutcha* houses or mud huts, 56 per cent in semi-*pucca* houses and only 22 per cent in *pucca* houses. In 71 per cent of the households, cooking was done in the living area and there was no separate kitchen. Although firewood was the main cooking fuel used by four-fifths of the households, only 13 per cent had smoke outlets.

Most of the households in the study depended on public water sources for their drinking water needs. About half the households (49%) depended on water from a public tap. Twenty-two per cent of the households fetched water from public hand pumps/borewells. About 5 per cent depended on open ponds and streams and only about a quarter of the households had a water source at home: well or tap.

Toilet facilities were almost non-existent, and a whopping majority (92%) of rural and a little more than half of urban households had no toilet facility and used open spaces. Even in urban areas, only 37 per cent of households had own toilets in their houses.

Assets Owned

Two thousand two hundred and twenty five (2225) households owned the houses in which they lived. Only 50 per cent owned any agricultural land; the average land owing of the sample was 2.9 acres. As already mentioned, Dharmapuri district is drought prone, and only 25 per cent of the land owned was irrigated, the remaining being rain-dependent. Only 2.6 per cent of the households had four or more acres of irrigated land. About 31 per cent of households owned livestock.

Ownership of household durable goods was limited to basic furniture (67%) and entertainment media such as radio (35%) and television (48%). The most common means of transport owned was the humble cycle (45%), followed by the motor cycle (15%) with less than 1 per cent possessing a car. Only 1 out of 10 households had a telephone connection. Only about 6 per cent of the households owned a 'productive' durable good such as irrigation motor, and less than 1 per cent owned a tractor, thresher or bullock cart (not included in Table 10.1).

Thirty-seven (37) per cent of households belonged to medium standard of living (SLI), another 37 per cent fell in low SLI and 26 per cent of households in the study belonged to the high standard of living group.

Population Characteristics

Total Population

Table 10.2 presents characteristics of the sample population. The population covered by the study was 11,039 (5624 males and 5415 females). The overall sex ratio was 962 females per 1000 males, which is higher than the integrated Dharmapuri district census figure (933 in 2001). The child sex ratio of 0-6 year population was 903 girls per 1000 boys,

Table 10.2

Characteristics of the Study Population

Variables	*Males*	*Females*	*Total*
Age group (years)			
< 15	1667 (29.6)	1514 (28.0)	3181 (28.8)
15-34	2033 (36.1)	2048 (37.8)	4081 (37.0)
35-59	1459 (25.9)	1440 (26.6)	2899 (26.3)
>=60	465 (8.3)	413 (7.6)	878 (8.0)
Educational Status			
Illiterate	1945 (34.6)	2712 (50.1)	4657 (42.2)
Primary or less	1230 (21.9)	1037 (19.2)	2267 (20.5)
Middle school	971 (17.3)	733 (13.5)	1704 (15.4)
High school	786 (14.0)	581 (10.7)	1367 (12.4)
Higher secondary	349 (6.2)	231 (4.3)	580 (5.3)
Higher education	343 (6.1)	121 (2.2)	464 (4.2)
Occupation			
Wage labourer	1501 (26.7)	1223 (22.6)	2724 (24.7)
Business/salaried employment	996 (17.7)	235 (4.3)	1231 (11.2)
Cultivation	567 (10.1)	341 (6.3)	908 (8.2)
Unemployed	582 (10.3)	329 (6.1)	911 (8.2)
Household work	0	1254 (23.2)	1254 (11.4)
Not in the work force	1978 (35.2)	2033 (37.5)	4011 (36.3)
Total	5624 (100.0)	5415 (100.0)	11039 (100.0)

Note: Percentages in brackets.

which is considerably higher than the district average (878 females per 1000 males). The mean age of the population was 28 years (27.9 years for males and 28.13 for females).

Overall, 58 per cent of the population above 7 years of age was literate, while 42 per cent was illiterate. The male and female literacy rates were 76 and 57 per cent respectively. A little more than one-fourth of males (26 per cent) and 17 per cent of females in the sample had more than 8 years of schooling. A fourth (25%) of the population (27% of men and 23% of women) worked as wage labourers in agriculture and other sectors.

Ever-married Women of Reproductive Age

In the study area, there were 2440 ever-married women in the reproductive age group of 15-49 years (Table 10.3). This was the population whose reproductive morbidity was studied. About 92 per cent of them were currently married and the remaining 8 per cent were either widowed or separated. The mean age of ever-married women was 31.7 years and about 6 per cent were 19 years or younger. Age at marriage of women is low in the study area, with more than one-fourth of the women in the 15-19 years age group currently married.

The average number of pregnancies per woman was 2.59, of children ever born 2.37 and of surviving children 2.18. Sixty-three per cent of currently married women were using contraception and all except a negligible proportion (less than 3%) have undergone sterilisation.

Morbidity

A little over 27 per cent of the population reported experiencing either acute or chronic morbidity or both during a recall period of 1 month, giving a prevalence rate of 276 per 1000 population. Acute morbidity alone was experienced by 9.5 per cent, 13.9 per cent experienced only chronic morbidity and 4.2 per cent experienced symptoms of both acute and chronic morbidities (Table 10.4).

Table 10.3

Characteristics of Ever-married Women in the Reproductive Age Group (15-49 Years of Age)

Variables		*Frequency*
Age (years)		
	15-24	567 (23)
	25-34	915 (38)
	35-44	728 (30)
	45-49	230 (9)
Marital status		
	Currently married	2236 (91.6)
	Widowed	135 (5.5)
	Divorced/separated	69 (2.8)
Age at marriage (years)		
	<18	1423 (58.3)
	18-19	556 (22.8)
	20-21	255 (10.5)
	22+	206 (8.4)
Type of family		
	Nuclear	1309 (53.7)
	Joint/extended	1131 (46.3)
Contraceptive use*		
	Non-users	835 (37.3)
	Users	1401 (62.7)
Total		2440

Note: * data available only for currently married women, n = 2236.

Table 10.4

Prevalence of General and Reproductive Morbidity

Morbidity	*Male*	*Female*	*Total*
General Morbidity			
Acute morbidity only	440 (7.8)	607 (11.2)	1047 (9.5)
Chronic morbidity only	699 (12.4)	837 (15.5)	1536 (13.9)
Acute and chronic	124 (2.2)	339 (6.3)	463 (4.2)
Any general morbidity (acute or chronic)	1263 (22.5)	1783 (32.9)	3046(27.6)
No general morbidity	4152 (77.5)	3841 (67.1)	7993 (72.4)
N	5415	5624	11039
Reproductive morbidity	Frequency (ever married women of reproductive age)		N
Any reproductive morbidity	1084 (44.5)		2440

Acute Morbidity

Prevalence of Acute Morbidity

Extent and Nature

About 14 per cent of the population in the sample households reported having symptoms of one or more acute illness, giving a prevalence rate of 137 per 1000 population (Table 10.4). 'Cold and cough' was the most frequently reported acute morbidity (36%), followed by severe aches and pains: headache, toothache, abdominal pain (31%). Overall, 1510 persons had 1650 morbidities and about 9 per cent had more than one illness. The mean number of morbidity per person was 1.09.

Most of the acute illness episodes (67.4%) were of short duration, i.e., 7 days or less. One-fifth suffered the problems for a duration of 8-14 days. The remaining 12 per cent had the diseases for more than 2 weeks. The mean and median duration of illness were 7 and 5 days respectively.

Correlates

Prevalence of acute morbidity was higher among females (17.5%) than among males (10%); among those belonging to most backward castes (15.5%) as compared to 'other' castes (13.5%) and SCs and STs (12.5%); and among those who had below average asset ownership (14.4%) as compared to 'above average' asset ownership (10.7%). All the differences were statistically significant at the 1 per cent level (Table 10.5).

Differences in prevalence of acute morbidity were also statistically significant by age, literacy status, and occupation and housing conditions. Those in the 15-34 age group had lower morbidity rates than those below 15 years as well as those above 35 years of age. Those who were literate and lived in above-average housing conditions had lower prevalence of acute morbidity than those who were illiterate and lived in below-average housing conditions. In terms of occupation, those who were in salaried employment had the lowest prevalence of acute morbidity (6.8%), while those working as labourers, self-employed or not engaged in remunerated work had double this prevalence rate or higher.

Table 10.5

Correlates of Acute and Chronic Morbidity

Variables		*Acute Morbidity*	*Chronic Morbidity*
Sex		**	**
	Male	564 (10.03)	823 (14.63)
	Female	946 (17.47)	1176 (21.72)
Caste		**	**
	SC/ST	467 (12.3)	556 (14.6)
	MBC	516 (15.5)	727 (21.8)
	Others	527 (13.5)	716 (18.4)
Assets		**	**
	Below average	1274 (14.4)	1149 (16.4)
	Above average	237 (10.7)	550 (24.7)
Age		**	**
	<15	451 (14.2)	152 (4.8)
	15-34	430 (10.5)	527 (12.9)
	35-59	470 (16.2)	933 (32.2)
	>=60	159 (18.1)	387 (44.1)
Literacy status		**	**
	Illiterate	831 (17.8)	1083 (23.3)
	Literate	697 (10.6)	916 (14.4)
Occupation		**	**
	Labourers	379 (13.9)	658 (24.2)
	Salaried employment	45 (6.8)	84 (12.8)
	Self-employment	231 (14.4)	458 (28.6)
	Unremunerated	855 (14.1)	799 (13.2)
Housing conditions		**	**
	Below average	954 (14.9)	1148 (17.9)
	Above average	556 (12.0)	851 (18.3)
Total N		11039	11039

Note: ** $p < 0.001$.

Stratified Analysis of Correlates of Acute Morbidity

Our next attempt was to understand whether there were differences in the nature and strength of association of different 'proximate' determinants of acute morbidity by gender, caste and ownership of assets. This was done through stratified analysis (Tables 10.6-10.8), yielding some interesting results.

There were major variations in the association of proximate determinants with acute morbidity in male and female respondents. For example, while for males the odds of being affected by acute morbidity decreased in the age groups 15-34 and 35-59 as compared to those below 15 years of age, for females the odds increased in the age groups 35-59 and above 60 years of age as compared to those below 15 years of age (Table 10.6). Being unremunerated and living in below-average housing conditions significantly increased the odds of acute morbidity for females but not for males. No such variations by gender were found by literacy status.

Table 10.6

Association of Independent Variables with Acute Morbidity Stratified by Sex

Variables	*Sex (Odds Ratio 95% CI)*	
	Male	*Female*
Age		
<15	Reference	Reference
15-34	0.43 (0.34-0.54) **	1.0 (0.80-1.20)
35-59	0.62 (0.50-0.78) **	1.79 (1.48-2.16) **
>=60	1.04 (0.78-1.40)	1.68 (1.28-2.21) **
Literacy status		
Literate	Reference	Reference
Illiterate	1.60 (1.34-1.91)**	1.72 (1.49-1.99) **
Occupation		
Remunerated	Reference	Reference
Unremunerated	0.71(0.59-0.84)**	1.36 (1.18-1.58)**
Housing conditions		
Below average	0.98 (0.83-1.17)	1.26 (1.08-1.48)*
Above average	Reference	Reference

Note: * $p < 0.05$; ** $p < 0.001$.

Variations by caste in the association of proximate determinants with acute morbidity were less striking, but nevertheless noticeable (Table 10.7). In all caste groups: SC/ST, MBC and other castes, the odds of prevalence of acute morbidity were significantly lower in the 15-34 age group as compared to the below 15 age group. However, while the risk of acute morbidity increased step-wise in the age groups 35-59 and above 60 years for SC/ST population, no such association was found for other castes.

Table 10.7

Association of Independent Variables with Acute Morbidity Stratified by Caste

Variables	*Caste (Odds Ratio 95% CI)*		
	SC/ST	*MBC*	*Other*
Age			
<15	Reference	Reference	Reference
15-34	0.70 (0.55-0.90)*	0.77 (0.60-0.97)*	0.65 (0.51-0.84)**
35-59	1.35 (1.06-1.73)*	1.13 (0.88-1.45)	1.04 (0.82-1.32)
>=60	1.54 (1.05-2.26)*	1.29 (0.91-1.83)	1.20 (0.87-1.65)
Literacy status			
Literate	Reference	Reference	Reference
Illiterate	1.85 (1.52-2.26)**	1.85 (1.53-2.24)**	1.75 (1.46-2.11)**
Occupation			
Unremunerated	Reference	Reference	Reference
Remunerated	1.08 (0.89-1.31)	0.93 (0.77-1.13)	0.72 (0.59-0.87)**
Housing conditions			
Below average	1.17 (0.96-1.43)	1.26 (1.03-1.54)*	1.39 (1.16-1.68)**
Above average	Reference	Reference	Reference

Note: * $p < 0.05$; ** $p < 0.001$.

Again, being engaged in remunerated work significantly lowered the risk of acute morbidity only for 'other' castes. For MBCs, the risk was slightly lower and for SC/STs, slightly higher for those in remunerated employment as compared to those engaged in unremunerated occupations. But these differences were not statistically significant. Below-average housing conditions significantly increased the risk of acute morbidity only for MBCs and 'other' castes.

Those with 'above-average' ownership of assets showed a much larger increase in risk of acute morbidity in older age (more than 60 years) as compared to those with 'below'-average assets. This is probably because of much lower levels of morbidity in the reference age group. Being illiterate and living in below-average housing conditions increased the odds of acute morbidity significantly in the 'below-average' asset ownership group.

Table 10.8

Association of Independent Variables with Acute Morbidity Stratified by Asset Ownership

Variables	*Assets owned (Odds Ratio 95% CI)*	
	Below Average	*Above Average*
Age		
<15	Reference	Reference
15-34	0.76 (0.65-0.88) **	1.20 (0.36-3.97)
35-59	1.53 (1.31-1.78) **	1.61 (0.49-5.29)
>=60	1.14 (0.90-1.45)	4.11 (1.22-13.76)*
Literacy status		
Illiterate	1.86 (1.65-2.1)**	1.54 (1.19-1.99)**
Literate	Reference	Reference
Occupation		
Unremunerated	1.09 (0.96-1.24)	0.61 (0.43-0.87)*
Remunerated	Reference	Reference
Housing conditions		
Below average	1.15 (1.01-1.32)*	1.34 (0.98-1.83)
Above average	Reference	Reference

Note: * $p < 0.05$; ** $p < 0.001$.

Treatment Seeking for Acute Morbidity

Rate and Source of Treatment Seeking

A large majority of those afflicted with acute morbidity (78.5%) sought treatment from a health care provider (Table 10.9). Those who did not seek treatment said either that the disease was not serious enough to seek external care or that they could not afford treatment. Almost everyone uses the allopathic system of treatment (98.5%) with only a negligible proportion using either *Siddha* or homeopathy.

More than half (55.7%) of those seeking treatment used a private facility or provider, and only 44.3 per cent went to a government facility. However, when examining the nature of private health care sought, we found that about two-fifths of them (37.6%) had used less than qualified health care providers. In effect, then, those who sought health care from a government provider were getting technically better care than those seeking care from private health providers.

Table 10.9

Treatment Seeking for Acute and Chronic Morbidity

Treatment Seeking	*Type of Morbidity*	
Of All Reporting a Morbidity	*Acute Morbidity*	*Chronic Morbidity*
Sought Treatment	1379 (78.5)	2967 (88.7)
Did not seek treatment	378 (21.5)	379 (11.3)
Total episodes	1757 (100.0)	3346 (100.0)
Of those seeking treatment, used		
Govt. facilities or provider	611 (44.3)	1254 (42.3)
Private facilities or provider	768 (55.7)	1713 (57.7)
Total	1379 (100.0)	2967 (100.0)
Of those seeking treatment, with private providers, those using		
Qualified private providers	479 (62.4)	1481 (86.5)
Less-than or unqualified providers	289 (37.6)	232 (13.5)
Total	768 (100.0)	1713 (100.0)

When analysing the reason for selecting a particular source of treatment, about 70 per cent of those using government facilities gave lack of money and free treatment as the most important reasons for their choice. More than 80 per cent of private service users quoted good quality of treatment and humane, caring behaviour of providers as reasons influencing their choice. Interestingly, these reasons were given also by those using less than qualified providers.

Correlates

Treatment seeking for acute morbidity did not vary significantly by sex or caste. Also, neither age nor occupation appears to make a difference to the proportion seeking treatment. The only two variables significantly associated with treatment seeking are ownership of assets and literacy status. A greater proportion of literate persons and those with 'above-average' ownership of assets sought treatment as compared to illiterate persons and those with below-average asset ownership (Table 10.10).

Table 10.10

Correlates of Treatment Seeking for Acute and Chronic Morbidity

Variables	*Sought Treatment for Episodes of Acute Morbidity*	*Total N (Episodes of Morbidity)*	*Sought Treatment for Episodes of Chronic Morbidity*	*Total N (Episodes of Morbidity)*
Sex				
Males	529 (80.5)	657	1179 (89.5)	1318
Females	850 (77.3)	1100	1788 (88.2)	2028
Caste			*	
SC/ST	433 (78.0)	555	736 (89.1)	826
MBC	454 (75.9)	598	1112 (86.7)	1283
Others	492(81.5)	604	1119 (90.5)	1237
Assets	**		**	
Below average	630 (75.4)	826	1541 (86.8)	1775
Above average	749 (81.3)	923	1426 (90.8)	1571
Age			**	
<15	401 (79.6)	504	197 (86.0)	229
15-34	372 (76.2)	488	691 (85.8)	805
35-59	448 (78.9)	568	1471 (90.9)	1618
>=60	158 (80.2)	197	608 (87.6)	694
Literacy status	*			
Illiterates	510 (75.7)	674	1609 (88.5)	1819
Literates	869 (80.2)	1083	1358 (88.9)	1527
Occupation				
Unremunerated	665 (80.1)	927	1196 (87.8)	1984
Remunerated	714 (77.0)	830	1771 (89.3)	1362
Total	1379 (78.5%)	1757	2967 (88.7)	3346

Note: * $p < 0.05$; ** $p < 0.001$.

Contrary to this result, source of treatment is influenced significantly by gender, caste, asset ownership, age, literacy status and occupation (Table 10.11). A greater proportion of females than males; SC/ST than MBC and other castes; those with below-average as compared to above-average asset ownership; older as compared younger persons; and illiterates as compared to literate persons used government health facilities.

An unexpected result is that a greater proportion of those in remunerated occupations used government health facilities as compared to unremunerated persons. The reason for this is not clear.

Table 10.11

Correlates of Source of Treatment for Acute and Chronic Morbidity

Variables	*Sought Treatment for Episodes of Acute Morbidity from*		*Total N (Treated Episodes of Morbidity)*	*Sought Treatment for Episodes of Chronic Morbidity from*		*Total N (Treated Episodes of Morbidity)*
	Govt. Facilities/ Providers	*Pvt. Facilities/ Providers*		*Govt. Facilities/ Providers*	*Pvt. Facilities/ Providers*	
Sex			*			
Males	214 (40.5)	315 (59.5)	529	477 (40.5)	702 (59.5)	1179
Females	397 (46.7)	453 (53.3)	850	777 (43.5)	1011 (56.5)	1788
Caste		**				
SC/ST	229 (52.9)	204 (47.1)	433	375 (51.0)	361 (49.0)	736
MBC	189 (41.6)	265 (58.4)	454	438 (39.4)	674 (60.8)	1112
Others	193 (39.2)	299 (60.8)	492	441 (39.4)	678 (60.6)	1119
Assets		**				
Below average	329 (52.2)	301 (47.8)	630	742 (48.2)	799 (51.8)	1541
Above average	282 (37.7)	467 (62.3)	749	512 (35.9)	914 (64.1)	1426
Age		**				
<15	162 (40.4)	239 (59.6)	401	76 (38.6)	121 (61.4)	197
15-34	138 (37.1)	234 (62.9)	372	226 (32.7)	465 (67.3)	691
35-59	223 (49.8)	225 (50.2)	448	621 (42.2)	850 (57.8)	1471
>=60	88 (55.7)	70 (44.3)	158	331 (54.4)	277 (45.6)	608
Literacy status		**				
Illiterates	269 (52.7)	241 (47.3)	510	775 (48.2)	834 (51.8)	1609
Literates	342 (39.4)	527 (60.6)	869	479 (35.3)	879 (64.7)	1358
Occupation						
Unremunerated	277 (41.7)	388 (58.3)	665	503 (42.1)	693 (57.9)	1196
Remunerated	334 (46.8)	380 (53.2)	714	751 (42.4)	1020 (57.6)	1771
Total	611 (44.3)	768 (55.7)	1379	1254 (42.3)	1713 (57.7)	2967

Note: *p < 0.05; ** p < 0.001.

Stratified Analysis of Correlates of Treatment Seeking

Analysis stratified by gender shows that males and females are differently affected by some of the determinants of treatment seeking (Table 10.12). While older age increases the odds of treatment seeking for acute morbidity among females, age does not influence treatment seeking among males. Again, being literate increases the odds of treatment seeking significantly among males but not among females.

Table 10.12

Association of Independent Variables with Treatment Seeking for Acute Morbidity Stratified by Sex

Variables	*Sex (Odds Ratio 95% CI)*	
	Male	*Female*
Age		
<15	Reference	Reference
15-34	1.32 (0.53-3.28)	1.15 (0.74-1.78)
35-59	1.57 (0.55-4.42)	1.64 (0.98-2.74)*
>=60	1.67 (0.54-5.13)	2.45 (1.19-5.02)*
Literacy status		
Illiterate	Reference	Reference
Literate	2.24 (1.34-3.73)*	1.18 (0.81-1.72)
Occupation		
Remunerated	1.45 (0.57-3.63)	1.39 (0.96-2.02)
Unremunerated	Reference	Reference

Note: * $p < 0.05$; ** $p < 0.001$.

The significant association between treatment seeking and literacy status found in bivariate analysis appears to hold only in the case of 'other castes' on analysis stratified by caste. Increasing age dramatically increases the odds of treatment seeking only in the higher asset owning group and not in those with below-average asset ownership.

Thus, different variables seem to be important in determining treatment seeking for acute morbidity among different groups.

Chronic Morbidity

Prevalence of Chronic Morbidity

Extent and Nature

Prevalence of chronic morbidity was substantially higher than prevalence of acute morbidity, with a rate of 181 per 1000 population. Painful joints affecting mobility, peptic ulcer and visual impairment were the three most commonly reported conditions. Overall, 1999 persons reported 2367 conditions and the mean morbidity per person was 1.18. About one-fifth (18%) had two or more chronic illnesses.

Nearly half of the persons with chronic illnesses had suffered from these problems for more than 2 years. A little more than 30 per cent suffered with the problems between 6 and 24 months. Only one out of five persons had been experiencing the reported chronic illness for less than 6 months. The median duration of chronic sickness was 24 months.

Correlates

In the case of correlates of prevalence of chronic morbidity, some associations were similar to those found for acute morbidity, while others differed (Table 10.5). Prevalence was much higher among females (21.7%) than males (14.6%) and more among MBCs (21.8%) than among 'other' castes (18.4%) and SCs and STs (14.6%). It was lower among the literate group (14.4%) than among the illiterate (23.3%).

Table 10.13

Association of Independent Variables with Treatment Seeking for Acute Morbidity Stratified by Caste

Variables	*Caste (Odds Ratio 95% CI)*		
	SC/ST	*MBC*	*Other*
Age			
<15	Reference	Reference	Reference
15-34	0.87 (0.45-1.68)	1.25 (0.66-2.35)	1.09 (0.57-2.09)
35-59	1.56 (0.72-3.38)	1.17 (0.56-2.43)	1.75 (0.81-3.78)
>=60	2.22 (0.78-6.27)	1.29 (0.51-3.21)	2.18 (0.83-5.75)
Literacy status			
Illiterate	Reference	Reference	Reference
Literate	1.72 (1.03-2.88)	0.94 (0.58-1.53)	2.02 (1.17-3.49)*
Occupation			
Unremunerated	1.04 (0.58-1.84)	1.37 (0.76-2.46)	1.48 (0.85-2.59)
Remunerated	Reference	Reference	Reference

Note: * $p < 0.05$; ** $p < 0.001$.

However, prevalence was higher among those with 'above-average' assets (24.7%) as compared to those with 'below-average' assets (16.4%); increased in a step-wise fashion with age, being highest in the above 60 age group; and was higher among those with above-average housing conditions and self-employed (28.6%) and labourers (24.2%).

Stratified Analysis of Correlates of Chronic Morbidity

Unlike in the case of acute morbidity, determinants of chronic morbidity do not vary for males and females. For both sexes, the odds of having chronic morbidity increases step-wise by age and is higher for illiterates than for literates. Those working in unremunerated occupations have twice the odds of being affected by a chronic morbidity than those working in remunerated occupations.

Again, neither caste nor asset ownership makes a major difference to determinants of chronic morbidity.

Treatment Seeking for Chronic Morbidity

Rate and Sources of Treatment Seeking

A much higher proportion of persons reporting a chronic morbidity had sought treatment (88.7%) as compared to those reporting acute morbidity (Table 10.5). A large majority (93%) sought allopathic treatment, 4 per cent had *Siddha* treatment and 3 per cent had taken recourse to traditional healers.

Private facilities or providers were the predominant source of care (57.7%) and 42 per cent sought care from government providers. Only a small proportion of the private health care providers for chronic morbidity were less-than qualified (13.5%). Eighty-seven per cent were private hospitals and clinics (Table 10.5).

As seen for acute illness, free treatment was the single most reason for choosing government health facilities (65%) followed by good treatment (25%) and close proximity (9.33%). Among users of private facilities, a majority (93%) mentioned good medical treatment and humane and caring behaviour of providers.

Correlates of Treatment Seeking

There were no significant differences by sex in whether treatment was sought for chronic morbidity. However, caste and ownership of assets were associated with treatment seeking for chronic morbidity, with MBCs and

Table 10.14

Association of Independent Variables with Treatment Seeking for Acute Morbidity Stratified by Asset Ownership

Variables	*Assets Owned (Odds Ratio 95% CI)*	
	Below average	*Above average*
Age		
<15	Reference	Reference
15-34	1.06 (0.61-1.83)	1.68 (0.59-4.79)
35-59	1.20 (0.65-2.19)	3.52 (1.25-9.93) *
>=60	1.35 (0.71-2.58)	12.36 (4.29-35.59)**
Literacy status		
Illiterate	Reference	Reference
Literate	1.37 (0.89-2.11)	1.39 (0.91-2.12)
Occupation		
Unremunerated	1.06 (0.70-1.59)	1.38 (0.91-2.10)**
Remunerated	Reference	Reference

Note: * $p < 0.05$; ** $p < 0.001$.

Table 10.15

Association of Independent Variables with Chronic Morbidity Stratified by Sex

Variables	*Sex (Odds Ratio 95% CI)*	
	Male	*Female*
Age		
<15	Reference	Reference
15-34	2.09 (1.60-2.71) **	3.99 (3.04-5.22)**
35-59	6.06 (4.72-7.78) **	14.25 (10.93-18.58) **
>=60	12.01 (9.00-16.01)**	21.16 (15.51.28-86) **
Literacy status		
Literate	Reference	Reference
Illiterate	1.24 (1.06-1.44)*	2.17 (1.89-2.48) **
Occupation		
Remunerated	Reference	Reference
Unremunerated	2.24 (1.90-2.63)**	2.46 (2.16-2.81)**
Housing conditions		
Below average	0.66 (0.57-0.77)**	1.11 (0.96-1.28)
Above average	Reference	Reference

Note: * $p < 0.05$; ** $p < 0.001$.

Table 10.16

Association of Independent Variables with Chronic Morbidity Stratified by Caste

Variables	*Caste (Odds Ratio 95% CI)*		
	SC/ST	*MBC*	*Other*
Age			
<15	Reference	Reference	Reference
15-34	3.08 (2.21-4.31)**	2.91 (2.16-3.93)**	2.89 (2.05-4.09)**
35-59	9.23 (1.06-1.73)**	9.60 (7.16-12.89)**	9.95 (7.17-13.8)**
>=60	12.70 (8.50-18.96)**	14.65 (10.29-20.84)**	19.03 (13.24-27.36)**
Literacy status			
Literate	Reference	Reference	Reference
Illiterate	1.94 (1.61-2.32)**	1.79 (1.51-2.11)**	1.72 (1.46-2.03)**
Occupation			
Unremunerated	Reference	Reference	Reference
Remunerated	2.49 (2.07-2.99)**	2.43 (2.04-2.88)**	1.40 (1.19-1.64)**
Housing conditions			
Below average	Reference	Reference	Reference
Above average	1.10 (0.91-1.32)	1.24 (1.05-1.47)*	0.83 (0.70-0.98)*

Note: * $p < 0.05$; ** $p < 0.001$.

Table 10.17

Association of Independent Variables with Chronic Morbidity Stratified by Asset Ownership

Variables	*Assets Owned (Odds Ratio 95% CI)*	
	Below Average	*Above Average*
Age		
<15	Reference	Reference
15-34	2.87 (2.36-3.50) **	1.68 (0.59-4.79)
35-59	11.67 (9.62-14.15) **	3.52 (1.25-9.93) *
>=60	13.17 (10.46-16.59)**	12.36 (4.29-35.59)**
Literacy status		
Illiterate	1.95 (1.74-2.19**	1.69 (1.40-2.05)**
Literate	Reference	Reference
Occupation		
Unremunerated	2.39 (2.12-2.68)**	0.46 (0.35-0.59)**
Remunerated	Reference	Reference
Housing conditions		
Below average	1.16 (1.02-1.32)*	1.54 (1.20-1.93)**
Above average	Reference	Reference

Note: * $p < 0.05$; ** $p < 0.001$.

those with below-average asset ownership having lower rates of treatment seeking (Table 10.10). There was also a statistically significant association between treatment seeking and age, with those above 35 years having a slightly higher rate.

Source of treatment (government or private provider) was significantly associated with caste, asset ownership, age and literacy status. It is interesting to note that while a lower proportion of those belonging to MBC sought treatment, a greater proportion of them used a private provider as compared to the SC/ST group. The latter has a much higher rate of utilisation of government facilities as compared to other caste groups (Table 11). A greater proportion of those with above-average assets, younger persons (below 35 years of age) and literate persons used private health care facilities as compared to those with below-average assets, above 35 years of age and illiterate persons.

Stratified Analysis of Correlates of Treatment Seeking for Chronic Morbidity

Age was associated with treatment seeking for males, but no such association was found for females. Males above 60 years of age had a significantly higher probability of seeking treatment for chronic morbidity (Table 10.18).

Table 10.18

Association of Independent Variables with Treatment Seeking for Chronic Morbidity Stratified by Sex

Variables	*Sex (Odds Ratio 95% CI)*	
	Male	*Female*
Age		
<15	Reference	Reference
15-34	1.70 (0.83-3.47)	0.67 (0.34-1.32)
35-59	1.59 (0.76-3.35)	1.50 (0.75-3.03)
>=60	1.95 (0.99-3.85)*	0.99 (0.48-20.02)
Education		
Illiterates	1.27 (0.86-1.88)	1.12 (0.80-1.56)
Literates	Reference	Reference
Occupation		
Unremunerated	1.12 (0.68-1.83)	1.00 (0.75-1.34)
Remunerated	Reference	Reference

Note: * $p < 0.05$; ** $p < 0.001$.

Table 10.19

Association of Independent Variables with Treatment Seeking for Chronic Morbidity Stratified by Caste

Variables	*Caste (Odds Ratio 95% CI)*		
	SC/ST	*MBC*	*Other*
Age			
<15	Reference	Reference	Reference
15-34	1.24 (0.58-2.62)	1.12 (0.59-2.15)	0.61 (0.26-1.45)
35-59	2.52 (1.19-5.34)*	1.39 (0.74-2.58)	1.31 (0.57-3.05)
>=60	1.14 (0.51-2.57)	0.96 (0.49-1.89)	1.07 (0.45-2.53)
Education			
Illiterates	0.88 (0.56-1.37)	0.99 (0.71-1.37)	1.16 (0.80-1.70)
Literates	Reference	Reference	Reference
Occupation			
Unremunerated	Reference	Reference	Reference
Remunerated	1.62 (1.04-2.52)*	0.86 (0.61-1.23)	1.51 (1.02-2.22)*

Note: * $p < 0.05$; ** $p < 0.001$.

Table 10.20

Association of Independent Variables with Treatment Seeking for Chronic Morbidity Stratified by Asset Ownership

Variables	*Assets Owned (Odds Ratio 95% CI)*	
	Below Average	*Above Average*
Age		
<15	Reference	Reference
15-34	0.81 (045-1.05)	1.22 (0.59-2.51)
35-59	1.46 (0.79-2.69)	1.87 (0.90-3.90)
>=60	1.18 (0.63-2.19)	1.33 (0.61-2.92)
Education		
Illiterates	Reference	Reference
Literates	1.20 (0.73-1.43)	1.24 (0.85-1.80)
Occupation		
Unremunerated	Reference	Reference
Remunerated	1.14 (0.84-1.57)	0.94 (0.64-1.36)

Note: * $p < 0.05$; ** $p < 0.001$.

Determinants of treatment seeking varied by the caste group: for SCs/STs, belonging to the 35-59 year age group and being in remunerated occupation increased the odds for treatment seeking for chronic morbidity, while for 'other' castes, remunerated employment was the only significant determinant. For MBCs, there were no major variations by age, literacy status or occupation (Table 10.19).

No variation in determinants of treatment seeking was observed by ownership of assets (Table 10.20).

Reproductive Morbidity

Prevalence of Reproductive Morbidity

Extent and Nature of Morbidity

In the sample households, there were 2440 ever-married women in the reproductive age group. Of them about 45 per cent (1086) had one or more gynaecological morbidities (Table 10.4). Overall 1086 women had 1466 morbidities; about one-fifth had two or more morbidities. The mean reproductive morbidity per woman was 1.4.

The most frequently mentioned complaints among ever-married women were menstrual problems (56%), white discharge (30%) and lower abdominal pain (10%). Another 2 per cent suffered from urinary tract infection. Of the rest, nine had uterine prolapse and another five had infertility problems. Fifty-six women (2.3%) had undergone hysterectomy. Six women who had undergone hysterectomy were below 35 years of age. This is an unusual occurrence and calls for further probing.

About 71 per cent of women reporting a reproductive morbidity had suffered from these problems for more than 1 year. Only 17.3 per cent of cases had experienced the problem for 6 months or less preceding the survey. The average (median) duration of illness was 3 years.

Correlates

An important finding that emerges is that many of the correlates of reproductive morbidity are different from factors associated with general morbidity (Table 10.21).

Table 10.21

Correlates of Reproductive Morbidity

Variables		*Prevalence of Morbidity*
Caste		*
	SC/ST	379 (45.6)
	MBC	366 (48.5)
	Others	341 (39.9)
Assets		
	Below average	1055 (44.6)
	Above average	31 (42.5)
Age		
	15-34	677 (45.7)
	35-49	409 (42.7)
Literacy status		*
	Illiterate	559 (47.4)
	Literate	527 (41.8)
Occupation		**
	Labourers	459 (47.9)
	Salaried employment	20 (20.8)
	Self-employment	186 (50.3)
	Unremunerated	421 (40.5)
Housing conditions		*
	Below average	772 (46.3)
	Above average	314 (40.7)
Family type		**
	Nuclear	639 (48.8)
	Joint/extended	447 (39.5)
Contraceptive use[a]		**
	Non-users	301 (36.0)
	Users	711 (50.7)
Parity		*
	0-2	596 (54.9)
	>=3	490 (45.1)
Total N		2440

Note: *p <= 0.05; ** p <=0.001.

a: calculated for currently married women only.

Table 10.22

Association of Independent Variables with Reproductive Morbidity Stratified by Caste

Variables	*Caste (Odds Ratio 95% CI)*		
	SC/ST	*MBC*	*Other*
Age			
15-34	1.15 (0.86-1.55)	1.04 (0.76-1.42)	1.39 (1.04-1.86)*
35-49	Reference	Reference	Reference
Education			
Illiterates	1.22 (0.91-1.63)	1.36 (1.01-1.85)**	1.20 (0.88-1.62)
Literates	Reference	Reference	Reference
Occupation			
Salaried employment	Reference	Reference	Reference
Labourers	2.08 (0.63-6.87)	2.67 (0.92-7.78)	1.81 (0.85-3.81)
Self-employment	3.00 (0.82-10.91)	2.24 (0.76-6.63)	2.72 (1.26-5.88)*
Unremunerated	1.54 (0.46-5.10)	1.93 (0.66-5.64)	1.68 (0.82-3.45)
Type of family			
Joint/extended	Reference	Reference	Reference
Nuclear	1.44 (1.28-1.68)	1.28 (1.11-1.49)	1.52 (1.32-1.72)
Housing conditions			
Above average	0.79 (0.59-1.07)	0.93 (0.66-1.30)	0.78 (0.59-1.04)
Below average	Reference	Reference	Reference
Contraceptive Use			
Ever users	2.21 (1.63-3.02)**	1.61 (1.19-2.18)*	1.80 (1.32-2.45)**
Non-users	Reference	Reference	Reference
Parity			
0-2	Reference	Reference	Reference
>=3	1.05 (0.80-1.39)	1.22 (0.91-1.64)	1.22 (0.92-1.63)

Note: * $p < 0.05$; ** $p < 0.001$.

Association with asset ownership and age are not statistically significant. Women who belonged to MBCs had a significantly higher prevalence of reproductive morbidity (48.5%) than their counterparts in 'other' castes (39.9%) and SC/ST (45.6%), and illiterate women had a higher rate of prevalence (47.4%) than literate women (41.8%). Similarly, those living in below-average housing conditions had a higher prevalence (46.3%) than their counterparts living in better housing conditions (40.7%).

Table 10.23

Association of Independent Variables with Reproductive Morbidity Stratified by Asset Ownership

Variables[a]	*Assets Owned (Odds Ratio 95% CI)*	
	Below Average	*Above Average*
Age		
15-34	1.22 (1.02-1.45)*	1.33 (0.46-3.84)
35-49	Reference	Reference
Education		
Illiterates	1.27 (1.07-1.50)*	6.61 (2.22-19.69)**
Literates	Reference	Reference
Occupation		
Remunerated	1.32 (1.12-1.55)**	2.08 (0.64-6.68)
Unremunerated	Reference	Reference
Housing conditions		
Below average	1.23 (1.03-1.47)*	2.38 (0.78-7.20)**
Above average	Reference	Reference
Family Type		
Joint/extended	Reference	Reference
Nuclear	1.23 (1.12-1.35)**	2.27 (1.87-2.76)**
Parity		
0-2	Reference	Reference
>=3		

Note: * $p < 0.05$; ** $p < 0.001$.

a: The variable 'contraceptive use' is not included in this table because of small numbers in the 'above average' asset ownership category.

Table 10.24

Treatment Seeking for Reproductive Morbidity

Treatment Seeking	
Of all reporting a morbidity	
Sought Treatment	956 (65.2)
Did not seek treatment	510 (34.8)
Total episodes	1466 (100.0)
Of those seeking treatment, used	
Govt. facilities or provider	463 (48.4)
Private facilities or provider	493 (51.6)
Total	956 (100.0)
Of those seeking treatment, with private providers, those using	
Qualified private providers	402 (81.5)
Less-than or unqualified providers	91 (18.5)
Total	493 (100.0)

The strongest associations of reproductive morbidity were with type of family, contraceptive use and parity. A greater proportion of women living in nuclear families suffered from reproductive morbidity (48.8%) as compared to women living in joint or extended families (39.5%). Use of contraception significantly increased prevalence of reproductive morbidity (50.7% as compared to 36% among non-users). More women with parity two or less suffered from reproductive morbidity (54.9%) as compared to their counterparts with parity 3 or more (45.1%).

Stratified Analysis of Correlates of Reproductive Morbidity

Stratified analysis by caste and asset ownership indicates some variations in determinants of reproductive morbidity. For women belonging to the SC/ST group, use of a contraceptive method is the only variable significantly increasing the odds of suffering from a reproductive morbidity. For women of MBCs, the determinants are literacy status and contraceptive use and for women of 'other' castes, younger age and being self-employed increase the odds of reproductive morbidity in addition to ever-use of contraception.

For women from low-asset households, younger age, illiteracy being in remunerated occupation, living in poor housing conditions and in a nuclear family increase odds of morbidity. For women from better-off households, age and occupation do not seem to matter, but illiteracy, poor housing conditions and living in a nuclear family increase the probability of suffering from reproductive morbidity.

Treatment Seeking for Reproductive Morbidity

Rates and Sources of Treatment Seeking

Of the 1466 episodes of reproductive morbidity reported, treatment was sought for 65 per cent (Table 10.24). This is much lower than the rate of treatment seeking for acute (78.5%) and chronic morbidity (88.7%). A little less than half of the women seeking treatment (48.4%) went to a government provider or facility, while just a little above half (51.6%) went to a private provider. About 19 per cent of those going to a private provider used a less than qualified provider, making government health facilities the main source of qualified care for women with reproductive morbidity.

Table 10.25

Correlates of Treatment Seeking for Reproductive Morbidity

Variables	*Proportion Seeking Treatment*	*N=Episodes of Reproductive Morbidity*
Caste		
SC/ST	313(64.0)	489
MBC	348(66.7)	522
Others	295(64.8)	455
Assets		
Below average	457(65.7)	696
Above average	499 (64.8)	770
Age	*	
15-34	568(62.7)	906
35-49	388(69.3)	560
Literacy status		
Illiterate	528(67.0)	788
Literate	428(63.1)	678
Occupation	**	
Unremunerated	323(60.1)	537
Remunerated	633(68.1)	929
Family type	*	
Nuclear	608(68.2)	892
Joint/extended	348(60.6)	574
Contraceptive use[a]		
Non-users	249(61.9)	402
Users	634(66.2)	957
Parity		
0-2	515(60.4)	805
>=3	441(66.7)	661
Total N	956 (65.2)	1466

Note: a: data available only for currently married women.
$p < 0.05$; ** $p < 0.001$.

About 71 per cent of women with reproductive morbidity gave proximity and free treatment as the most important factors underlying their choice of a government provider or facility for treatment. Immediate attention and humane treatment were main reasons for choosing private hospitals/doctors. Of the 510 women who did not take any treatment for a

Table 10.26

Correlates of Source of Treatment for Reproductive Morbidity

Variables	*Sought Treatment from*		*Total N (Treated Episodes of Reproductive Morbidity)*
	Govt. Facilities/ Providers	*Pvt. Facilities/ Providers*	
Caste			**
SC/ST	180 (57.5)	133 (42.5)	313
MBC	167 (48.0)	181 (52.0)	348
Others	116 (39.3)	179 (60.7)	295
Assets		**	
Below average	262 (57.3)	195 (42.7)	457
Above average	201 (40.3)	298 (59.7)	499
Age			
15-24	66 (41.0)	95 (59.0)	161
25-34	197 (48.4)	210 (51.6)	407
35-44	175 (53.0)	155 (47.0)	330
45-49	25 (43.1)	33 (56.9)	58
Literacy status		**	
Illiterate	280 (53.0)	248 (47.0)	528
Literate	183 (42.8)	245 (57.2)	428
Occupation		*	
Unremunerated	138 (42.7)	185 (57.3)	633
Remunerated	325 (51.3)	308 (48.7)	323
Family type			
Nuclear	285 (46.9)	323 (53.1)	608
Joint/extended	178 (51.1)	170 (48.9)	348
Contraceptive use		**	
Non-users	85 (34.1)	164 (65.9)	249
Users	341 (53.8)	293 (46.2)	634
Parity		**	
0-2	222 (43.1)	293 (56.9)	515
>=3	241 (54.6)	200 (45.4)	441
Total N	463 (48.4)	493 (51.6)	956

Note: * $p < 0.05$; ** $p < 0.001$.

reproductive health problem, 55 per cent reported that they did not think it was necessary to seek treatment for the problem: this was especially true for menstrual problems and severe abdominal pain. Lack of money was the second most reason for not taking treatment and another 14 per cent intended seeking treatment but had not found the time to do so. A quarter of the women suffering from reproductive tract infections did not seek treatment because they were embarrassed to report the condition to a health provider.

Correlates of Treatment Seeking for Reproductive Morbidity

Many of the correlates of treatment seeking for reproductive morbidity were different from those for acute or chronic morbidity. Neither caste nor asset ownership showed an association, nor did literacy status. Age, occupation, family type, contraceptive use and parity were significantly associated with treatment seeking. There was an increase in treatment seeking by age. A higher rate of treatment seeking was found among women in remunerated occupations as compared to those in unremunerated occupations, those living in nuclear families as compared to those in joint/extended families and ever-users of contraception as compared to never-users of contraception.

Source of treatment appears to be associated with a different set of factors. For example, caste and asset ownership are associated with source of treatment, with women from SC/ST more likely to use government providers/facilities and 'other' castes and MBCs more likely to use private providers or facilities. As may be expected, those with above-average assets and were literate had a greater proportion seeking treatment from the private sector in health. Users of contraception and those of higher parity also tended to use government facilities more than private facilities. The association of remunerated occupation with use of government facilities is unexpected and needs further analysis.

Stratified Analysis of Correlates of Treatment Seeking for Reproductive Morbidity

Do correlates of treatment seeking for reproductive morbidity vary by caste and asset ownership?

There are variations by caste in correlates of treatment seeking for reproductive morbidity. For SC/ST women, the odds of treatment seeking increase significantly with increasing age, and residing in a nuclear family

Table 10.27

Association of Independent Variables with Treatment Seeking for Reproductive Morbidity Stratified by Caste

Variables	*Caste (Odds Ratio 95% CI)*		
	SC/ST	*MBC*	*Other*
Age			
15-34	Reference	Reference	Reference
35-49	1.22 (0.83-1.79)	1.38 (0.94-2.02)	1.44 (0.96-2.15)
Education			
Illiterates	Reference	Reference	Reference
Literates	1.32 (0.84-2.05)	0.73 (0.47-1.12)	1.33 (0.84-2.10)
Occupation			
Unremunerated	Reference	Reference	Reference
Remunerated	1.29 (0.84-1.98)	1.61 (1.04-2.51)*	1.28 (0.83-1.96)
Contraceptive Use			
Non-users	Reference	Reference	Reference
Ever users	0.82 (0.49-1.37)	1.26 (0.79-1.99)	0.98 (0.60-1.60)
Parity			
0-2	Reference	Reference	Reference
>=3	1.20 (0.82-1.73)	1.15 (0.79-1.66)	1.05 (0.70-1.58)
Type of family			
Joint/extended	Reference	Reference	Reference
Nuclear	1.57 (1.19-2.08)**	1.39 (1.04-1.85)*	1.37 (1.04-1.80)*

Note: * $p < 0.05$; ** $p<0.001$.

increases the odds of treatment seeking. For women, belonging to MBC, being in a remunerated occupation and residing in a nuclear family increase the odds of treatment seeking significantly, while for women from 'other' castes, only belonging to a nuclear family matters (Table 10.27). As for variations by asset ownership, older age, having a remunerated occupation and living in a nuclear family increase the odds of treatment seeking. No significant correlates were found for those with below-average asset ownership (Table 10.28).

Table 10.28

Association of Independent Variables with Treatment Seeking for Reproductive Morbidity Stratified by Asset Ownership

Variables	*Assets Owned (Odds Ratio 95% CI)*	
	Below Average	*Above Average*
Age		
15-34	Reference	Reference
35-49	1.12 (0.77-1.64)	1.41 (0.99-1.99)*
Education		
Illiterates	1.02 (0.70-1.48)	0.97 (0.69-1.35)
Literates	Reference	Reference
Occupation		
Unremunerated	Reference	Reference
Remunerated	1.44 (0.98-2.10)	1.35 (0.98-1.86)*
Contraceptive use		
Non-users	Reference	Reference
Users	1.21 (0.82-1.77)	0.97 (0.67-1.39)
Parity		
0-2	Reference	Reference
>=3	1.07 (0.70-1.63	1.47 (0.97-2.23)
Type of family		
Joint/Extended	Reference	Reference
Nuclear	1.26 (0.91-1.74)	1.51 (1.11-2.03)*

Note: * $p < 0.05$; ** $p < 0.001$.

Discussion and Conclusions

Summary and Discussion

This study sought to examine differences by caste, class and gender in prevalence and correlates of morbidity and in rates and correlates of treatment seeking for morbidity, using information on self-reported morbidity gathered from a health interview/survey carried out in Dharmapuri district.

The reported morbidity rate in the survey was relatively high as compared to other studies in India. NSS data for Tamil Nadu (1995-96) reported the prevalence of any ailment in the population to be 54 per 1000 as compared to 276 per 1000 in the present study (Mishra and Dilip, 2004).

Prevalence of acute as well as chronic morbidity was significantly associated with age, literacy, occupation and housing conditions, all variables identified as 'proximate' determinants of health in the study. All associations were in the expected direction, with age above 35 years, illiteracy, unremunerated occupation and poor housing conditions associated with higher prevalence.

There were significant differences in the prevalence of acute and chronic morbidity by caste, ownership of assets and gender. Females and those with lower level of assets had higher prevalence than males and those who were economically better-off. A higher prevalence of morbidity for females is observed also in NSSO 52nd round (Mishra and Dilip, 2004). In the case of caste, it was not the SCs and STs but the MBC group that had a significant disadvantage. This is usually interpreted as being the result of under-reporting by socially backward castes. However, this is not what we found.

An analysis of the characteristics of the MBC group as against SC/ST and 'other' castes gives some indication as to the reasons. In the study sample, the MBCs have a lower level of literacy (53.3%) as compared to SC/ST (56.1%). A higher proportion of MBCs (64%) live in poor housing as compared to those belonging to the SC/ST group (60.5%). Further, the SC/ST group has a higher proportion of population below 15 years of age (37%) as compared to the MBC group (31%). All three factors are correlated with a higher prevalence of morbidity. This is a significant finding in that it indicates that material conditions and access to resources are sources of inequities in health, rather than membership of a caste *per se*.

Reproductive morbidity was associated significantly with literacy, occupation and housing conditions, but not with age. Contraceptive use was associated with increased reproductive morbidity, a phenomenon noted in several studies especially when the method of contraception is female sterilisation (Bhatia and Cleland 1995, C.V. Sowmini dissertation). There was also significantly higher prevalence of reproductive morbidity in women of lower parity and those residing in nuclear families. The reasons for these associations are not clear.

As in the case of acute and chronic morbidity, women belonging to MBCs suffered higher levels of reproductive morbidity. However, it is interesting to note that economic status was not associated with reproductive morbidity.

Many of the findings on correlates of reproductive morbidity differ from those found in NFHS-2 with some exceptions. NFHS-2 also finds a slightly higher prevalence among women of lower parity as found in the present study. In NFHS-2 for Tamil Nadu, standard of living is the only variable associated significantly with prevalence of reproductive morbidity which is contrary to our findings above. Further it also finds that none of the background characteristics such as age, residence, education and work status made a difference to reproductive morbidity (IIPS and ORC Macro, 2001b), unlike in the present study.

Levels of treatment seeking in this population were high for acute as well as chronic morbidity. Literacy was associated with treatment seeking for acute morbidity, while for chronic morbidity, higher proportions from the older age groups sought care rather than from the younger age groups.

Caste and gender did not make a difference to whether treatment was sought for acute or chronic morbidity, only asset ownership was significantly associated. However, caste, gender as well as asset ownership significantly influenced where treatment was sought. Females and those with lower assets tended to depend more on government facilities. Among caste groups, it was those belonging to SC/ST who were more likely to use government health facilities. Thus, government health facilities appear to play an important role in making health care accessible to socially vulnerable populations.

Treatment seeking for reproductive morbidity by women in the present study was 65 per cent, considerably higher than the findings in NFHS-2, of 49 per cent. The proportion seeking treatment increased significantly with increasing age, remunerated occupation and residence in a nuclear family. Residing in a nuclear family may increase a woman's ability to take decisions concerning treatment seeking.

Neither caste nor asset ownership influenced whether treatment was sought, but significantly influenced the source of treatment, with SC/ST women using government facilities significantly more than women from

Table 10.29

Correlates of Morbidity Stratified by Caste, Asset Ownership and Gender

Type of Morbidity	*Caste*			*Ownership of Assets*		*Gender*	
	SC/ST	*MBC*	*Other*	*Below Average*	*Above Average*	*Male*	*Female*
Acute	Age (+) Literacy: higher for illiterate	Age, literacy and housing conditions (higher for poorer housing)	Age, literacy, occupation, housing conditions	Age Literacy Housing conditions	Age Literacy Occupation	Age Literacy Occupation	Age Literacy Occupation Housing conditions
Chronic	----	-----	Literacy: higher for literate	Age, literacy, Occupation, housing conditions	Age, literacy, Occupation, housing conditions	Literacy: higher for literates	Age: increases with age
Reproductive	Contraceptive use (+)	Literacy: higher for illiterate, contraceptive use	Age, occupation, contraceptive use	Age, literacy, occupation, housing conditions	Literacy, housing conditions	NOT APPLICABLE	

Table 10.30

Correlates of Treatment Seeking Stratified by Caste, Asset Ownership and Gender

Type of Morbidity	*Caste*			*Ownership of Assets*		*Gender*	
	SC/ST	*MBC*	*Other*	*Below Average*	*Above Average*	*Male*	*Female*
Acute	--Nil--	--Nil--	Literacy	--Nil--	Age, occupation	Literacy	Age
Chronic	Age, occupation	--Nil--	Occupation	--Nil--	--Nil--	Age	-Nil-
Reproductive	Age, type of family	Occupation, type of family	Type of family	--Nil---	Age, occupation, type of family	NOT APPLICABLE	

the MBC group and 'other' castes, and a greater proportion of women from households with lower assets using government facilities as compared to their better-off counterparts.

Stratified analysis shows that determinants of morbidity as well as treatment seeking may differ by caste, class and gender. Tables 10.29 and 10.30 summarise these differences. If this means that pathways to poorer health status and factors influencing access to health care differ by gender, caste and class then interventions to improve health will have to factor in these differences.

Conclusions

Caste, class and gender are significantly associated with prevalence of acute and chronic morbidity, and caste was a significant variable associated with reproductive morbidity. Treatment seeking was high overall and did not differ significantly either by gender or caste but only by economic status as indicated by ownership of assets. However, dependence on government health facilities was significantly higher for females, MBCs and those with lower assets, indicating the crucial role played by public health facilities in ensuring access to care of socially vulnerable groups.

The study thus found inequities in health status by caste, class and gender, but less so in treatment seeking, thanks to availability of low-cost or free treatment. Access to resources needed for remaining healthy seems to contribute to a large part of inequities in health. Bridging these health gaps would require addressing their social determinants: education, remunerated work, better housing conditions and economic resources. For women, in addition to these, improved quality of care in family planning should be another major focus of attention to remove avoidable reproductive morbidity.

References

Bandewar, Sunita and Shelly Saha (2000). *Studies in Reproductive Health Services in India (1990-1999): Selected Annotated Bibliography*. Mumbai: Centre for Health Education and Allied Themes.

Bhatia, Jagdish C. and John Cleland (1995). "Determinants of Maternal Care in a Region of South India", *Health Transition Review* 5(2): 127-42.

Census of India (2001). *Sex Ratio and Population Density in 1991 and 2001 State: Tamil Nadu*. At: *http://www.censusindia.net/cendata1*. Accessed 3 January 2006.

Daniels, N., B. Kennedy and I. Kawachi (1999). "Justice is Good for Our Health: How Greater Economic Equality would Promote Public Health", *Botston Review*.

Deogaonkar, Milind (2004). "Socio Economic Inequality and Its Effect on Health Care Delivery in India: Inequality and Health Care", *Electronic Journal of Sociology*.

Deshpande, R.V. (1998). "Morbidity Differentials in Rural Karnataka", *The Journal of Family Welfare* 44(4): 9-14. December. Location SNDT Churchgate.

Directorate of Census Operations—Tamil Nadu. Primary—Census Abstract—Census 2001. Retrieved December 30, 2005, from *http://www.census.tn.nic.in/downloads/Dharmapuri.pdf*.

Duggal, R. and S. Amin (1989). *Cost of Health Care: An Household Level Survey in an Indian District*. Bombay: Foundation for Research in Community Health.

Duraisamy, P. (1998). "Morbidity in Tamil Nadu", *Economic and Political Weekly* xxxiii(17): 982-90.

Duraisamy, P. (2001). "Health Status and Curative Health Care in Rural India", *Working paper* series No.78. New Delhi: National Council of Applied Economic Research.

Ghose, Soumitra (2004). "Levels and Differentials of Morbidity in West Bengal", MPS thesis. Mumbai: International Institute of Population Studies.

Government of Tamil Nadu, Department of Evaluation and Applied Research (2000). "Vital Rates in Tamil Nadu". Retrieved January 4, 2006, from *http://www.tn.gov.in/dear/part2/health6.pdf*.

Gupta, Indrani (2003). *Inequities in Health Care in India: Can the Poor Hope for a Respite?* Delhi: Institute of Economic Growth. December.

International Institute for Population Sciences (IIPS) and ORC Macro (2001a). *National Family Health Survey (NFHS-2), India, 1998-99*. Mumbai: IIPS.

International Institute for Population Sciences (IIPS) and ORC Macro (2001b). *National Family Health Survey (NFHS-2), Tamil Nadu, 1998-99*. Mumbai: IIPS.

Iyer, Aditi and Gita Sen (2000). "Heath Sector Changes and Health Equity in the 1990's", in Shobha Raghuram (ed.), *Health and Equity Effecting Change*. Technical Report Series 1.8. The Netherlands: Human Institute for Co-operation with Developing Countries.

Kannan, K.P., K.R. Thangappan, V.R. Kutty *et al.* (1991). *Health and Development in Rural Kerala. Kerala:* Kerala Sastra Sahitya Parishad (KSSP).

Kreiger, N., D. Rowley, A. Herman *et al.* (1993). "Racism, Sexism and Social Class: Implications for Studies of Health, Disease and Well-being", *American Journal of Preventive Medicine* 9: 82-122.

Krishnamoorthy, S. (2004). *Inequalities in Health Status and in Access and Utilisation of Healthcare Services in Tamil Nadu: Evidences from the National Family Health Surveys*. Tamil Nadu: Rural Women's Social Education Centre.

Legge, David (n.d.). "Health Inequalities in the New World Order". *People's Health Assembly: Issue Paper LaTrobe University*. Retrieved December 29, 2005, from *http//www.phmovement.org/pha2000/presentations/legge.html*.

Lynch, J., G. Kaplan, E. Pamuk *et al.* (1998). "Income Inequity and Mortality in Metropolitan Areas of the United States", *American Journal of Public Health* 88(7): 1074-80.

Madhiwala, N., S. Nandraj and R. Sinha (2000). *Health Households and Women's Lives: A Study of Illness and Child Bearing among Women in Nasihk District*. Mumbai: Centre for Enquiry into Health and Allied Themes.

Marmot, M.G., M. Kogevinas and M.A. Elston (1987). "Social Economic Status and Diseases", *Annual Review of Public Health* 8: 111-35.

Mishra, U.S. and T.R. Dilip (2004). *Health Inequities in Tamil Nadu: Some NSSO based Evidence*. Tamil Nadu: Rural Women's Social Education Centre.

Muntaner, C. (1999). "Invited Commentary: Social Mechanisms, Race and Social Epidemiology", *American Journal of Epidemiology* 150(2): 121-6.

Muntaner, C. and J. Lynch (1991). "Income Inequity, Social Cohesion and Class Relations", *International Journal of Health Services* 29: 59-82.

National Council for Applied Economic Research (NCAER) (1992). *Household Survey of Medical Care*. New Delhi: NCAER.

National Sample Survey Organisation (1998). *Morbidity and Treatment of Ailments*. New Delhi: Department of Statistics, Govt. of India (report no. 441).

Pappas, G., S. Queen, W. Hadden, *et al.* (1993). "The Increasing Disparity in Mortality between Socioeconomic Groups in the United States, 1960 and 1986", *New England Journal of Medicine* 329(2): 103-9.

Population Research Centre (PRC), Gandhigram Institute of Rural Health and Family Welfare Trust and Indian Institute of Population Studies (2001). Tamil Nadu: Reproductive and Child Health Project. Rapid Household Survey 1998–99.

Rao, P.S. and J. Richard (1984). "Socioeconomic and Demographic Correlates of Medical Care and Health Practices", *Journal of Biosocial Science* 16(3): 344-55.

Sen, A. (1999). *Development as Freedom*. New York; Knopf; republished, Oxford: Oxford University Press.

Sen, Gita (2001). "Health Deteriorates, 1995-2001", *The Hindu*. Retrieved December 30, 2005, from *http://www.dawn.org.fj/publications/docs/Indiahealth.doc*.

Sen, Gita, Aditi Iyer and Asha George (2002). "Class, Gender and Health Equity: Lessons from Liberalisation in India". Harvard Center for Population and Development Studies Working Paper Series Volume 12, Number 3, February.

Sundar, A. (1995). "Household Survey of Health Care Utilisation and Expenditure", Working Paper No.53, NCAER, March.

Vaguet, A., F. Richard and E. Eliot (1995). Health and Culture in an Urban Indian Context. *Space, Populations, Societie* 1: 81-90.

Visaria, Leela (n.d.). *Innovations in Tamil Nadu*. Retrieved January 3, 2006, from *http://www.india-seminar.com/2000/489.htm*.

Willams, D. (1996). "Race/Ethnicity and Socioeconomic Status: Measurements and Methodological Issues", *International Journal of Health Services* 26(3): 483: 505.

11 Changing Landscape of Higher Education in Tamil Nadu

P. Geetha Rani

Growth of Higher Education

The system of higher education in India is one of the largest in the world. The system of education in India inherited a poor educational infrastructure from colonial masters in the 19th century. Colonial policy focused neither on mass education nor on higher education. As a consequence, the country had to begin from scratch soon after its independence. In order to meet the requirements of professional and technical manpower in a developing economy, the government set up the Indian Institutes of Technology, regional engineering colleges, medical colleges, arts and science colleges and universities. However, to begin with, there were only 20 universities and 500 colleges at the time of independence. In 1990-91, there were 179 university level and research institutions which grew to 543 in 2004-05. During the same period, the colleges grew from 4152 to 16009 in the country (see Table 11.1).

At the national level, between 1980 and 2004, the number of universities has trebled (at an annual rate of 4.5% pa) and that of colleges has grown fourfold (by 6.8% pa). Over the same period, Tamil Nadu has registered higher growth rates in the number of both universities (5.1% pa) and colleges (7.7% pa). Enrolment in higher educational institutions of Tamil Nadu has also been much faster (8.7% pa) than in the country as a whole (6.8% pa).

Despite this, growth of institutions and enrolment in higher education in India were only 10 per cent during 2004-05. The gross enrolment ratio in higher education in Tamil Nadu is more than the national average and the third highest after Himachal Pradesh and Maharashtra, but still only 11.5 per cent compared to 50 per cent or more in a majority of the developed countries. If India aspires to become a developed nation by 2020, the threshold level of the age group entering higher education must at least be 25 per cent. Neither India nor Tamil Nadu is near this threshold level.

Table 11.1

Growth of Higher Educational Institutions and Enrolment in India and Tamil Nadu

	India				*Tamil Nadu*			
	Univs and R. instns	*Colleges*	*HEIs*	*Enrolment**	*Univs and R. instns*	*Colleges*	*HEIs*	*Enrolment**
1980-81	179	4152	4358	2.76	8	382	390	0.19
1985-86	198	5232	5043	3.83	8	395	403	0.21
1990-91	233	6627	6289	5.03	16	608	624	0.24
1995-96	290	9033	8247	6.38	20	716	736	0.36
2000-01	331	11304	10515	10.00	23	986	1009	0.42
2001-02	351	14232	11497	9.74	26	989	1015	0.59
2002-03	385	14913	12161	10.01	28	1558	1586	0.56
2003-04	389	15274	10716	10.23	28	1530	1558	0.61
2004-05	543	16009	16552	11.77	42	1642	1684	0.81
Gth. Rates	4.52	6.77	6.70	6.86	5.13	7.67	7.61	8.73

Note: * enrolment in millions; growth rates (in %) are estimated by fitting semi-log liner trend regressions from 1990-91 to 2003-04.

HEIs: higher education institutions; R. instns: research institutions.

Source: *Selected Educational Statistics*, various issues.

Enrolment ratio of girls is much lower than of boys at the national level as well as across states except Kerala and Punjab (Table 11.2). This gender differential is somewhat lower than the national average in Tamil Nadu.

The state's policy has been to promote wider participation of women at all levels of higher education, especially the levels that require special talents, knowledge and skill. Overall, female students enrolled in higher education have increased at an annual rate of 10 per cent which compares with 6 per cent annual rate of growth of male students (Table 11.3). During 2004-05, about 48 per cent of the student strength of the state was women, which was only 37 per cent during 1990-91. However, the current rate of female enrolment is hardly 10 per cent.

Table 11.2

GER in Higher Education in Selected States in India, 2004-05*

States	*2004-05*		
	Boys	*Girls*	*Total*
Himachal Pradesh	14.6	13.7	14.1
Maharashtra	15.2	10.9	13.2
Tamil Nadu	13.0	10.0	11.5
Karnataka	12.7	10.4	11.6
Haryana	11.1	10.1	10.6
Gujarat	11.9	9.3	10.7
Andhra Pradesh	14.6	8.6	11.5
Punjab	9.4	11.2	10.2
Kerala	8.2	10.0	9.1
India	11.6	8.2	10.0

Note: * includes polytechnics.
GER: gross enrolment ratio.
Source: *Selected Educational Statistics*, 2001-02; 2004-05.

Table 11.3

Enrolment in Higher Educational Institutions by Gender in Tamil Nadu

(in '000s)

	Boys	*Girls*	*All*	*% of Girls in Total*
1990-91	149.91	90.04	239.95	37.5
1995-96	202.85	153.87	356.71	43.1
2000-01	215.43	203.84	419.27	48.6
2001-02	326.60	266.14	592.74	44.9
2002-03	302.63	255.87	558.50	45.8
2003-04	321.60	291.57	613.18	47.6
2004-05	283.51	260.19	543.70	47.9
GR	6.01	9.85	7.60	

Note: GR: growth rate.
Source: same as Table 11.1.

In order to attain the threshold levels of gross enrolment ratio in higher education, there needs to be a concomitant qualitative expansion not only in higher education but also in school education. But what is happening is quantitative expansion of the private unaided sector. The policy changes paved the way for expanding self-financing or the private unaided sector. Further, state funding was highly inadequate with just around 3.5 per cent of its gross domestic product (GDP) invested on education. With the combined forces of macroeconomic reform policies known by the acronym LPG—denoting liberalisation, privatisation and globalisation—and the rise in social demand, the private sector and also the 'private' dimension of higher education have been growing. To what extent the private unaided sector has grown in Tamil Nadu since 1990s is examined in the following section.

Management Structure and Institutional Type

The structure of higher education in Tamil Nadu, as at the national level and in many other states, consists of universities and research institutions, and deemed to be universities which are at the highest level of higher educational institutions. Altogether the state has over 1700 higher educational institutions, of which, 35 are university level institutions. The rest are colleges, of which, some 490 (35% of all higher educational institutions)[1] are general arts and science colleges affiliated to universities under the overall purview of the University Grants Commission (UGC) (Table 11.4). Professional colleges including engineering, medical, pharmacy, agriculture, law, management and education constitute another 35 per cent. These professional colleges fall under the purview of various bodies—engineering and management colleges and computer application programmes are to get the approval of All India Council for Technical Education (AICTE); medical colleges from the Medical Council of India; and law colleges from the Bar Council of India.

There is considerable overlap of various regulatory bodies in higher and professional education. For instance, management and computer application courses attached to general arts and science colleges which fall under the purview of UGC need to get the approval of AICTE. As noted by Singh (2004) and others, the Centre has set up more than a dozen professional councils. Each one of them has specific powers relating to the area with which it is concerned. Each one of them has a specific role to play

1. Even though UGC is the regulatory body of all such colleges in the country at the federal level, the state governments play a vital role at the policy level.

in regulation and it is for the Ministry of Human Resource Development to deal with how they coordinate their functioning with one another.

Table 11.4

Structure of Higher Educational Institutions by Type of Management in Tamil Nadu in 2006-07

Institutions	*Govt. (in %)*	*Pvt. Aided (in %)*	*Self-fing. (in %)*	*Total (in numbers)*	*% of Institution Type in Total Institutions*
	(2)	*(3)*	*(4)*	*(5)*	*(6)*
Univs. including DU.	57.1	11.4	31.4	35	2.48
Arts and Science colleges	12.2	27.1	60.6	490	34.78
Engineering Colleges	4.0	1.2	94.8	248	17.60
Polytechnics	10.3	18.2	71.5	214	15.19
Medical colleges	60.0	0.0	40.0	25	1.77
Ayurveda colleges	0.0	40.0	60.0	5	0.35
Dental colleges	5.9	0.0	94.1	17	1.21
Homoeopathy	10.0	0.0	90.0	10	0.71
Law colleges	72.7	0.0	27.3	11	0.78
Management*	8.2	1.4	90.4	146	10.36
Agriculture Colleges	72.7	27.3	0.0	11	0.78
Colleges of Education	4.4	8.8	86.9	160	11.36
Colleges of Physical edn	0.0	37.5	62.5	8	0.57
Others	6.9	41.4	51.7	29	2.06
All	11.8	15.3	73.0	1409	100.00

Note: DU: Deemed Universities; *: Management institutes are part of the existing institutions except 44 additional individual business schools (includes hotel mgt) (see Saravanan, 2007).

Source: *www.ugc.nic.in*; based on Government of Tamil Nadu (2007). *Statistical Handbook of Tamil Nadu, 2006*.

Educational institutions in India and in the states are categorised into three groups based on funding: (i) government institutions set up and funded by the state; (ii) private-aided institutions under private management but funded partially by government; and (iii) privately managed and wholly self-financed institutions. This type of management reflected simultaneous dominance of private-aided and the state. During 1970s, until the middle of 1980s, government and private- aided institutions dominated the field. The latter were set up and managed by religious, charitable and philanthropic organisations termed as fused private-public entities. Wholly self-financing private institutions cater both to elites and non-elites. The latter category has become increasingly important from the 1990s especially in professional education, because government and government-aided institutions have been unable to meet the rapidly growing demand for higher education from middle and lower middle classes (Geiger, 2004; Levy, 2006).

Around half of the enrolled students are in general arts and science colleges with another 22 per cent in engineering and 10 per cent in medical courses (Figure 11.1). It is important to note this distribution because most 'private investment' in higher education is concentrated in engineering, medicine and management.

Figure 11.1

Distribution of Higher Educational Institutions by Discipline in 2004-05 in Tamil Nadu

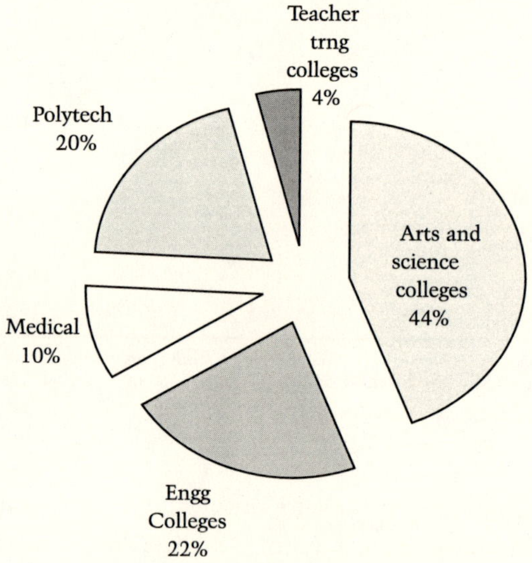

Source: Same as Table 11.1.

Self-financing institutions in Tamil Nadu exploit the circumstances and emerge as something similar to for-profit higher education in the United States wherein students and families buy higher education services in the market. They now account for more than 90 per cent of the total engineering and management colleges in the state (Table 11.4). Even among the general arts and science colleges, 60 per cent are self-financing. Among all higher educational institutions, about three-fourths of them are the self-financing type of institutions. Given this dominant share of private self-financing institutions in higher education, the following section attempts to look at the growth of such institutions over a period of time, from 1990-91 to 2006-07.

Pattern of Growth: The Trend

This section examines the pattern of growth under various levels from university level institutions to colleges by discipline in higher education in the state.

Universities

University level institutions comprise institutions of national importance; state universities; Deemed to be Universities with government funds, deemed universities without government funds or self-financing or private universities. Tamil Nadu houses two institutions of national importance, Indian Institute of Technology and Dakshin Bharat Hindi Prachar Sabha, both funded by the Ministry of Human Resource Development (MHRD) and another two deemed universities getting UGC funds. Higher education is the concurrent responsibility of the centre and states, with the latter playing an important role in establishing the contours of the higher education institutions. The number of institutions of national importance and deemed universities getting government aid has not increased in Tamil Nadu since 1990-91. Among 18 state universities, only 12 of them get plan funds or development assistance from the UGC (see Table 11.5). Only recently a central university was established in the state, its first.

Table 11.5

Growth of University Level Institutions by Funding Type in Tamil Nadu

Type	*1990-91*	*1995-96*	*2000-01*	*2006-07*	*Funding Source*
Institutions of National Importance	2	2	2	2	MHRD
State Universities	13	14	16	18	State govt/ UGC
Deemed Universities with govt funds	2	2	2	2	State govt/ UGC
Deemed Universities	7	10	10	13	Self-financing
All	24	28	30	35	

Source: Based on UGC *Annual Reports*, various issues and *www.ugc.nic.in* downloaded as on 17.05.2007.

New state universities established since 1990-91 do not seem to have obtained any central assistance. The state did not (until recently) have any central university with full funding of plan and non-plan assistance by UGC. Central government assistance to states for higher education is provided by the MHRD and UGC.[2] UGC assistance has increased in absolute terms but its share in total higher education expenditure in the state has averaged around 10 per cent and fluctuated between 7.5 per cent and around 12.5 per cent in the last one and half decades (see Figure 11.2). The centre has followed a policy of shifting greater responsibility for funding and managing public higher education from federal to state governments and state government to private sector.

Figure 11.2

Share of Expenditure on General Higher Education by Government of Tamil Nadu and University Grants Commission

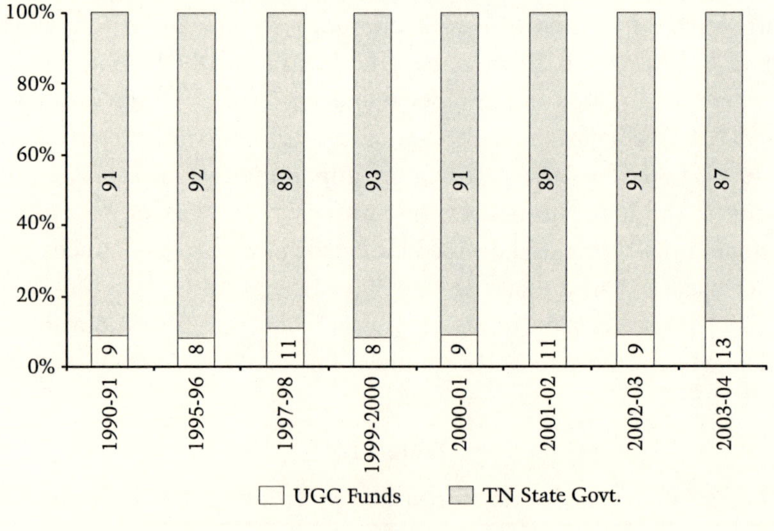

Source: Based on analysis of budgetary expenditure on education and UGC *Annual Reports*, various issues.

2. The information on total central government transfers to higher education by states is not readily available. From UGC annual reports, one can cull out information from the fund allocation to state universities and colleges in Tamil Nadu. However, similar information is not available from MHRD annual reports.

The number of deemed universities have almost doubled in the state from 1990-91 to 2006-07. It is to be noted that the expansion is predominantly under self-financing universities. Private institutions that initially specialised in one academic field expanded into other revenue-generating disciplines and virtually became self-financing universities. Under Section 3 of the UGC Act, 2003, deemed universities are required to possess viability and a management capable of contributing to university ideas and traditions. Under this scheme, a number of private institutions have been granted the status of deemed university. In addition, AICTE has also given deemed university status to many private engineering colleges that did not even have basic engineering laboratories and other necessary facilities. As a result, some of the engineering and also medical colleges in the state have metamorphosed into deemed universities. These were small institutions that were clearly demand-absorbing and transformed into a university by the policy changes. At present, none of the 13 deemed universities in the state receive UGC plan funds.

Arts and Science Colleges

Currently, around one-eighth of arts and science colleges in Tamil Nadu are government institutions; 30 per cent are government aided and nearly 60 per cent are private unaided colleges (Table 11.6). Opening of self-financing general arts and science colleges started in the state in 1994-95 (GoTN, 2003). The annual growth rate of private unaided or the self-financing colleges is rapid at the rate of 20 per cent during the period 1990-91 to 2004-05. Share of government- and private-aided colleges during 1990-91 was 86 per cent which drastically decreased to 43 per cent during 2004-05. The self-financing colleges started to occupy more than 50 per cent share since 2000-01.

Private unaided colleges have been growing much faster than other categories both in terms of numbers and enrolment. But, their share in enrolment is consistently much less than their share in number of colleges. More than 70 per cent of the students were enrolled in government- and private-aided colleges even in 2004-05 (Table 11.6). Private unaided colleges tend to be more expensive and are free to charge fees to cover costs. They offer courses oriented to high end jobs like Bachelor of Business Management (BBM), Master of Business Administration (MBA),

Biotechnology, and the like. (Private-aided colleges are also allowed to charge on a self-financing basis for specified job-oriented courses.) High cost of such courses restricts the demand for them to the better-off classes. This probably explains the smaller enrolment per college in this category.

Table 11.6

Growth of Arts and Science Colleges and Enrolment therein in General Higher Education by Type of Management (in %)

	Institutions				*Enrolment*			
	Govt.	*PA*	*PUA*	*Total**	*Govt*	*PA*	*PUA*	*Total**
1990-91 ^	25	61	13	215	27.2	69.1	3.7	207042
1995-96	21	47	32	280	26.7	63.0	10.3	317213
2000-01	14	31	55	426	21.7	54.2	24.1	410508
2001-02	14	30	56	440	21.4	54.0	24.5	421012
2002-03	14	30	56	440	21.0	54.2	24.9	436642
2003-04	14	30	56	441	21.1	53.6	25.3	461026
2004-05	13	30	57	444	19.2	51.5	29.3	513222
GR**	1.0	0.1	20.4	7.1	2.3	3.9	15.8	6.0

Note: * total in numbers; ^ prior to 1990-91 there is no separate information available for private-aided and unaided colleges; ** growth rate is estimated by fitting a semi-log-linear trend regression.

Source: *Statistical Handbook of Tamil Nadu*, Chennai.

The rapid growth of private colleges is in part due to the strain on government finances. Both the Centre and the States were under severe pressure to take measures to contain and reduce fiscal deficits. The central Fiscal Responsibility and Budget Management (FRBM) Act mandated elimination of the revenue deficit and brought down fiscal deficit to manageable levels by 2008-09. Tamil Nadu enacted the FRBM Act in the same year as the Central Act. This fiscal reform has led to a heavy compression on the public budgets on education sector, more specifically so on higher education. Publicly funded institutions had at the same time to meet rising costs in the face of strong resistance to increasing fees. Under these conditions, their ability to expand capacity to meet the rapid increase in social demand for higher education was severely restricted. With demand growing much faster than available capacity, pressures grew for major changes in policy that facilitated and encouraged private sector expansion. This led to permitting aided colleges to start self-financing courses and opening the field for wholly self-financed private colleges.

Engineering Colleges

These factors have been an even stronger reason for the spectacular growth of private self-financing colleges in engineering and other professional disciplines. Private engineering colleges have expanded rapidly in all states but their growth has been exceptionally rapid in Andhra Pradesh, Tamil Nadu and Karnataka along with Maharashtra. In the 1980s, when the Central and State Governments were finding it difficult to cope with the need to expand technical education in the country, governments of these states took a decision to permit private registered societies and trusts to establish and run technical institutions on a self-financing basis. A large number of private self-financing institutions came into existence in these states in the early 1980s itself (AICTE, 1999). All these institutions were established with the permission of the respective state governments and were affiliated to the universities of the region and/or to the State Boards of Technical Education.

Figure 11.3

Growth of Engineering Colleges by Management Type in Tamil Nadu

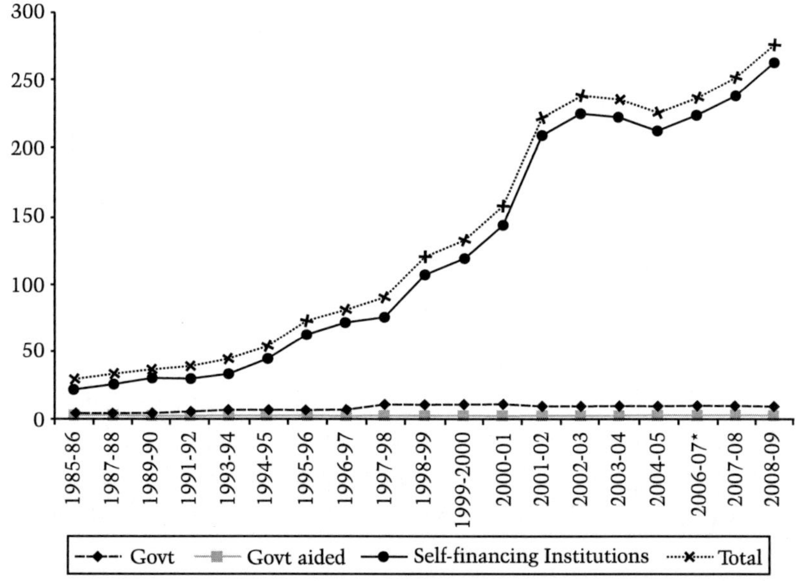

Source: *Statistical Handbook of Tamil Nadu*, Chennai.

Table 11.7

Per cent Share of Institutions and Enrolment in Engineering Colleges and Enrolment per Institution by Type of Management in Tamil Nadu (in %)

	Institutions			*Enrolment*		
	Govt.	*PUA*	*All**	*Govt.*	*PUA*	*All**
1997-98	11.6	88.4	86	12.9	87.1	21674
1998-99	8.7	91.3	127	10.8	89.2	22873
1999-2000	8.3	91.7	132	9.4	90.6	30463
2000-01	7.2	92.8	153	7.8	92.2	38893
2001-02	5.0	95.0	218	7.6	92.4	48887
2002-03	4.3	95.7	234	6.6	93.4	61042
2003-04	3.9	96.1	231	7.4	92.6	48106
2004-05	4.0	96.0	226	7.1	92.9	49466

Note: * in numbers.
Source: *Statistical Handbook of Tamil Nadu*, Chennai.

In Tamil Nadu, prior to this change of policy, engineering colleges were mostly government institutions. There were also several private colleges set up by the initiatives of Christian missions and Nattukottai Chettiar community. But since the 1980s, there has been unfettered and unregulated growth of private self-financing colleges promoted and run by registered societies and private trusts controlled by politicians, industrialists and wealthy individuals. The number of engineering colleges rose from about 30 in 1984-85 to 86 in 1997-98 and further to 226 in 2004-05. The number of government and aided private colleges has remained more or less constant and they account for barely 7 per cent of total enrolment. Practically the entire increase in the number of colleges has been in the self-financing sector. Much the same is true of enrolment: the total increased nearly two and a half times between 1997 and 2004; enrolment grew by less than 30 per cent in government colleges, while in private colleges it grew two and a half times. Practically the entire increase in enrolment has been in the private sector which now accounts for close to 95 per cent of enrolment in this category. Engineering education in the state is now almost entirely in self-financing colleges (Table 11.7).

It is important to note that the government colleges have significantly better facilities and quality of education than the self-financing colleges.

Management Colleges

Management education in colleges affiliated to universities started in Calcutta in 1954, quickly followed by the universities of Bombay, Delhi and Madras. In order to meet the growing demand for management education, AICTE permitted from 1993-94, a large number of MBA and Postgraduate Diplomas in Business Management (PGDBM) programmes on self-financing basis. Tamil Nadu was again in the race along with Maharashtra and Andhra Pradesh, these three states alone accounted for nearly 60 per cent of the full-time seats. Private societies and trusts in these states had the experience of establishing and managing diploma and degree level engineering colleges and therefore were quick in taking the lead in the sector of self-financing management education (AICTE, 1999). Management educational institutions first began to appear in 1987-88 in Tamil Nadu and grew many fold between 1994 and 1999 but the growth gradually stagnated. Among the 146 institutions in 2005-06, 91 per cent of them are self-financing institutions and do not get any grant from State or Central Governments (Table 11.8).

Table 11.8

Management Educational Institutions by Type of Management in Tamil Nadu

Management Type	*1990s*	*Since 2001*	*1990s*	*Since 2001*
	(in numbers)		*(in %)*	
Govt (state colleges, univ depts. DU, Central govt)	4	8	3.9	5.4
Private aided	1	2	1.0	1.4
PUA (including private DUs)	98	138	95.1	93.2
Total	103	148	100	100

Source: Based on *www.aicte.nic.in* downloaded as on 20.5.2007.

Medical Colleges

A similar trend is observed in medical and paramedical education as well. A total of 243 medical and para-medical Institutions exist in Tamil Nadu (2006-07). Both the government and private unaided institutions are affiliated to the Tamil Nadu Dr M.G.R. Medical University. Government medical and paramedical colleges in the state account for 11 per cent, while medical colleges owned and run by private unaided managements share 88 per cent (Table 11.9).

Table 11.9

Medical Colleges and Enrolment by Management in Tamil Nadu as on 2006-07

Courses	*Colleges (numbers)*			*Enrolment (000)*		
	Govt.	*Private*	*Total*	*Govt.*	*Private*	*Total*
Medical	66.7	33.3	21	78.6	21.4	1965
Siddha	40	60	5	62.5	37.5	240
Homoeopathy	10	90	10	10	90	500
Unani	100	0	1	100	0	26
Ayurveda	0	100	5	0	100	150
Dental, Pharmacy, Nursing	5.9	91.3	132	9.5	90.5	5175
Physiotherapy and Others	4.3	95.7	69	2	98	2782
Total	11.1	88.5	243	19.3	80.7	10072

Source: Based on *www.tnmgr.univ.org.*

Out of these 243 institutions, 91 institutions offer postgraduate/diploma courses. Within these 91 postgraduate institutions, the majority, that is, 82 per cent of them, are in the private sector. The specialty courses such as Dental, Pharmacy, Nursing, Physiotherapy, and Occupational Therapy are almost within the private sector (*www.tnmgr.univ.org*). The Government of Tamil Nadu plans to start three new medical colleges in the state. Besides, it proposes to increase MBBS (Bachelor of Medicine, Bachelor of Surgery) seats in five medical colleges. The Government accorded sanction for the creation of an additional 315 seats in the MBBS course (GoTN, 2004).

Agricultural Colleges

Agriculture education in Tamil Nadu has been primarily state funded. There are 11 government and two affiliated agricultural colleges (GoTN, 2007). However, the privatisation process has already begun there as well. For instance, the Tamil Nadu Agricultural University (TNAU) has introduced master's degree and doctoral programmes on self-supporting basis (*www.tnau.ac.in*).

Law Colleges

There are five government law colleges in the state at present. Besides, a few of the university departments provide legal education at the postgraduate level. Private law colleges are limited in the state (GoTN, 2006b). The private sector in legal education, like that of agricultural education, is limited in the state.

As the growth pattern suggests, private sector in the case of Tamil Nadu is found to have substituted the public sector in the state by absorbing the excess demand. It is amply clear that the institutional landscape of higher education is changing drastically, the number and share of government colleges and universities are declining persistently while self-financed (for-profit) institutions are growing in strength, strongly tied to broader processes of LPG. An important aspect of this policy has been to allow the private sector to attract a growing number of students who do not qualify in the entrance examinations to public institutions. Even though this has not been an explicitly stated policy, by limiting the intake of public higher education institutions without expanding the government institutions gave a green signal to the expansion of the private sector. Given this trend, the thrust of the rest of the paper is on the salient characteristics which emerge and the response from the Government of Tamil Nadu.

Emerging Salient Characteristics

Emerging characteristics of private higher education are examined within the perspectives of three crucial players, namely the institutions, individuals (students and the broader economy) and the state. At the institutional level, academic, finance and infrastructure issues are discussed. At the student level, the issue of choice and at the economy level, commercial orientation and the mismatch in the labour market are discussed. At the state level, the regulatory aspect, that is the response from the state government, is examined.

Institutional Dynamics

The institutional dynamics of the private higher education institutions is examined by raising three questions: What do these private institutions provide? And at what cost? And what is the outcome?

Infrastructure

The academic excellence of higher educational institutions depends upon the physical infrastructure, human resources (teacher strength and quality) and also the impetus for research. These three important components are rarely considered significant in the private higher education institutions as their focus is mainly on profit. For the private sector, the expenditure on buildings and infrastructure is a capital investment. Besides, they incur the recurring expenditures on major items such as salaries of teachers. Indeed, the private institutions work as profit centres cutting down all long-term investments. There is no information base on these physical facilities in higher education unlike the All India Education Surveys focusing on schools conducted by National Council of Education Research and Training (NCERT). Infrastructure and other physical facilities in private higher education institutions are generally weak. In some of these private higher education institutions, not even proper buildings (if not a campus) are in place, leave alone the quality components of library and laboratories.

With regard to human infrastructure, the share of teachers in the private unaided sector in general arts and science colleges is high with 43 per cent with an annual rate of growth of 18.5 per cent, while the private aided sector has depicted a negative growth rate of 2.5 per cent per annum during the same period. On the contrary with regard to private unaided sector, the number of teachers has grown rapidly by 18.5 per cent (Table 11.10).

Table 11.10

Growth of Teachers in Arts and Science Colleges in General Higher Education and in Engineering Colleges by Type of Management in Tamil Nadu (in %)

	General Arts and Science Colleges				*Engineering Colleges*			
	Govt.	*PA*	*PUA*	*Total**		*Govt.*	*PA*	*Govt. and PA*
*1990-91^*	*29.1*	*67.1*	*3.8*	*15738*	*1994-95*	*344*	*298*	642
1995-96	26.4	63	10.5	17270	1995-96	339	298	637
2000-01	21.4	45.9	32.7	21728	1996-97	330	298	628
2001-02	21.8	44.5	33.7	22424	1997-98	317	298	615
2002-03	21.8	43.7	34.5	23627	1998-99	271	306	577
2004-05	19.9	36.8	43.3	22523	1999-2000	257	317	574
GR	0.5	-2.5	18.5	3.3	GR	-6	1.1	-2.5

Note: * total in numbers; ^ prior to 1990-91 there is no separate information available for private-aided and unaided colleges; ** growth rates estimated by fitting a semi-log-linear trend regression.

Source: *Statistical Handbook of Tamil Nadu*, Chennai.

The salary bill of the teachers in private unaided colleges in general arts and science colleges is around the salary of one-fifth of the regular teachers. They are generally provided with a contractual appointment. They neither have job security nor a voice in academic decision making. However, very recently in 2007, a large number of teachers in government colleges were recruited. With regard to teachers in engineering colleges, there is no published information available on the numbers unlike in the general arts and science colleges. With respect to teachers in government engineering colleges, there has occurred a negative growth rate of 6 per cent and government aided colleges showed a positive but marginal growth rate of 1.1 per cent per annum during 1994-95 to 1999-2000 (Table 11.13). Technical education was facing acute shortage of qualified faculty. "In engineering alone, the demand is for 1.20 lakh teachers, but the system today has hardly 7,000 Ph.Ds, 20,000 M.Techs and rest, fresh B.Tech degree holders. This is mainly because engineering graduates consider teaching as the last career option" (The Telegraph, 2006). Because of the rapid growth of professional education, there is an acute shortage of experienced and qualified faculty, on account of which most of the colleges have to depend heavily on part-time and visiting faculty from business and industry. Competent faculty can come and be retained at higher and attractive levels of salary, which is absent in the private institutions.

Cost

To finance the physical and human infrastructure, fee income is the main source for these private unaided institutions. From the private institutional perspective, they charge commercial fee rates and 'capitation' fees which are not accounted for by receipts nor do they follow a transparent admission procedure. In addition, the private institutions collect exorbitant and compulsory fees of many forms and kinds in the name of transport, canteen, library, textbooks, marks sheets, caution deposits, degree certificates, hall tickets, association fees, etc. It would be extremely difficult to estimate these costs based on very limited and scanty knowledge except from the National Sample Survey Organisation (NSSO).[3] It is a known fact that these institutions rarely part with such information and there

3. There is some information available on the private or unorganized education services in terms of their size, type, workers full time and part time and by gender, income generated (value added) by enterprise and by worker (NSSO, 2003a; 2003b). The major problem here is the whole of education sector is considered without looking at them by levels of education and hence, not utilised in the present paper.

is no effort on the part of the government to collect and document this information. Further, on this fee front, judicial interventions complicate the issue.

Judicial Interventions

The system of capitation fee began first in the state of Karnataka and soon spread to Maharashtra, Tamil Nadu, Kerala and Andhra Pradesh. These states have also enacted legislation that prohibits the charging of capitation fees. The legislation was enacted in 2004 in Kerala, but the Acts were enacted before the Supreme Court declared charging capitation fees as illegal in the Unnikrishnan case in 1993. The idea behind the Unnikrishnan judgment in devising the free and payment seat scheme was to provide enhanced opportunities to meritorious students who may otherwise not be able to pay the enhanced fee prescribed by the government for such colleges.

However, the case of T.M.A. Pai and others vs. the state of Karnataka in 2002 reversed the earlier judgment. It has legally clarified that private institutions are free to charge fees which cover their operating costs and allow surplus to accrue which can be ploughed back for the development/ expansion of the institutions. Thus technically, the only ban on the management of these institutions is that they cannot invest surpluses in businesses (outside the Trust). Later in 2005, the Supreme Court in the Inamdar Case ruled that the governments have no right to ask for government quota in private unaided professional institutions. This case in 2005 defines capitation fee as "something taken over and above what the institution needs by way of revenue and capital expenditure plus a reasonable surplus." This judgment seems to indicate that the state cannot regulate unaided institutions, who are free to set their fees as they wish as long as they do not term any part of their fee as a capitation fee, and as long as they only make a reasonable surplus. Even the National Knowledge Commission (2006) recommends land grants, tax exemptions, no restriction on utilisation of income and autonomy to set fees and tap other sources, etc., for the private unaided institutions.

As against this, the fee structure for private unaided medical colleges in Tamil Nadu has been fixed by a statutory committee. In August 2004, the Permanent Committee for Fixation of Fees in Self-Financing

Professional Colleges had fixed ₹ 1.3 lakhs per annum as fee for students admitted under the government quota in private unaided medical colleges. However, there was no restriction with regard to the fees collected from students admitted under the management quota and the non-resident Indian (NRI) quota. The structure was to be in place from 2004 to 2007. When the three private institutions sought review of the direction, a single judge of the High Court passed an interim order permitting them to collect ₹ 4 lakhs per year. Collecting fees in excess of the structure laid down by the Committee was nothing but collection of capitation fee, and the court added that the self-financing institutions should not challenge the fees fixed by the Committee, even while enjoying the freedom of collecting fees of their choice from the management quota and NRI quota students. By and large, the judicial interventions paved way for higher cost recovery from students. Besides the huge cost recovery from students, these private institutions enjoy considerable amount of hidden subsidy from the government.

Hidden Subsidy

Government assistance is not direct, but indirect in terms of land, tax concession and facilities under the Societies and Charitable Trust Act, etc. A major difficulty in the Indian case is whether most private institutions that claim tax-exemption status qualify as "philanthropic." No distinction can now be readily made between private institutions which work on commercial lines and those which do not and recent court judgments have further clouded this distinction. The basic difficulty is that invariably all such institutions are registered as non-profit institutions (trusts or societies) and are legally permitted to generate revenues which cover their costs and permit accumulation of surpluses. This has been a major legal conundrum and judicial decisions have done little to add clarity to the issue. This makes for a very thin legal dividing line between philanthropic and for-profit institutions (Kapur and Mehta, 2004).

Further, these private institutions that are legally non-profit pass on large sums to family members and others officially on the staff or spend money on lavish facilities. They sometimes lobby successfully for public funding, for instance, in the form of land grants. One of the key recommendations of the National Knowledge Commission (2006) is land grants and use of land to generate revenue. Already in India and also in the state of Tamil Nadu, privatisation takes place in the mask of philanthropy. Anandakrishnan (2006) notes that only a quarter of such institutions genuinely function as public trusts or charitable societies, committed to educational excellence and conscious of their responsibility. Since there is no distinction between the philanthropic and profit-making institutions, the rationale of the state extending subsidies to them is questionable. In any case, any form of subsidy needs to be open, rather than hidden.

If the self-financing institutions recover their full cost from students, then the private sector's contribution to higher education would indeed be *notional*. No recent information is available to highlight the extent of household contribution to higher education. In any case, the moot question is: does this contribution of households indicate their willingness and ability to pay or should it be taken as forced commercialisation? What is the motivation of these institutions as providers of education? Is it the land available at subsidised rates or the income tax exemptions? If they are fully recovering the cost from students, are they net contributors of funds? Is it rather to exploit the maximum profit potential in a situation of excess demand?

A major disturbing feature has been lack of motivation on the part of some educational entrepreneurs to serve the cause of education leading in turn to a lack of commitment to intellectual excellence. This was because their focus was 'profit making'. Since the norms for fixation of fees are vague, the quantum of fees charged has no rational basis. While the illegal capitation fees range from 2 to 8 lakhs for some of the courses, the regular fees also vary considerably among courses and across colleges as well (Anandakrishnan,2006). Since, private institutions are privately owned and financed, they are governed very little by the state. In other words, since they are owned and financed by private groups (either business groups or family) and also governed by them, it should not be a surprise that (Levy, 1992) academic excellence is not pursued as the principal aim.

Outcome

Academic Orientation: Bulk of private higher education remains concentrated on undergraduate teaching and training with a subject bias towards engineering, management, computer applications, a few applied sciences—biotechnology, microbiology, etc., which are geared to the growing service economy. However, the rapid expansion of such programmes also indicates a new type of social demand that requires merely a certificate to compete in the labour market. Private institutions concentrate more substantially on the provision of diplomas and professional education than in postgraduate education and research. For instance, students enrolled in private self-financing colleges at the diploma level (above graduate) range from 26 per cent among the urban male to as high as 42.8 per cent among the urban female[4] (see Table 11.11). The percentage of students currently attending self-financing institutions is minimal at graduate levels and above ranging from 10.2 to 22.4 per cent during 2004-05.

Table 11.11

Students in Higher Education in Private Unaided Educational Institutions in India[5] in 2004-05 (in %)

	Grad and above	*Diploma (Below Grad.)*	*Diploma (Above Grad.)*	*Professional (Engg, Medicine, etc.)*
Rural				
Male	10.6	12.6	30.0	25.5
Female	10.2	17.6	42.0	19.9
Person	10.4	14.5	33.5	23.5
Urban				
Male	22.4	14.2	26.8	27.9
Female	20.5	15.2	42.8	24.9
Person	21.5	14.6	32.2	26.6
All				
Male	14.3	13.4	28.3	27.0
Female	14.2	16.2	42.5	23.5
Person	14.2	14.5	32.8	25.6

Source: NSSO (2006).

Besides their expansion, another equally important aspect is how effectively the private higher education delivers. Mere attendance rate does

4. It is interesting to note that there is no difference in the participation rate among rural and urban females.

5. There is no such state-specific information available from NSSO (2006).

not provide information about what happens to these students after they are enrolled.

Unsatisfactory Quality

Unsatisfactory quality of these mushrooming private colleges is a serious problem. The turnout rate is one of the process indicators that, to a large extent, indicates the holding power of the system. The ability of an educational system to maximise (minimise) the number of turnout (dropouts) is a strong indication of its development and growth. For instance, in technical education, the per cent of postgraduate turnout was 70 per cent during 1996, which has drastically declined to 58 per cent at the beginning of the new millennium. At the graduate level, the situation is still worse, even during 1996 only 37 per cent of the enrolled completed their graduation. This low turnout rate has further deteriorated during 2000 to 31 per cent (Table 11.12).

Table 11.12

Growth and Outturn of Technical Manpower in Tamil Nadu

	Postgraduate			*Graduate*		
	Intake	*Outturn*	*% Outturn in Intake*	*Intake*	*Outturn*	*% Outturn in Intake*
1996	4162	2923	70.2	20605	7679	37.3
1997	4479	3115	69.5	22366	9111	40.7
1998	4805	3328	69.3	24820	11941	48.1
1999	5153	3565	69.2	34170	13106	38.4
2000	5814	2805	48.2	48240	14992	31.1

Source: *Tamil Nadu Economic Appraisal 1999-2000* and *2000-01*.

The turnout or the completion rate even in engineering education itself was deteriorating from 1996 to 2000. Further, the issue of performance is problematic. In Tamil Nadu, the minimum percentage of marks required to pass the final examination is around 40. The average pass rate was 42.6 per cent for all the 229 private unaided engineering colleges (Table 11.13). It may be noted that only 21 per cent of the private unaided colleges could get more than 50 per cent pass rate. Out of 229, 32 private unaided engineering colleges had less than 16 per cent pass rate. In a majority, that is 65 per cent of the private unaided colleges, the pass percentage ranged between 25 and 50 per cent.

Table 11.13

Pass Per cent of Private Unaided Engineering Colleges in Tamil Nadu 2003-04

Pass % Range	*No. of Colleges*	*No. Appeared*	*No. Passed*	*Pass %*
80-100	0	-	-	-
70-80	5	6669	4983	74.7
60-70	21	24826	15872	63.9
50-60	22	21861	11866	54.3
40-50	31	24457	11168	45.7
30-40	66	42502	15087	35.5
20-30	52	26680	6926	26.0
10-20	27	10364	1629	15.7
0-10	5	1343	132	9.8
Total	229	158702	67663	42.6

Source: Anna University as reported in Anandakrishnan (2004).

Since these colleges are now affiliated to Anna University, this being Asia's biggest technical education university, they clearly exhibit the deficiency in the quality of teaching and learning in these engineering colleges. Lack of qualified, experienced and competent teachers is found to be one of the major factors. The evidence clearly brings out that while the activities of the private sector have increased stupendously, their quality is extremely fragile as there is no accountability of these institutions in terms of performance. The state is unable or unwilling to make them accountable to the society and regulate their performance. While a few of them make significant contributions to the need for a highly skilled workforce, others merely exploit the situation.

Students' Demand: Second Choice

Even though the private sector is expanding, it is rarely the number one choice for aspirants. The private higher education sector is less prestigious and primarily demand-absorbing. Even though it is interpreted as spontaneous demand, a deeper look at it would clearly suggest that the students and parents opt for private higher education only as a second alternative certainly not the first best choice (Rani, 2007). For instance, the average size of enrolment in government and aided colleges is much higher compared to private unaided colleges both in arts and science and in engineering colleges (see Table 11.14).

Table 11.14

Average Size of Enrolment per Institution by Type of Management in General Arts and Science and Engineering Colleges in Tamil Nadu

	General Arts and Science			*Engineering Colleges*		
1996-97	*Govt*	*PA*	*PUA*	*Govt*	*PUA*	*All*
1997-98	1343	1379	418	279	248	252
1998-99	1358	1457	380	224	176	180
1999-2000	1306	1583	488	259	228	231
2000-01	1486	1674	424	277	252	254
2001-02	1504	1710	418	337	218	224
2002-03	1526	1778	439	401	255	261
2003-04	1618	1845	473	393	201	208
2004-05	1642	1989	598	392	212	219

Source: *Statistical Handbook of Tamil Nadu*, Chennai.

This clearly suggests that the students and parents opt for private higher education only as a second alternative. All over the world including India, the rapid expansion of private higher education is in the form of excess demand and/or differentiated demand and demand-absorbing type. The private sector in higher education has emerged out of compulsion, as there was no corresponding public provision to cater to excess demand. This needs to be viewed in a macro context where three-fourths of investments in the economy are now flowing from the private sector.

Deepening Market Forces

Financial constraints emanating from the FRBM law coupled with inefficiency and waste in public service deliveries have led to increasing space for the private sector. The market forces have become very active and deepened within the private colleges and have also penetrated into the public higher education institutions. For instance, within 146 management institutions, only 41 (28%) of them are independent or new institutions in Tamil Nadu. The rest 72 per cent of the institutions are part of already existing engineering colleges. This comprises 32 per cent of government (which are few in number) and private unaided colleges.

Another 26 per cent of the institutions are under private arts and science colleges. This denotes extending the privateness in the existing self-financing institutions. Government arts and science colleges and university departments constitute another 7 per cent of the management institutions. This indicates the privatisation of the already very few public colleges and universities (Table 11.15).

Table 11.15

Type of Management Institutions in Tamil Nadu in 2005-06

Type of Institutes	*No. of Instns.*	*In Per cent*
Engg. College Depts	46	32
Individual business schools	41	28
Univ. depts.	8	05
Pvt arts and science	38	26
Govt. arts and science	3	02
DU	9	06
Central Govt. insts	1	01
Total	146	100

Source: Saravanan (2007).

Deepening *privateness* within the existing private colleges is taking place. The inter-linkages between private and government colleges have further allowed the markets forces to penetrate into the government colleges as well. Private sector increasingly intrudes on the domain of public higher education. This presents the public institutions with a critical dilemma. Do they rearticulate and reassert their public values or do they try to emulate the private universities by becoming more 'commercial'. As set out in Kirp (2003), the former carries the risk that no one may be listening. The latter also carries the risk that they may lose what is most valuable about them. Despite being commercial, these institutions are unlikely to provide the skills that are required in the market.

Commercial Orientations *versus* Mismatch in the Labour Market

Most private institutions claim to be commercially oriented, preparing graduates for the job market. Professional institutions promise potential students lucrative positions in their field of choice upon graduation, but there is no guarantee that they can ensure their claims. It is because the market is not able to find the kind of talent it is looking for. The unfettered growth in engineering colleges coupled with mismatch in the labour market has perhaps led to a glut of seats. For instance, AICTE notes that 30,000 seats remain vacant in technical institutes, with 1.5 lakhs students going abroad for higher education (The Telegraph, 2006). The story is similar in engineering education in Tamil Nadu which is going through a period of crisis. In 2003-04, 33 per cent of the sanctioned seats remained vacant in self-financing colleges (see Table 11.16).

Table 11.16

Sanctioned and Admitted Seats in Engineering Colleges in Tamil Nadu

	Sanctioned Intake	*Admitted*	*Vacancy*	*Vacancy as % Intake*
1997-98	22192	22594	-402	-1.81
1998-99	22192	22873	-681	-3.07
1999-2000	32735	31463	1272	3.89
2000-01	42892	38893	3999	9.32
2001-02	60470	48887	11583	19.15
2003-04	71460	48106	23354	32.68
2004-05	68190	49466	18724	27.46

Source: *Statistical Handbook of Tamil Nadu*, Chennai.

It is because the sanctioned intake has grown three and a half times from 22,192 students in 1997-98 to 71,460 students in 2003-04. Indeed, the state has the second largest intake capacity in the country in engineering education. A challenge for engineering colleges in Tamil Nadu is how to tackle decreasing demand which is to the tune of above 25 per cent of the intake capacity. Based on the market forces of demand and supply, colleges are now offering much lower fees (price) than that fixed by the Government to attract students and yet there are not many takers (The Hindu, 2003). As discussed earlier, the most prominent reason is many engineering colleges do not have trained faculty. With these serious constraints, it is irrational to find that the total number of seats have been increased from 47,417 in 2003 to 69,100 in 2004 despite the fact that 21,505 seats remained vacant in 2003. Why has the capacity increased despite the steep fall in demand? This raises the structural issue of economic viability of the institutions. This kind of expansion takes place in the midst of discontent against the lack of accountability by private higher education providers which comes out very strongly in the state.

The state governments and the AICTE have not seriously looked into permitting so many engineering colleges in the state, without relating the capacity creation for engineering education to the pattern of industrial growth in the state/country and requirements of qualified engineers. This also speaks of the approach of the Government of Tamil Nadu in promoting higher education, mainly higher technical education, to create manpower for export which has boomeranged. The rapid growth of private engineering colleges and management institutions has produced not high-quality scientific and technical manpower but IT labourers, who contribute very little in the national and international markets. The overall result is a glut in the labor market. The chaos of international, political and economic events causes panic among students, particularly those who studied with a view to going abroad.

Responses from the State

Against this backdrop, it is important to note that the Government of Tamil Nadu plays an active role in governance if not in regulation. A couple of interventions namely single window system and abolition of common entrance test are noteworthy in this context.

Single Window System of Admission

State regulation has been in an incremental approach, resulting in piecemeal additions to programmes that are already in place. When private self-financing institutions came in large numbers in the 1980s in the four states of Andhra Pradesh, Tamil Nadu, Karnataka and Maharashtra, there was no effective mechanism to control their functioning, nor was there a systematic admission procedure, except in Andhra Pradesh, where all seats were filled up by the Government on merit basis. In other states, 50 per cent seats were filled up by the respective governments and for the remaining seats, large sums of money were collected as donations. Since the demand for admissions continued to increase and there was no effective control, the situation led to commercialisation of technical education. The above situation continued even after all institutions were brought under the AICTE's control. Later, the Supreme Court, in a historical judgment in 1993, defined the norms for admission and the fee structure for all self-financing engineering colleges. As per the Supreme Court directive, all admissions to self-financing private colleges are to be done by the respective state governments based on merit. Fifty per cent of the seats are "free seats" for which the fee structure is the same as those of government institutions in the state (AICTE, 1999: 151).

Following this, the Government of Tamil Nadu introduced a single window system of admission of students to engineering colleges during 1997-98 and streamlined the admission procedure on the basis of merit of the students. The planning and execution of the single window system of engineering admissions has been executed by Anna University (GoTN, 2006a). However, in conducting examinations and evaluation, these colleges were under Madras University and operating independently until 2002. In 2003, the State Government brought all these colleges under Anna University. The State Legislature has passed an amendment bill disaffiliating all the engineering colleges from the six general purpose universities of the state and affiliating the same to Anna University. The bill also contains a provision for transfer of all the government engineering colleges to Anna University as constituent colleges. Belatedly in 2001, the state came up with a common entrance test (CET) covering all management colleges along the lines of engineering colleges when the Anna University Amendment Bill was passed. Not only the engineering colleges but also all arts and science colleges are part of an affiliating university, whose main function is to act as a regulating and an examining body in Tamil Nadu.

Abolition of Common Entrance Test

The CET system for admissions to professional courses in Tamil Nadu was introduced in 1984 in order to infuse transparency in the admission process, at least with regard to the government quota seats in unaided professional education institutions. The CET system evolved over time and got its present structure in the early 1990s. Admissions to courses in medical, paramedical, engineering, veterinary and agriculture and allied sciences were based on a combination of marks obtained in the higher secondary examinations and the CET. This CET is largely urban biased and did not consider the larger interest and welfare of the student community. This resulted in mushrooming of coaching centres and fleecing parents in the name of entrance examinations. To lessen the burden and hardship faced by students in view of CET, the government constituted a high-level expert committee headed by the former Anna University Vice-Chancellor M. Anandakrishnan to recommend measures to be taken for the abolition of CET from 2007-08.

Following the recommendations of the committee, the State Government enacted the Tamil Nadu Regulation of Admission in Professional Courses Act 2006 whereby the CET was abolished for students clearing the State Board Examination. The students of other boards such as the Central Board of Secondary Education were required to write the CET for admission to professional courses. It may be noted that as in 2007-08, Tamil Nadu is the only state which abolished CET. However, these are a few lukewarm measures, given the intensity of the nexus between high fees combined with poor quality and no accountability of the private institutions.

Concluding Remarks

Tamil Nadu, with the 70 per cent share of private higher educational institutions and above 50 per cent share of enrolments in the private sector, still operates in a largely unregulated space, beyond reasonable quality control in the midst of still unreformed and underfunded institutions. The most acute problem is quality on account of lack of competent faculty. This coupled with no accountability raises serious doubts as to its ability to address the huge latent demand for quality higher education in the state. What is troubling is the raw power that money—and an ethic that gives pride of place to the things that money can buy—directly exerts over so many aspects of higher education. As aptly put, "There is a place for the market, but the market must be kept in its place" (Kirp, 2007). Hence, a more effective regulatory framework needs to be developed to address the problem of imperfect information on the quality of teaching and student learning. While improved information sharing on academic quality would be an obvious regulatory mechanism, some form of 'enforced self-regulation' is needed for more effective private higher education. This would entail government incentives and sanctions designed to reform and strengthen institutional and professional mechanisms for assuring academic quality, expressed as early in the middle of 19th century by J.S. Mill (1965).

Hence, it is important to regulate market through both short-term and long-term policies. In the short run, it needs to focus on ensuring quality and accountability of the private higher education system immediately. In the long run, it should raise some fundamental and forgotten intrinsic values such as the positive externalities, the social purpose that higher education serves, the nation building role it performs, the public good and the human rights nature of higher education are to be brought back. Given these inherent and intrinsic values of higher education, some basic questions like: should the expansion of private higher education continue? How much responsibility does it owe to the public good? How to revive the abandoned scholarship? How to save the core of the ideals of modern higher education in the face of market forces serving private interests rather than the public good? etc. These are to be the policy concerns in the middle and long run.

References

Anandakrishnan, M. (2004). *Equity, Quality and Quantity in Higher Education, in Issues in Higher Education*, Vol. II. Hyderabad: ICFAI University Press.

———. (2006). "Privatisation of Higher Education: Opportunities and Anomalies", presented at the National Seminar on Privatisation and Commercialisation of Higher Education, NIEPA, New Delhi, May 2.

AICTE (1999). *Technical Education in India in Independent India: 1947-1997. A Compendium to Commemorate the 50th Anniversary of Independence.* New Delhi: All India Council for Technical Education.

Geiger, Roger L. (2004). "The Publicness of Private Higher Education", CHER Meeting, Enschede, Netherlands.

Government of Tamil Nadu (GoTN) (2003). *Tamil Nadu Human Development Report*. Delhi: Social Science Press.

———. (2004). "Policy Note: Demand No.18 Chapter 2, Medical Education 2004-05", Health and Family Welfare Department, Chennai.

———. (2006a). "Policy Note: Demand No: 20, Higher Education, 2006-07", Higher Education Department of Government of Tamil Nadu, *Chennai.*

———. (2006b). "Policy Note: Legal Education, 2006-07", Government of Tamil Nadu, Chennai.

———. (2007). "Policy Note, 2006-07, Agriculture Department, Demand No. 5, Policy Note 2007-08". Government of Tamil Nadu, Chennai.

Government of Tamil Nadu (various year). *Statistical Handbook of Tamil Nadu*, various issues. Chennai: Government of Tamil Nadu.

Government of Tamil Nadu (various year), *Economic Appraisal of Tamil Nadu, 1999-2000 and 2000-01*. Chennai: Government of Tamil Nadu.

Kapur, D. and P.B. Mehta (2004). "Indian Higher Education Reform: From Half-Baked Socialism to Half-Baked Capitalism", Working Paper No 108, Centre for International Development, Harvard University, September.

Kirp, D. (2003). *Shakespeare, Einstein and the Bottom Line: The Marketing of Higher Education.* Cambridge, MA: Harvard University Press,

———. (2007). "The Corporation of Learning: Nonprofit Higher Education Acquires Lessons from Business", CSHE Research & Occasional Paper Series.

Levy, D.C. (1992). "Private Institutions of Higher Education", in B. Clark and G. Neave (eds.), *The Encyclopedia of Higher Education*, Vol. 2. New York, NY: Pergamon Press. pp.1183-95.

———. (2006). "The Unanticipated Explosion: Private Higher Education's Global Surge", *Comparative Education Review* 50(2): 218-40.

Mill, J.S. (1965). *Principles of Political Economy With Some Applications to Social Philosophy* (Collected Works, vols. II and III). Toronto: University of Toronto Press and Routledge.

MHRD (2005). *Selected Educational Statistics*, 2004-05. New Delhi: Government of India.

MHRD (various year). Analysis of Budgetary Expenditure on Education 2004-05. various issues. New Delhi: Government of India.

National Knowledge Commission (2006). "National Knowledge Commission Report to the Nation, 2006", Government of India.

NSSO (2003a). *Unorganised Service Sector in India 2001-02, Salient Features*, Report No. 482, NSS 57th Round, Government of India.

———. (2003b). *Unorganised Service Sector in India 2001-02, Characteristics of Enterprises*, Report, No. 483, NSS 57th Round, Government of India.

———. (2006). *Status of Education and Vocational Training in India 2004-05*, Report No 517, NSS 65th Round, Government of India.

Rani, Geetha (2007). "Transforming Role of State and Market in India: The Case of Privatisation and Private Sector in Higher Education", in *Transformation, Transition or Stagnation: Understanding Change in a Globalizing Economy*, Chennai: Madras Institute of Development Studies.

Saravanan, S. (2007). A Study on Mushroom Growth of Two-year Management Programme and Its Impact on Quality of Management Education in Tamil Nadu, W.P. No. 2007-02-01, February 2007, Indian Institute of Management, Ahmedabad, India.

Singh, A. (2004). "Challenges in Higher Education", *Economic and Political Weekly* 34(21): 2155-58.

The Hindu, 28 July, 2003.

The Telegraph, 06 February, 2006.

University Grants Commission (various year). *UGC Annual Reports*, various years.

www.ugc.nic.in

www.aicte.nic.in

www.tnmgr.univ.org

www.tnau.ac.in.

The author would like to thank Prof A. Vaidyanathan, Prof V.K. Natraj and Prof Ramakrishnan for critical discussions and for encouragement to work on this paper.

12 Globalisation and the Social Sector

An Analysis of the Tamil Nadu Case

V.K. Natraj and J. Jeyaranjan

Preamble

On two aspects of economic reforms, there is agreement at least among its critics. Firstly, reforms tend to dilute the role of the state. And some argue that this is one of its cardinal planks. Secondly, they are essentially anti-poor partly because it is the poor who depend on the state and therefore any dilution in its active role and intervention in the working of the economy must have an adverse impact upon these sections. Following from this, an obvious candidate for inquiry is the nexus between reforms and expenditure on the social sector. The latter can conveniently and justifiably be taken as a valid proxy for a proactive and pro-poor state. This paper focuses on these dimensions of reforms and bases itself upon the performance of the state of Tamil Nadu in relation to the social sector. Tamil Nadu is selected for a variety of reasons among which the more important ones are the following:

- Tamil Nadu is an advanced state with an impressive socio-economic profile.
- It has a very good record in terms of the social sector and provision of major safety nets.
- Both the political parties which have been in power continuously since 1967 have generally redeemed their electoral promises thereby rendering these more than mere 'pre-poll gimmicks or populist measures'.

Tamil Nadu has stood out as a major champion of the federal principle and believes that the much vaunted 73rd and 74th amendments to the Constitution do not genuinely promote decentralisation.

The paper begins by sketching very briefly the macro backdrop to India's economic reforms. In this, we examine the relationship between globalisation and the role of the state. This is followed by the specific case of Tamil Nadu in the social sector. The changes that took place in this area soon after the 2001 elections and the reversal of these policy changes a little later are discussed. The run-up to the 2006 elections and its effects are then summarised. Since the 2001 and 2006 elections appear to represent landmarks in social sector policy, the paper concentrates on them. The 2011 election and its aftermath are not discussed in detail. The final section summarises the principal conclusions.

Macro Backdrop

India's economic reforms were formally adopted in 1991. It is eminently arguable that their origins go back to the 1980s but interesting though that dimension is, we shall not be able to concern ourselves with it here. The quintessential point about the reforms is that they have aimed at diluting the role of the state. The other features can be described as logical corollaries to this basic construct. However, the degree to which the centrality of the state has been reduced is a matter for discussion on its own and like in so many aspects of the debate on reforms, several conflicting views have been put forward (for instance see Harriss in *Globalisation and the Indian State 2005*).

The reforms (often abbreviated as the acronym LPG connoting liberalisation, privatisation and globalisation) are controversial two decades after they were formally adopted. Debate around them recall to mind a prescient remark of Albert Hirschman speaking of the price (market) mechanism that while one school extols it, the other practically vilifies it. With some changes, this could be said of LPG. Its supporters speak glowingly of the positive effects of reforms and cite by way of evidence the impressive growth rates posted by India after their initiation. Critics point to the fragile foundations of these 'successes' and place before us the persistence of poverty, inequality, unemployment and other serious maladies, all too familiar to require recapitulation here. A major issue in the debate relates to the role of the state and critics of reforms argue that the state has withdrawn from spheres that ought to be its principal if not exclusive concern and responsibility. Good examples are social security and provision of safety nets, health care, education, etc. Before entering into the vortex of that discussion, we should take note of the antecedents of reforms. There is a view that it was a sudden and transformative process which caused a striking change in India's economic profile. There is another view that holds that while the reforms were in some ways an epochal event, their origins are traceable to the 1980's which ushered in some loosening of the control regime and also to what is described as 'reforms by stealth', that is changes introduced without being openly acknowledged as reforms. The position we take is that while the origins of the reforms can be traced back by a decade or so, it was an epochal event, although not transformative in the degree often urged by some authors.

Two features of the Structural Adjustment Programme (SAP)/ globalisation debate are of particular importance. One is that critics see in the process the root of the country's most stressful problems and there are those who suggest that India's autonomy in the sphere of policy-making has suffered deep erosion (Prabhat Patnaik, 2006; Utsa Patnaik, 2006). There is also the often expressed view that what has occurred after the adoption of SAP is a visible withdrawal from the Nehruvian vision of the state, economy and the country. The state is experiencing a steady whittling down of its role and this has presaged a pronounced retreat from the dirigiste regime, which marked India's policy in the 1950s and 1960s and continued in some degree through the 1970s. Secondly, there are those who critique globalisation by positing the view that it does not promote democracy. Put another way, democracy and globalisation are seen as confronting each other (*Globalisation and the Indian State* 1(2): 2005). The statement ushering in the project of which this paper is a part poses the question in the following terms: "Globalisation is often opposed in the name of democracy, and democracy is often bypassed for fear that it may slow down globalisation". Further, globalisation is seen as "a force that will lead to a re-colonisation of the country, making it once again subservient to the diktat of foreign capital and multinational corporations" (Ibid). Behind all of this and indeed underlying SAP is the premise that there should occur some dilution in the state's role, although it would perhaps be a mistake to suppose that this is some kind of a *sine qua non* for greater integration of the national with the global economy. We have the striking example of China where a 'strong state' guides its economy towards global integration. This view is also endorsed by John Harriss who, in an insightful passage, remarks: "—the history of globalisation shows that those countries that have done well have done so, so to speak on their own terms" and "—successful globalisation has called for strong states" (*Globalisation and the Indian State* 1(1)) Harriss argues further that there is no solid ground to contend that there has taken place the decline of the Indian state; on the contrary, what has transpired are changes in the role and function of the state. He has cited evidence which supports the perception that even in the present era of globalisation, people, especially those who are not part of the globalising process (say the non-middle classes), have high expectations of the state. Therefore, following this line of reasoning, we may question the view that the state is tending to become smaller (and not necessarily more effective) and that its place is being filled by civil society. We need to distinguish those who are part of from those who are not integral to the globalising process. It may make for better logic than to look at globalisation as a process which has a similar impact on all sections of society.

We have referred to above to the view posited by John Harriss to the effect that there are vital areas in which the state is still expected to be active. The issue is whether there is anything intrinsic to economic reforms that drives them in the direction of state withdrawal from essential spheres of policy—the social sector is an excellent example---and also leads to the interests of the vulnerable being neglected or at the very least underemphasised? In addressing these issues, a prefatory observation is in order. The dynamics that led to the adoption of economic reforms in India consisted of internal as well as external factors. While the latter comprising the advice of the Fund-Bank combination is frequently discussed, we should remember that the former set is equally important. The factors adverted to above are meant to urge the point that the paradigms in which policy was framed in the 1970s and early 1980s are no longer wholly relevant. And for a variety of reasons not discussed here, the currently emphasised ingredients of good governance such as transparency, participation, accountability and decentralisation indicate major changes in our perception of the state and at the same time, these represent a confluence of several strands of thought and policy preferences which may not always have been intended.

Also relevant to our discussion is the concept of social security. This has experienced an important change. Today the concept refers to all social policy measures which aim to prevent deprivation. It is no longer confined to what is conventionally regarded as denoting deprivation. This is in line with the manner in which our understanding of development has steadily altered. From the early days of the discipline of development studies when there was almost exclusive concern with rates of growth, we have traversed a vast territory crossing several landmarks. Important among them are human capital, equity and access, gender justice, human development and finally development as freedom (Dev and Mooij, 2002; Ghosh, 2006)

Social Sector Expenditure

We find that in India, the expenditure on the social sector by government, both the centre and states, has never been significantly impressive. Total public expenditure as a percentage of gross domestic product (GDP) is no doubt much higher in India when compared with averages of other groups, but the share of public expenditure allotted to social services is lower than in East Asian countries and as compared with all developing countries (Dev and Mooij, 2002). The expenditure on health is low in comparison with South Asian countries. It was mentioned above that a major criticism of economic reforms in India is that the state has come to play a smaller role in several areas. In this context, the following is of interest. In the pre-reform period, expenditure on the social sector in the states was 39 per cent of aggregate disbursements and above 7 per cent of GDP. After the reforms were introduced, this went down to 37 and 7 respectively. It is interesting as Dev and Mooij (2002) demonstrate that social sector expenditure as a proportion of the gross state domestic product (GSDP) began falling from the mid-1980s onwards. It would seem that after the reforms commenced, this trend was aggravated. It is also shown that right through the 1990s, the average level of expenditure on the social sector as a percentage of aggregate expenditure was less than in the 1980s. While certain trends may have been aggravated after the commencement of reforms, it is not always justifiable to argue that all negative trends are attributable to liberalisation and globalisation. It may also be pointed out that a reconsideration of the role of the state in fact started in the 1980s coinciding with changes in the perception of development. An important inference from all of this is that the process of globalisation cannot be understood if it is studied without reference to the internal or domestic constellation of forces impinging on policy making. It is eminently possible that a government in power may utilise external factors in order to introduce changes, which are its preference, but which it apprehends may prove to be politically risky.

The Economic Growth–Human Development Nexus

From the perspective of this study, an important factor is that the nexus between economic growth and human development is no longer analysed from what was practically accepted practice a few decades ago, namely, studying the impact of economic growth on human development and not often looking at it the other way round. Admittedly there were thinkers in the 1970s and even earlier—two outstanding names are Dudley Seers and Gunnar Myrdal—who saw that equity would have beneficial effects on growth but in today's discourse, it is seen much more routinely. For this reason, there are numerous studies nationally and across countries that attempt to assess how human development exercises an impact on growth (See Ghosh, 2006). In this context, it is worth digressing briefly into the reasons for Tamil Nadu's expenditure pattern and priorities taking the shape they did. They are to a considerable extent rooted in the state's ethos.

The Dravidian parties since the late 1960s when they first tasted power had to create and nurture a constituency for themselves. Logically this had to comprise those groups in society which were left out of the Nehruvian vision. Harriss and Wyatt (2004) expressing this idea cite with the approval of Narender Subramanian (2002) who argues that the Congress' constituency and support rested "on a thin foundation—large-scale industrialisation, pan-Indian nationalism and the aggregation of already organised interests". Sudipto Kaviraj (1996) expresses something similar by pointing to what the Nehruvian vision missed, namely, a single political language, mytho-history and what he calls 'common thinker-weness'. Also as Harriss and Wyatt argue, neither of the Dravidian parties exploited cleavages in society. One reason for this was (and indeed continues to be) that issues like language do not lend themselves to such use mainly because an overwhelming number in the state speak Tamil, and, further, language was used highly effectively in the late 1960s to confront the domination of Hindi and the North. Secondly, unlike in states like Karnataka, Tamil Nadu has two features in relation to caste which must be factored into the discussion. One is that there were always some castes that could and did challenge Brahmanical hegemony. Additionally Tamil Nadu does not have dominant intermediate castes like, for example, the Vokkaligas and Lingayats in Karnataka or the Kammas and Reddys in Andhra Pradesh. These have contributed, along with the economic factors adumbrated above, to the Dravidian parties focusing strongly on the social sector. It is arguable that it is the pursuit of this policy frame that has succeeded in providing to the vulnerable a cushion or collection of safety nets which have helped them negotiate the difficult terrain of the transition influenced by the reforms. Elections in the recent past have brought about changes in the support bases of the principal parties but there is no significant alteration in the development model presented to the people. Only recently (May 2013), the present Anna Dravida Munnetra Kazhagam (ADMK) government brought out a list of its achievements and a perusal affirms the point made above.

We may also draw attention to the fact that Tamil Nadu has one of the highest rates of indebtedness of cultivator households but farmers' suicides have been less numerous than in the neighbouring states of Karnataka and Andhra Pradesh (Rao, 2006).

Tamil Nadu: Investment/Expenditure on the Social Sector

An analysis of the expenditure on the social sector reveals the following major trends. In the recent past, the state appears to have relied more upon rising rates of growth of GSDP to increase per capita expenditure on what may be broadly described as the human development sectors. The White Paper of 2002 drew pointed attention to the prospect of the state becoming financially vulnerable. It went on to add that this might not only reverse all the socioeconomic gains made by Tamil Nadu in the past five decades but was likely to affect adversely its capacity in the future to discharge basic duties. The Social Priority Ratio (SPR) or the share of human development expenditure on elementary education, primary health care, nutrition and water supply has declined noticeably in the past few years. The per capita real expenditure on elementary education has declined since 1993-94. Intra-state/inter-district divergences are visibly sharp in this sector. There are problems relating to high dropout as well as completion rates in elementary education. With respect to health, a feature worth noting is the following. The National Health Policy suggests that the expenditure of the states on health in the primary, secondary and tertiary sectors should be in the following proportion: 55, 35 and 10 per cent respectively but in Tamil Nadu the proportions are 44, 25 and 26 per cent respectively. An outcome of the relatively low level of expenditure on the primary and secondary sectors is that the poor may be moving away from public to private health care. This is possibly encouraged by the perception that the public system is inferior to its private counterpart. At the same time, Tamil Nadu has performed well in terms of the infant morality rate (IMR) and not nearly so well with reference to the maternal morality rate (MMR). In relation to malnutrition the State Government has enunciated its policy in a document titled Towards a Malnutrition Free Tamil Nadu (2002). The problem is that while there is impressive provision of nutritional supplements to children and expectant mothers, these do not address the problem of malnutrition comprehensively (for details, see Finance and Accounts of Tamil Nadu, 2006).

The overall public expenditure on the poor through pro-poor programmes stands at present at around 24 per cent of all expenditure. It is seen that there has occurred an increase in capital expenditure and this appears to be accounted for by higher levels of expenditure on rural water supply programmes. This is particularly because of expenditure on water supply in tribal areas. On the whole, there has been a slight decrease in pro-poor revenue expenditure. It is also arguable that in the recent past the state has encouraged expenditure promoting growth directly as compared to pro-poor intervention programmes. Even if this be true, it may serve as a corrective to the earlier trends in the beginning of the 1990s when capital expenditures suffered a degree of neglect because of the predominant share of pro-poor expenditures (see Guhan, 1992). In education and health as illustrated above, Tamil Nadu has registered significant progress. On several health indicators, the state is close to achieving the targets set out in the

Millennium Development Goals (MDG). On the social welfare and social security fronts, Tamil Nadu has done well. A number of schemes introduced by the state show that there is a commitment to welfare which is more than tokenism. It may be stated here that this is one important reason that we refrain from calling this populist. The programmes under the social sector attract many criticisms; the most common one being with respect to poor quality of services, inadequate staffing and lack of supervision. Studies have commented on this with reference, for instance, to the flagship programme, namely, the mid-day meal scheme (Swaminathan *et al.*, 2004). There is also the observation that possibly the health programmes benefit the better-off sections slightly more than the poorer ones especially in the rural areas. Some of these would apply across the country to most state sponsored and delivered programmes but that is no reason for complacency. In this context, we may take note of the following. It is only in 2001 that the Government explicitly noted that it was necessary to introduce "measures to reduce the ratio of subsidy in total expenditure" and added that this was "a crying need" (Economic and Functional Classification, Government of Tamil Nadu, 2001). In contrast in the previous report for 2000-01, the following statement was made: social service is the "thrust area of the State government". The need to reduce subsidies was reiterated in subsequent reports. In 2002-03, for instance, the report stated that the "Government is conscious of reducing the proportion of subsidy going to non-merit goods". It is worth noting that the ratio of subsidies and other transfers has altered over the years. Up to 2000-01, it stood at 65:35 but later it altered to 40:60. The major subsidy payments are public distribution system (PDS), free power to farmers, incentives to farmers in the Cauvery Delta, absorption of losses in irrigation, and incentives to Khadi and handloom industries. Other transfers include aid to educational institutions, grants to local bodies and co-operatives and assistance to specially identified groups such as destitute women, widows, etc. Further, subsidy towards social services decreased from 2001 onwards.

State's Financial Crisis and Response

In assessing the impact of globalisation on Tamil Nadu's policy towards the social sector, the state's financial crisis which reached its height in 2001 has to be borne in mind. The ADMK which came to power in the summer of that year admitted candidly that the state was in the grip of a severe financial crunch which required immediate and strong counteractive measures. It is believed that even had the Dravida Munnetra Kazhagam (DMK) returned to power, it would have had no choice except to go in for some drastic measures but that is in the nature of a counter-factual and highly speculative. Suffice it to state that the White Paper on Tamil Nadu's finances (Government of Tamil Nadu, 2001) which the government brought out soon after assuming office was a fairly comprehensive and candid analysis of the parlous state of Tamil Nadu's finances. The Paper drew attention to the following as disquieting features.

The gross fiscal deficit of the state increased only marginally from ₹ 1126 crore in 1990-91 to ₹ 1255 crore in 1995-96 but then grew alarmingly to a level of ₹ 5781 crore in 2000-01. In absolute terms, the revenue deficit—gap between revenue receipts and revenue expenditure—declined from ₹ 553 crore in 1990-91 to ₹ 311 crore in 1995-96 and rose sharply in the next five years to ₹ 3922 crore in 2000-01.

- The 16.2 per cent annual rate of growth of revenue receipts during 1991-96 declined to 11.7 per cent during 1996-2001, without a concomitant reduction in growth of revenue expenditure.
- The average share of development expenditure in the budget declined from 77.9 per cent in 1991-92 to 57.8 per cent in 2000-01.
- The revenue deficit of the Government was 16 per cent of the total revenue receipts in 2000-01 as against 2.7 per cent in 1995-96.

The Government was forced to regulate its cash outflows through a system of treasury control, wherein prior concurrence of the Finance Department was made mandatory before any bill exceeding ₹ 2 lakh in value was cleared for payment.

The PDS network in Tamil Nadu had at that time a universal coverage, it was untargeted. Operated through a network of co-operatives, most of them found it difficult to meet the costs and therefore looked to the State Government for support. The White Paper took the view that such a universal and untargeted food subsidy system was a severe drain on the exchequer. This apart it noticed that due to then vast difference between the issue and open market prices, there was a thriving black market. From this came the inevitable conclusion that if the system could be targeted towards the needy and poor, better results could be achieved. Of course, there are many social scientists who felt that this could be the proverbial thin end of the wedge and quite likely signalled the dismantling of the system.

Among other features which the White Paper dealt with critically were power subsidies, transport subsidies and the working of public sector undertakings (PSUs). Much of the criticism was that the subsidies were untargeted. Another area which came in for critical scrutiny was the handloom sector. It was pointed out that the free saree and *dhoti* scheme was misutilised and there was a large incidence of the free ride problem. For instance, while the scheme benefited 75 lakh families, the National Sample Survey (NSS) estimate was that there were only 42 lakh families eligible for subsidy. On local bodies, the White Paper was critical of the fact that most of them had not made adequate efforts to mobilise resources. It is interesting that while the general tone of the White Paper was to reduce the free ride problem and recommend targeted subsidies, it did not make any direct recommendation for reducing the expenditure on the social sector. As a consequence of the severity of the financial crisis and the readiness of government to confront it head-on, several major changes were introduced from 2001-02 onwards. Apart from the inescapable severity of the problem, the Government (read ruling party, ADMK) must have been assisted by the fact that it had won only a few months ago an impressive electoral victory and there was no electoral battle on hand just then. The following new policies and practices were brought in after the White Paper:

- A bi-yearly budget review.
- Expenditure Commission constituted.
- Attempt to identify surplus staff in government.
- Aim to achieve fiscal correction and stabilisation.
- Regulation of subsidies.
- Regulation and/or withdrawal of facilities enjoyed by government employees such as leave travel concession etc.
- Budget presentation altered so as to reflect more accurately the state's financial situation.

- Fiscal Responsibility Act enacted, the third state in the country to do so.
- Medium-term Fiscal Programme presented along with the budget in 2004.

The state's finances did show a turn for the better after 2001-02. A drastic policy measure, not necessarily connected with the policy measures, was the temporary termination of the services of a very large number of government employees including teachers who resorted to a strike in 2003. But in 2004 in the elections to Parliament, the ruling ADMK suffered a crushing defeat. As a reaction, several of the 'reforms' were rolled back. The Government's publication: *Achieving Fiscal Correction and Stabilisation 2004-05,* undertook a candid examination of the manner in which the rollback took place. In the aftermath of the debacle in the parliamentary elections, free power was restored, electricity tariff was reduced, bus passes also were restored and the PDS was once again freed from targeting and made universal. As the document referred to above states, the rollback meant that the stabilisation aims which prompted the Government to take up the reforms were unlikely to be realised in the medium term. At a conference in October 2004 sponsored by the Government, the then Finance Secretary argued, with enviable frankness, that one of the problems confronting policy advisors was how to convince the political authority of the soundness of their advice. In fact in the ensuing discussions, attention was given to this dimension as well as to the need for the bureaucracy/ advisors and political authority to appreciate each other's compulsions and perspectives (*The Hindu*, October 8, 2004).

Why were New Measures Rolled Back?

It is worth considering the bundle of factors which constituted the rationale for the rollback of the severe measures introduced in the wake of the first White Paper. One proximate explanation is that the party in power was influenced by the parliamentary elections in 2004. The party was routed in these polls and thereafter had its attention focused on the assembly polls due in 2006. Does this connote merely electoral politics or is there a significant element of bowing to public pressure? In one sense, it is difficult to separate the two and treat one as independent of the other.

Given the fact though that the welfare element has always been strong in the policy of the state almost regardless of which party is in power, there are differences between the welfare orientations of the two Dravidian parties and these are adverted to below in the text—it is plausible to argue that in a broad sense, the reversal of some of the harsher reforms represented a response to public pressure. Also as some authors have argued redeeming poll promises is a characteristic of Tamil Nadu politics, in other words, all promises made in the manifestos are not to be treated lightly as 'pre-poll gimmicks'. As mentioned above after the rollback of 2004, the ruling party's focus was on the elections to the state assembly due in May 2006. As the 2004-05 document states with a candour not generally encountered in government statements, financial adjustment has to face several risks. Principal among them is political resistance. The correction of distortions and fiscal excesses entails large costs especially in the short term. The perceptions regarding these costs are intensified when elections are round the corner. Resistance, the document states, is particularly strong in relation to the levy of user charges. Over and above these difficulties, the State Government has had to contend with macro level developments including decline in Central Government transfers. Added to this is the fact that Tamil Nadu agriculture has been vulnerable to drought.

Run-up to the 2006 Elections

It was only to be expected that as the 2006 elections drew nearer both the ruling party and its principal competitor the DMK tried to reach out to the electorate through promises of various kinds. In the last year of its power, the ADMK Government introduced new schemes in the social sector such as free bicycles for school girls. Not to be outdone, the DMK in its election manifesto promised rice at ₹ 2 per kg, free colour TV sets to the poor as well as gas stoves and subsidised liquid petroleum gas (LPG) connections. We do not propose delve deeply into the course of fortunes of the major parties in the elections or attempt to explain the final result. We shall only make note of the following. Both the DMK and ADMK pursued what may be called the welfare route; we prefer this to the more commonly used term populism which in our view has a negative flavour to it. Several social sector schemes are of long standing. The DMK took the lead in reaching out to the electorate through its manifesto. Apart from the Karunanidhi factor, the manifesto with its studied emphasis on welfare measures worked to the party's advantage. It requires to be noted that the DMK has taken a violently proactive position on the issue of reservation for the other backward classes (OBCs). This too should properly be regarded as part of the Government's 'welfarist' agenda, although this is not meant to argue that the Government's position is unequivocally correct.

From the foregoing, it should be obvious that Tamil Nadu has always been in the frontline insofar as expenditure on the social sector is concerned. It is therefore no surprise that Ghosh (2006) finds that in this state, there is a positive two-way relationship between growth and human development. It is time now to ask what has caused this particular type of development paradigm to be pursued in Tamil Nadu. One explanation offered is that the state lacked the traditional investment avenues such as irrigation and therefore the social sector stepped in to fill this vacuum. However this does not serve to explain in full the Tamil Nadu reality. Also it does not incorporate the impact of the transformations that Tamil Nadu has been undergoing as well as that of the changing sociopolitical configurations in the state and society. We shall consider these issues in what follows.

Distinctive Features of Tamil Nadu

To begin with, we require to take note of some characteristic features of Tamil Nadu. One is that the state has been endowed with an indigenous and efficient entrepreneurial class. This class has certainly helped the state achieve impressive progress on the industrial front. In terms of education, especially higher education, it has been a leading state. It should surprise none that in recent times, it is a leader in attracting foreign direct investment (FDI). Presently it is the third most important destination in India for FDI. Strenuous efforts are being made now to develop the city of Chennai into an information technology (IT) hub rivalling Hyderabad and Bangalore. The social movements of the early part of the last century such as the non-Brahmin movement spearheaded by the Justice Party and the rationalist/modern complexion imparted to it by Periyar ensured that the demands of the non-Brahmins did not stay confined merely to reservations in jobs but succeeded in giving them a competitive edge in the professions. In addition to the development of the industrial-entrepreneurial class referred to above, the state also developed an efficient bureaucracy and even today, Tamil Nadu enjoys the reputation of being one of the best administered states in the country. Not to be forgotten is the fact that Tamilians have an impressive diaspora which must have contributed its share to the state's development by virtue of making available to its citizens, though obviously only in a small part, valuable contacts and a global (distinct from globalising) perspective or world view. Further Tamil Nadu has for long had an impressive array of leaders of consequence at the national level. It has been in the forefront of the demand for greater adherence to the federal principle in the polity and has now become a major player in national politics. Another feature of interest is that, cutting across party lines, there is a uniform disapproval of the 73rd Amendment which is seen not as a decentraliser but yet another instrument to be used by the centre to control the states. Both the DMK and ADMK abstained from voting on the amendment and the state cannot lay claim to being highly committed to devolution of power to local government institutions. At the political level, the state has been governed from 1967 by the Dravidian parties, DMK and AIADMK, with intermittent spells of President's rule. It is one of the few states where the Congress has lost ground quite comprehensively and today marks its political presence only as a DMK or ADMK ally.

Attention was drawn above to the view that the state's investment vacuum and the social sector and welfare measures serving as an effective substitute are an incomplete explanation of the Tamil Nadu model of development. We now return to this theme. Tamil Nadu's industrial growth has resulted from an efficient group of entrepreneurs as argued above but the state did provide a climate favourable for investment. Of particular importance has been the provision of infrastructure and an efficient administrative system. The state, the earlier Madras Presidency and its successor did not witness state capitalism in terms of industrial investment with the exception of Central Government initiatives. However, the state has been experiencing a series of transformations; not all of which are noticed since they have tended to be somewhat silent transitions. Their effects though are there. The occupational diversification among the working population in the state is one of the highest in the country. While the agrarian crisis could be the push factor, the emergence of numerous clusters and the booming urbanisation process are the pull factors that work in tandem in transforming the economy. Apart from such changes from within the boundaries of the state, it is also experiencing one of the highest rates of offshore migration. The number of labour migrants to destinations like West and South Asia from the state is the highest in the country. From an economic perspective, it would make sense, in such a context, for a government to give serious attention to providing social welfare nets to the vulnerable sections of the population. This appears even more easily understandable if we juxtapose this with certain important social and political factors. Prior to moving into that discussion, it is necessary to note a few other factors which have made Tamil Nadu a favourable pitch for experiencing some of the beneficial effects of globalisation. The state has quite a long history of industrial growth. Today its industrial profile as shown by the following indicators is indicative of its record.

- Second most industrialised state after Maharashtra.
- Accounts for over 11 per cent of the country's industrial output. Shares in all-India output: 21 per cent in cars, 26 per cent in two-wheelers, 30 per cent in auto components, leather products 75 per cent, cotton yarn 32 per cent, 14 per cent in software.
- Large number of export-oriented industries: in 2004-05 state's exports valued at $6.5 billion.
- A well spread out industrial base unlike other industrialised states like Maharashtra and Gujarat.
- A blend of traditional and modern industry.
- A policy environment conducive to industrial growth.

Both the DMK and ADMK are described by some writers as populist. A distinction though is sought to be made between the 'empowerment populism of the DMK' and the 'protection populism of the ADMK'. Swamy (1998) who makes this distinction says: "I use the term empowerment populism to refer to a style of political rhetoric that describes society as a conflict between 'the common people' and narrow elite demanding greater privileges for outgroups on behalf of 'the people'. By protection populism, on the other hand, I mean a rhetoric that emphasises themes of vulnerability, offering to protect 'the weak' and 'truly needy'". Without entering the contentious domain of what precisely constitutes populism, it is certainly arguable that these policies have won for both parties electoral victories but equally important they have brought politics into the domain of the common people quite effectively. Despite all these, political decentralisation is quite weak and this in our view represents a conundrum.

The state's success, despite limitations, is due to the following blend: continuous commitment to pro-poor policies, capacity of government institutions and the bureaucracy to administer the policies effectively, and with relatively lower levels of leakages. However, there are tensions. "A tightrope act is implied by the tensions to between the need to maintain fiscal health in public finances and the need to provide benefits in a state where many traditional jobs have dried up and more than five million people are registered as unemployed" (Harriss and Wyatt, 2004).

The welfare programmes in Tamil Nadu are too numerous to list. However a few comments are in order. One of the more important programmes relates to food security which is provided through the PDS. As mentioned above, the state has a universal untargeted PDS. Along with the Noon Meal Scheme, this should be regarded as a flagship programme of the state. Despite this in most analyses, the outlay on PDS does not seem to be included as part of the overall expenditure on the social sector. The Tamil Nadu Human Development Report (HDR) also does not accord specific treatment to this as part of the social safety net provision.

Translation of Social Sector Programmes to Actuality

There are numerous social sector programmes that touch upon the various facets of human life in the state. They look very impressive on paper as programmes. How do they translate into reality? We undertook a quick but not an exhaustive field survey in Palayampudur village of Dharmapuri District. It is not a random selection but a purposive and convenient one. We prepared a detailed ethnographic account of the village for a different research work. Our results that are presented below benefited both from the present assessment and from the earlier ethnographic account. The salient findings of the survey are the following. This part of the study was conducted during 2005-06.

- Both our field inquiry and the earlier more detailed study clearly show that people do entertain substantial expectations from the state. What actually constitutes 'state' in the popular conception is largely context determined but we do not find hard evidence to suggest the state has started to disappear (Natraj and Ganesh Prasad, 2008).

- The local government structure has little to do with the welfare programmes in the state. This is essentially because Tamil Nadu has not encouraged *panchayats* to play a proactive role in development and governance. Yet it is not uncommon for people to take their grievances in relation to welfare programmes to elected *panchayat* representatives. On the whole, the implementation of welfare programmes is through the line departments of the government. One instance where the *panchayat* system was involved was in enhancing enrolment and retention rates in schools but this too was at the initiative of the Collector of the district.
- Awareness about various welfare programmes is not all at the same level among the population. While generic programmes like PDS and noon meal are known among all, awareness about specific programmes like marriage assistance schemes, etc., was much lower.
- People in general did not complain much about undue illegal transaction costs entering into the programme.
- There were complaints about the quality of the services but no outright condemnation. For instance, the quantity of any ration supplied through PDS suffers from underweight or the quality of meal served in the noon meal centre usually has a lower quantum of vegetable and dal. People do complain about these inadequacies but hurry to acknowledge the importance of these programmes in their everyday life particularly in a hostile and insecure livelihood environment in the rural areas due to the prolonged agrarian distress.
- There are leakages in the implementation of the programme at various levels. It is due to the familiar problem of lack of accountability and transparency.

- One of the problems with the PDS is that the Fair Price Shop does not receive the supply it requires. As a consequence, it is reported by our respondents that roughly only about 50 per cent are able to purchase rice. Further, there is the problem of people having more than one card where one is pledged with the local moneylender.
- In innovative programmes like the Cradle Baby Scheme, we find that the hospital staff counsel parent/s who feel unable to bring up a child not to leave it behind but instead take it back home. However we have to add that we have no information as to what happened to the children in 42 cases where the counselling was successful.

Concluding Remarks

The foregoing account of Tamil Nadu's development profile shows that investment and expenditure on the social sector has been one of its leading characteristics. It is fashionable to describe such policies dismissively as 'populist'. A major implication of this is that such policies do not add to an enhancement of the economy's productive capabilities and further that they make people dependent upon largesse from the state. However it is eminently arguable that the state's policy towards the social sector has helped the vulnerable sections navigate the problems posed by the transition that the economy has experienced. For instance, the severity of the crisis in agriculture has been mitigated by the cushions provided by the state. For it should be noted that the indebtedness of agricultural households in Tamil Nadu is high (Rao, 2006). Some other costs have been described in the text. It is therefore not reasonable to argue that Tamil Nadu has encouraged populism in the sense of making people dependent. Of course the policy can be critiqued on various grounds like that the different components are not cohesive and often not properly implemented but these are criticisms that can be laid at the door of all social sector policies in the country. Is Tamil Nadu exceptional or is it an exception in respect of readiness to avail itself of the new environment of the 1990s which afforded an opportunity to embrace a more market friendly, less control-driven framework? In the absence of an analysis of other states in a comparative framework, it is difficult to answer this question definitively. But all in all the following inferences are justifiable. Tamil Nadu has benefited from the blend of industrial entrepreneurship leading to well spread out development of industries which have contributed in significant measure to the state's overall growth. Its status in terms of per capita income is quite high in comparison with the all-India figures. And this has meant that the state can afford to invest in policies and programmes which contribute to welfare. Put another way, the state can manage poverty alleviation programmes not least because in relation to most other states, Tamil Nadu has good coverage for the vulnerable. And this concern on the human development front, far from being detrimental to the overall development and growth of the state appears to be proving beneficial. A most important factor is of course the sociopolitical configuration in the state and the commitment of the two major political parties to the promotion of welfare-oriented policies and programmes.

The Central Government has started, in the past few years, a number of social sector schemes as centrally sponsored initiatives. Prominent among them are MGNREGS, SSA, NRHM, Midday meals scheme, Antyodaya Anna Yojana, etc. It is possible that the Centre was adopting some of the steps taken over the years by Tamil Nadu especially with regard to the midday meal scheme or designing programmes related to health and education.

Tamil Nadu has performed well because of its historical antecedents which have been discussed in some detail in the text. Its political maturity (with occasional lapses) accompanied by economic dynamism and administrative efficiency has resulted in a favourable utilisation of the opportunities presented by the reform process. Above all, we should remember that while the reforms are a central initiative, their implementation is almost entirely a state responsibility. And this, in the final analysis, is what separates the leaders from the 'also ran'.

References

Arora, Balveer (2006). "From Reluctant to Robust Federalism", in Mary John *et al.* (eds.), *Contested Transformations*. Tulika Books.

Dev, S. Mahendra and Jos Mooij (2002). "Social Sector Expenditures in the 1990s", *Economic and Political Weekly*. March 2-8.

Ghosh, Madhusudan (2006). "Economic Growth and Human Development in Indian States", *EPW*, 26 September.

Globalisation and the Indian State Quarterly Newsletter 1(1&2), 2005.

Government of Tamil Nadu (2001). White Paper on State Finances.

———. *An Economic-cum-Functional Classification of the Tamil Nadu Government Budgetary Transactions 2001, 2002, 2003, 2004 and 2005*. Chennai: GoTN.

———. *Achieving Fiscal Correction and Stabilisation 2004-05*. Chennai: GoTN.

———. *Finance and Accounts 2006*. Chennai: GoTN.

Guhan, S. (1992). "State Finances in Tamil Nadu-1960-1990", in Amaresh Bagchi *et al.* (eds.), *State Finances in India*. Vikas.

Harriss, John (2006) *Power Matters*. Oxford.

Harriss, John and Andrew Wyatt (2004). "Politics of Tamil Nadu in the 1990s", *Conference on State Politics in India in the 1990s*, December.

Irschick, Eugene (1986). *Tamil Revivalism in the 1930s*. Crea.

Kaviraj, Sudipto (1996). "Dilemmas of Democratic Development in India", in A. Leftwich (ed.), *Democracy and Development Polity*. Cambridge.

Natraj V.K. and G.S. Ganesh Prasad (2008). "Situating the State in Rural India", *The Hindu*, January 30.

Patnaik, Prabhat (2006). "The Meaning of Contemporary Globalisation", in Mary John *et al.* (eds.), *Contested Transformations*. Tulika Books.

Patnaik, Utsa (2006). "Unleashing the Market: Capitalism, Deflation and Agrarian Crisis in Developing Countries", in Mary John *et al.* (eds.), *Contested Transformations*. Tulika Books.

Saraswathi, S. (1995). *Government, Politicians and People: Linkage Politics of Tamil Nadu*. New Delhi: Manak.

Subba Rao, K.G.K. (2006). "Indebtedness of Cultivator Households", *Economic and Political Weekly*, August 12-18.

Subramanian, Narendar (1999). *Ethnicity and Populist Mobilisation: Political Parties, Citizens and Democracy in South Asia*. Delhi: Oxford.

———. (2002). "Identity Politics and Social Pluralism: Political Sociology and Political Change in Tamil Nadu", *Commonwealth and Comparative Politics* 40: 125-39.

Swaminathan, Padmini *et al.* (2004). "Tamil Nadu's Midday Meal Scheme", *Economic and Political Weekly*, October 30-November 6.

Swamy, A.R. (1998). "Parties, Political Identities and the Absence of Mass Political Violence in South India", in A. Basu and A. Kohli (eds.), *Community Conflicts and the State in India*. New Delhi: Oxford.

Environment

13 State of Environment

K.S. Kavi Kumar

Introduction

Tamil Nadu is at the crossroads in terms of sustainable development. On the one hand, the state has registered impressive economic growth along with significant progress in human development in recent years. It is endowed with rich biodiversity that is protected and conserved through a network of five national parks, 20 wildlife sanctuaries and two biosphere reserves. On the other hand, the state has the highest level of urbanisation in India bringing with it a plethora of associated environmental problems. High level of industrialisation has also brought to the forefront pollution concerns. A long coast line with dense population will always put the region in a vulnerable position with respect to natural hazards and the Tsunami havoc (2004) highlighted this. Thus, natural and anthropogenic factors are putting the environment of Tamil Nadu into a precarious position threatening sustainable development. A few examples of the long list of the state's environmental concerns caused by anthropogenic factors include the following:

- A recent report by the Blacksmith Institute included Ranipet in Tamil Nadu among the top 10 worst polluted places[1] of the world (Blacksmith Institute, 2006). While the State Government has ordered closure of Tamil Nadu Chromates and Chemicals Limited a decade ago, the legacy of the same still continues with no solution still in sight for the safe disposal of 1,500,000 tonnes of solid waste generated by the factory over two decades before its

1. Worst polluted places are selected on the basis of size of affected population, severity of the toxin involved, impact on children's health and development, evidence of a clear pathway of contamination and existing and reliable evidence of health impact. While the top 10 list is not based on a comprehensive database, it may not be prudent to debate the methodology *per se*.

closure. The Blacksmith Institute and Asian Development Bank estimate 3.5 million people as potentially affected people due to ground and surface water contamination.

- Within a radius of 5 km around 68 tanneries operate in Dindigul leading to severe groundwater pollution. Tannery effluents are reported to have left only 16 out of 56 wells in Kamatchipuram village uncontaminated forcing people to walk long distances for water. The water and soil pollution from the tannery effluents has the potential to affect about 450,000 people.

How to take stock of the environment of a region, so that 'effective' actions could be initiated? As the above examples illustrate, the anthropogenic activities causing environmental degradation are legitimate economic activities, and their impact can only be ascertained after a time lag. Moreover the fact that the environmental goods are non-marketed in nature makes the valuation extremely difficult. The 'effective' interventions should ideally be chosen by appropriately weighing the costs of intervention with the benefits of avoided environmental degradation. Given the large gestation periods associated with such detailed analysis, studies aimed at providing policy insights often adopt an indicator-based approach to identify the 'hot spot' areas within a region.

Mukherjee and Kathuria (2006), for instance, compared economic growth in major states of India against the observed environmental degradation. The environmental quality is captured through integration of some 14 indicators and the environmental degradation in each state is assessed in terms of the change in the environmental quality over 1990s. Figure 13.1 shows the trade-off between economic growth and environmental quality across Indian states. The study concludes that Tamil Nadu, along with West Bengal and Karnataka, registered higher economic growth during 1990s at the cost of environmental quality.

Several recent studies used pressure-state-impact-response (PSIR) framework to analyse the state of the environment of a region. In the PSIR framework: (a) pressure indicators as observed now point to future deterioration and reflect historic (non) responses undertaken; (b) indicators as observed now point to future likely impact and reflect historic pressures; (c) impact indicators as observed now point to responses needed and reflect historic state of affairs; and (d) response indicators as observed now point to likely changes in future pressures, restoration of state and amelioration of impact. Some studies also add an additional set of indicators under the head 'driver' and analyse the state of the environment using driver-pressure-state-impact-response (DPSIR) framework (Segnestam, 2002).

Figure 13.1*

Economic Growth versus Environmental Degradation

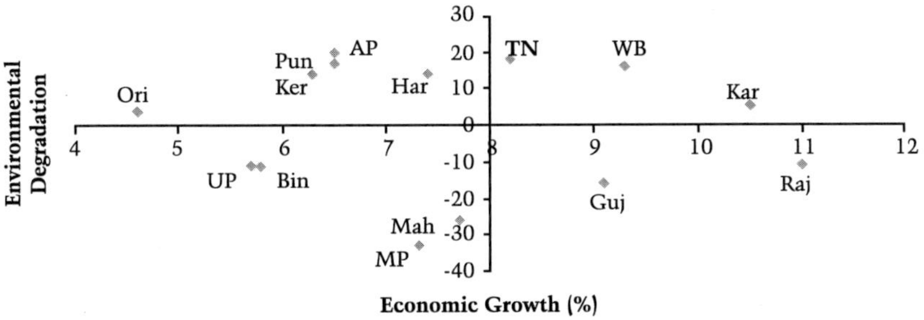

Note: * All figures and tables are based upon compilations of the author from various secondary sources..
Source: Adopted from Mukherjee and Kathuria, 2006.

Most state governments in India have also used, and are using, the PSIR framework while preparing State of Environment (SoE) reports. The recent SoE report prepared by the Department of Environment, Government of Tamil Nadu, has also made an attempt to use the PSIR framework (SoERTN, 2006). However instead of focusing on each environmental medium, a sectoral approach is adopted here. Some of the critical environmental issues concerning the rural and urban environments of Tamil Nadu are discussed by identifying, wherever possible, the pressure, state, impact and response indicators.

The vulnerability of the state to natural climatic hazards such as drought, cyclone and flood is analyzed through vulnerability assessment. Since Tamil Nadu is relatively more vulnerable to drought and cyclone, a few recent studies in this context are reviewed and the transition of the state in the last decade in its vulnerability to these hazards is analysed. For the vulnerability assessment, the conceptualisation suggested by the Intergovernmental Panel on Climate Change is used and key components and indicators representing the three broad dimensions of vulnerability, namely, exposure, sensitivity and adaptive capacity, are aggregated in developing the overall vulnerability index.

Finally, the threats and opportunities for the state in the context of global climate change are discussed. While the potential changes in the rainfall, temperature and sea level could cause significant impact in the climate-sensitive sectors such as agriculture, health and coastal resources, the emerging carbon market through a clean development mechanism also offers opportunities for the state to embark on a sustainable development path.

Rural Environment

Tamil Nadu has witnessed a significant drop in the share of the agricultural sector in the state domestic product in the last 40 years—13 per cent in 2004-05 as against 52 per cent in 1960-61. However, like in other states of India, agriculture continues to be the major employment provider with more than 50 per cent of the workforce still dependent on agriculture for livelihood. Stagnant (or declining) yields of major crops over the years, when seen in the context of rising input use, raise concerns about the sustainability of agriculture. Spread of agriculture through forest clearing, overexploitation of groundwater and other resources and indiscriminate application of fertiliser and pesticides result in the development of some direct linkages between agriculture and the environment. Spread of resource stress and pollution created through rapid industrialisation in rural areas lead to additional linkages between agriculture and the environment. The rural environment is also marked by significant dependence of the population on biofuels for cooking. The resulting indoor air pollution is proving to be a dominant factor contributing to the health burden. These and a few other related issues concerning the rural environment in Tamil Nadu are discussed in the following sections.

Rainfall and population are two of the overall drivers that have a bearing on the agriculture-environment issues discussed here, and it is worth taking stock of these drivers. Tamil Nadu receives limited rainfall from the South-West monsoon, but the North-East monsoon provides rainfall to the coastal districts mainly through cyclonic storms formed in the Bay of Bengal. The North-East monsoon contributes about 47 per cent of rainfall, while the South-West monsoon accounts for about 33 per cent, with the remaining rainfall occurring during the rest of the year. In 4 out of the past 7 years, the state experienced deficient rainfall, with significant variability across the years in terms of the source of rainfall deficiency. There is a wide spatial disparity also in rainfall, with the normal rainfall in interior districts such as Erode, Namakkal, Coimbatore and Karur below 800 mm, and the same in the coastal districts going above 1200 mm. However as Figure 13.2 shows, the spatial variability in rainfall does not stick to this overall pattern in any one year leading to varying drought conditions across the state.

Figure 13.2

Rainfall Anomaly across Districts, 2004-05

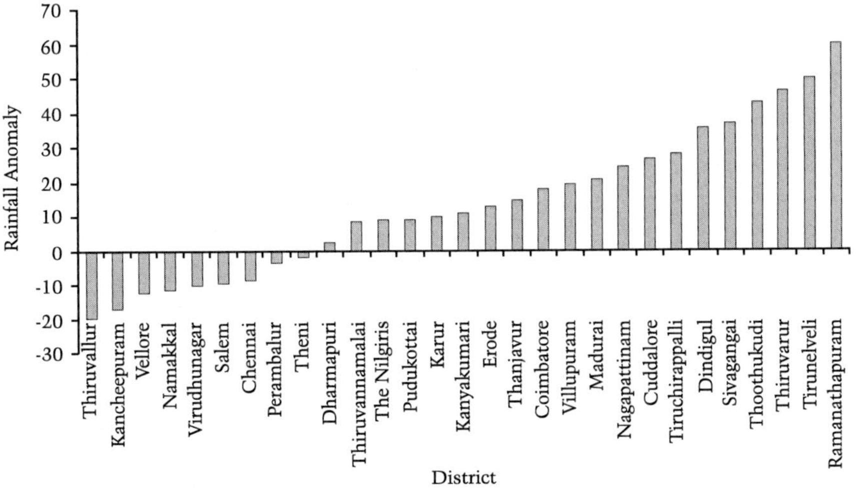

Tamil Nadu is the sixth largest state in India in terms of population. Over the last two decades population growth has declined significantly in the state. The decadal growth of population during 1981-1991 and 1991-2001 is 15.39 and 11.19 per cent respectively and is well below the national average of 21.34 per cent during 1991-2001. However population density in Tamil Nadu is among the highest in the country, with several coastal districts having significantly higher population density than the interior districts in 1991 and 2001 (Figure 13.3).

Figure 13.3

Population Density across Districts, 1991 and 2001

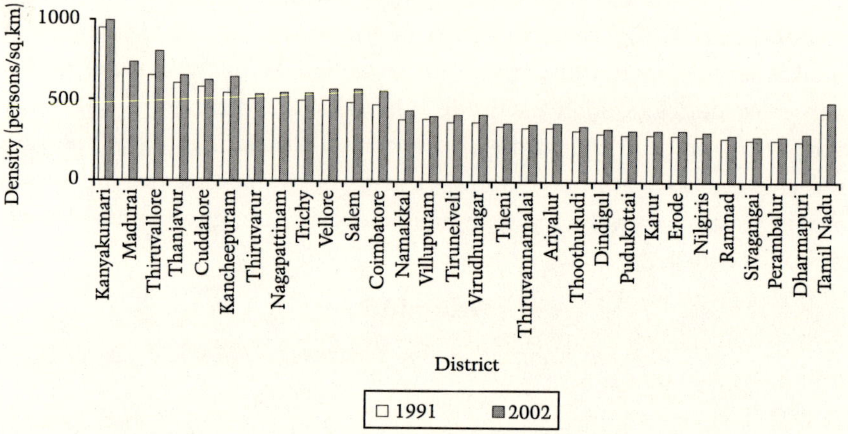

Land Resources

Competing uses of land resource for forestry, agriculture, human settlements and industries has led to significant land degradation in India (Sehgal and Abrol, 1994), and Tamil Nadu is no exception to this all-India trend. Some of the prominent features of land use change in Tamil Nadu include the following:

a) *Increase in fallow lands*: The per capita land availability is a mere 0.19 ha. Yet it is interesting that land is sub-optimally utilised as revealed by increase in fallow lands in the state. In the last two decades, total fallow lands crossed the 20 lakh ha mark accounting for about 15 per cent of total geographic area of the state and almost one-third of the net sown area. An exploration to identify the factors (pressures) contributing towards this state of the natural resource indicates that urbanisation and labour scarcity (manifested through higher wages) are among the principal causes for the sub-optimal utilisation of land. This has led to shift in the cropping pattern in several pockets of the state with less labour-intensive but more water-intensive crops such as coconut and sugarcane replacing the more conventional crops. For instance, the area under coconut has increased by as much as 450 per cent in the last 40 years, while area under sugarcane registered a 300 per cent increase during the same period. Possible response strategies to arrest increase in fallow lands include efforts to increase mechanisation of labour-intensive activities.

b) *Decline in soil fertility*: Soils need both major and minor nutrients for retaining fertility. While the major nutrients are typically supplied through inorganic fertilisers, the minor nutrients could be replenished through organic manure. One of the main sources of organic manure is the livestock grazing the fields. However, the scarcity of labour has diverted the workforce engaged in livestock grazing to other profitable endeavours resulting in decreasing supply of organic manure to the soil. For instance in Tamil Nadu, the organic manure supplied is about 200 lakh tonne as against a normal requirement of about 500 lakh tonne. This has resulted in the addition of only 0.25 lakh tonnes of micro nutrients to the soils as against the requirement of about 2 lakh tonnes. While excess supply of fertilisers (and pesticides) is a cause of worry from the pollution perspective,[2] lower supply of fertiliser is likely to result in mining of soil nutrients. Several farm level soil studies conducted by the Tamil Nadu Agricultural University have established this fact. Nutrient mining is likely to result in lower soil productivity and hence contribute to crop yield decline.

Water Resources

There are 17 major river basins in the state with 61 reservoirs and about 41,948 tanks (SoERTN, 2006). Despite rich resource availability, the per capita water availability in the state at 900 cubic meters a year is way below the national average of 2200 cubic meters a year. Agriculture continues to be the single largest user (75 per cent) of available water resources with increasing demands from both domestic and industrial sectors. Both quantity and quality issues relating to this resource are of environmental concern in the state.

---

2. See the following for further discussion of this aspect.

Groundwater Exploitation

The Institute of Water Studies has prepared a water resource plan of Tamil Nadu for the period 1994-2044. Of the annual water potential of 46,540 million cubic meters (MCM), surface flows account for about half. Most of the surface water has already been tapped, primarily for irrigation. About 24 lakh ha are irrigated by surface water through major, medium and minor schemes. The utilisation of surface water for irrigation is about 90 per cent. Despite need for bringing more area under surface irrigation, inadequate and improper maintenance of irrigation facilities coupled with inefficient use of irrigation water (both in terms of quantum and timing of application) are widely considered limiting factors. Also, poor drainage in several irrigation facilities is considered to be responsible for continuation of water-intensive paddy which can withstand water stagnation, even during water scarce conditions.

On the other hand, the utilisable groundwater recharge in Tamil Nadu is 22,423 MCM. The utilisation expressed as net groundwater draft of 13,558 MCM has increased from about 60 per cent of the available recharge in 1993 to 64 per cent in 2003. While much of the groundwater is used for drinking purposes—for instance, in 2001 about 80 per cent of annual drinking water demand was met through groundwater, increasingly groundwater is also tapped for irrigation. The state of groundwater conditions in Coimbatore district exemplifies the situation that prevails over most parts of the state. Between 1960-61 and 2004-05, the number of wells tapping groundwater has doubled from about 1.09 lakh to 2.42 lakh. Such indiscriminate tapping fuelled by free power supply for irrigation pump sets has also resulted in a significant number of 'failed' wells. According to Central Groundwater Board statistics, the number of districts recording more than 20 cm fall in the groundwater table per year has increased from 15 during 1980-2000 to 27 during 1995-2004. Figure 13.4 shows district-wise groundwater development and highlights the seriousness of overexploitation in some areas that is not evident from the state-level average data.

One of the immediate manifestations of groundwater exploitation can be perceived in the availability of drinking water. Over the period 1998-2003, the percentage of safe blocks has declined from 35.6 to 25.2

Figure 13.4

District-wise Groundwater Development, 2001

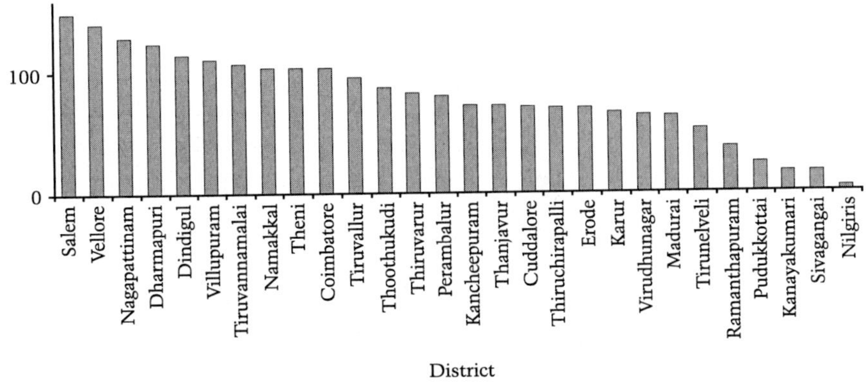

while the semi-critical blocks have gone up by a similar percentage (see Table 13.1). Overexploitation has already occurred in more than a third of the blocks while eight blocks have turned saline. The water level data reveal that the depth of the wells ranges from an average of 0.93 meters in Pudukottai district to 43.43 meters in Erode.

Table 13.1

Block-wise Groundwater Status in Tamil Nadu, 1998 to 2003

Status	*No. of Blocks as on Jan. 1998*	*Percentage*	*No. of Blocks as on Jan. 2003*	*Percentage*
Safe	137	35.6	97	25.2
Semi-critical	70	18.2	105	27.3
Critical	35	9.1	37	9.6
Overexploited	135	35.0	138	35.8
Saline	8	2.1	8	2.1
Total	385	100	385	100

Source: Central Groundwater Board, 2003.

Vaidyanathan (2006) points out yet another ramification of the groundwater exploitation for irrigation purposes. He argues that since digging borewells is a typically capital-intensive activity, it is mainly the rich farmers who have had capacity to avail themselves of the option, leaving the poor farmers to depend on shallow wells. Thus, groundwater exploitation could have long-term socioeconomic implications in terms of increasing social tensions.

Deterioration of Water Quality

Deterioration of groundwater quality is a major concern. According to an analysis carried out by the Tamil Nadu Water Supply and Sewerage Board in 2000-01, non-potable samples were in excess of 20 per cent in 20 out of the 29 districts in the state. Water contamination is mainly due to high levels of total dissolved solids, iron, fluoride and nitrate.

More than 66 per cent of the samples tested in Ramanathapuram district turned out to be non-potable. Besides the natural factors such as saline aquifer and coastal influence, the samples reported high total dissolved solids (TDS) possibly due to overexploitation of groundwater and indiscriminate disposal of domestic waste water. Dependence on untreated rainwater for drinking purpose is making people in Ramanathapuram district vulnerable to water borne diseases.

Nineteen out of 29 districts were affected by fluoride contamination. Dharmapuri, Salem and Erode were the most severely affected districts. Western districts were also affected by nitrate. Among other things, the pollution from tanneries in the Palar Basin contributes towards groundwater contamination in these districts. Agriculture also contributes towards groundwater contamination through excessive dependence on chemical fertilisers and pesticides. For instance, total chemical fertiliser consumption in the state has increased from 7.43 lakh tonnes in 2002-03 to 9.52 lakh tonnes in 2004-05. Figure 13.5 shows the disparity across districts in terms of total fertiliser consumption in 2002. All the three pollutants could cause significant health burden—fluoride pollution, for instance, could lead to ageing, cancer and arteriosclerosis; continuous exposure to TDS could result in kidney stones.

Indoor Air Pollution

Large numbers in rural India continue to depend on biofuels for cooking. A number of inherent disadvantages of the traditional fuels are widely reported, and these include arduous and time-consuming nature of fuel collection, difficult to control combustion process and inefficient heat

Figure 13.5

Chemical Fertiliser Consumption across Districts, 2002

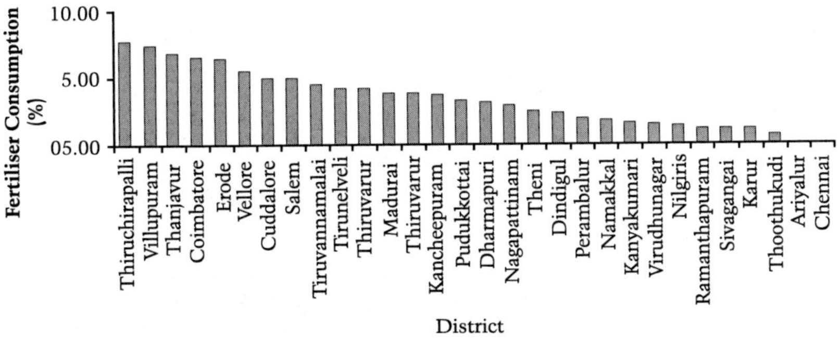

exchange. For instance, cooking with firewood on open fire captures only 15 per cent of thermal energy, while on the other hand, about 60 per cent of energy is captured while cooking with liquid petroleum gas (LPG). Even more important is the serious health threat that traditional fuels pose for the persons involved in cooking. Cooking with biofuels on an open fire within a confined space can lead to acute respiratory problems, particularly for women and children. Studies in India show that as many as 500,000 premature deaths annually in children under five and women could be attributable to the indoor pollution caused by the use of biofuels (Smith, 1998).

While there is some evidence to suggest that dependence on biofuels is declining over time, Viswanathan and Kumar (2005) argue that several parts of rural India still widely use these 'dirty' fuels. Using household level data from the National Sample Survey (NSS) rounds corresponding to the years 1983, 1993-94 and 1999-2000, they analyse expenditure shares of 'clean' and 'dirty' fuels across decile groups. The 'clean' fuels include kerosene, gobar gas and LPG, whereas the 'dirty' fuels include firewood, coal, dung and coke. Figure 13.6 shows the expenditure shares of 'clean' and 'dirty' fuels in rural and urban areas of Tamil Nadu.

Parikh and Laxmi (2000) based on detailed personal exposure studies conducted across 500 households argue that personal exposure to respirable dust ranged from around 70 mg/m^3 in houses using 'clean' fuels to around 2000 mg/m³ in houses using 'dirty' fuels. Such high exposure could have adverse health impact. Possible response strategies to enable shift towards cleaner fuels especially in rural areas include among other things promotion of improved stoves and removal of urban bias in supply of kerosene. Viswanathan and Kumar (2005) highlight pro-rich, pro-urban bias in kerosene supply through PDS.

Figure 13.6

Expenditure Shares of 'Clean' and 'Dirty' Fuels

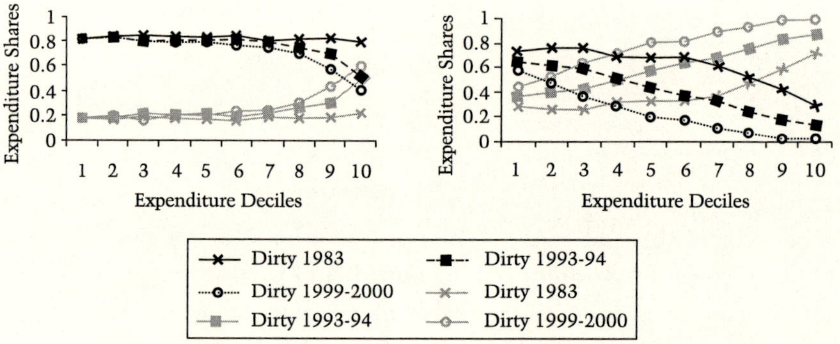

Source: Viswanathan and Kumar, 2005.

Industrial Pollution

More than 3000 industrial units in Tamil Nadu are classified under 'red' category of high pollution potential. The pollution released by tanneries located in Vellore, Kancheepuram, Dindigul and Erode Districts have received widespread attention. The Palar Basin bore the brunt of the pollution from these tanneries. Similarly the bleaching and dyeing units of the textile industries in Tiruppur, Erode and Karur have caused significant damage in the Noyyal river basin.

The impact of tannery pollution on agricultural land was analysed by the Loss of Ecology Authority, Government of India. About 36,000 individuals were identified by the Authority for paying compensation to the tune of ₹ 35 crore by the tanneries. Similarly the impact of pollution from textile units on agricultural production was analysed through several studies at the Madras School of Economics and significant losses were reported.

Following strict directives from the High Court that polluting industries should not release their treated effluent into the waterways, it has become somewhat common practice to use the treated and semi-treated water for irrigation purposes. This has resulted in significant contamination of groundwater and not only in loss to agricultural output but also in rendering the groundwater unsuitable for drinking (Mukherjee and Nelliyat, 2006). Amarnath and Krishnamoorthy (2001) have estimated the loss in yield of paddy and sugarcane crops in Vellore district and attributed more than 90 per cent of the loss to water pollution.

Sand Mining

Besides direct pollution effects, the agricultural lands are also affected by the sand quarrying for construction activities and mining of top soil among other things for brick manufacture. Sand quarrying has received particularly wide attention in both river beds and coastal areas. The boom in construction activities in the urban areas appears to be triggering the indiscriminate mining of sand. Despite the Government Order in 2002 regulating sand mining, the activity is continuing in several river basins. The sand mining in river basins is considered responsible for impairment of water flow, bed erosion, collapse of banks and mix-up of sewerage flows with river water. In coastal areas, unscientific methods of sand mining are considered responsible for loss of valuable silicon sand. It also leads to conflict of interest between sand miners and the fishing community. The high-level committee constituted by the Government of Tamil Nadu has recommended a 'single' agency to oversee the issuance of permits for sand mining as against the current practice involving several departments (e.g., geology and mining, revenue and public works).

Pressure from urbanisation has not only resulted in competition for scarce resources like land and water but also affected their quality. For instance, increasing demand for bricks has resulted in removal of topsoil in the fertile agricultural lands prompting the farmers to apply chemical fertilisers in an attempt to replenish the loss of nutrient. Farm level studies have indicated that removal of topsoil has resulted in loss of major nutrients like phosphorous (20%) and nitrogen (35%), along with micro nutrients. However as discussed earlier in the section Land Resources, it is often difficult to replenish the loss of micro nutrients and as a result, the productivity loss due to topsoil removal is almost permanent. Kathuria (2005) quantifies the implications of loss of topsoil for agricultural productivity and estimates the loss to be about ₹ 3250 per acre. (The discussion on sand mining may be profitably read along with Neelakantan's paper in this volume on the Amaravati basin: Editors.)

Urban Environment

Tamil Nadu leads the rest of the country in urbanisation (2001 census). The extent of urbanisation is as much as 44 per cent with 2.72 crores out of the total population of 6.21 crore living in urban areas. Compared to 1991 census, Tamil Nadu catapulted to the first place in 2001, outperforming Maharashtra and Gujarat, mainly due to the Nagar Palika Act of 1994 wherein all the town *panchayats* were brought under the category of statutory towns whether they satisfy the demographic norms of being urban or not. Figure 13.7 shows the extent of urbanisation across districts in Tamil Nadu. Kancheepuram, Theni, Thiruvallur, Madurai, Kanniyakumari and Coimbatore have shown significant jump in the urbanisation levels bringing with it a plethora of environmental problems.

Figure 13.7

Urbanisation across Districts of Tamil Nadu, 2001

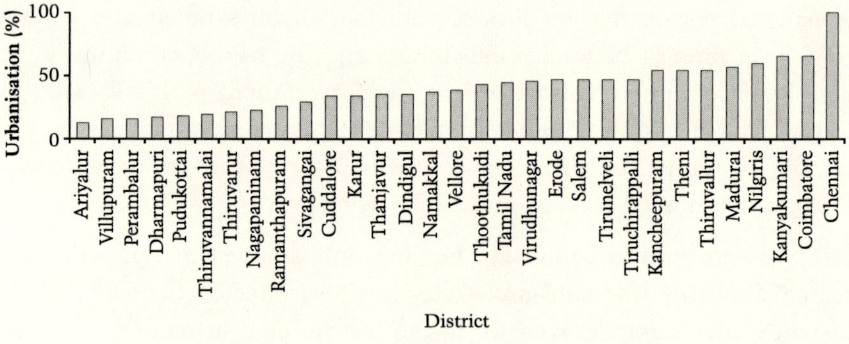

Despite this definitional controversy surrounding the level of urbanisation, the pressure created by the urban population on the environment resource is ever increasing. The structure of economic activity is also fast changing towards 'urban' with the role being played by industry and service sectors both in terms of value added and employment potential. The urban population through its increasing use of land and water resources puts significant pressure on the environment. Due to concentration of wastes generated in the urban systems, the environmental damage caused by urban activities is often serious. Air pollution from vehicles and industries, water pollution from industries, solid waste from households and conflict between peri-urban and urban dwellers for scarce resources like water are some of the fast emerging concerns.

Vehicular Pollution

One of the immediate manifestation of urbanisation can be seen in terms of increase in the vehicular population. The number of motor vehicles has increased in Tamil Nadu from 46.0 lakh in 1999-2000 to 67.5 lakh in 2003-04. Major cities like Chennai, Coimbatore, Salem, Madurai, Tiruchirapalli and Tirunelveli accounted for almost half of the total vehicles, and Chennai itself has a quarter of all the registered vehicles in the state. The registered vehicular population has increased more than twofold during the year 1996-2004. Figure 13.8 records distribution of registered vehicles across districts in the year 2001 and shows relatively uniform distribution across districts excluding Chennai and Coimbatore.

Figure 13.8

Distribution of Registered Vehicles across Districts, 2001

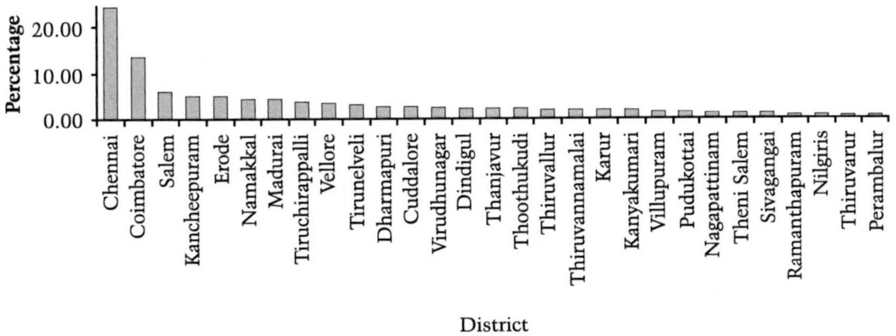

The ambient levels of major pollutants like suspended particulate matter, respirable suspended particulate matter, oxides of nitrogen and sulphur are regularly monitored in several major cities but concentration levels of toxic chemicals like benzene and lead are not monitored. Among the monitored pollutants, SPM (suspended particulate matter) and RSPM (respirable suspended particulate matter) levels are often found to be in excess of the standard in cities like Chennai and Madurai mainly due to increased vehicular population. Epidemiological studies have shown serious health effects due to this pollution and have advocated regular monitoring of toxics such as lead and benzene.

Industrial Pollution

Industrial activity in the state has traditionally been among the top in India and it has occupied the top position among the major states of India in recent years. Thermal power plants are among the most pollution-intensive industries and there are five thermal power stations in the state at Ennore, North Chennai, Mettur, Neyveli and Tuticorin. Table 13.2 shows the level and intensity of emissions from these five power plants. There is wide divergence between the five plants indicating significant potential for efficiency improvements. While the ambient levels of pollution in several parts of the state are below the standard, the health problems caused by the prevailing pollution load are still a cause for worry. It may be noted that the standards are typically set in such a way that they trade-off the marginal cost of abatement with the marginal damage cost. Hence compliance with

Table 13.2

Thermal Power Plant Emissions in Tamil Nadu

Emissions	*Ennore*	*Mettur*	*Neyveli*	*North Chennai*	*Tuticorin*
CO_2 Emission per day (thousand tons)	4282	19635	10710	14994	23919
CO_2 Emission (kg/KWH)	12.852	10.2812	8.711	10.282	10.139
SO_2 Emission per day (thousand tons)	0.0304	0.1304	0.2347	0.0999	0.1565
SO_2 Emission (kg/KWH)	0.0086	0.005	0.019	0.0069	0.0066
HO Emission per day (thousand tons)	0.039	0.168	0.087	0.116	0.205
NO Emission (kg/KWH)	0.0101	0.0081	0.0065	0.0082	0.0078
Soot Emission per day (thousand tons)	0.00027	0.00123	0.00068	0.00093	0.00139
Soot Emission (kg/KWH)	0.000077	0.000062	0.000054	0.000063	0.000061
SPM Emission per day (thousand tons)	0.01	0.04	0.007	0.03	0.05
SPM Emission (kg/KWH)	0.003	0.002	0.0006	0.002	0.002

the standards need not necessarily imply absence of social damage cost imposed by the polluting unit.

Another feature of the industrial pollution that is gaining increasing attention in the recent past is hazardous waste. As pointed out in the beginning of this chapter, Tamil Nadu has a significant presence of hazardous-waste-generating units. While Coimbatore and Erode Districts have a large number of hazardous-waste-generating units, Thoothukudi and Thiruvallur Districts contribute a large share of the waste generated. Figure 13.9 shows the distribution of generating units and waste generated across districts of Tamil Nadu.

Figure 13.9

Distribution of Hazardous Waste and Generating Units across Districts

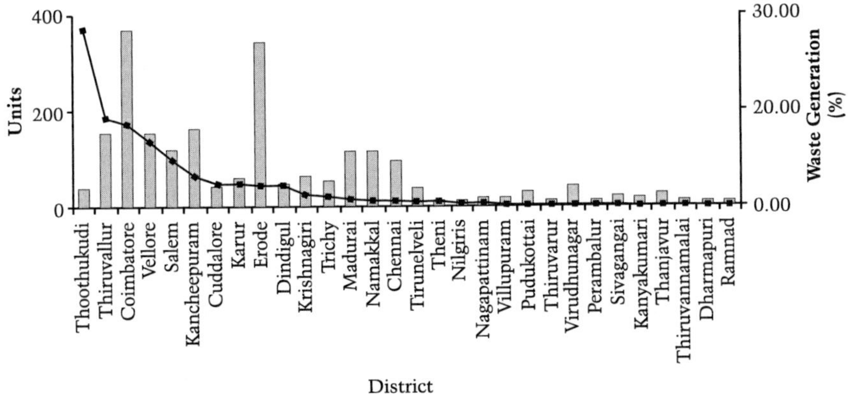

Another feature of industrial activity in Tamil Nadu is the presence of several small-scale units. In 2002-03, the number of registered small-scale industries in Tamil Nadu stood at 4.74 lakh, with dense concentration in a few pockets. Absence of pollution control measures is a typical feature of small-scale industries. This when coupled with difficulty in monitoring the large number of units makes regulation virtually impossible in the small-scale sector. Some of the innovative instruments such as common effluent treatment plants used in the Tiruppur area for controlling pollution from the tanneries have given mixed results so far.

Solid Waste Management

Improper management of solid waste has become a feature of urban areas in most developing countries and cities in Tamil Nadu are no exception. Per-capita generation of waste is higher in urban areas and the high density results in large quantities of waste that need to be collected and disposed of properly. Table 13.3 provides an estimate of the solid waste generated in tonnes per day in the six corporations of Tamil Nadu.

Table 13.3

Solid Waste in Major Cities of Tamil Nadu

Sl. No.	*City*	*Quantity (tonnes/day)*
1.	Chennai	3,500
2.	Coimbatore	710
3.	Madurai	711
4.	Tiruchi	408
5.	Salem	330
6.	Tirunelveli	210

Source: SoERTN (2006).

While collection is adequate in most of the cities, disposal can at best be described as inadequate. In most cities, the solid waste is disposed of in open sites leading to inefficient utilisation of scarce land resource. Further open disposal can result in loss of soil productivity and amenity loss. Other disposal options such as incineration while being capital intensive could result in unwanted gaseous emissions leading to health problems in the neighbourhood of the disposal site. The Municipal Solid Waste Rules of 2000 prescribe composting of organic waste and disposal of the inerts/ residuals in a sanitary landfill. However, none of the cities in Tamil Nadu including Chennai have a sanitary landfill.

In the midst of growing despair on solid waste management, the case of Namakkal stands tall and provides optimism that if properly addressed with people's involvement, these issues can be solved with considerable ease. Namakkal is a small district headquarter town situated on the main highway from Salem to Dindigul. It is the first municipality in the country involved in privatisation of all components in solid waste management. By institutionalisation of door-to-door collection with segregation at source, manufacturing of vermi-compost from organic waste and sale of recyclable inorganic waste, Namakkal has the distinction of becoming the only zero-garbage town in the country. Some of the main features of solid waste management in Namakkal include the following:

- Door-to-door collection with segregation at collection point;
- Levy of service charges on heavy polluters such as hotels and commercial complexes;
- Manufacture of vermi-compost from organic waste through voluntary organisations and private agencies on BOT (build-operate transfer) basis and selling inorganic recyclable garbage.

Besides household solid waste and hazardous waste, two emerging waste categories in the urban areas include biomedical waste and electronic waste. The biomedical waste in Tamil Nadu is handled in an unscientific manner at present, with the municipal solid waste and biomedical waste often carried and disposed of together. Given the high risk for the sanitary workers and residents around the disposal site, it is essential that the public and private hospitals strictly adhere to the regulations laid down by the Ministry of Environment and Forests regarding biomedical waste.

Water Conflicts

Several areas surrounding the urban regions (peri-urban areas) often face the brunt of urban environmental problems in terms of providing scarce resources like water to the urban areas and also absorbing considerable amounts of effluent from the cities. Palar river basin provides an interesting case for conflicts that arise between urban, peri-urban and rural areas in the context of water. In the upper Palar basin, the conflict is between agricultural, industrial and domestic users of water, whereas in the lower basin, it is between urban domestic users and farmers. While the tannery pollution in the upper Palar basin area and the resulting impact on agriculture are well documented and discussed (see section Industrial Pollution above), the case of lower Palar basin deserves special mention in the context of the growing rural-urban divide.

An estimated 40 mld of water is transported from the peri-urban areas to cities drawing groundwater from the river bed aquifer. The peri-urban dwellers lured by short-term gains enter into the water market potentially at the cost of their future, as continuous pumping of water can cause permanent damage to the ecology of the area. For even those who wish to retain water for long-term use, there is little hope as the water in the aquifer is like a public good and hence carries with it the perils of public goods. For instance, non-participation in the water trade by an individual may not provide the intended benefits as her neighbours continue to exploit the resource for short-term gains. Sand mining also adds to the problems in the river bed. The existing institutional mechanisms are inadequate to handle the situation and a small section of 'new' beneficiaries in the peri-urban areas (such as the water sellers) exercise considerable power with relatively short-term vision.

Thus the conflict of interest in the use of water presents a changing picture of transportation of urban environmental problems into peri-urban areas, demanding urgent policy intervention.

Vulnerability to Climate Extremes

In the context of climate change, several studies in the recent past focused on the notion of vulnerability, without necessarily using the same conceptualisation. Janssen *et al.* (2005) note that in the past decades, more than 700 articles in the global change literature have used the term vulnerability as a key word. The natural hazard literature uses the term vulnerability to denote the risk faced by regions to extreme natural events. In the context of Tamil Nadu, these events include cyclones and drought. Several studies analysed the vulnerability of coastal districts in India to cyclones (see Kumar and Tholkappian, 2006; Patnaik and Narayanan, 2005; Hossain and Singh, 2002) and noted the high vulnerability of several coastal districts of Tamil Nadu to cyclonic storms.

Hossain and Singh (2002) used the geographical information system approach to categorise the coastal areas across India into low, moderate, high and extreme vulnerable categories based on their exposure to cyclonic storms. Table 13.4 shows the summary statistics of their analysis for Tamil Nadu. A large proportion of the coastal population in the state is either highly or extremely vulnerable and the state also constitutes a large percentage of India's total vulnerable population.

Table 13.4

Vulnerability to Cyclonic Storms: Summary Statistics

Vulnerability Level	*Percentage of State Coastal Population*	*Percentage of All India Vulnerable Population*
Moderate	4.5	1.15
High	71.1	16.6
Extremely	24.4	28.9

Source: Hossain and Singh (2002).

Kumar and Tholkappian (2006) in a recent study analysed district level vulnerability to cyclonic storms in Tamil Nadu. For the purpose of index calculation, vulnerability is hypothesised to be a function of *impact* on the district, and *resistance* and *resilience* of the district in responding to the impact it experiences. District-specific data on the following parameters (which are considered to influence vulnerability) is assembled.

- *Demographic*: (a) Population density based on 2001 census; (b) annual growth rate of population.
- *Physical*: (a) Coast length; (b) Insularity (defined as ratio of coastal length to the area of the district); (c) frequency of cyclones (weighted to account for cyclones of different intensities) based on historical data; (d) probable maximum surge height; (e) area at risk of inundation due to sea level rise; (f) vulnerable houses—both at the risk of damage and collapse (based on 1991 census).
- *Economic*: (a) Agricultural dependency (expressed in terms of population dependent on agriculture and other primary sectors); (b) income.
- *Social*: Literacy rate.

While most of the above indicators capture the *impact* characteristic of vulnerability, the indicators listed under the heading 'Economic' and 'Social' indicate the ability of districts to *resist* and *bounce back*. Table 13.5 shows the assembled district-specific data on all the above parameters. It may be noted that some of the districts are combined

Table 13.5

Characteristics of Coastal Districts in Tamil Nadu

Sl no.	District	Population 2001	Popn. Growth Rate 1991-2001	Popn. Density 2001	Literate 2001	Coast Length (km)[1]	Agri. Labour Force 1991	Share of Agri. in Value Added	Income[2]	Cyclone Freq.[3]	PMSH[4]	No. of Vulnerable Houses[5]	
												Damaged	Destroyed
1	Chengalpattu	5608905	20.53	714	68	152.9	51.20	11.58	258011	15	3	100471	366459
2	Kanyakumari	1669804	4.34	992	79	65	58.82	10.74	73601	2	2.7	25134	0
3	Madras	4216316	9.76	24231	73	17	0.94	0.00	376698	15	5.45	86650	91635
4	Ramanathapuram	1209593	5.73	280	64	186.2	74.21	40.48	48915	3	11	22111	1725
5	South Arcot	5224367	7.09	480	60	79.4	80.16	37.32	153419	5	3	94603	219049
6	Thanjavur	6309967	7.70	488	67	225.9	73.03	30.49	224617	13	7	259674	62062
7	Tirunelveli	4366995	10.34	382	70	163.3	55.64	17.95	216787	2	6	56973	0

Notes: 1. Calculated using GIS.

2. Estimated using state level gross domestic product (GDP).

3. Based on data from India Meteorological Department.

4. Probable Max Surge Height; from Vulnerability Atlas (1997).

5. Vulnerability Atlas (1997).

for data consistency.[3] The composite index is calculated by taking the average of all the standardised observations of each district over all the components. The averaging procedure implies that equal weights are assigned to each component. The procedure is similar to that followed in the construction of the Human Development Index by the United Nations Development Programme (UNDP). The index computations are made for a range of combinations of the parameters listed above. Table 13.6 shows the vulnerability index and vulnerability rank (across all the coastal districts in India). The vulnerability rankings are relatively robust independent of the specification and the results highlight significant disparity across coastal regions in terms of their vulnerability to cyclones.

Table 13.6

Vulnerability to Cyclonic Storms: Tamil Nadu Districts

Sl. No.	*District*	*V1*	*V1 Rank*	*V2*	*V2 Rank*	*V3*	*V3 Rank*
1	Chengalpattu	0.4063	7	0.3802	8	0.4533	7
2	Kanyakumari	0.2894	26	0.2611	28	0.3645	21
3	Madras	0.5349	4	0.5042	4	0.5578	4
4	Ramanathapuram	0.3853	11	0.3443	13	0.4518	8
5	South Arcot	0.2942	22	0.2719	21	0.3622	23
6	Thanjavur	0.3957	8	0.3680	9	0.4466	9
7	Tirunelveli	0.2760	32	0.2609	29	0.3408	37

Note: V1 is estimated using insularity, population density, population growth, population in agriculture, literate population, vulnerable houses (total), PMSH and cyclone frequency as indicators; V2 and V3 are estimated using all the indicators used in the computation of V1 and income as vulnerability indicator and resilience indicator, respectively.

The way indicators are combined together in the above-mentioned studies is somewhat arbitrary. In order to conceptualise vulnerability of an entity as a function of its exposure, sensitivity and adaptive capacity (McCarthy *et al.*, 2001), the indicators capturing these three dimensions can be developed in a more structured manner. The dimensions can be visualised along several components and each component in turn can be represented by several indicators. For instance, the indicators in the context of vulnerability to drought can be understood as follows:

3. Pudukottai District is combined with Thanjavur District and Chidambaranar District with Tirunelveli-Kattabomman District.

- Exposure is better understood in terms of the components such as (i) the characteristics of the stimulus (namely drought); (ii) exposed population (e.g., agricultural farmers); and (iii) exposed activity (e.g., agricultural activity). The components can then be measured in terms of
    - o Characteristics of the stimulus: (a) percentage area under stress—that is, say, where the ratio of water withdrawal to water availability exceeds a norm, and (b) rainfall deviation from the normal.
    - o Exposed population: (a) rural population density and (b) percentage of population engaged in farming activity (i.e., cultivators and agricultural labourers).
    - o Exposed activity: (a) percentage of rainfed agriculture and (b) size of agricultural sector (i.e., percentage of GDP).
- Sensitivity can be described in terms of socioeconomic features of the exposed population and characteristics of the exposed activity. Thus sensitivity is better understood in terms of components such as (i) socioeconomic characteristics; (ii) characteristics of existing technology; and (iii) characteristics of activity. Note that the sensitivity (which is the effect of stresses) is captured through its effect on entity and its present practice of water use. The components can then be measured in terms of
    - o Socioeconomic characteristics: (a) income/household expenditure; (b) inequality coefficient (say, Gini coefficient); and (c) percentage of socially (and/or economically) backward population in the total population.
    - o Characteristics of existing technology: (a) fertiliser (total of N+P+K) use per hectare; (b) pesticide use per hectare; and (c) number of tractors per hectare.
    - o Characteristics of activity: (a) percentage of high-yielding variety (HYV) crop area in net sown area and (b) percentage of commercial crop area in net sown area.
- Adaptive Capacity can be described in terms of the ability of the exposed population to protect themselves, physical access to

appropriate coping measures as well as entity's ability to avail itself of such options. Thus adaptive capacity is best understood in terms of components such as (i) human capacity; (ii) governance; and (iii) coping options. The components can then be measured in terms of

- Human capacity: (a) percentage of literate population in the total exposed population; (b) percentage of expenditure on education in total expenditure in the region; and (c) number of schools per 100 sq km.
- Governance: (a) tax revenue as percentage of total GDP of the region; (b) research and development expenditure in agriculture as percentage of GDP of the region; (c) number of agricultural extension service centres per 100 sq km; and (d) expenditure on drought management programmes as percentage of total expenditure of the region.
- Coping options: (a) percentage of rural labour force in non-agricultural sector and (b) agricultural loans disbursed as percentage of total savings of the region.

The functional relationships between various measures and vulnerability can be described as follows. To start with, vulnerability increases with exposure and sensitivity, and declines with improvements in adaptive capacity. Exposure itself increases with increase in stress, exposed population and exposed activity. In terms of the measures, one can argue that as probability of drought and rainfall anomaly increases, the stress itself intensifies. Similarly with increases in workforce dependent on agriculture and rural population, the exposed population to the stress increases. As agricultural dependency of the economy increases along with increase in rainfed agriculture, the activity affected by the stress (namely, agriculture) increases. Sensitivity increases as socioeconomic characteristics deteriorate and decreases as better technology is used for agriculture and more commercialisation takes place. Socioeconomic characteristics improve with increase in income, but decline with increase in inequality. Technology used in agriculture can be hypothesised to improve with higher utilisation of fertilisers, pesticides[4] and tractors. Increasing share of fruits and vegetables and total oilseeds in the agricultural produce indicates greater commercialisation of agriculture. Adaptive capacity increases with improvements in human capacity, capacity of government and greater access to coping options. Human capacity in turn increases with improvement in literacy rates and higher spending on education by the state. Increasing tax revenue indicates growing capacity of the Government to handle stresses. Increase in percentage of labour force in household industries indicates better access to coping options for the population that is otherwise dependent on agriculture.

Using data for 16 states in India for two time points, 1990-91 and 1999-2000, Kumar (2006) assessed vulnerability to extreme climate events. Figure 10 shows the changing profile of vulnerability of Tamil Nadu to drought and cyclones across the time periods along with the corresponding changes in the key dimensions of vulnerability—namely, exposure, sensitivity and adaptive capacity.

The tsunami that devastated the costal districts of Tamil Nadu in December 2004 further highlighted the vulnerability of the state to climate extremes. While the magnitude of the physical impacts was staggering—7995 deaths, 69,1000 people affected, 2487 ha area affected and 9,1037 dwelling units affected—the estimated economic losses highlighted the long-term consequences of such an event. The estimated total damages and losses (including both direct and indirect effects) in the state were US$ 815 million (Asian Development Bank, United Nations and World Bank, 2005). The study further highlighted that about 44 per cent of the total damages and losses could be attributed to loss in livelihood, indicating the long-term nature of the impacts.

Global climate change that is likely to manifest itself in terms of increase in temperature, rise in sea levels and increase in frequency and intensity of extreme climate events is expected to result in similar kinds of risks in Tamil Nadu, especially on the coast. While there are no recent

4 Higher use of pesticides need not imply better technology as intensive pesticide use has adverse environmental implications. In fact data show that over the 1990s, most states showed sharp decline in pesticide consumption per hectare possibly due to environmental pressures. Given this in the final analysis, pesticide consumption is not included as an indicator of technology.

Figure 13.10

Vulnerability to Drought and Cyclone in Tamil Nadu: 1990-91 and 1999-2000

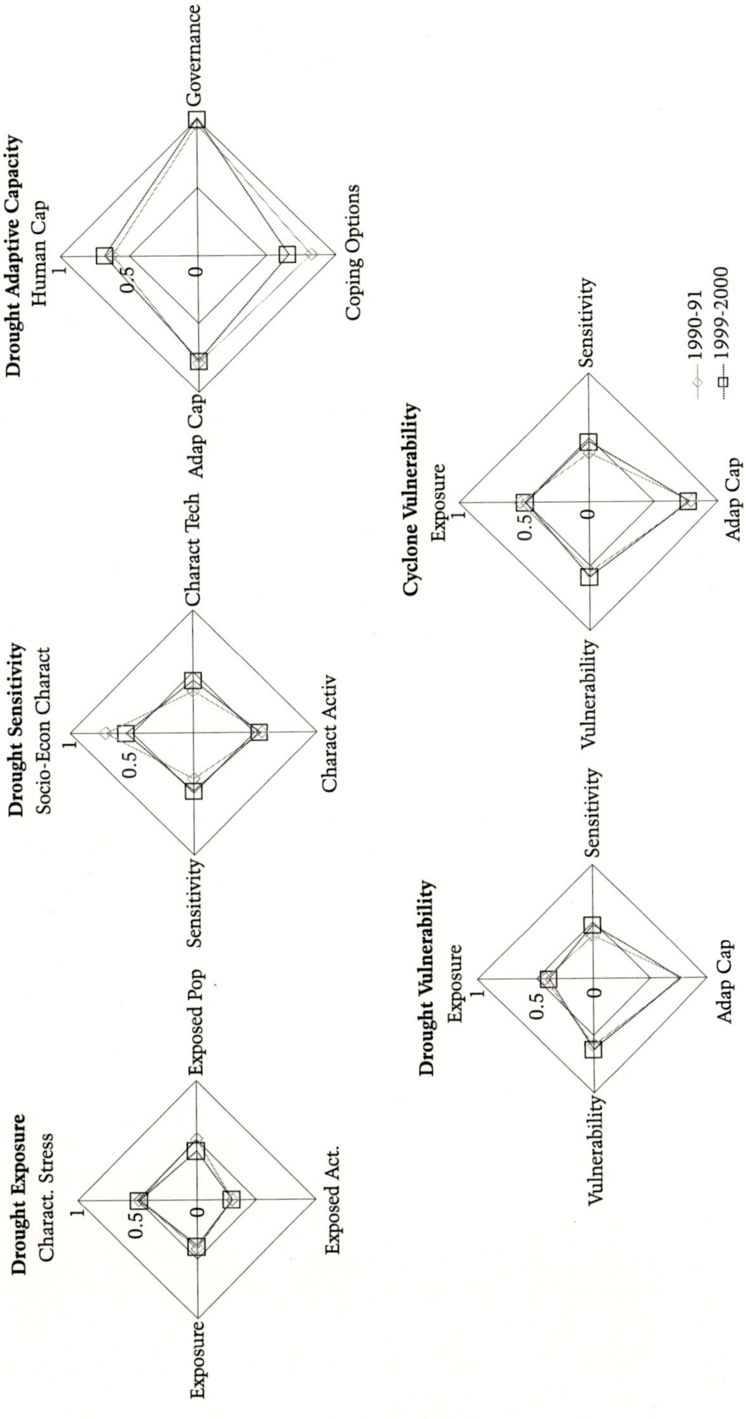

studies to assess the climate change impact on coastal regions through sea level rise, a dated but detailed study carried out by Jawaharlal Nehru University (JNU, 1993) corroborates this point. Table 13.7 shows the district-wise area that faces the threat of inundation due to sea level rise along with population at risk. The agricultural sector also is likely to get adversely affected by the rising temperature and erratic rainfall patterns. Some recent studies have also shown that the atmospheric brown cloud over the Indian sub-continent had adversely affected the agricultural production in southern states of India, especially Tamil Nadu.

On the other hand, the greenhouse gas mitigation efforts have created some opportunities for sustainable development in developing countries through the clean development mechanism (CDM). Through CDM, the industries in developed countries generate greenhouse gas emission credits through investment in the industries in developing countries in the form of provision of efficient technology and finance. Access to better technology is expected to enable the developing countries to leapfrog towards sustainable development. Several industries in Tamil Nadu are currently in the process of entering into CDM projects. Power generation projects through renewable technologies, especially wind, are gaining prominence.

Table 13.7

Impacts of 1-m Sea Level Rise: Tamil Nadu

Sl. No.	*District*	*Area Inundated due to 1-m SLR (ha)*
1	Chengalpattu	13440
2	Kanniyakumari	117
3	Madras/Chennai	3378
4	Ramanathapuram	9908
5	South Arcot	4272
6	Thanjavur	14300
7	Tirunelveli	21585
Total		67000
Area inundated as percentage of total area		0.52
People affected as percentage of total population		2.91

Source: JNU (1993).

Conclusions

What have been the response strategies in Tamil Nadu so far? Are they adequate? What kind of proactive strategies should the state adopt to improve the state of the environment? These are some of the issues that this section tries to address. The response strategies can be seen through three broad categories: (a) strategies towards reducing the pressure; (b) strategies aimed at restoring the state of the environment; and (c) strategies targeted towards the amelioration of impacts caused by the environmental degradation.

Strategies Towards Reducing Pressure

Several air, water and solid waste control acts were primarily aimed at reducing the pressure through reduction of pollution. Some of the policies have also attempted to control the driving forces that create pressure. But on the whole such policies have at best been inadequate. For instance, while there have been several measures to reduce vehicular emission through adoption of stricter control norms, little effort is directed towards control of increase in the number of vehicles. Improvement in public transport facilities can go long way in reducing the pressure on the environment with the added benefit of easing traffic congestion. This essentially calls for a more integrated approach in designing the response strategies.

Strategies Towards Restoring the State of the Environment

Regular monitoring of the ambient environment has been a feature of the policies aimed at restoring the state of the environment. However, often the deterioration of environmental goods is not correlated with the potential driving forces. Awareness is important but may not be sufficient to galvanise required changes. As far as the policies aimed at physical restoration of environmental goods are concerned, the typical approach has been to deal with the 'hot-spot' area in an isolated manner. While such an approach is useful for managing the situation, it may also create a 'special' status for the environmental good under consideration and hence may not work towards avoidance of recurring deterioration.

Strategies Towards Amelioration of Impacts

The polluter-pays principle has been effectively enforced in the case of compensation awarded to the victims of tannery pollution by the Loss of Ecology Authority. Besides this, however, the policies aimed at reducing the impact caused by environmental degradation have largely been in the form of compensation given by the state. For instance, in the case of climate extremes, there has been little effort towards encouraging the potential victims to participate in insurance schemes. In the case of agriculture, the new initiatives in the microfinance sector undertaken by non-governmental organisations like Dhan-foundation and BASIX deserve more attention.

References

Amarnath, J.S. and S. Krishnamoorthy (2001). "Study on Relationship between Productivity, Inputs and Environmental Quality in Tannery Effluent Affected Farms of Tamil Nadu", *Water Resources Management* 15: 1–15.

Asian Development Bank, United Nations and World Bank (2005). *India Post Tsunami Recovery Programme: Preliminary Damage and Needs Assessment*. Retrieved from *http://www.undp.org.in/dmweb/media/india-assessment-full-report.pdf*

Blacksmith Institute (2006). *The World's Worst Polluted Places*. New York.

Hossain, S.M.N. and A. Singh (2002). *Application of GIS for Assessing Human Vulnerability to Cyclone in India*. Retrieved from *http://gis2.esri.com/library/userconf/proc02/pap0701/p0701.htm*

Janssen, M.A., M.L. Schoon, W. Ke, and K. Borner (2005). "Scholarly Networks on Resilience, Vulnerability and Adaptation within the Human Dimensions of Global Environmental Change", paper presented at the workshop, *Key Challenges for Human Dimensions Research*, 9-11 February, Arizona State University, Tempe, AZ.

Jawaharlal Nehru University (JNU) (1993). *Impact of Greenhouse Induced Sea Level Rise on the Islands and Coasts of India*. Project report submitted to the Ministry of Environment and Forests, Government of India, Delhi.

Kathuria, V. (2005). *Utilisation of Fly-ash by Brick Manufacturers—Environmental Costs Vs. Benefits*. Project report submitted to the Ministry of Environment and Forests, Government of India, Delhi.

Kumar, K.S. Kavi (2006). *Vulnerability to Drought, Cyclone and Flood in India*, Research report submitted to Winrock International, New Delhi.

Kumar, K.S. Kavi and S. Tholkappian (2006). "Relative Vulnerability of Indian Coastal Districts to Sea Level Rise and Climate Extremes", *International Review of Environmental Strategies* 6(1).

McCarthy, J.J., O.F. Canziani, N.A. Leary, D.J. Dokken and K.S. White (eds.) (2001). *Climate Change 2001: Impacts, Adaptation and Vulnerability*. Contribution of Working Group II to the Third Assessment Report of the Intergovernmental Panel on Climate Change, Cambridge University Press, Cambridge, UK, x+1032 pp.

Mukherjee, S. and P. Nelliyat (2006). "Groundwater Pollution and Emerging Environmental Challenges of Industrial Effluent Irrigation: A Case Study of Mettupalayam Taluk, Tamil Nadu", *Working Paper No.* 7/2006. Chennai: Madras School of Economics.

Mukherjee, S. and V. Kathuria (2006). "Is Economic Growth Sustainable?Environmental Quality of Indian States Post 1991", *Working Paper* 6/2006, Chennai: Madras School of Economics.

Parikh, J. and V. Laxmi (2000). "Biofuels, Pollution and Health Linkages: A Survey of Rural Tamil Nadu", *Economic and Political Weekly*, November 18.

Patnaik, U. and K. Narayanan (2005). "Vulnerability and Climate Change: An Analysis of Eastern Coastal Districts of India", *Human Security and Climate Change* workshop, Oslo, June.

Segnestam, L. (2002). "Indicators of Environment and Sustainable Development: Theories and Practical Experience", *Environmental Economics series paper* no.89 Washington DC: The World Bank Environment Department.

Sehgal, J. and I.P. Abrol (2002). *Soil Degradation in India: Status and Impact*. New Delhi: Oxford and IBH.

Smith, K.R. (1998). *Indoor Air Pollution in India: National Health Impacts and Cost Effectiveness of Intervention*, Report prepared for Capacity 21 Project of India, Indira Gandhi Institute of Development Research, Mumbai.

State Ground and Surface Water Resources Data Centre and Central Groundwater Board (2003). "Report on Dynamic Groundwater Resources of Tamil Nadu", Chennai: Government of Tamil Nadu.

State of Environment Report Tamil Nadu (SoERTN) (2006). *State of Environment Report Tamil Nadu—2005*, Department of Environment, Government of Tamil Nadu.

Vaidyanathan, A. (2006). "Farmers' Suicides and the Agrarian Crisis", *Economic and Political Weekly*, September 23.

Viswanathan, B. and K.S. Kavi Kumar (2005). "Cooking Fuel Use Patterns in India: 1983-2000", *Energy Policy*, 33(8).

Vulnerability Atlas of India (1997). A Report of the Expert Group, Ministry of Urban Affairs and Employment, Government of India.